W9-BCQ-837

Build Your Own Website

Build Your Own Website

A Comic Guide to HTML, CSS, and WordPress

Nate Cooper
with art by Kim Gee

no starch
press

San Francisco

Build Your Own Website. Copyright © 2014 by Nate Cooper.

All rights reserved. No part of this work may be reproduced or transmitted in any form or by any means, electronic or mechanical, including photocopying, recording, or by any information storage or retrieval system, without the prior written permission of the copyright owner and the publisher.

18 17 16 15 14   1 2 3 4 5 6 7 8 9

ISBN-10: 1-59327-522-6
ISBN-13: 978-1-59327-522-8

Publisher: William Pollock
Production Editor: Serena Yang
Developmental Editor: Tyler Ortman
Technical Reviewer: Shay Howe
Copyeditor: Rachel Monaghan
Compositor: Serena Yang
Proofreader: Kate Blackham
Indexer: BIM Indexing & Proofreading Services

For information on distribution, translations, or bulk sales, please contact No Starch Press, Inc. directly:
No Starch Press, Inc.
245 8th Street, San Francisco, CA 94103
phone: 415.863.9900; fax: 415.863.9950; info@nostarch.com; http://www.nostarch.com/

Library of Congress Cataloging-in-Publication Data

```
Cooper, Nate, 1980- author.
  Build your own website : a comic guide to HTML, CSS, and WordPress / by Nate Cooper.
      pages cm
  Includes index.
  ISBN 978-1-59327-522-8 -- ISBN 1-59327-522-6
  1.  Web sites--Design--Humor. 2.  Web site development--Humor.  I. Title.
  TK5105.888.C66 2014
  006.7--dc23
                                                        2014019597
```

No Starch Press and the No Starch Press logo are registered trademarks of No Starch Press, Inc. Other product and company names mentioned herein may be the trademarks of their respective owners. Rather than use a trademark symbol with every occurrence of a trademarked name, we are using the names only in an editorial fashion and to the benefit of the trademark owner, with no intention of infringement of the trademark.

This book is not authorized or endorsed by the WordPress foundation or Automattic Inc. WordPress is a trademark of the WordPress Foundation.

The information in this book is distributed on an "As Is" basis, without warranty. While every precaution has been taken in the preparation of this work, neither the author nor No Starch Press, Inc. shall have any liability to any person or entity with respect to any loss or damage caused or alleged to be caused directly or indirectly by the information contained in it.

All characters in this publication are fictitious or are used fictitiously.

About the Author

Nate Cooper is a writer and consultant in New York City. After working in retail marketing at Apple Inc., Nate has established himself within the New York tech and entrepreneurial commu-nity, writing on the subject of business strategy. His company Simple Labs consults with businesses on WordPress implemen-tation and content strategy, and regularly draws audiences for events on the topics of communications and technology.

Photo credit: Amanda Ghanooni

About the Illustrator

Kim Gee is an illustrator and graphic designer, currently living in New York City with her boyfriend and her pet dog, Tofu. In 2010 she created her eponymous web comic and has since self-published a graphic novel and mini-comic collecting her work.

Contents

4
Kim Explores WordPress City

5
Customizing WordPress

6
The Big Launch 217

A Note from the Author

When I started my consulting business, I anticipated a demand for basic web skills in the design community. Graphic designers who'd been able to get by knowing just Photoshop, Illustrator, and InDesign would tell me that their clients started expecting them to know how to write HTML and CSS. As companies started shifting over from proprietary content management systems to general CMSs like WordPress, the need for designers to have basic tech knowledge grew. Today, designers must be able to create content both for print and for the Web, and that means knowing HTML and CSS.

When seen against the media's transition from print to Web, perhaps this shouldn't be shocking. What surprised me, however, is how much interest in these skills has spread beyond the design and media communities. If you're as old as I am, you might remember a time and place when office desks didn't always have computers on them. I remember visiting my dad's office at a community college while I was still in high school. He was considered forward-thinking because he not only had a computer on his desk but he actually read his own email, which was unheard of by certain college administrators.

We don't live in that world anymore. It didn't take very long for the Internet, desktop computers, word processing, typing skills, and email to become standard tools for nearly every single job in existence. Now, not only designers, but all sorts of professionals are required to produce content for the Web using basic HTML and CSS. The Web is taking over, but that doesn't mean learning about it has to be a pain.

My hope is that this book will appeal to those people feeling left behind as well as those who want to get ahead. We live in an ever-changing world where the skills you learn today aren't guaranteed to carry you into the future. To succeed in the jobs of the future, you'll have to learn not only what's needed for the task at hand, but also how to adapt and learn new skills. Learning shouldn't be a chore! Once you figure out how to make learning a fun experience, you'll crave it.

Whether you're a designer, writer, student, or anyone else who's new to website design, I hope you find this comic funny and interesting, but I also hope it inspires you to adopt the mantra *learning is awesome*!

Looking forward to the future! :)

Nate Cooper
July 2014

Acknowledgments

This book started as a Kickstarter project. Though the project has evolved quite a bit since the original plan, I wanted to express my sincere thanks to those who initially supported me in my goal of writing an educational comic book.

These early adopters proved that people want this book to exist and put their money where their mouth is. I thank them for believing in me, and in this concept.

A special thanks to my top funders: Matthew Bergman, Dwight Bishop, Dean Cooney, James Cropcho, Sue Maisonneuve, Steven Morrison, Edward O'Neill, and Johan Uhle.

Thanks also to: Gail Amurao, Angie Hall Anderson, Ari Arsyadi, Tony Bacigalupo, Stephen Bennett, Claire Burns, Nicole Calasich, Luke Chamberlin, Sara Chipps, Ernie Cooper, Jessica Cooper, Katrina E. Damkoehler, Colin Deeb, Martha Denton, Amy Donnelly, Danny Dougherty, Tarynn Farmer, Edward G, George Haines, Steven Hodas, Jim Hopkinson, Bill Johnson, Raygan Kelly, Mitch Kocen, Marissa Levy Lerer, Jonathan Levin, Anna Lubrecht, Michelle Mazzara, Colette Mazzucelli, Brenna McLaughlin, Lura Milner, John Murch, Stefan Nickum, Jason Nou, Paul Orlando, Eric Pan, Craig Plunkett, Julie Roche, Seth, Marny Smith, Shakti Andrea Smith, Kimberly Ann Southwick, Bobby Stoskopf, Erica Swallow, Harrison Swift, Kara Szalkowski, Sean Talts, Sophia Teper, Jennifer Tzahi, Jeremy Wadhams, Joe Watkins, Stefan Wehrmeyer, and Katy Zack.

I would also like to thank Shay Howe for his valuable feedback throughout the writing process, and everyone at No Starch Press who helped to turn this book into a reality.

The First Day of Class

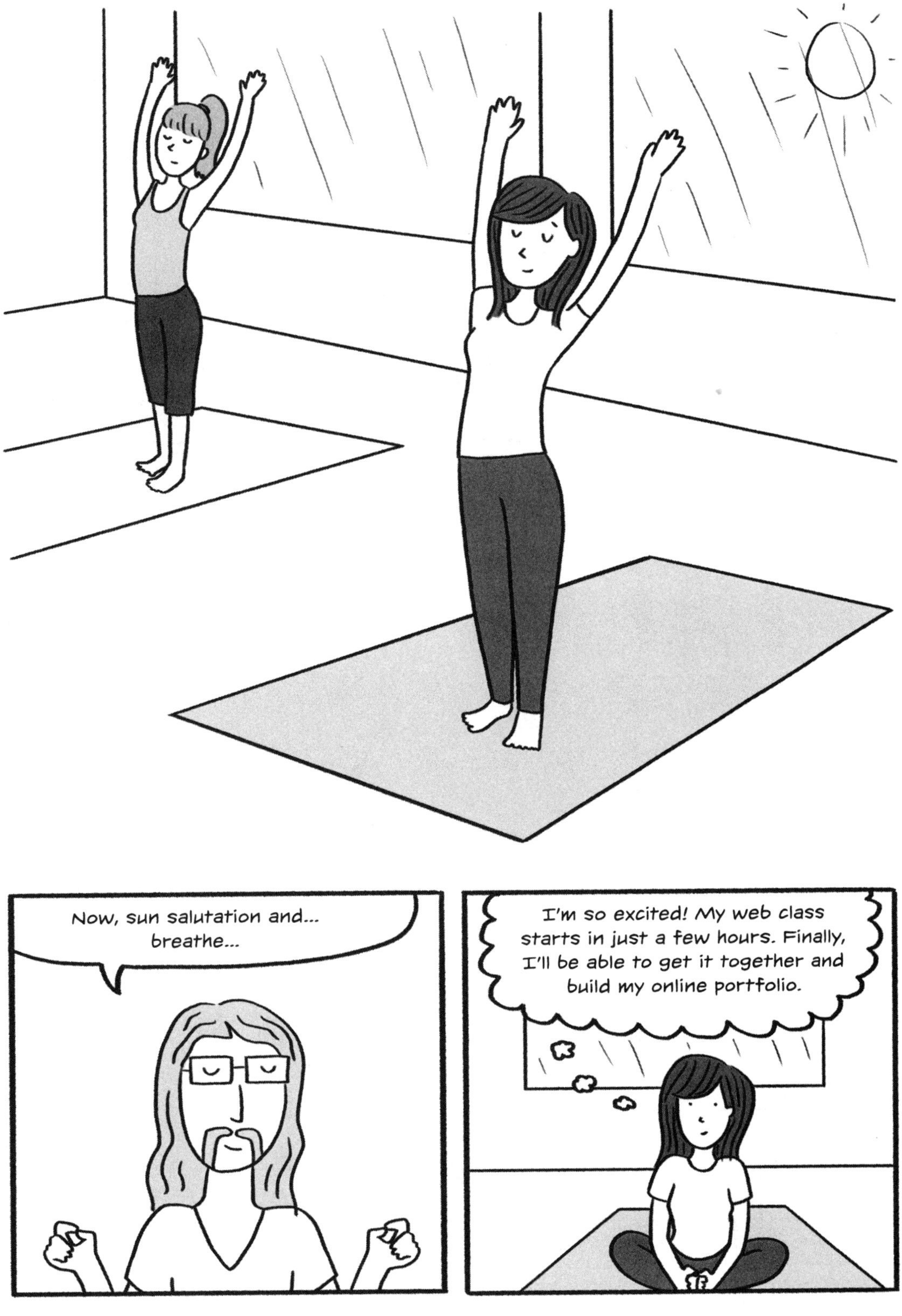
Now, sun salutation and...
breathe...
I'm so excited! My web class starts in just a few hours. Finally, I'll be able to get it together and build my online portfolio.

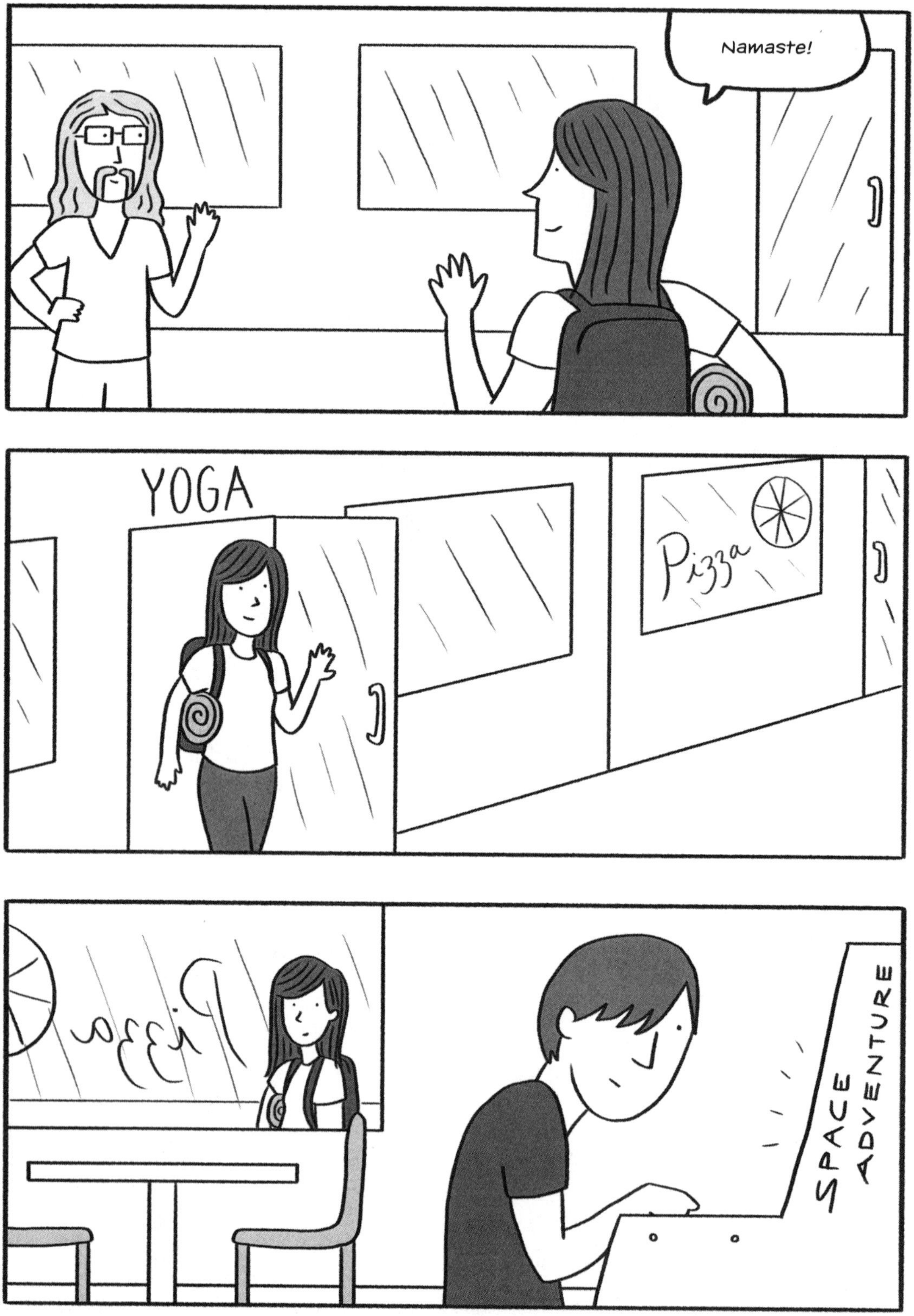
Namaste!
YOGA
Pizza
SPACE ADVENTURE

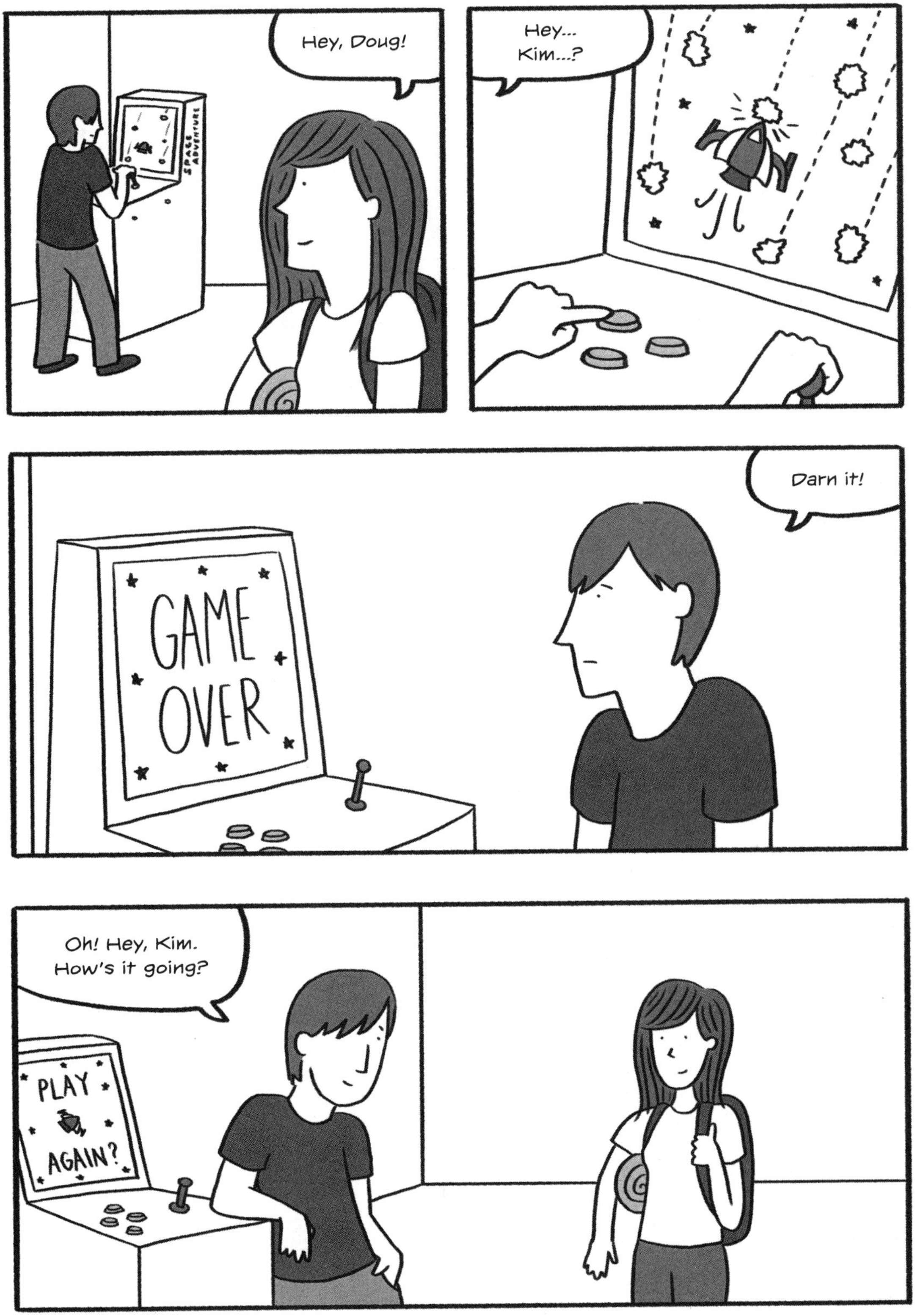
Hey, Doug!
SPACE ADVENTURE
Hey...
Kim...?
Darn it!
GAME OVER
Oh! Hey, Kim.
How's it going?
PLAY AGAIN?

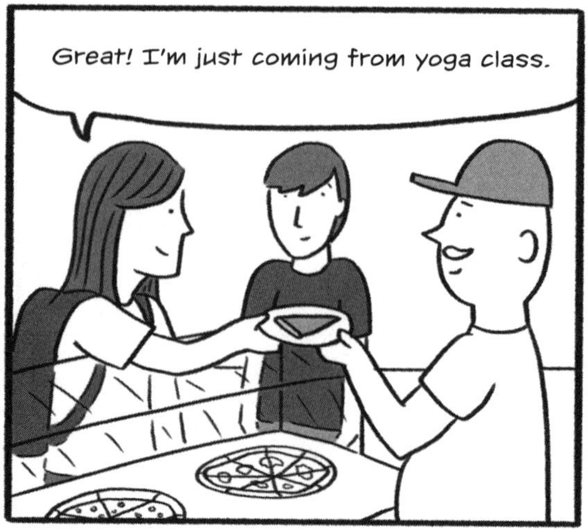
Great! I'm just coming from yoga class.

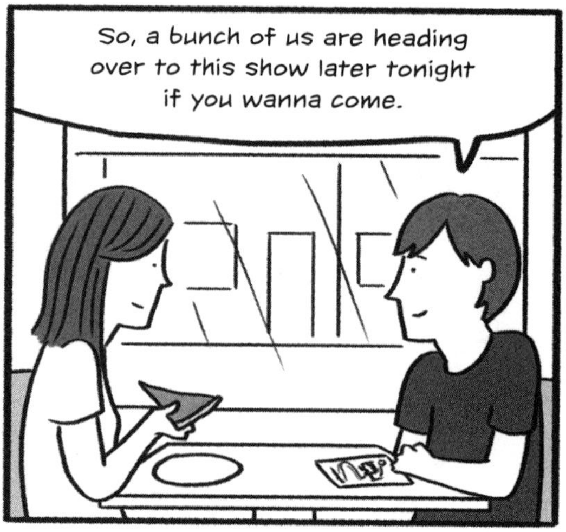
So, a bunch of us are heading over to this show later tonight if you wanna come.

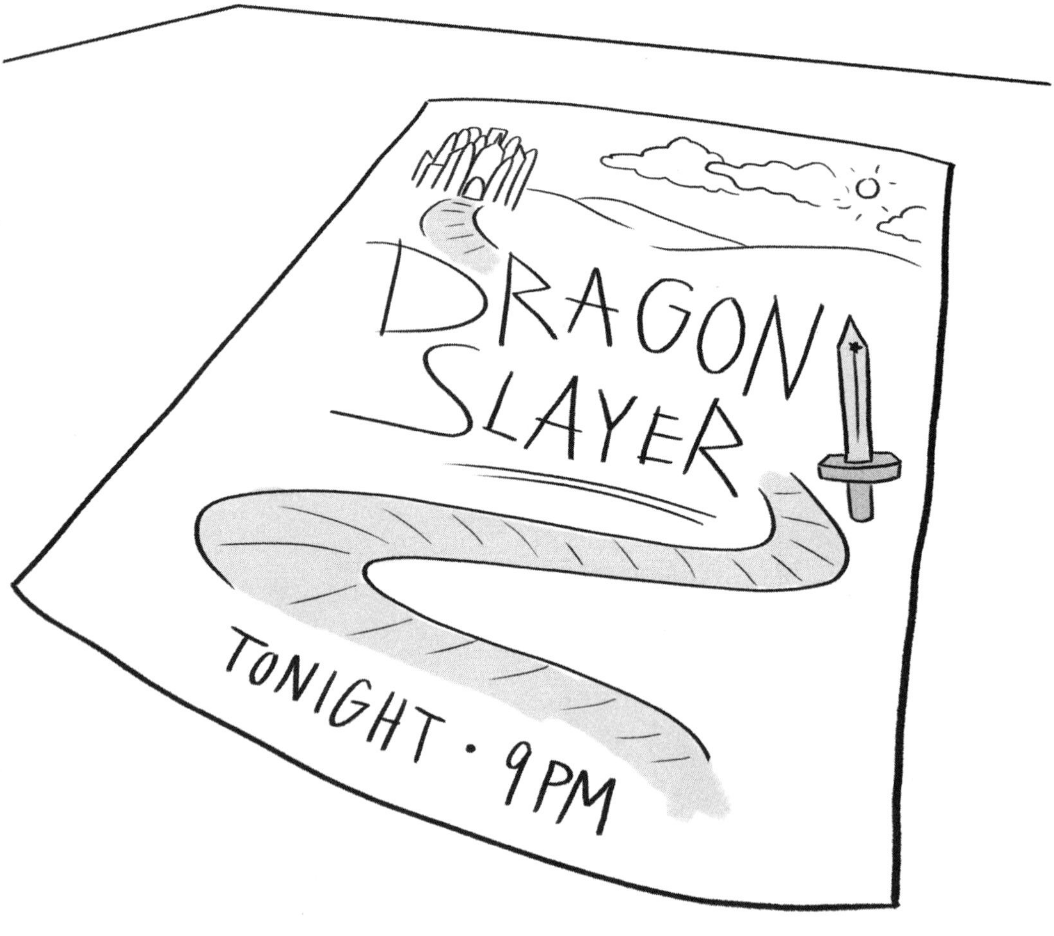
DRAGON SLAYER
TONIGHT • 9PM

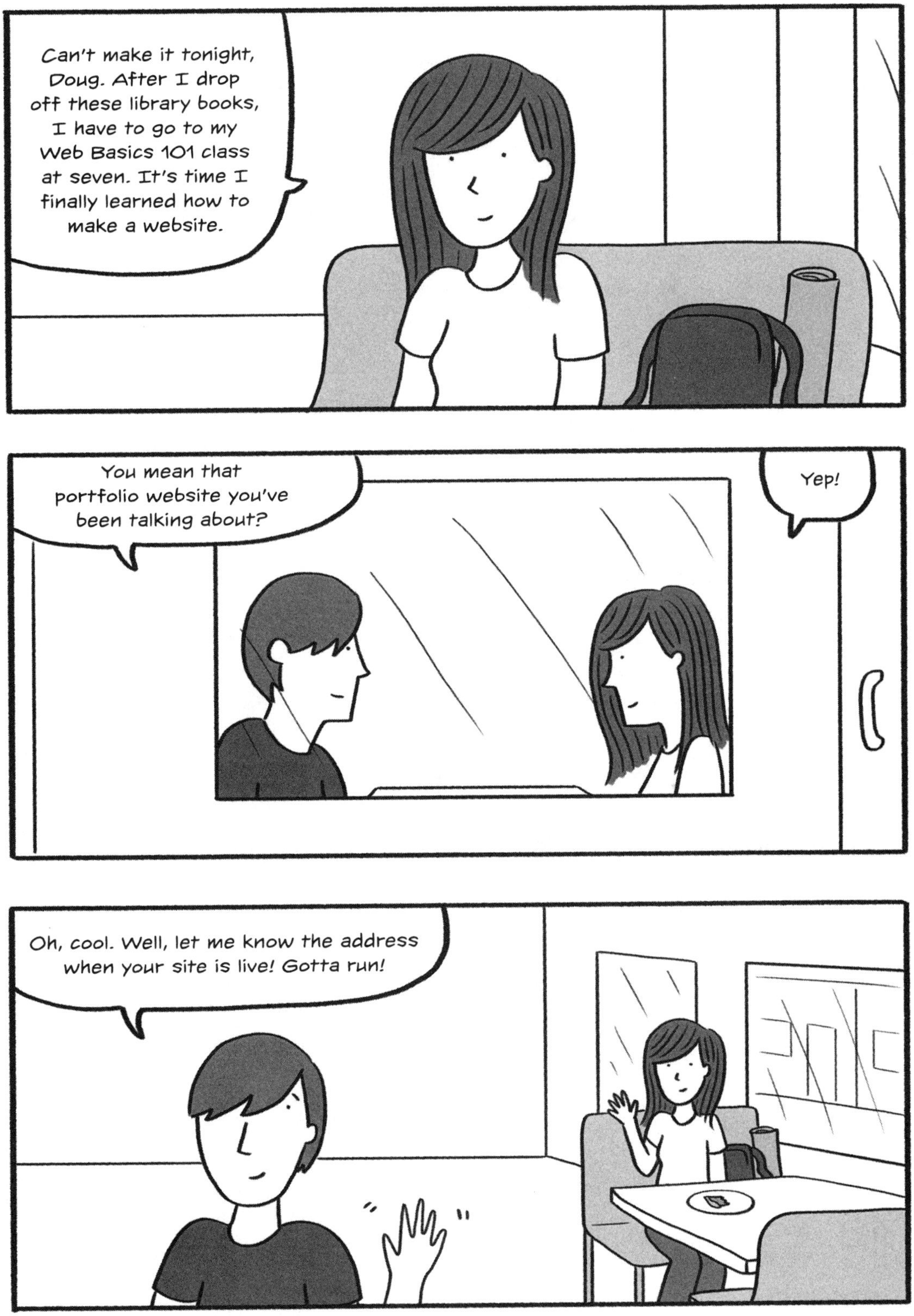
Can't make it tonight, Doug. After I drop off these library books, I have to go to my Web Basics 101 class at seven. It's time I finally learned how to make a website.
You mean that portfolio website you've been talking about?
Yep!
Oh, cool. Well, let me know the address when your site is live! Gotta run!

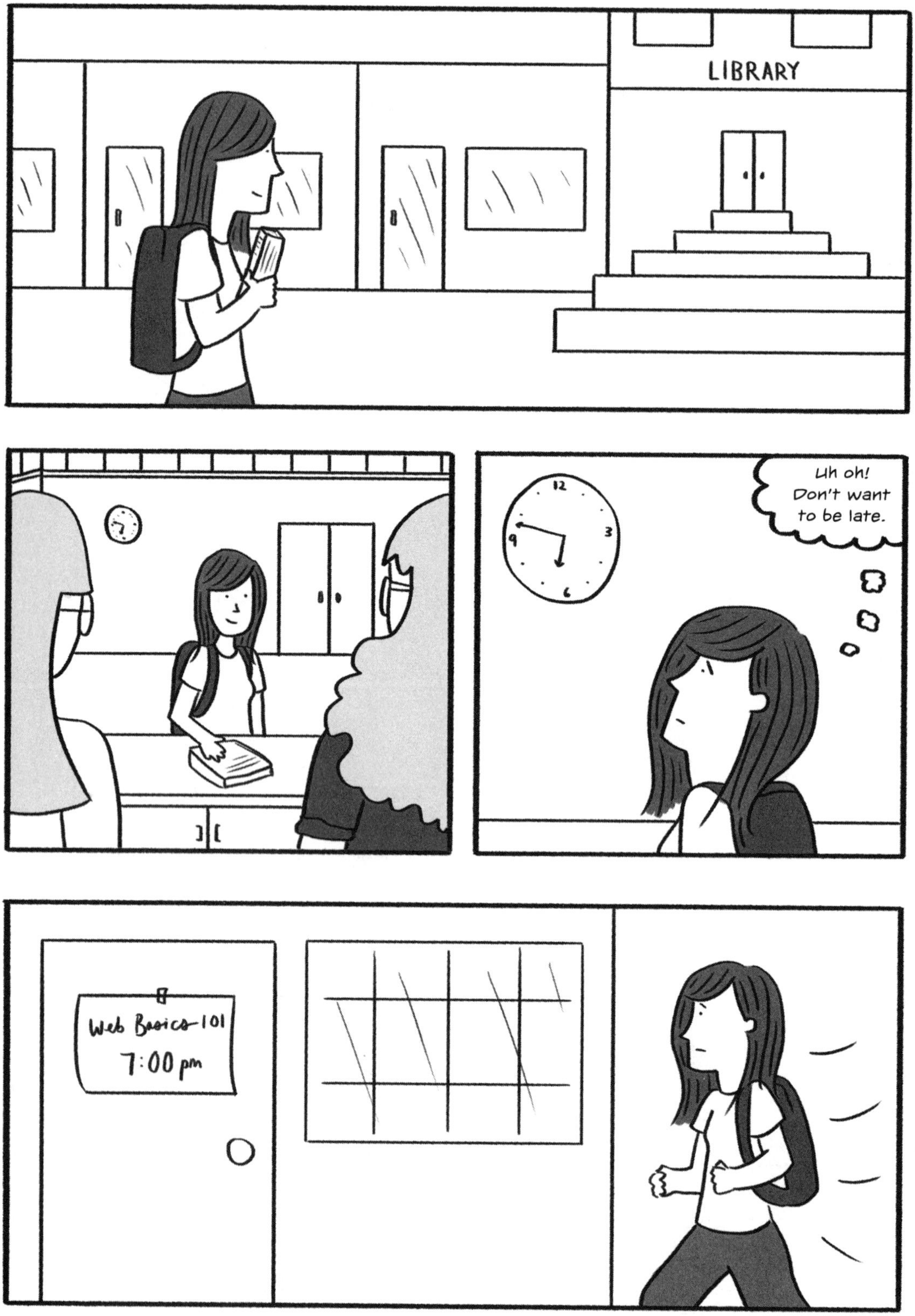
LIBRARY
Uh oh! Don't want to be late.
Web Basics 101
7:00 pm

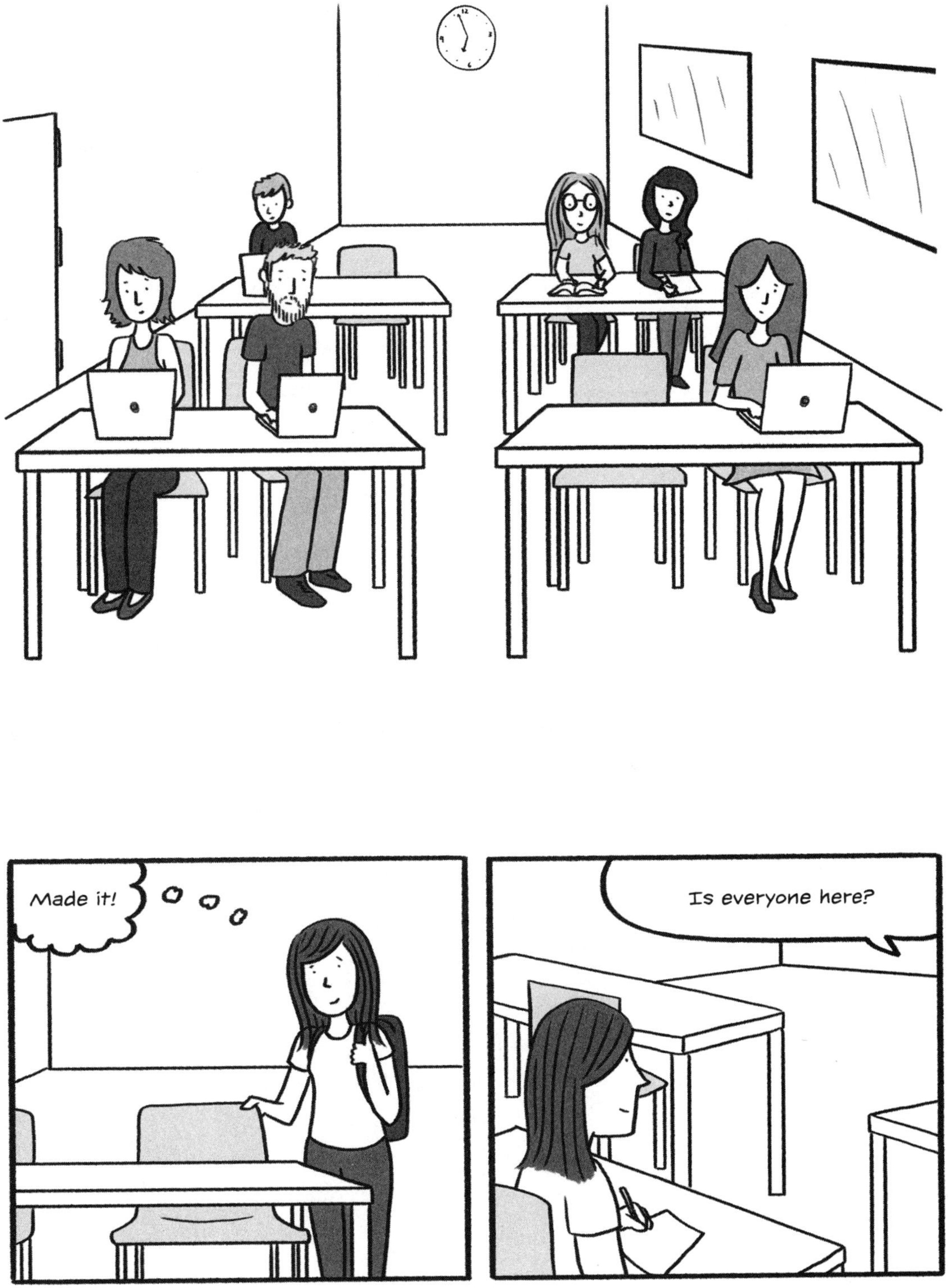
Made it!
Is everyone here?

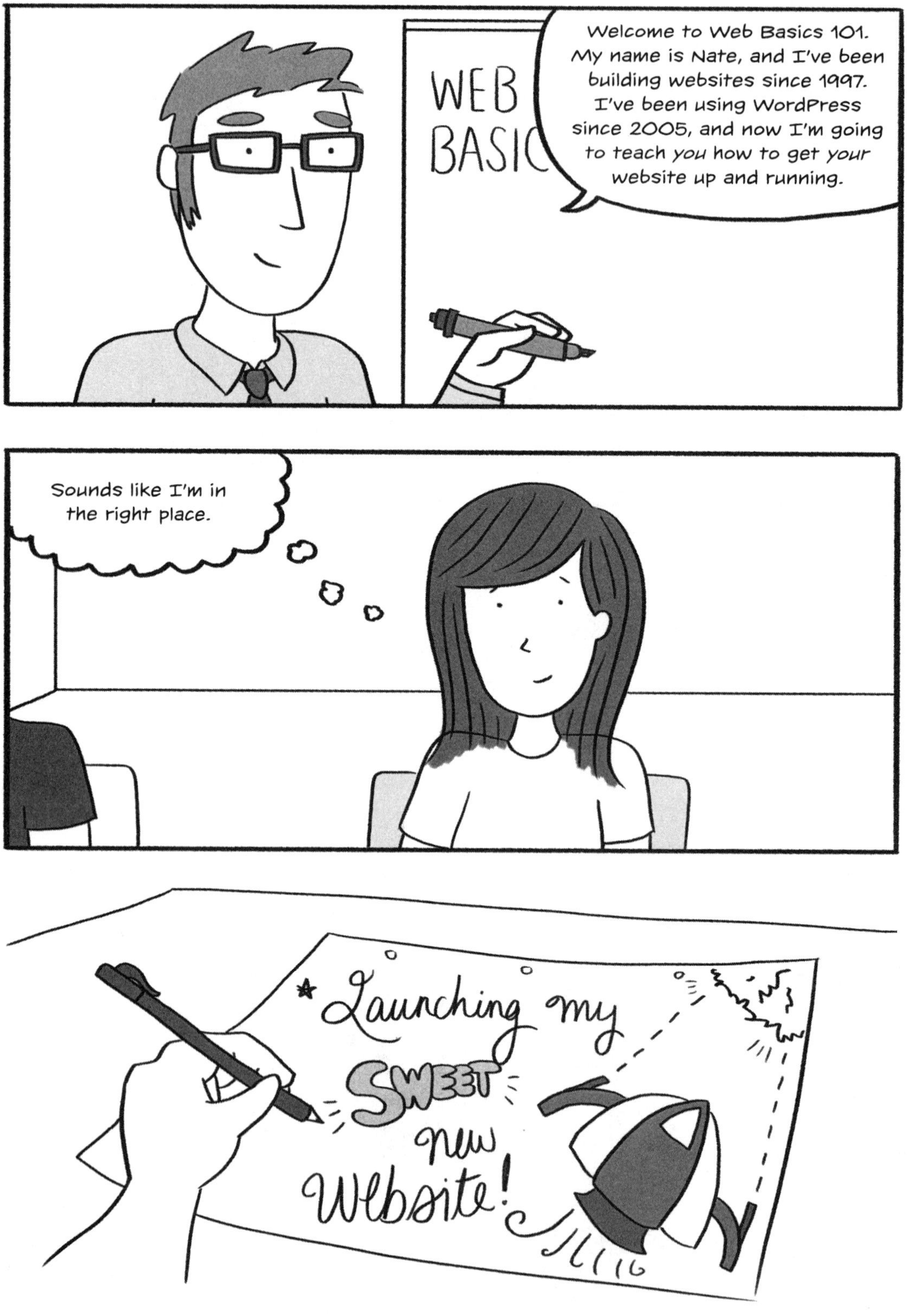
WEB
BASIC
Welcome to Web Basics 101. My name is Nate, and I've been building websites since 1997. I've been using WordPress since 2005, and now I'm going to teach *you* how to get *your* website up and running.
Sounds like I'm in the right place.
Launching my
SWEET
new
Website!

What You Need

In this book you'll learn the fundamental concepts that go into building a website. We'll discuss the basics of HTML, CSS, and WordPress. By the time you're finished, you will have everything you need to launch your very own website. One little book can't teach you everything about developing websites, though. Learning is a process, and I hope that this book is a helpful beginning on your journey to becoming a web guru.

It's up to *you* to do the exercises and to make sure you get the practice you'll need. This book takes the "learn by doing" approach. You'll need a couple of things on your own computer to follow along.

A Web Browser

First, you'll need a web browser. A *web browser* is what you use to view web pages online. If you're running Windows, I recommend you download Chrome, Firefox, or Safari and not use Internet Explorer. Many older versions of Internet Explorer are not equipped to handle modern conventions for the Web. While most of what we're doing in this book will work fine in Internet Explorer, if you go deeper into web development you'll be glad that you started using these other browsers.

If you're on a Mac, you already have Safari installed and can stick with that if you'd like. But you may also want to get Firefox or Chrome to test out your work. Even though this is an extra step, you may find that you prefer some Firefox or Chrome features.

Having more than one browser is a great idea so you can see the differences between them, as well as see how your website will appear to visitors using different browsers.

A Text Editor

Next, you'll need a text editor or code editor of some kind. Why bother getting a program just to write boring old text? A good code editor is designed to help you with the tricky parts of writing HTML and CSS. When you open a text editor, at first glance it may look similar to Microsoft Word or other word processors. But once you dig in, you'll see that it is specially designed to display code, as Figure 1-1 shows.

```
<p>Word processor without <em>code highlighting</em>.</p>

2
3
4    <p>Code editor with <em>code highlighting</em>.</p>
5
6
7
```

Figure 1-1: Don't use Word or another word processing program to write HTML (top)! A good code editor makes your job easier (bottom). It will highlight pairs of tags, use a monospaced font, and save the files in the right way.

If you're on a PC running Windows, NotePad++ is a great free option (available at *http://www.notepad-plus-plus.org/*). If you're on a Mac, you can download Text Wrangler for free (*http://www.barebones.com/products/textwrangler*). Sublime Text is an excellent free code editor that works on both Macs and PCs (*http://www.sublimetext.com/*) and one I would highly recommend. Choose an editor you like, and get to know it.

A web browser and a text editor are all you need to follow along with the chapters on HTML and CSS. If you get comfortable using a code editor, it can pay off down the line if you pursue a more advanced scripting language, like PHP, JavaScript, or Ruby.

Stuff to Know

In this book, I assume you can use a file browser (Finder on Mac, Explorer on Windows) to open and save files and install programs, and that you generally know your way around a computer. There are some other basics you'll also need to know.

How Do You Read an Address?

You've probably seen a website address before. It looks like *http://nytimes.com/*, *http://en.wikipedia.org/*, or *http://nostarch.com/websitecomic*. Because we geeks like fancy names, we call this a *URL*, which is short for *uniform resource locator*. We'll just call it a link or an address for now, though.

As you move to new places on the Web, this address changes, just as your location changes as you walk around big city blocks and go to new stores.

Let's take a closer look at what each part of an address does:

$$http://nytimes.com/articletitle$$

↑　　↑　　↑　　　↑
❶　　❷　　❸　　　❹

❶ First, there's the **http://**. That lets us know that we're using *HTTP*, the *HyperText Transfer Protocol*. That's a fancy way of saying that the web browser should expect to receive an HTML document. We'll write some of our own HTML in Chapter 2.

HTTP is the most common protocol you'll see on the Web. Another one worth knowing is *HTTPS*, which means *Secure HyperText Transfer Protocol*. You should see this protocol used on pages where you're entering confidential information, like credit cards or passwords. You might also see other protocols from time to time, like *ftp://* (short for *File Transfer Protocol*, which is described in "An FTP Client" on page 14).

❷ Then we have the domain name. Here, that's **nytimes**.

❸ The **.com** that follows means that this site is commercial. While *.com* is still the most popular kind of top-level domain, you'll see all sorts of different top-level domains these days.

❹ The rest of the URL points to an article, blog post, or other particular resource or page.

What Are Clients and Servers?

Ever wonder what's on the other end when you go to a website, or what makes the Web work? It's just a bunch of computers talking to one another.

When you visit Wikipedia, your computer talks to the Wikipedia server. It works a little bit like this:

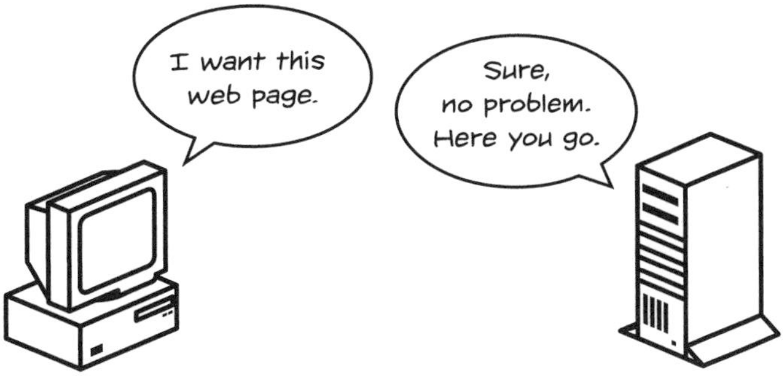
I want this web page.
Sure, no problem. Here you go.

When you ask your web browser to pull up a Wikipedia article, Wikipedia's server (shown in Figure 1-2) brings you the article, just like the server at a restaurant brings you a menu or a croissant when you ask.

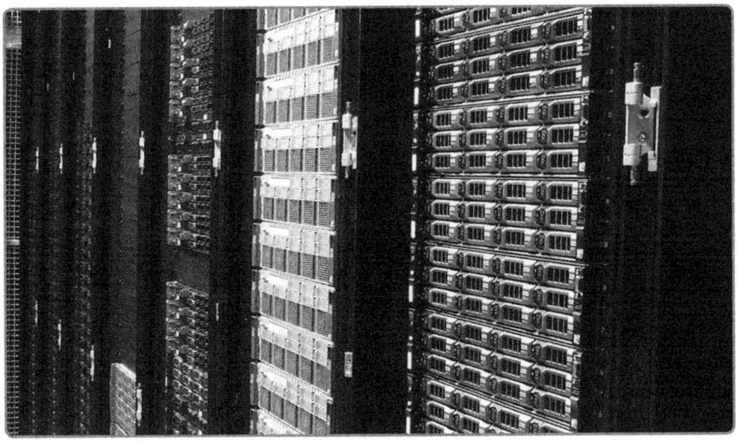

Figure 1-2: A server can be a simple desktop computer, or it can be racks of specialized computers like the servers in this photo, which serve up Wikipedia pages. The more traffic your website gets, the bigger and better server you'll need. (Photo credit: Victorgrigas)

Until today, you've probably been mostly acting as a client, requesting pages from the Web. Well, now you're going to be serving up those pages. But you might be wondering where you'll get your own server.

What's a Host?

To make sure the web pages you create can be seen by the world, you'll need to have a server of your own. Running a server can be a pain, so people often buy space on someone else's server. A company that sells space on a server is called a *web host*. For a fee, a web host stores your web pages and keeps them up and available 24/7 to anyone who wants to access them. Usually, setting up a host involves two steps. First, you register a domain (like *www.natecooper.co*) for a fee, and then you pick a host and pay a monthly or yearly fee for the hosting.

An FTP Client

Eventually, you'll need a way of sending files to your host. This is how you'll add pages and edit articles. For that you'll need an *FTP (File Transfer Protocol)* program. A great free FTP program available for both Windows and Mac is FileZilla (*http://www.filezilla-project.org/*). Once you've signed up for hosting, you'll get the login information from your host and be able to connect remotely via FTP. You don't need an FTP client yet, but you may find yourself needing one later when you have your first website.

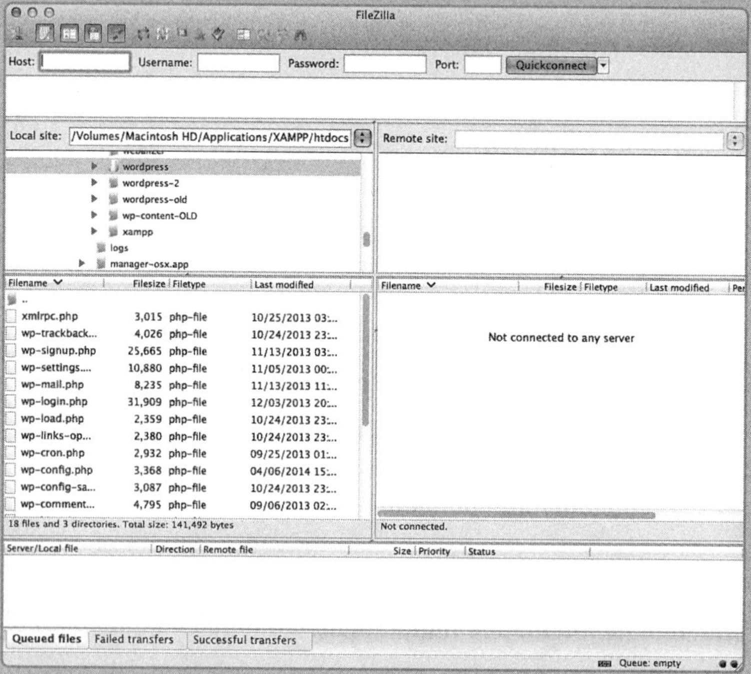

Figure 1-3: FileZilla is a free FTP application that lets you upload files from your computer to a remote server.

But you don't need to spend any money to follow along with everything covered in this book. As we build web pages in HTML and CSS, you'll be testing them on your computer using your web browser. That means you'll just be checking how your web pages look on your own computer, without having those pages broadcast on the Internet.

When we start playing with WordPress in Chapter 4, you'll need a host because WordPress uses technology that requires a server in order for it to work. To follow along you can use a free WordPress account from WordPress.com, or if you sign up for hosting with a third-party site like Host Gator, you can set up WordPress for free (see Chapter 6).

We'll revisit some particulars of how to buy a host in the last chapter of this book. For now, file that away in the to-do list in your mind. If you've installed your web browser and a code editor, all you need now is a sense of adventure. Get ready to learn!

The Trouble with HTML

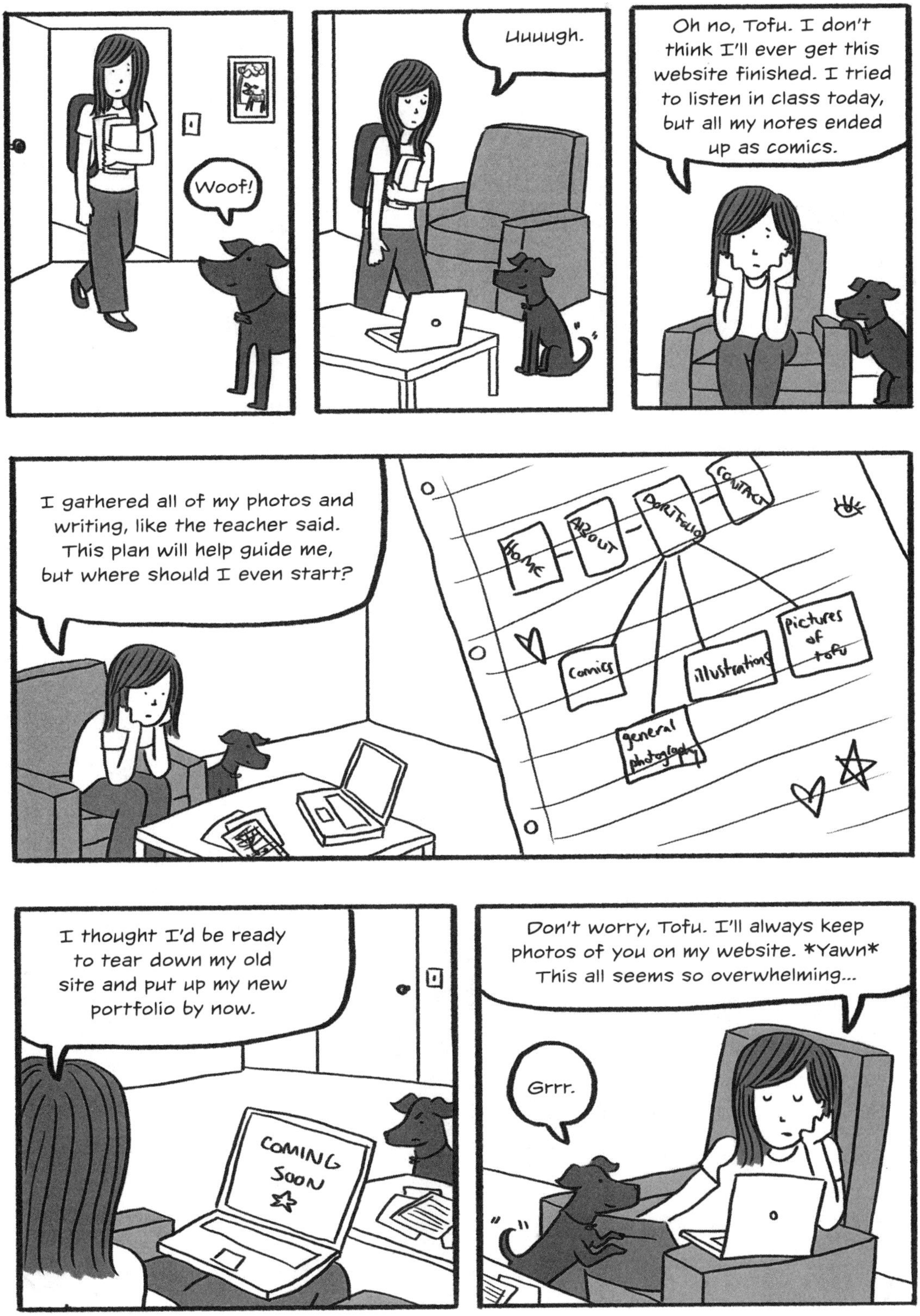
Woof!
Uuuugh.
Oh no, Tofu. I don't think I'll ever get this website finished. I tried to listen in class today, but all my notes ended up as comics.
I gathered all of my photos and writing, like the teacher said. This plan will help guide me, but where should I even start?
HOME
ABOUT
PORTFOLIO
CONTACT
comics
illustrations
pictures of tofu
general photography
I thought I'd be ready to tear down my old site and put up my new portfolio by now.
COMING SOON
Don't worry, Tofu. I'll always keep photos of you on my website. *Yawn* This all seems so overwhelming...
Grrr.

Kim Learns Basic HTML Tags

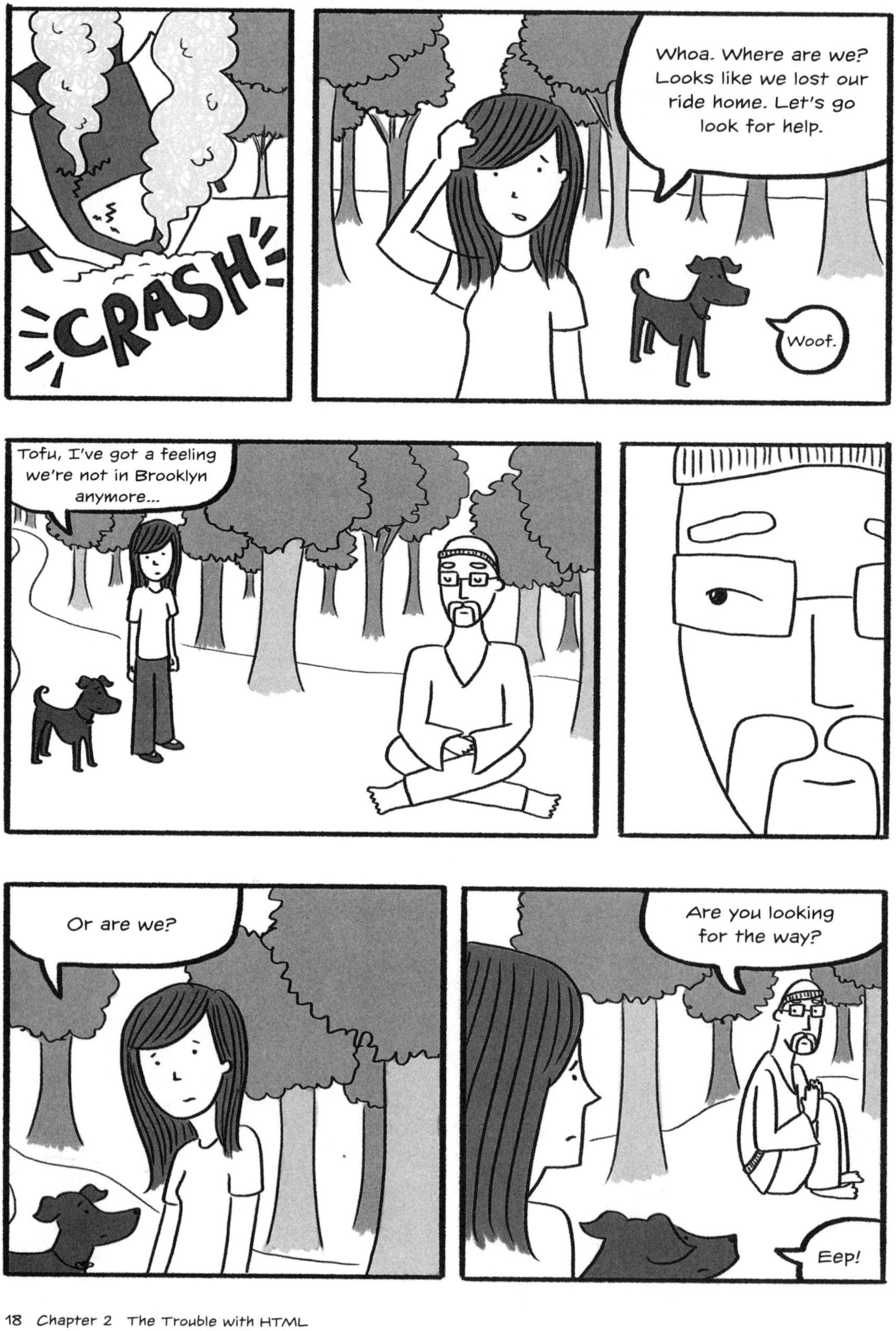
CRASH
Whoa. Where are we? Looks like we lost our ride home. Let's go look for help.
Woof.
Tofu, I've got a feeling we're not in Brooklyn anymore...
Or are we?
Are you looking for the way?
Eep!

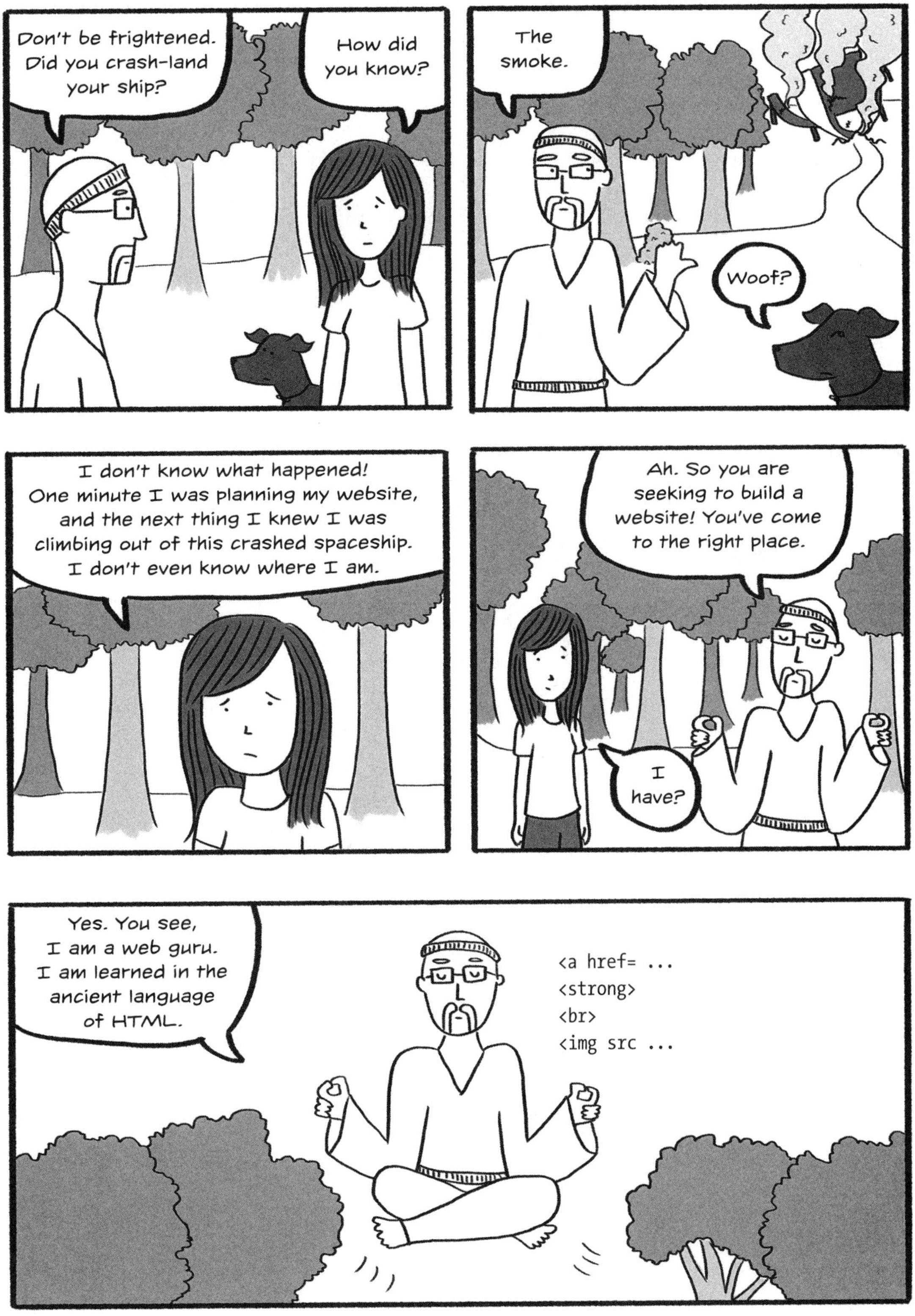
Don't be frightened. Did you crash-land your ship?
How did you know?
The smoke.
Woof?
I don't know what happened! One minute I was planning my website, and the next thing I knew I was climbing out of this crashed spaceship. I don't even know where I am.
Ah. So you are seeking to build a website! You've come to the right place.
I have?
Yes. You see, I am a web guru. I am learned in the ancient language of HTML.
<a href= ...
<strong>

<img src ...

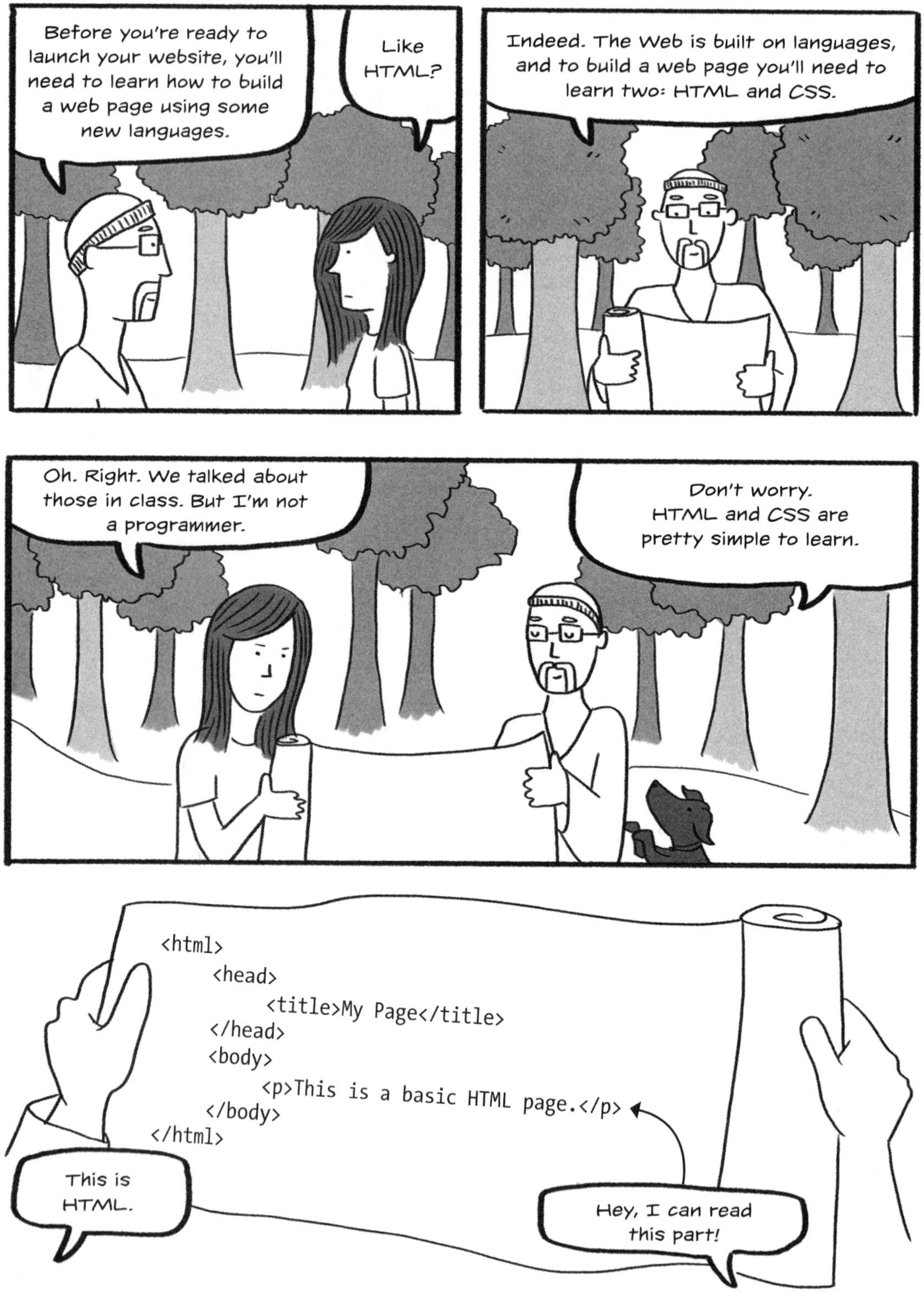
Before you're ready to launch your website, you'll need to learn how to build a web page using some new languages.
Like HTML?
Indeed. The Web is built on languages, and to build a web page you'll need to learn two: HTML and CSS.
Oh. Right. We talked about those in class. But I'm not a programmer.
Don't worry. HTML and CSS are pretty simple to learn.
<html>
<head>
<title>My Page</title>
</head>
<body>
<p>This is a basic HTML page.</p>
</body>
</html>
This is HTML.
Hey, I can read this part!

That's right. HTML is a markup language. That means it's a language that gives structure to regular old text. The acronym HTML stands for *HyperText Markup Language*.

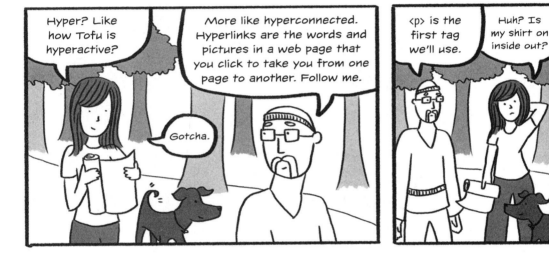

Hyper? Like how Tofu is hyperactive?

More like hyperconnected. Hyperlinks are the words and pictures in a web page that you click to take you from one page to another. Follow me.

Gotcha.

<p> is the first tag we'll use.

Huh? Is my shirt on inside out?

Ha! No, not your shirt tag. Markup tags surround the text in your document to change the words between them.

So, for example, if *we use* <em>the text in here is italic</em>, <em> stands for *emphasis*. <p> stands for *paragraph*.

That's how we make a new paragraph!

Exactly!

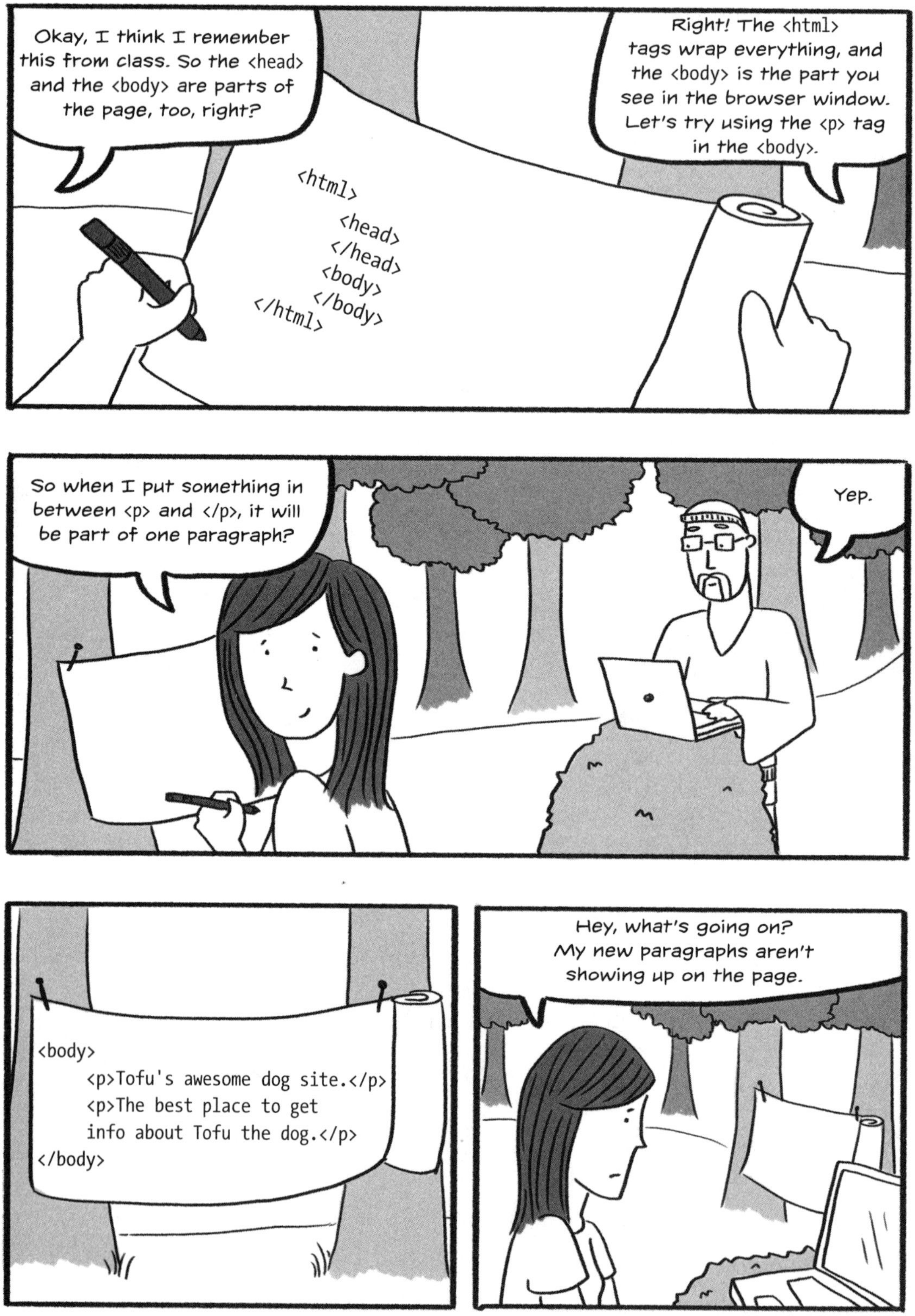
Okay, I think I remember this from class. So the <head> and the <body> are parts of the page, too, right?
Right! The <html> tags wrap everything, and the <body> is the part you see in the browser window. Let's try using the <p> tag in the <body>.
<html>
<head>
</head>
<body>
</body>
</html>
So when I put something in between <p> and </p>, it will be part of one paragraph?
Yep.
<body>
<p>Tofu's awesome dog site.</p>
<p>The best place to get info about Tofu the dog.</p>
</body>
Hey, what's going on? My new paragraphs aren't showing up on the page.

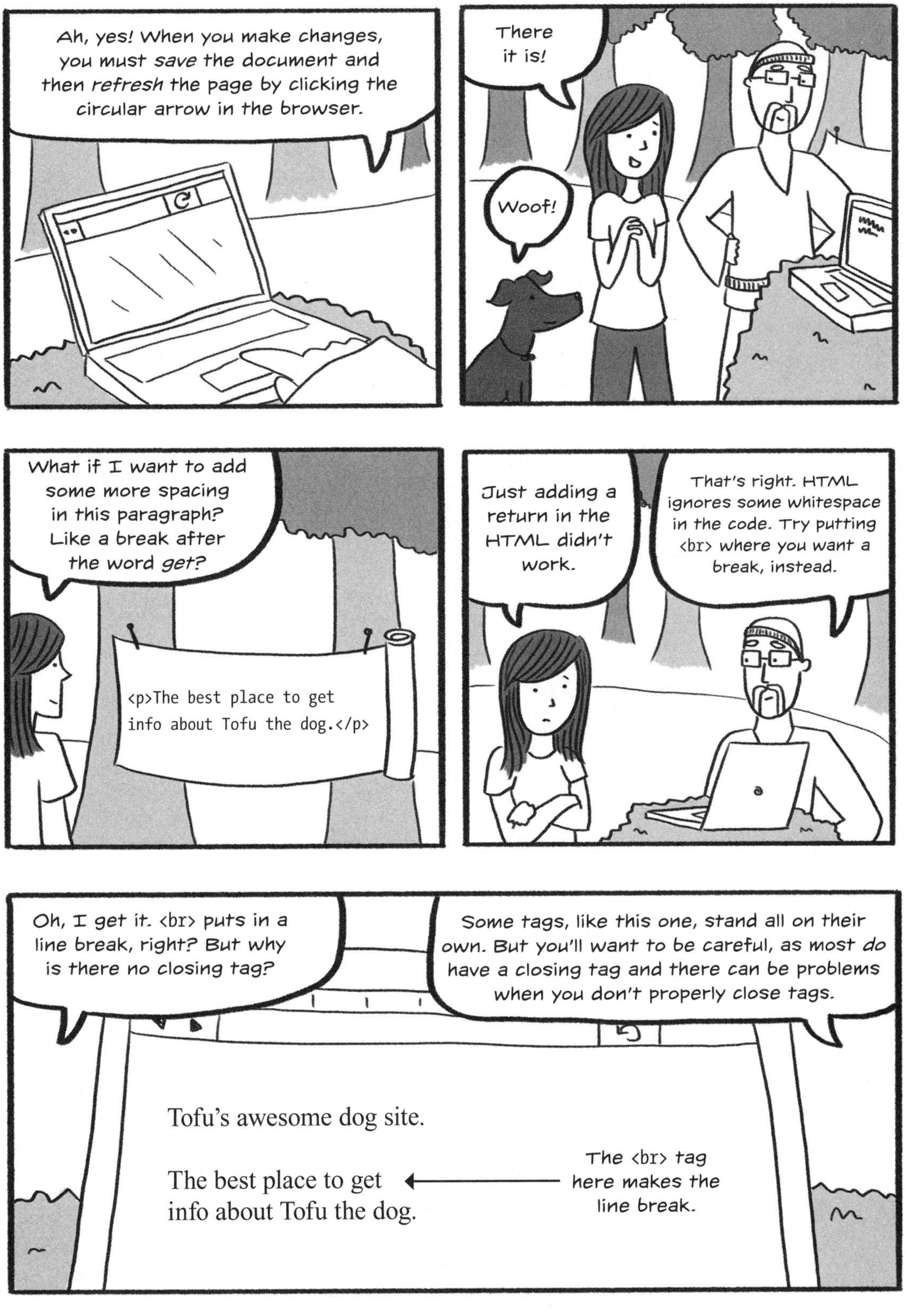

Ah, yes! When you make changes, you must *save* the document and then *refresh* the page by clicking the circular arrow in the browser.
There it is!
Woof!
What if I want to add some more spacing in this paragraph? Like a break after the word *get*?
<p>The best place to get info about Tofu the dog.</p>
Just adding a return in the HTML didn't work.
That's right. HTML ignores some whitespace in the code. Try putting <br> where you want a break, instead.
Oh, I get it.
 puts in a line break, right? But why is there no closing tag?
Some tags, like this one, stand all on their own. But you'll want to be careful, as most *do* have a closing tag and there can be problems when you don't properly close tags.
Tofu's awesome dog site.
The best place to get info about Tofu the dog.
The <br> tag here makes the line break.

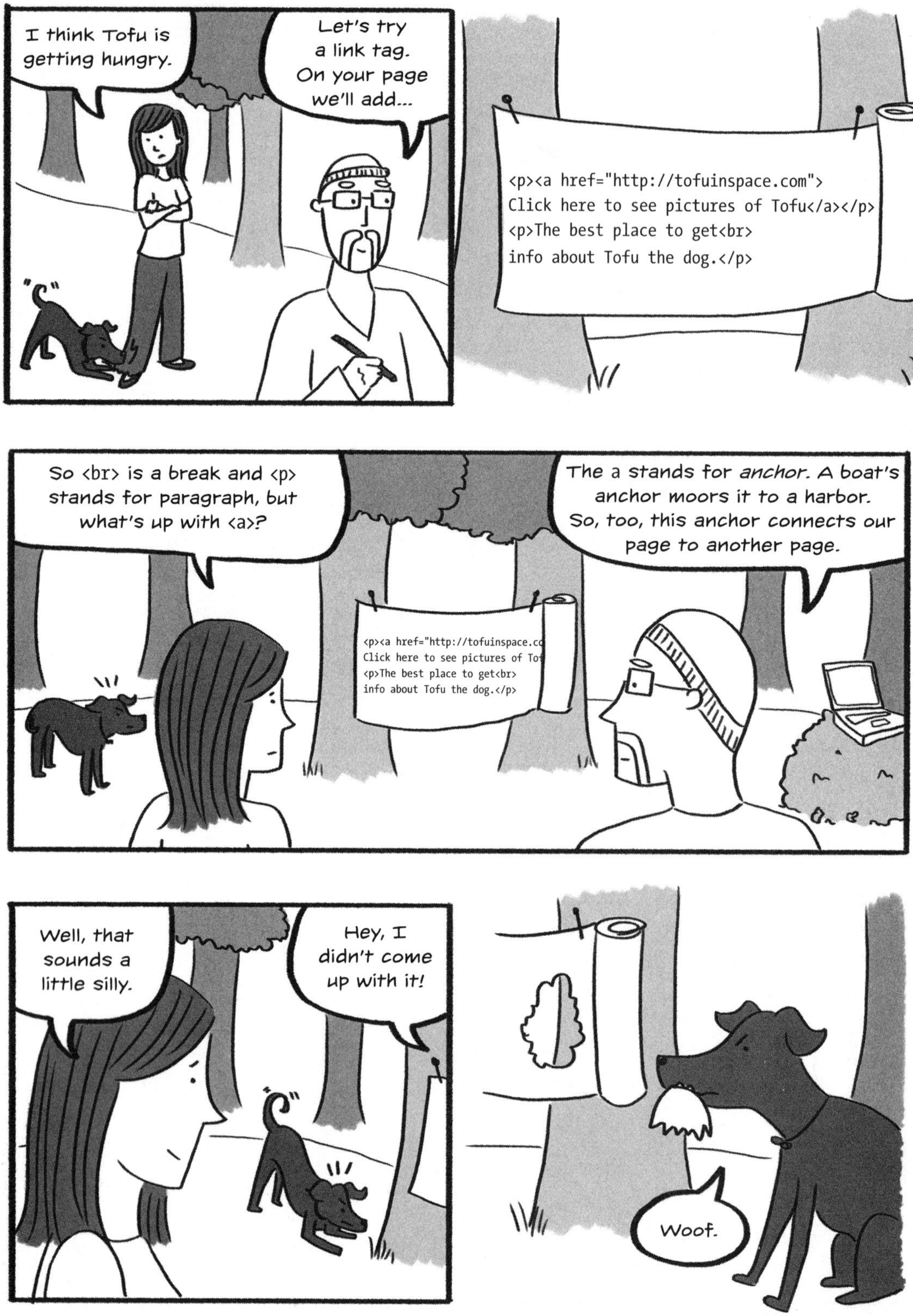
I think Tofu is getting hungry.
Let's try a link tag. On your page we'll add...
<p><a href="http://tofuinspace.com">
Click here to see pictures of Tofu</a></p>
<p>The best place to get
info about Tofu the dog.</p>
So <br> is a break and <p> stands for paragraph, but what's up with <a>?
The a stands for *anchor*. A boat's anchor moors it to a harbor. So, too, this anchor connects our page to another page.
<p>The best place to get
info about Tofu the dog.</p>
Well, that sounds a little silly.
Hey, I didn't come up with it!
Woof.

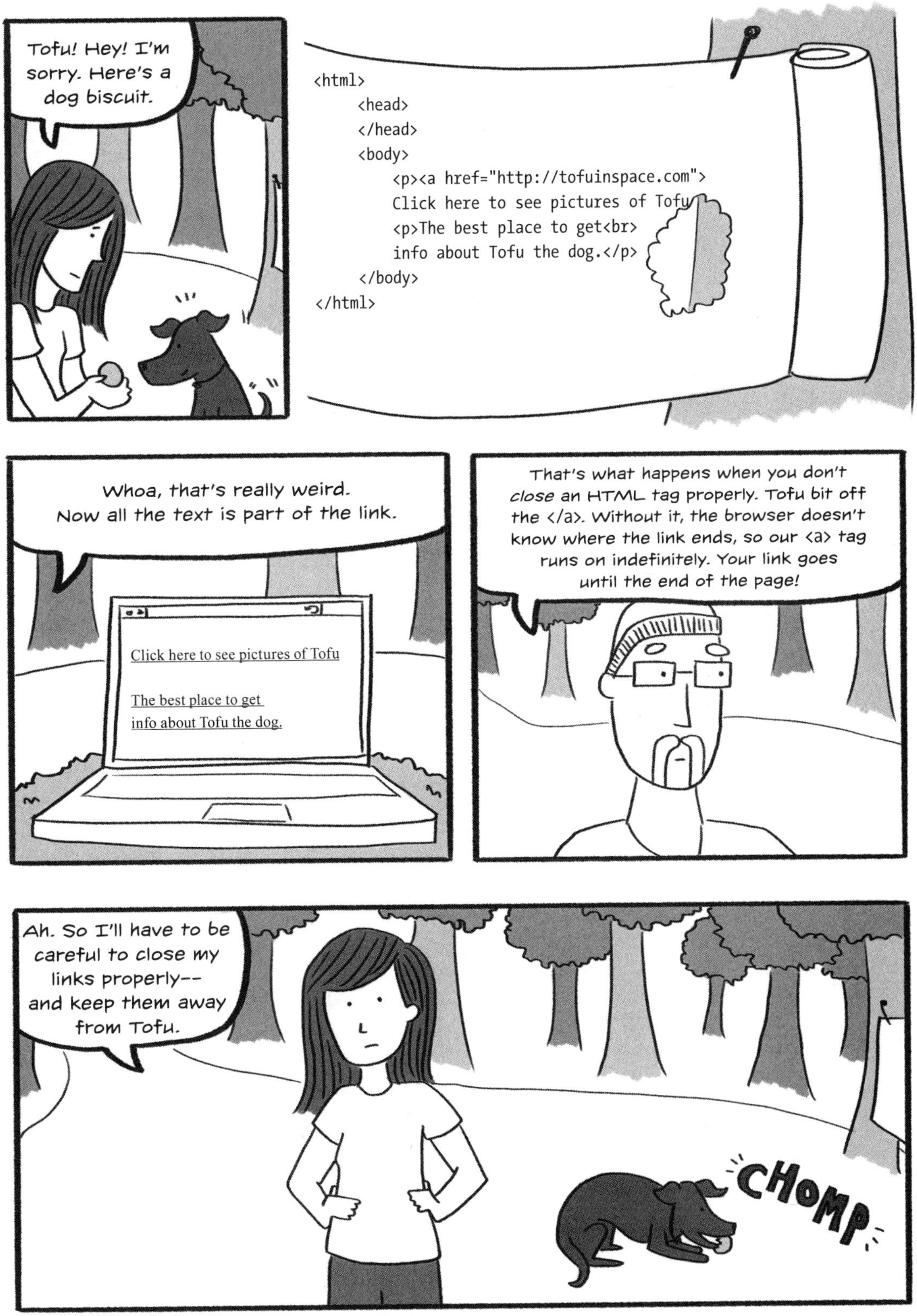
Tofu! Hey! I'm sorry. Here's a dog biscuit.
<html>
<head>
</head>
<body>
<p><a href="http://tofuinspace.com">
Click here to see pictures of Tofu
<p>The best place to get
info about Tofu the dog.</p>
</body>
</html>
Whoa, that's really weird. Now all the text is part of the link.
Click here to see pictures of Tofu
The best place to get
info about Tofu the dog.
That's what happens when you don't *close* an HTML tag properly. Tofu bit off the </a>. Without it, the browser doesn't know where the link ends, so our <a> tag runs on indefinitely. Your link goes until the end of the page!
Ah. So I'll have to be careful to close my links properly-- and keep them away from Tofu.
CHOMP

Paths and Naming Conventions

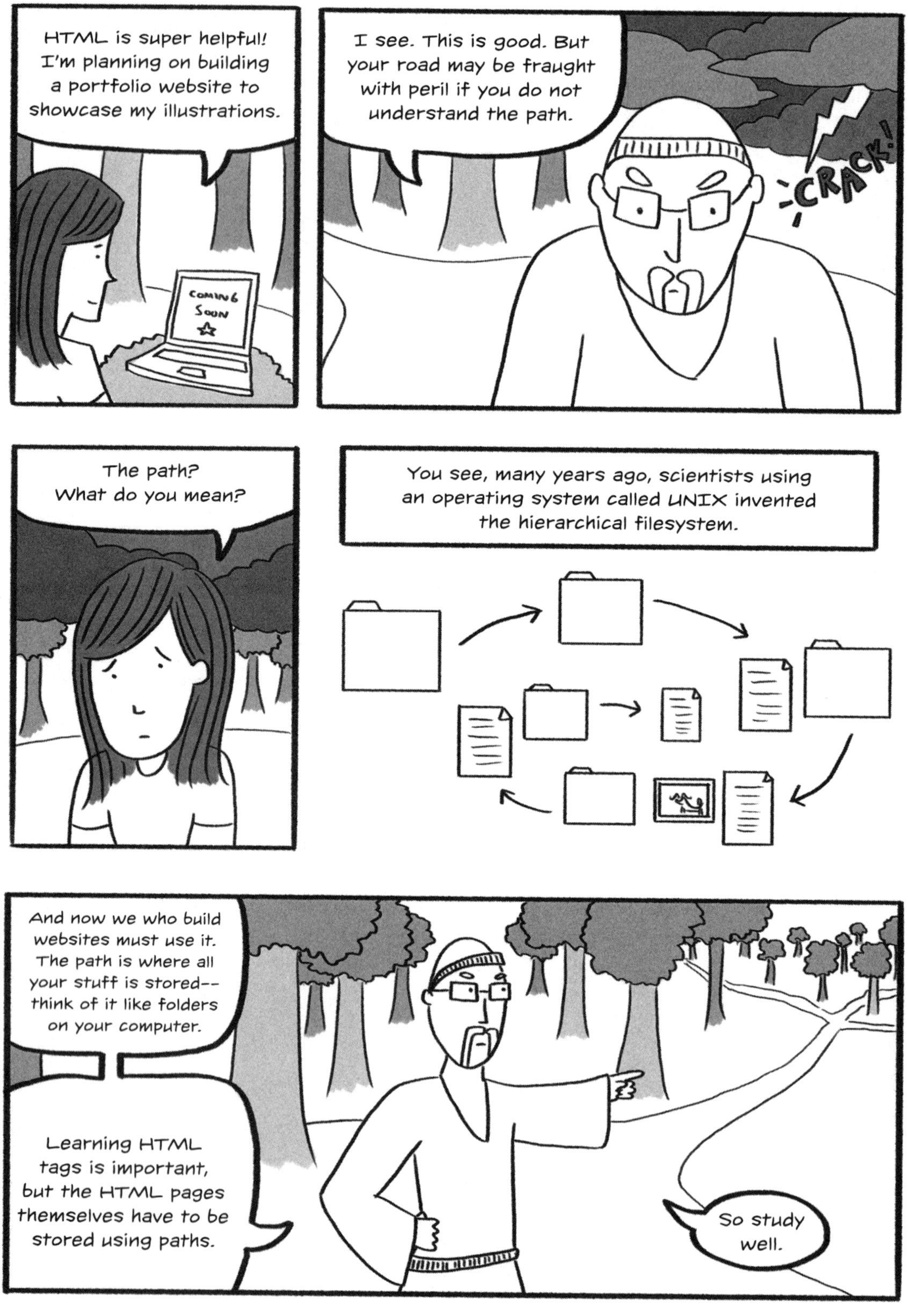
HTML is super helpful! I'm planning on building a portfolio website to showcase my illustrations.
COMING SOON
I see. This is good. But your road may be fraught with peril if you do not understand the path.
CRACK!
The path? What do you mean?
You see, many years ago, scientists using an operating system called UNIX invented the hierarchical filesystem.
And now we who build websites must use it. The path is where all your stuff is stored-- think of it like folders on your computer.
Learning HTML tags is important, but the HTML pages themselves have to be stored using paths.
So study well.

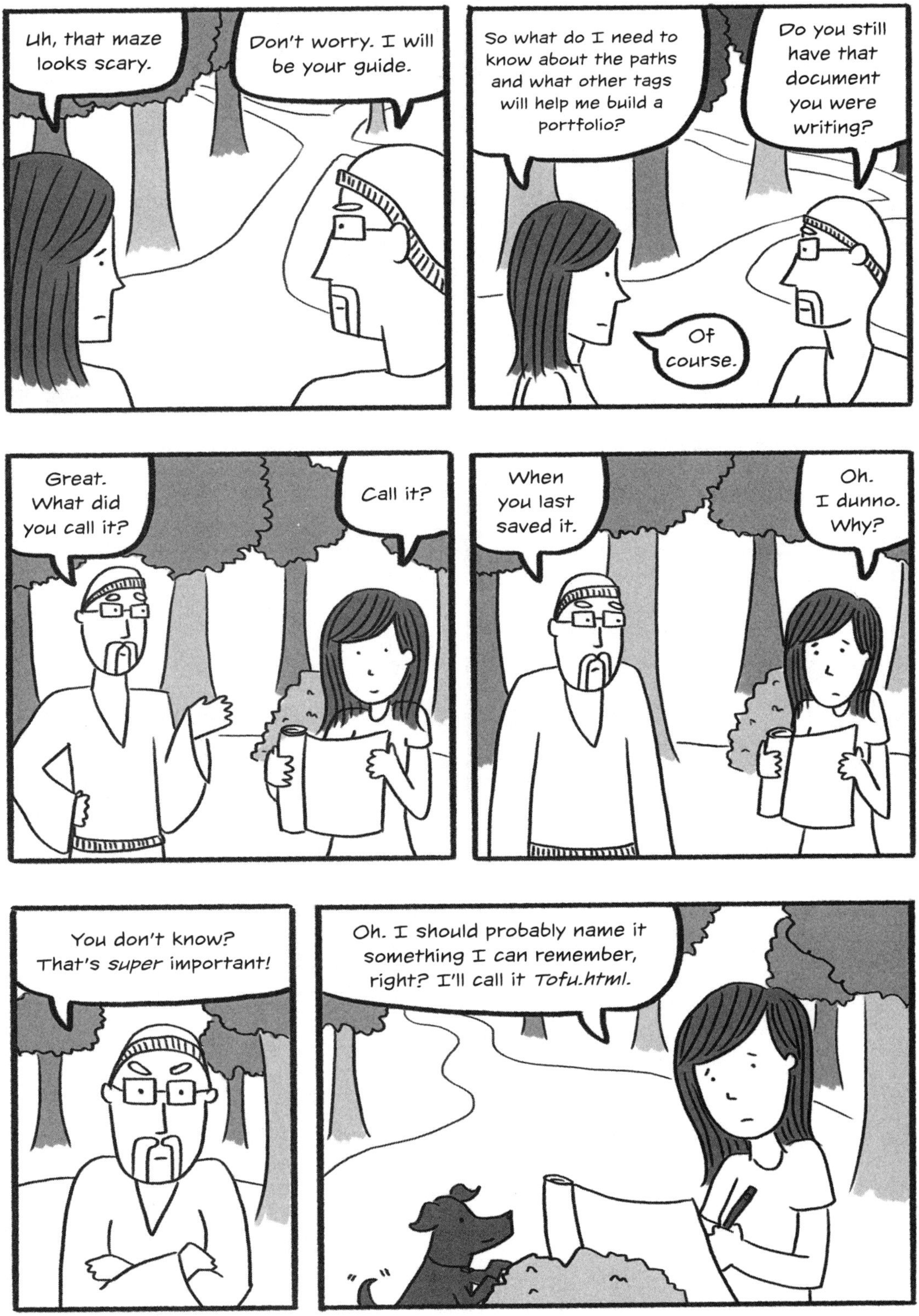
Uh, that maze looks scary.
Don't worry. I will be your guide.
So what do I need to know about the paths and what other tags will help me build a portfolio?
Do you still have that document you were writing?
Of course.
Great. What did you call it?
Call it?
When you last saved it.
Oh. I dunno. Why?
You don't know? That's *super* important!
Oh. I should probably name it something I can remember, right? I'll call it *Tofu.html*.

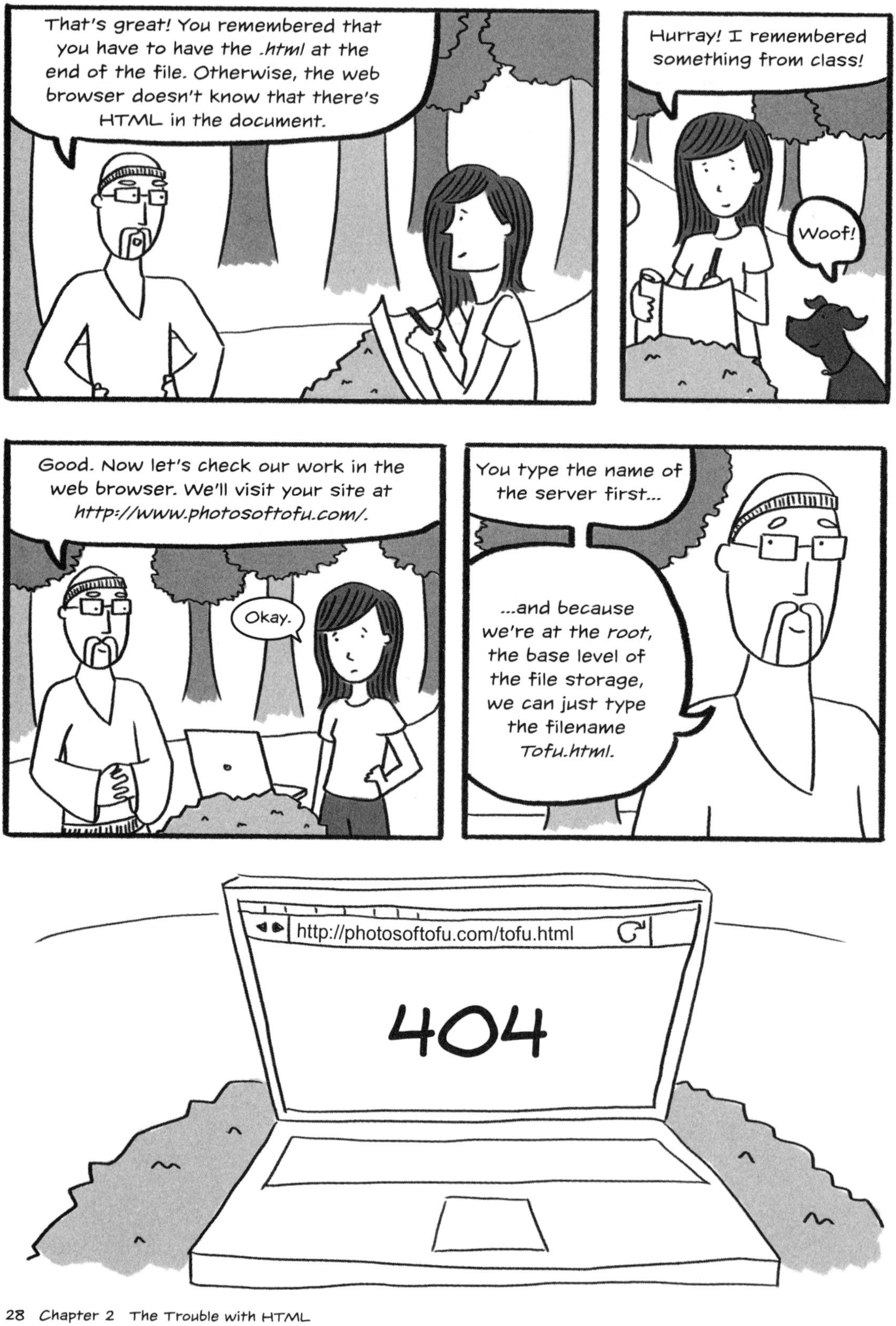
That's great! You remembered that you have to have the *.html* at the end of the file. Otherwise, the web browser doesn't know that there's HTML in the document.
Hurray! I remembered something from class!
Woof!
Good. Now let's check our work in the web browser. We'll visit your site at *http://www.photosoftofu.com/*.
Okay.
You type the name of the server first...
...and because we're at the *root*, the base level of the file storage, we can just type the filename *Tofu.html*.
http://photosoftofu.com/tofu.html
404

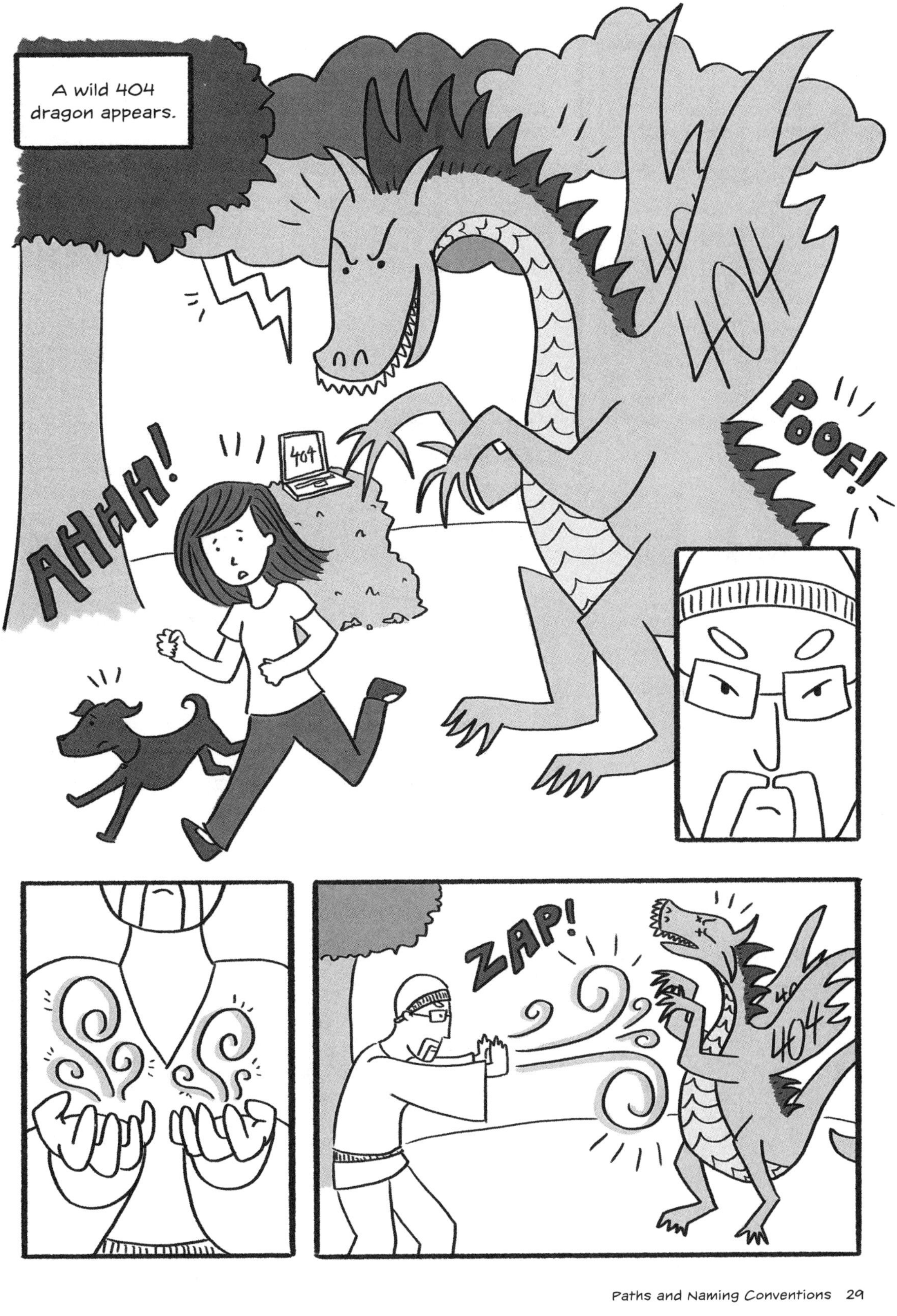
A wild 404 dragon appears.
AHHH!
404
404
POOF!
ZAP!
404

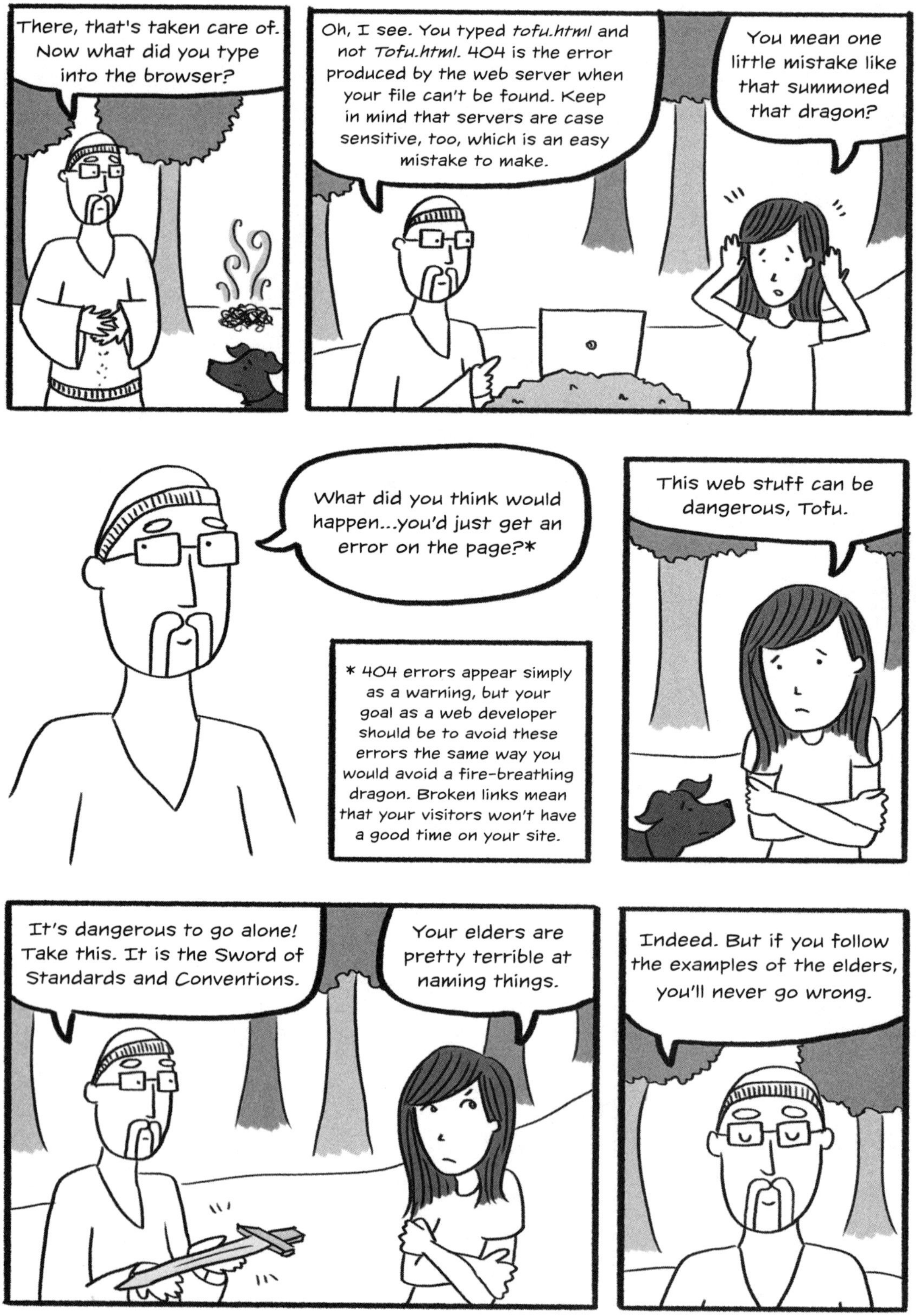
There, that's taken care of. Now what did you type into the browser?
Oh, I see. You typed *tofu.html* and not *Tofu.html*. 404 is the error produced by the web server when your file can't be found. Keep in mind that servers are case sensitive, too, which is an easy mistake to make.
You mean one little mistake like that summoned that dragon?
What did you think would happen...you'd just get an error on the page?*
* 404 errors appear simply as a warning, but your goal as a web developer should be to avoid these errors the same way you would avoid a fire-breathing dragon. Broken links mean that your visitors won't have a good time on your site.
This web stuff can be dangerous, Tofu.
It's dangerous to go alone! Take this. It is the Sword of Standards and Conventions.
Your elders are pretty terrible at naming things.
Indeed. But if you follow the examples of the elders, you'll never go wrong.

Naming Conventions for HTML Documents

If you follow a few tips when naming your document, you'll end up defeating dragons (errors) or avoiding them altogether.

*   Be consistent with capitalization. If you have a choice, don't use any capitals in your document names. So, for example, *Tofu.html*, *ToFu.html*, and *TOFU .HTML* are all different names. It's easiest to consistently name your pages all in lowercase, like *tofu.html*.

*   Don't use spaces in filenames. If you have a file named *tofu in space.html* on your computer, it will likely show up as *tofu%20in%20space.html* when viewed in a web browser. However, this is not guaranteed to work on all computers.
    Play it safe. Don't use spaces, or if you must, substitute hyphens like so: *tofu-in-space.html*.

*   Files named *index.html* are special. An index file is the *default file* for the folder and will load if no other file is specified.

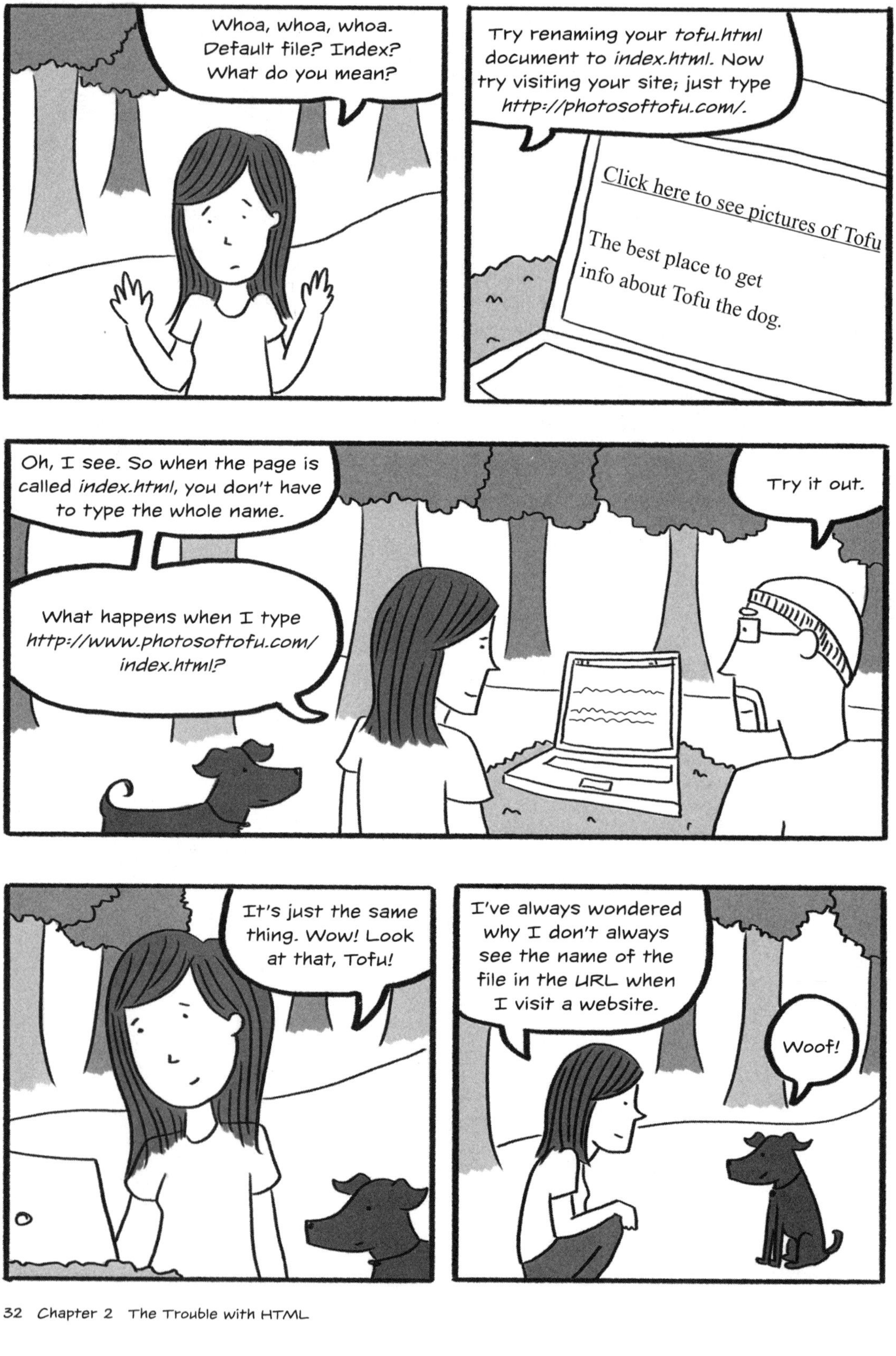
Whoa, whoa, whoa. Default file? Index? What do you mean?
Try renaming your *tofu.html* document to *index.html*. Now try visiting your site; just type *http://photosoftofu.com/*.
Click here to see pictures of Tofu
The best place to get info about Tofu the dog.
Oh, I see. So when the page is called *index.html*, you don't have to type the whole name.
What happens when I type *http://www.photosoftofu.com/index.html*?
Try it out.
It's just the same thing. Wow! Look at that, Tofu!
I've always wondered why I don't always see the name of the file in the URL when I visit a website.
Woof!

Adding Pictures

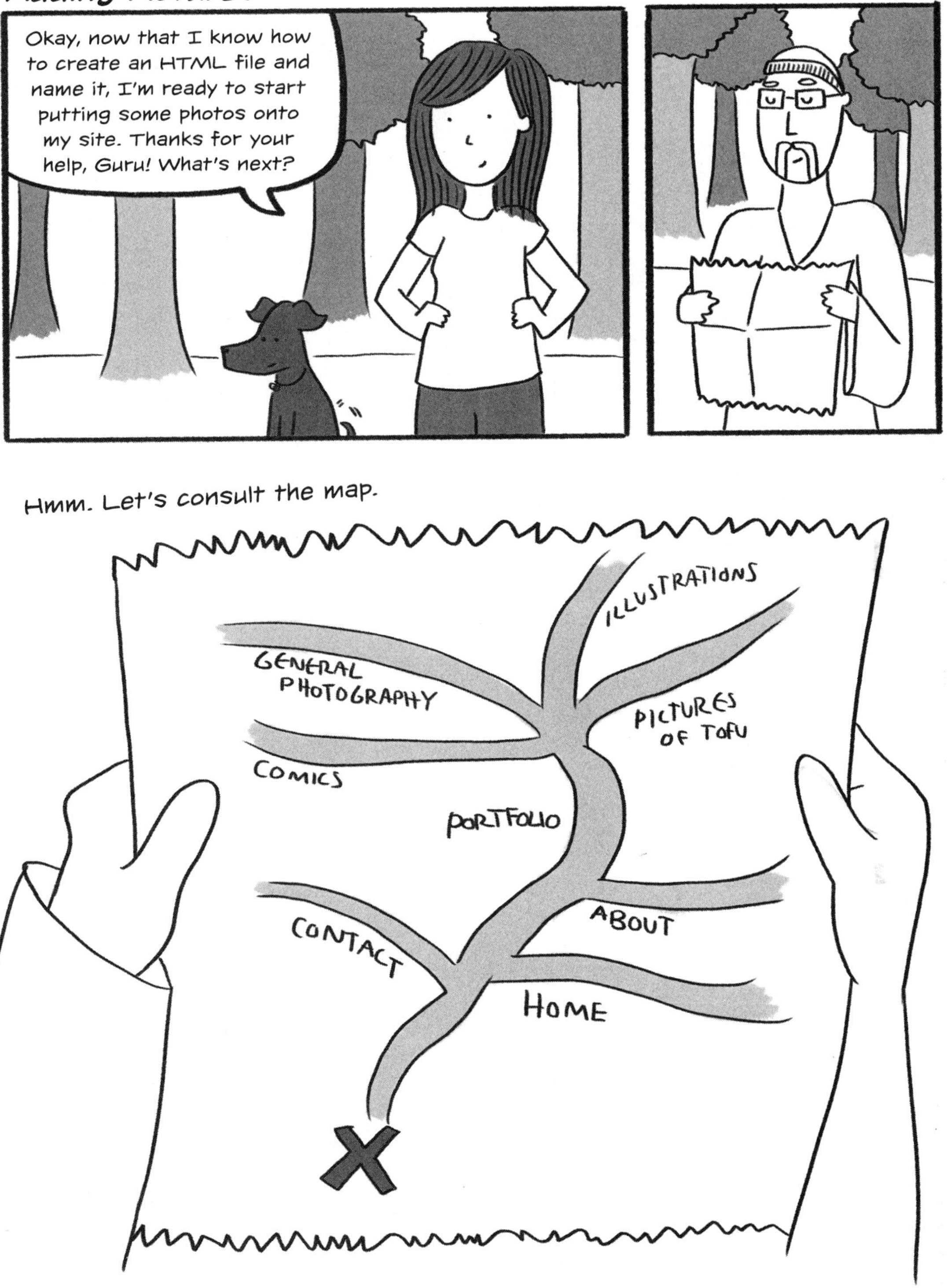
Okay, now that I know how to create an HTML file and name it, I'm ready to start putting some photos onto my site. Thanks for your help, Guru! What's next?
Hmm. Let's consult the map.
ILLUSTRATIONS
GENERAL PHOTOGRAPHY
PICTURES OF TOFU
COMICS
PORTFOLIO
ABOUT
CONTACT
HOME
X

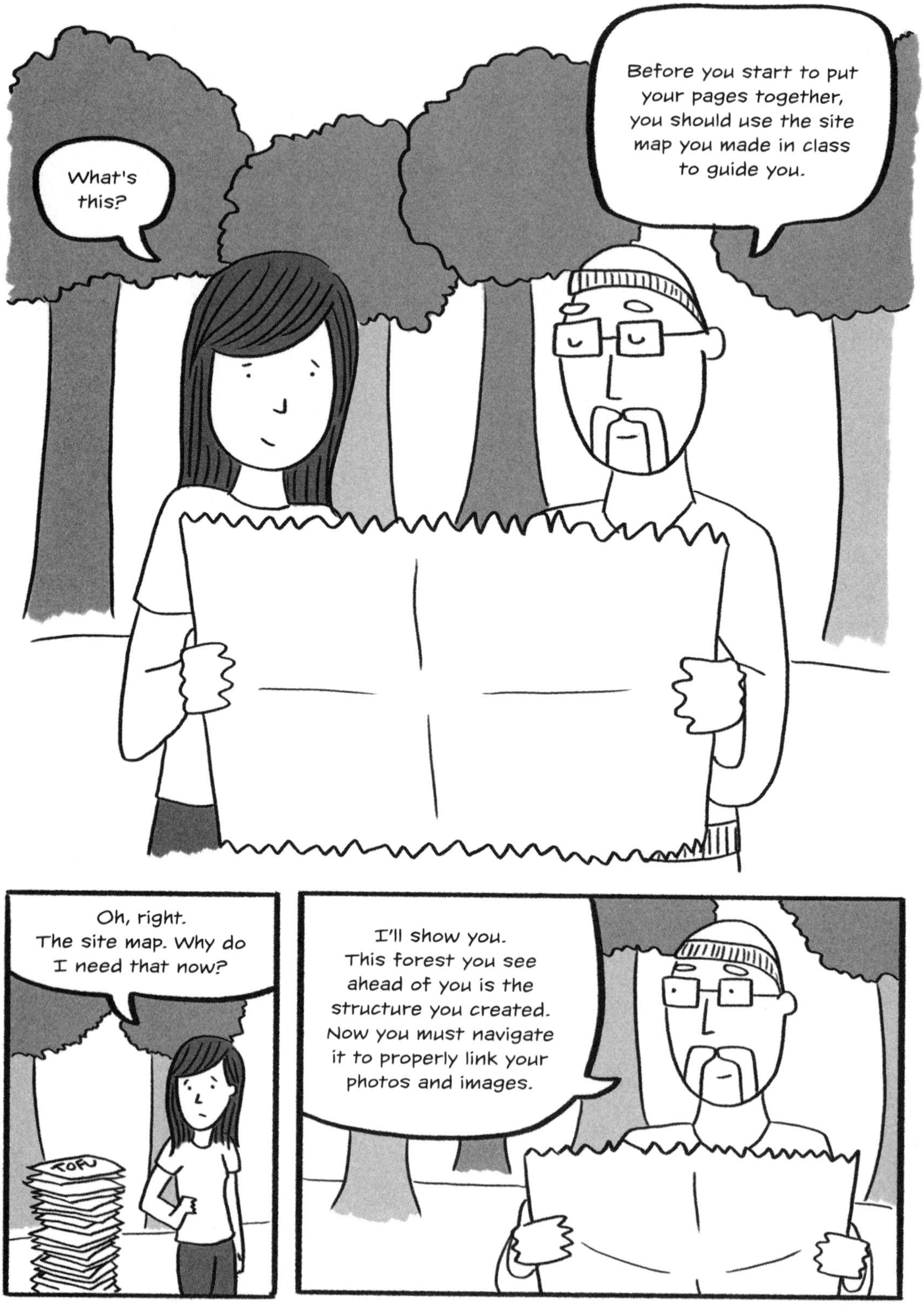
What's this?
Before you start to put your pages together, you should use the site map you made in class to guide you.
Oh, right. The site map. Why do I need that now?
TOFU
I'll show you. This forest you see ahead of you is the structure you created. Now you must navigate it to properly link your photos and images.

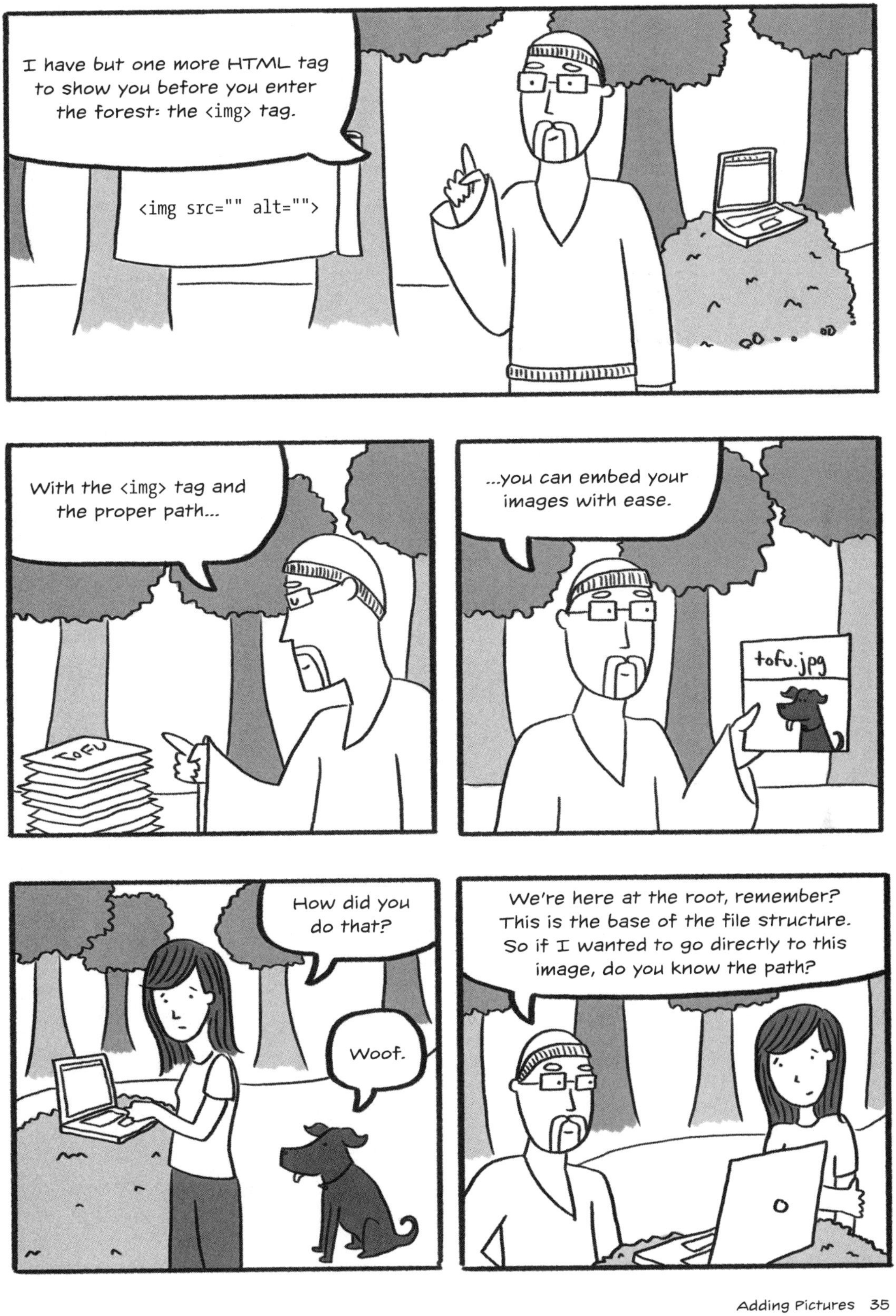
I have but one more HTML tag to show you before you enter the forest: the <img> tag.
<img src="" alt="">
With the <img> tag and the proper path...
TOFU
...you can embed your images with ease.
tofu.jpg
How did you do that?
Woof.
We're here at the root, remember? This is the base of the file structure. So if I wanted to go directly to this image, do you know the path?

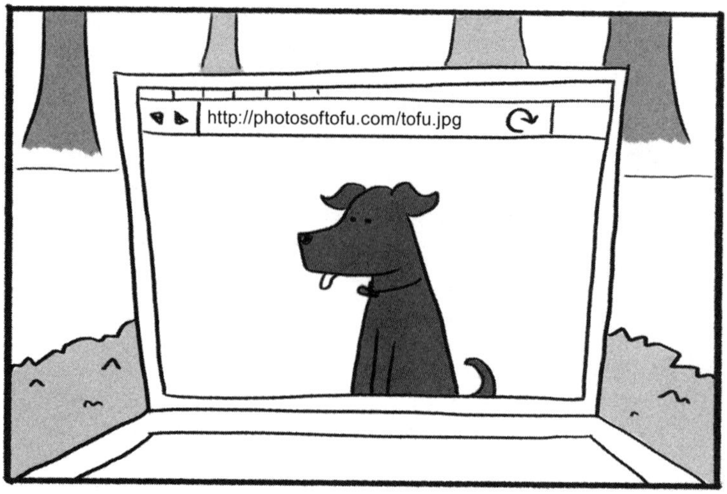
http://photosoftofu.com/tofu.jpg

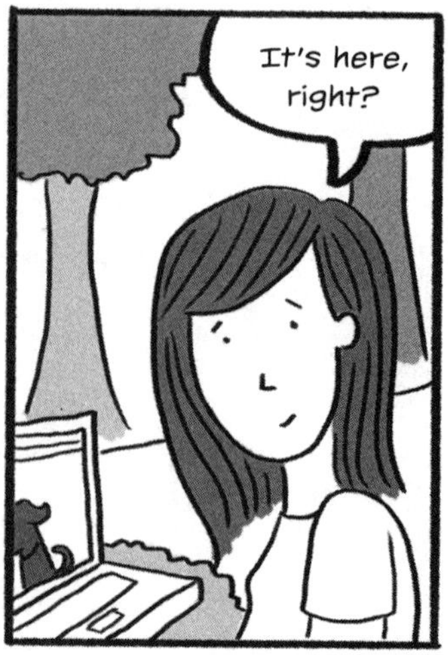
It's here, right?

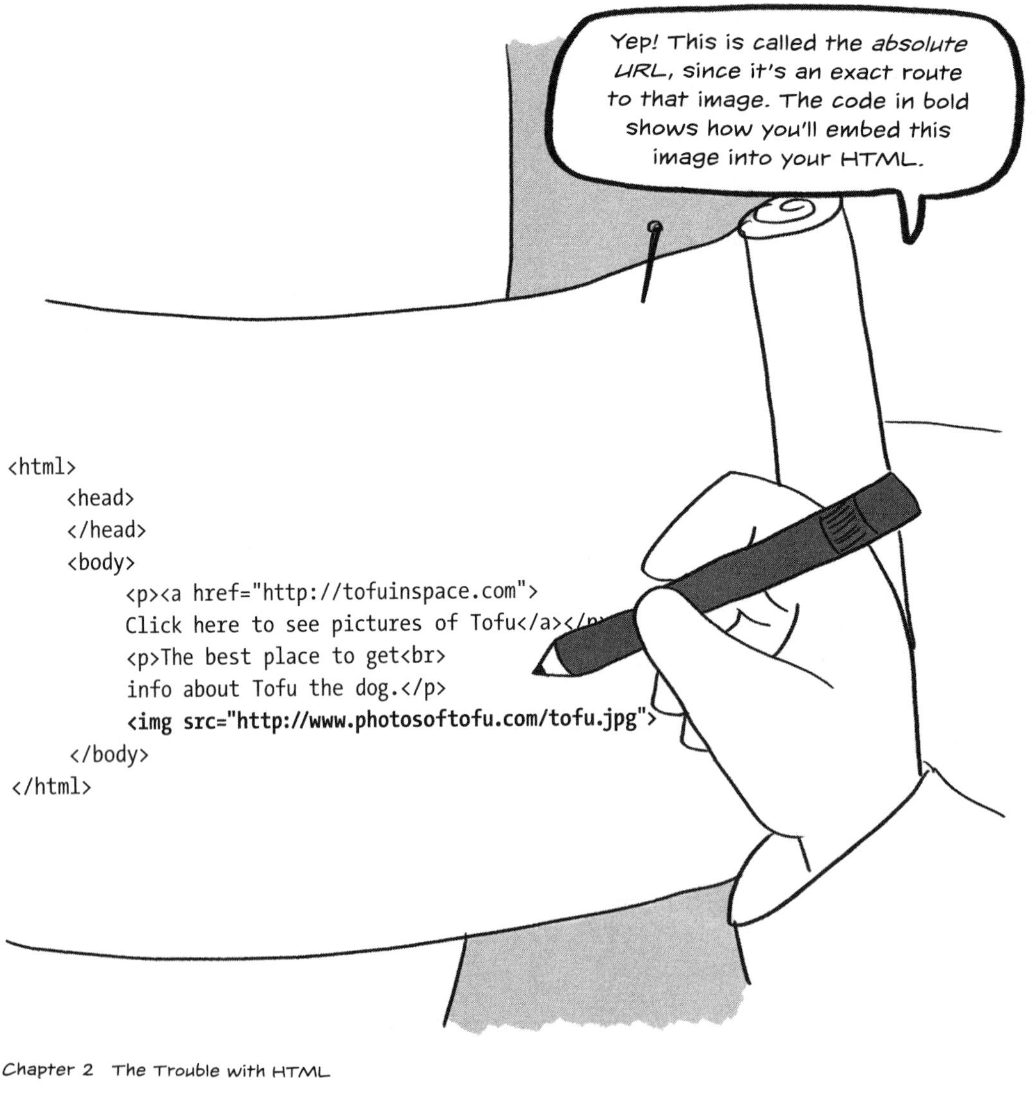
Yep! This is called the *absolute URL*, since it's an exact route to that image. The code in bold shows how you'll embed this image into your HTML.
<html>
<head>
</head>
<body>
<p><a href="http://tofuinspace.com">
Click here to see pictures of Tofu</a></p>
<p>The best place to get
info about Tofu the dog.</p>
<img src="http://www.photosoftofu.com/tofu.jpg">
</body>
</html>

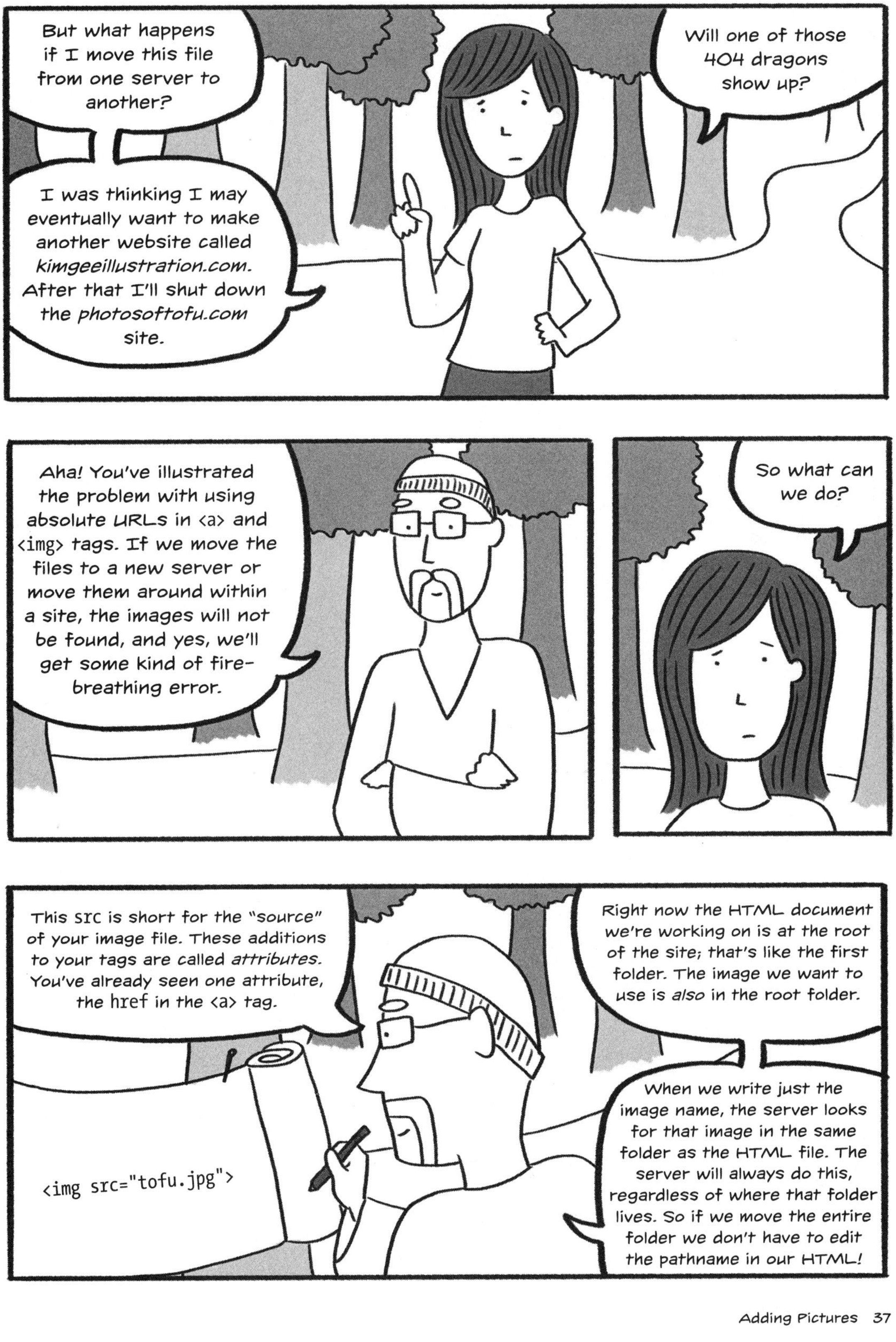
But what happens if I move this file from one server to another?
I was thinking I may eventually want to make another website called *kimgeeillustration.com*. After that I'll shut down the *photosoftofu.com* site.
Will one of those 404 dragons show up?
Aha! You've illustrated the problem with using absolute URLs in <a> and <img> tags. If we move the files to a new server or move them around within a site, the images will not be found, and yes, we'll get some kind of fire-breathing error.
So what can we do?
This src is short for the "source" of your image file. These additions to your tags are called *attributes*. You've already seen one attribute, the href in the <a> tag.
<img src="tofu.jpg">
Right now the HTML document we're working on is at the root of the site; that's like the first folder. The image we want to use is *also* in the root folder.
When we write just the image name, the server looks for that image in the same folder as the HTML file. The server will always do this, regardless of where that folder lives. So if we move the entire folder we don't have to edit the pathname in our HTML!

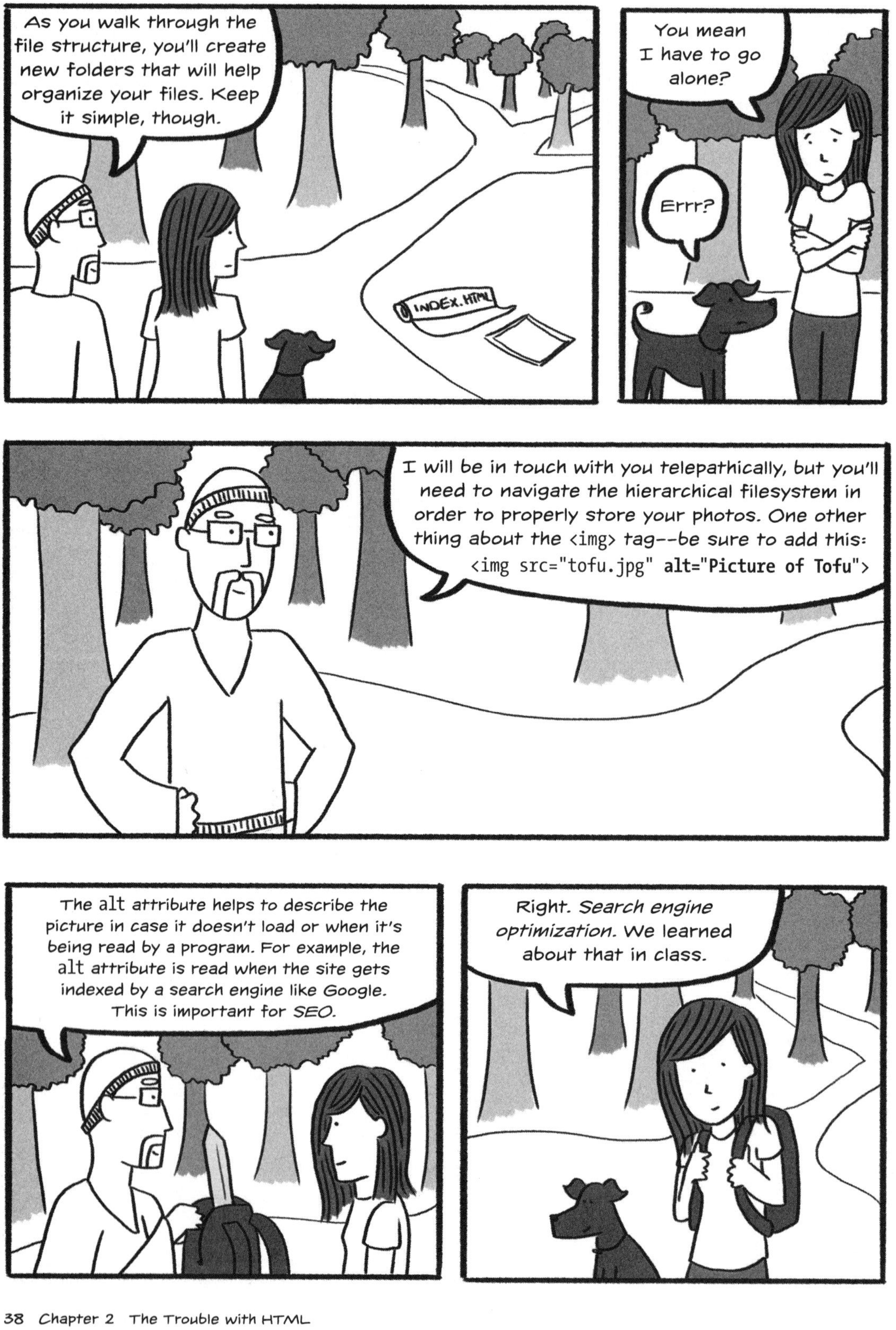

As you walk through the file structure, you'll create new folders that will help organize your files. Keep it simple, though.
INDEX.HTML
You mean I have to go alone?
Errr?
I will be in touch with you telepathically, but you'll need to navigate the hierarchical filesystem in order to properly store your photos. One other thing about the <img> tag--be sure to add this:
<img src="tofu.jpg" alt="Picture of Tofu">
The alt attribute helps to describe the picture in case it doesn't load or when it's being read by a program. For example, the alt attribute is read when the site gets indexed by a search engine like Google. This is important for SEO.
Right. Search engine optimization. We learned about that in class.

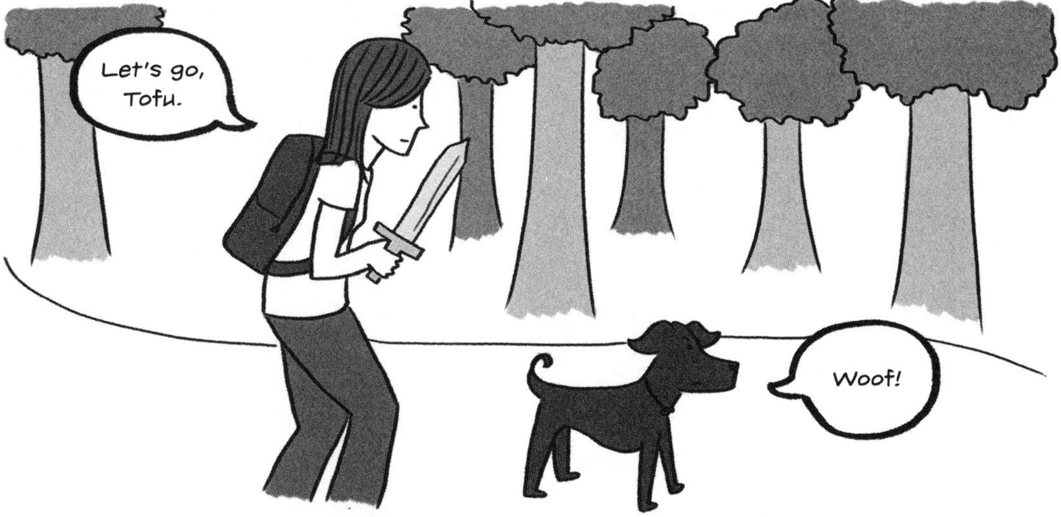
Let's go, Tofu.
Woof!

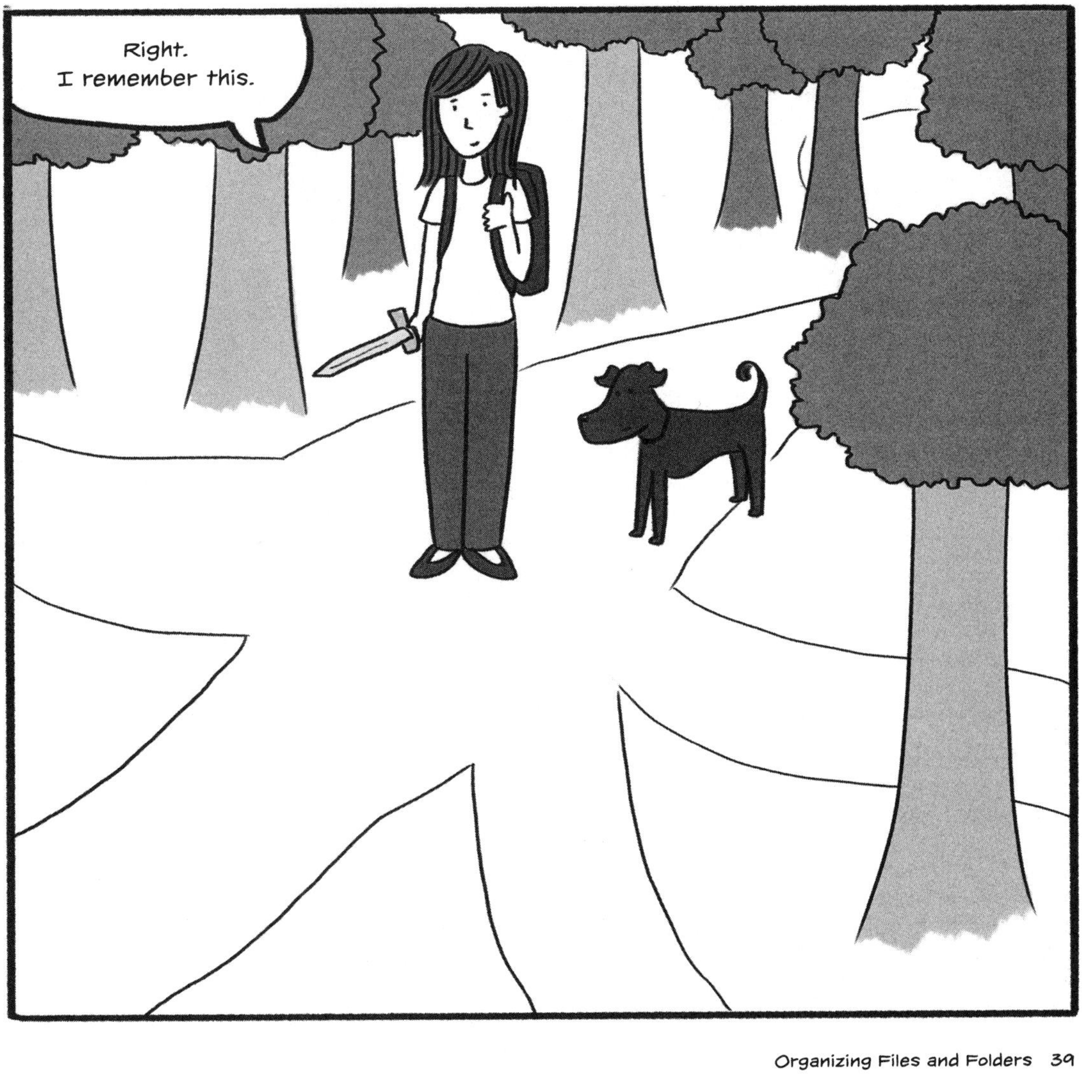
Right.
I remember this.

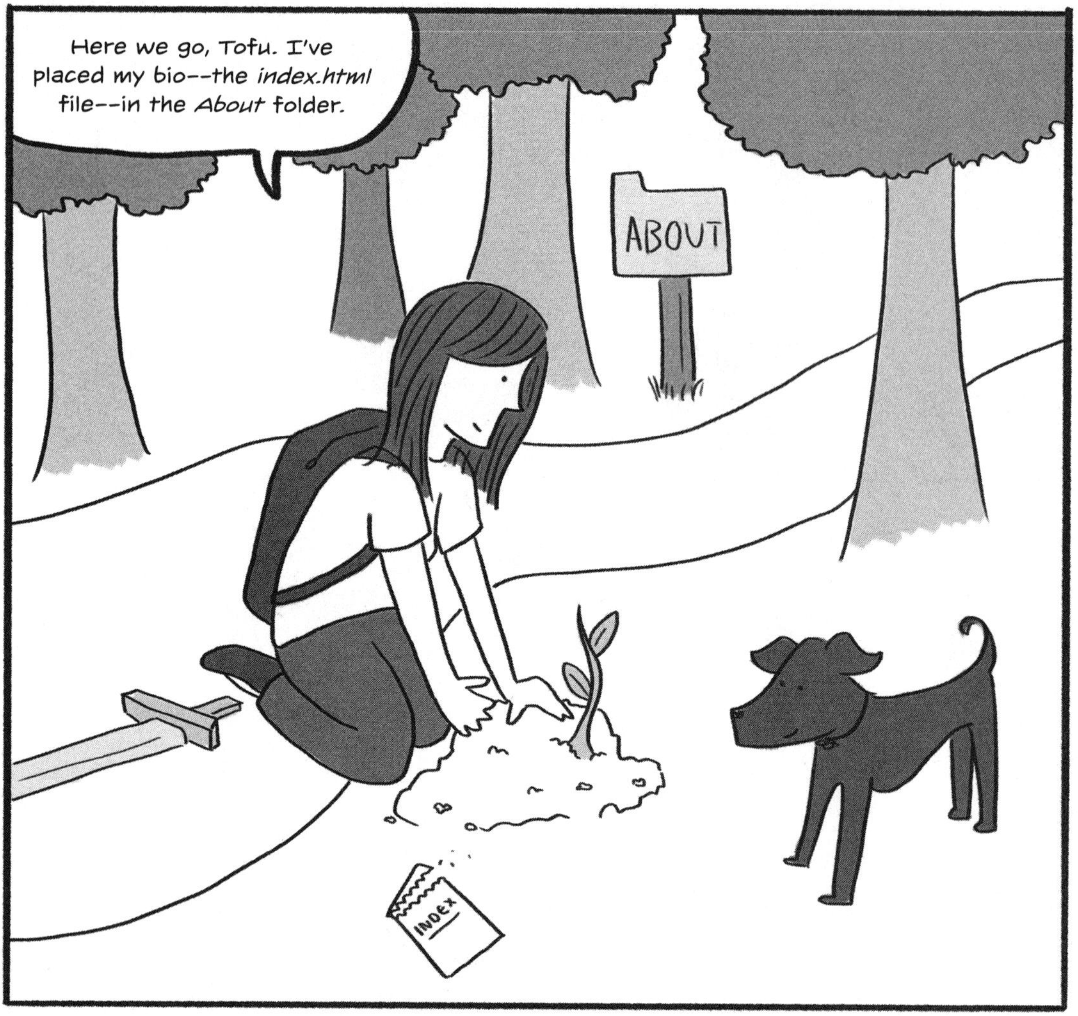
Here we go, Tofu. I've placed my bio--the *index.html* file--in the *About* folder.
ABOUT
INDEX

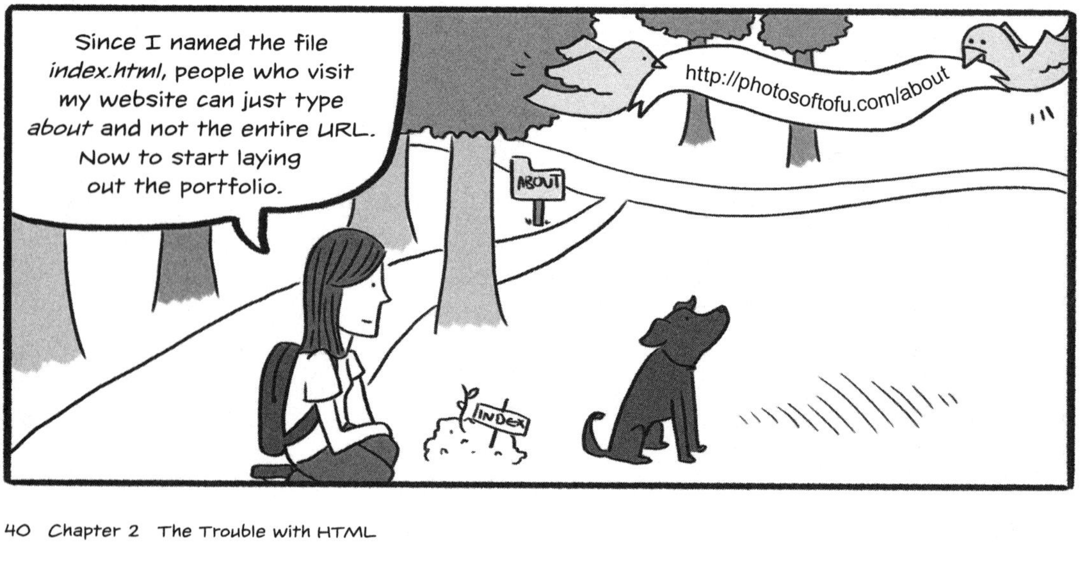
Since I named the file *index.html*, people who visit my website can just type *about* and not the entire URL. Now to start laying out the portfolio.
http://photosoftofu.com/about
ABOUT
INDEX

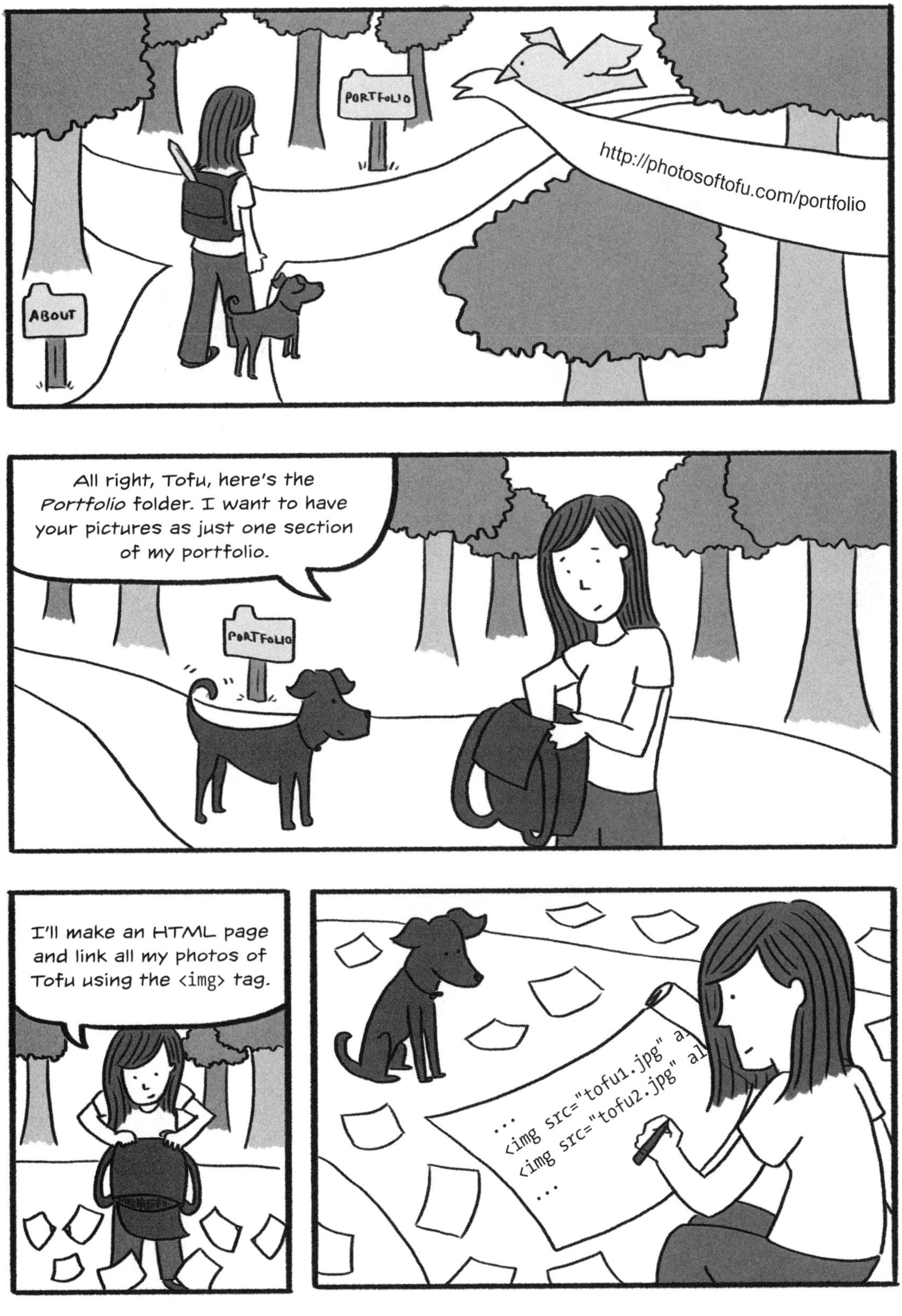
PORTFOLIO
http://photosoftofu.com/portfolio
ABOUT
All right, Tofu, here's the *Portfolio* folder. I want to have your pictures as just one section of my portfolio.
PORTFOLIO
I'll make an HTML page and link all my photos of Tofu using the <img> tag.
...
<img src="tofu1.jpg"
<img src="tofu2.jpg"
...

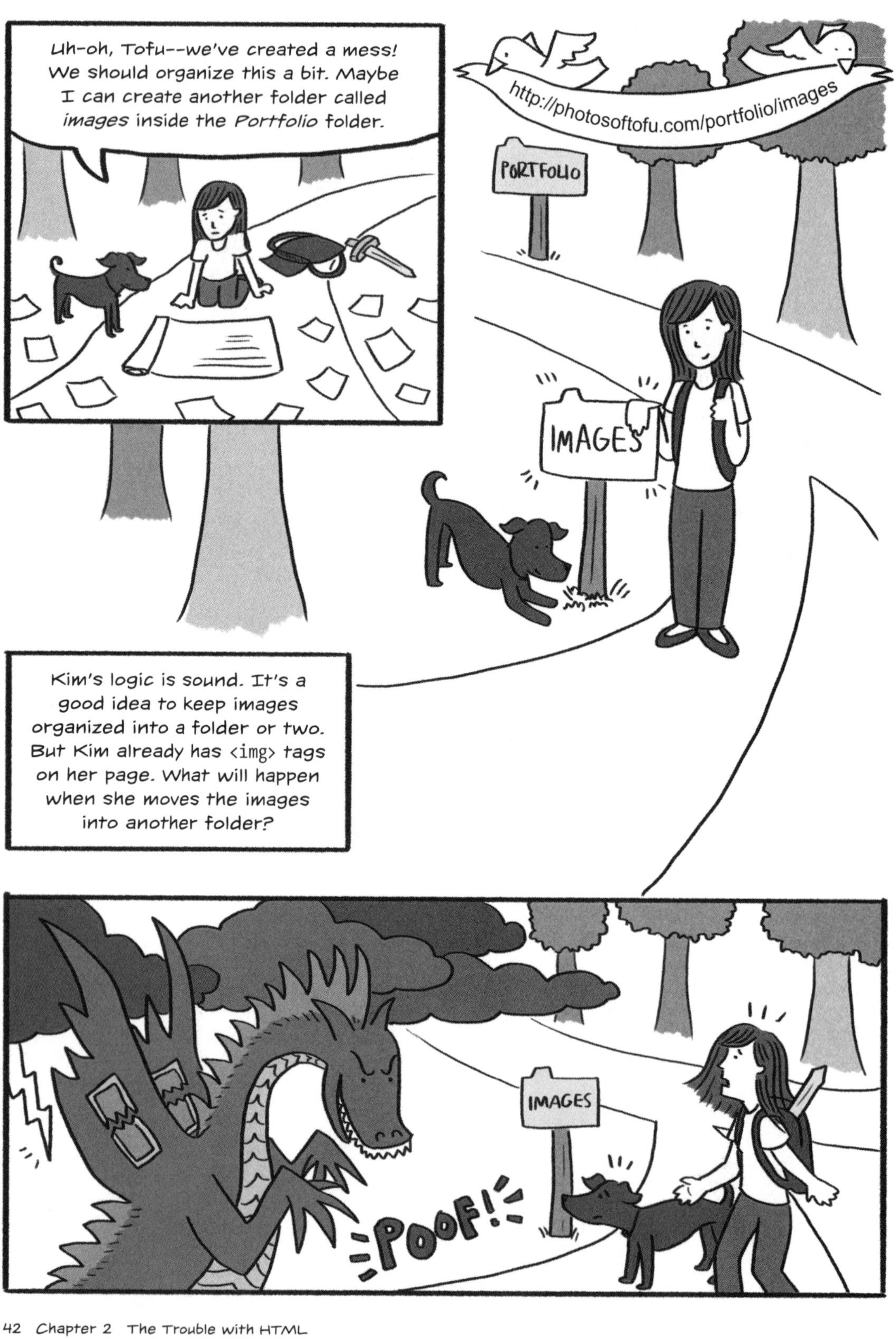
Uh-oh, Tofu--we've created a mess! We should organize this a bit. Maybe I can create another folder called *images* inside the *Portfolio* folder.
http://photosoftofu.com/portfolio/images
PORTFOLIO
IMAGES
Kim's logic is sound. It's a good idea to keep images organized into a folder or two. But Kim already has <img> tags on her page. What will happen when she moves the images into another folder?
IMAGES
POOF!

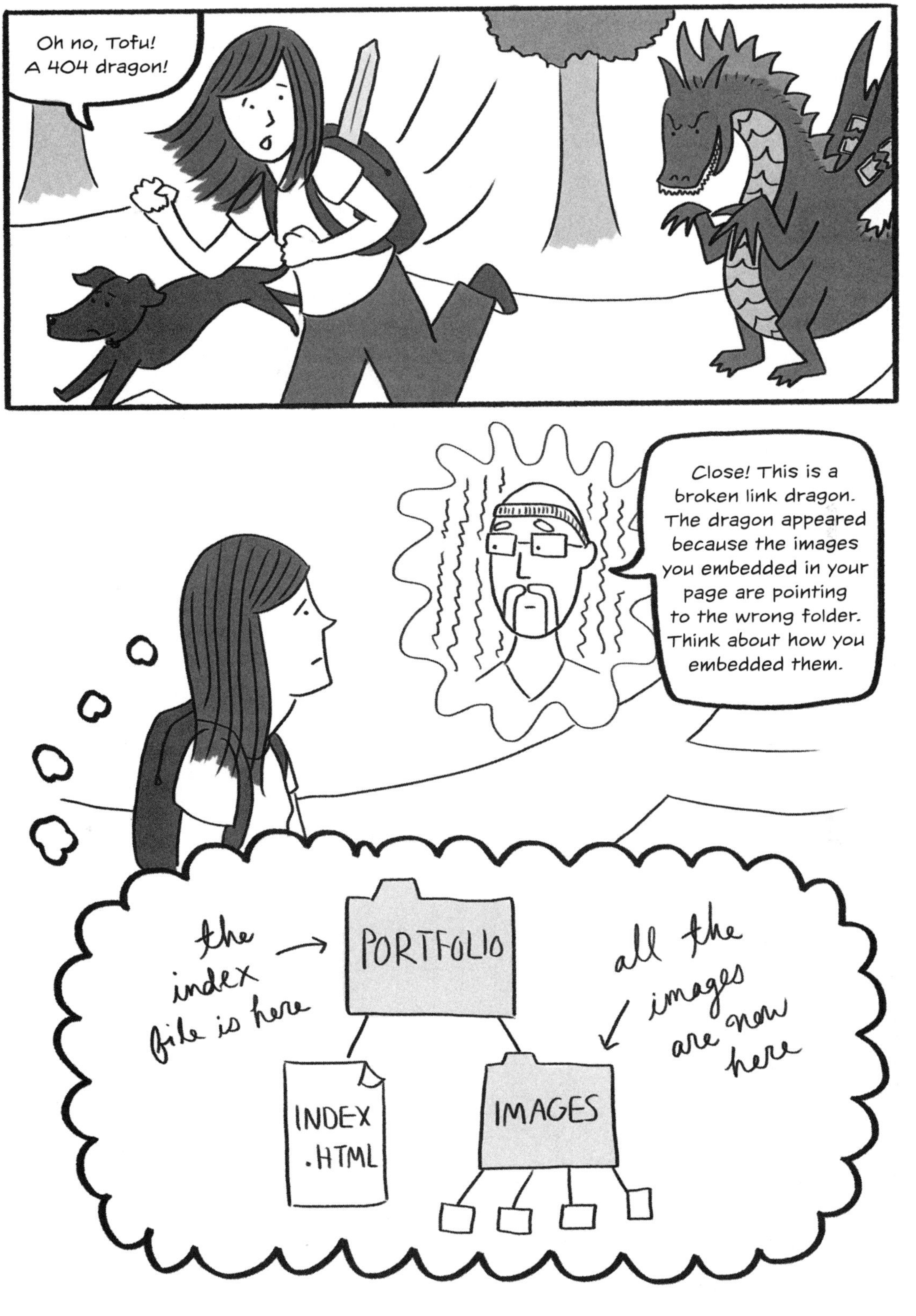
Oh no, Tofu! A 404 dragon!
Close! This is a broken link dragon. The dragon appeared because the images you embedded in your page are pointing to the wrong folder. Think about how you embedded them.
the index file is here
PORTFOLIO
all the images are now here
INDEX .HTML
IMAGES

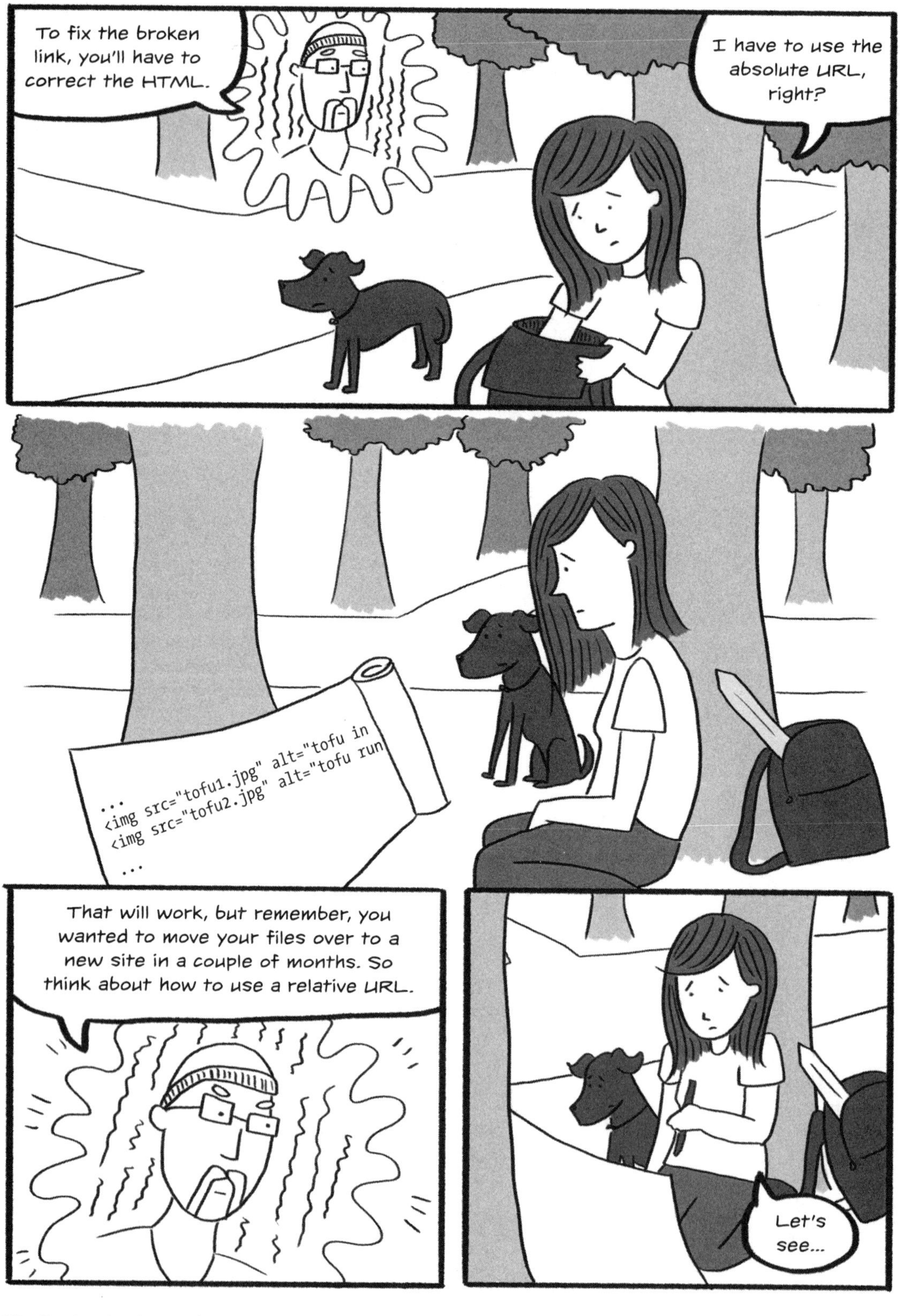
To fix the broken link, you'll have to correct the HTML.
I have to use the absolute URL, right?
...
<img src="tofu1.jpg" alt="tofu in
<img src="tofu2.jpg" alt="tofu run
...
That will work, but remember, you wanted to move your files over to a new site in a couple of months. So think about how to use a relative URL.
Let's see...

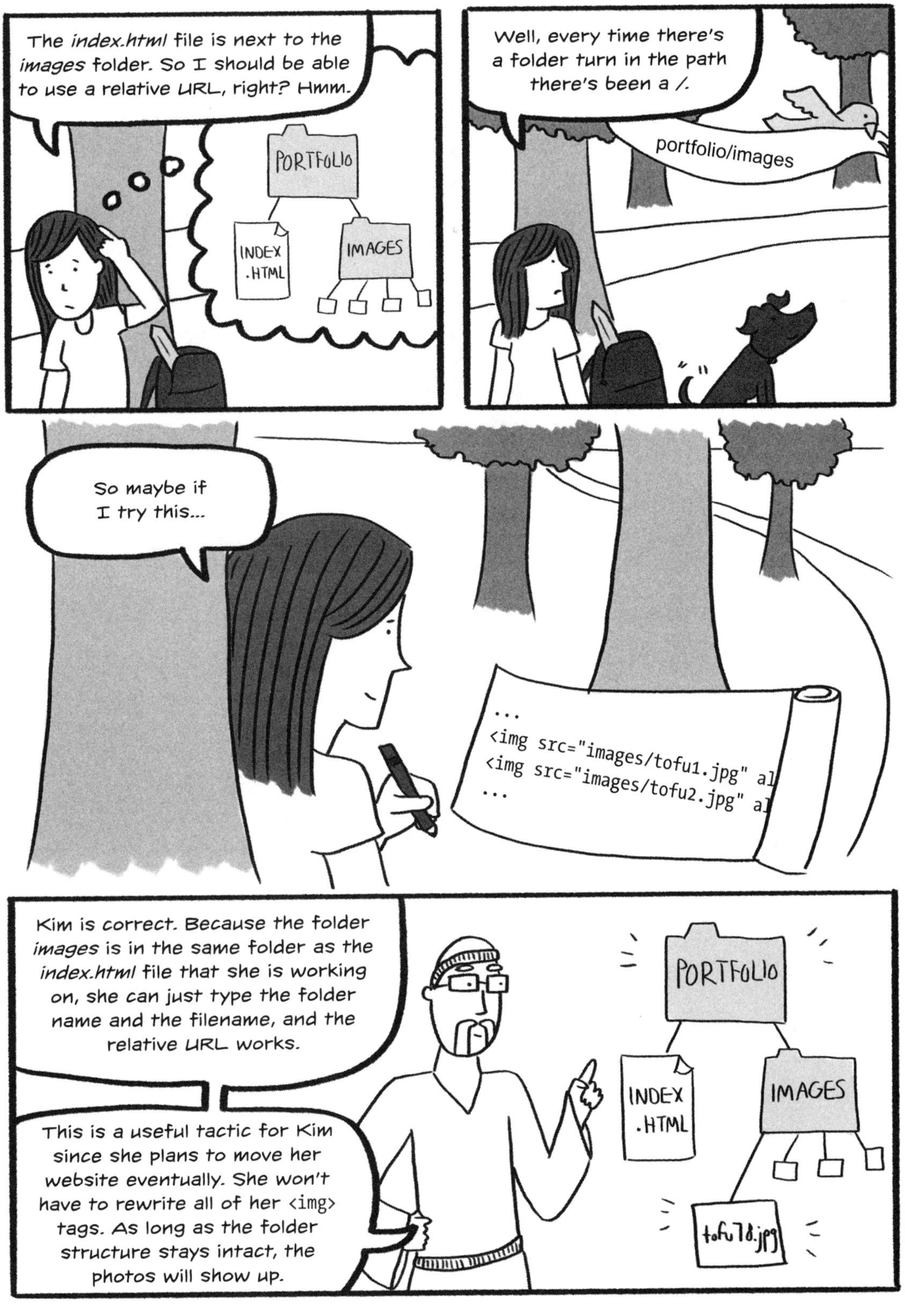
The *index.html* file is next to the *images* folder. So I should be able to use a relative URL, right? Hmm.
PORTFOLIO
INDEX .HTML
IMAGES
Well, every time there's a folder turn in the path there's been a /.
portfolio/images
So maybe if I try this...
...
<img src="images/tofu1.jpg" al
<img src="images/tofu2.jpg" al
...
Kim is correct. Because the folder *images* is in the same folder as the *index.html* file that she is working on, she can just type the folder name and the filename, and the relative URL works.
This is a useful tactic for Kim since she plans to move her website eventually. She won't have to rewrite all of her <img> tags. As long as the folder structure stays intact, the photos will show up.
PORTFOLIO
INDEX .HTML
IMAGES
tofu78.jpg

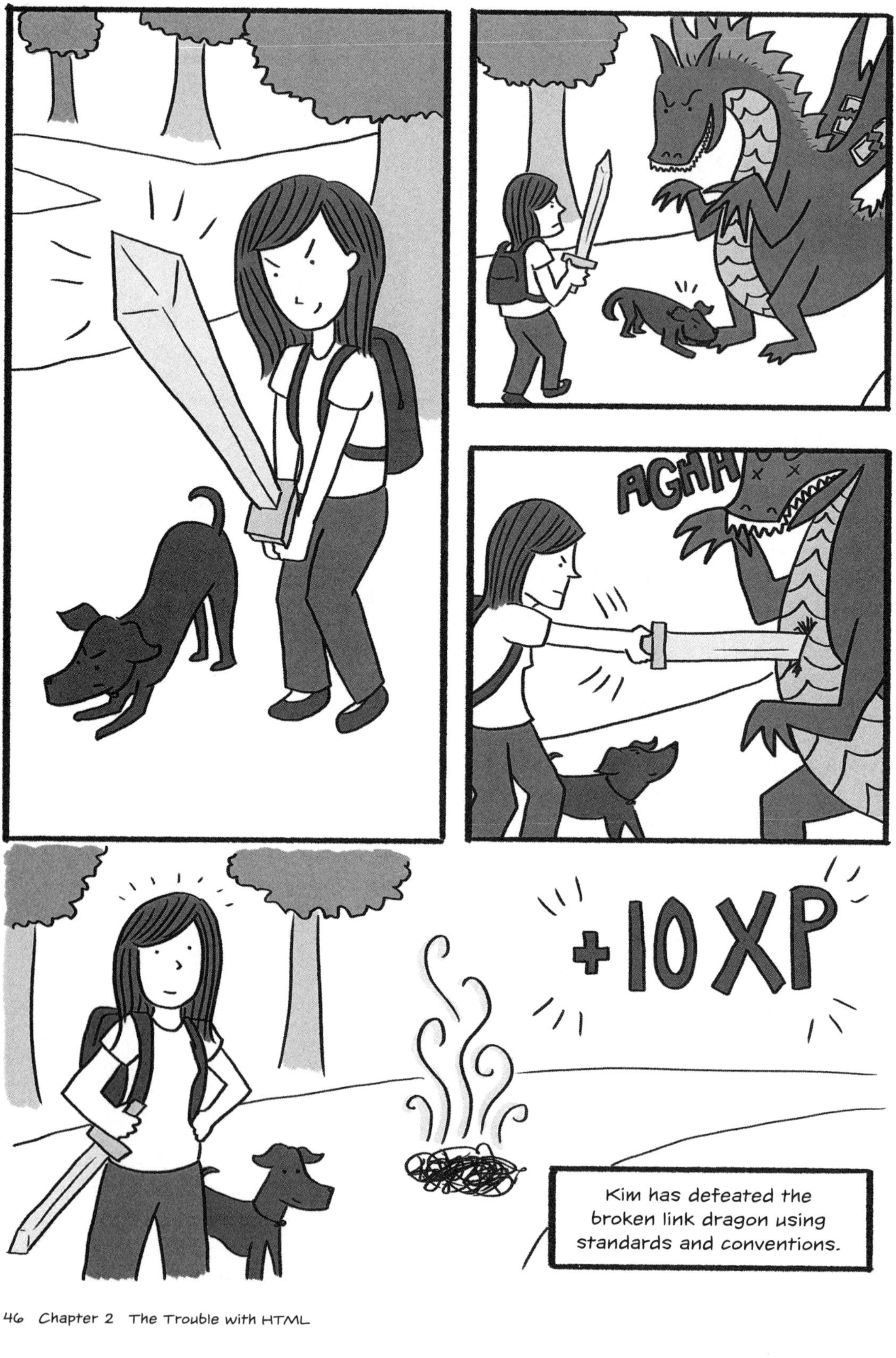
AGHH
+10 XP
Kim has defeated the broken link dragon using standards and conventions.

Playing with HTML

Building a website doesn't have to be complicated, but it does require some forethought. Even though HTML was new to Kim, she was able to use her plan to avoid errors. The journey of building a website starts with a single web page, and all web pages use HTML.

But what is HTML? *HyperText Markup Language* is the foundational language of the World Wide Web. An HTML document is text, which means you can often open it and read large sections of it without having any coding knowledge. The markup part appears in angle brackets (<>), which are interpreted by a web browser. When a web browser sees an HTML bracket within a page, it recognizes the value of the bracket and changes the text that follows according to a set of rules.

Once you've chosen a code editor, building an HTML page simply requires some common sense and memorization. Let's use some basic tags to start building a web page. Open your text editor and follow along.

Getting Started

All web pages start with a document declaration called a **DOCTYPE**. This tells the web browser which version of HTML you are using so that it knows which set of rules to obey. In this book we use HTML5. The **DOCTYPE** for HTML5 is `<!DOCTYPE html>`, so this should be the very first line on your HTML document. This simple declaration prepares your visitor's web browser so it knows which version of HTML it's about to receive. HTML5 is the fifth iteration of the language! Web designers improve their tools over time, so HTML evolves and tags fall in and out of fashion just as words in English do.

The next bit of HTML you'll write is where the exciting markup really begins. Use the `<html></html>` tags to begin and end your document. All of the HTML for this page will go between those bracketed tags. Add some text between the `<html>` tags (this process is called *marking up*), as shown here:

```
<!DOCTYPE html>
<html>


        My first web page! Allllll right!


</html>
```

Remember that HTML is not whitespace dependent. By leaving blank lines between the `<html>` and `</html>` tags, we've given ourselves room to write more content for our page. Whitespace (like paragraph returns and tab spaces) will be ignored by the browser, but it makes it easier for us humans to read. You can now save the document and name it *test.html*.

When naming an HTML page, avoid using spaces and special characters (like #, $, &, and *). If you want to use more than one word in the filename, use a hyphen (-) to separate each word (for example, *my-first-test.html*). HTML filenames are case sensitive, so for consistency's sake we will keep all of our filenames lowercase.

This page should work in our browser, but it's missing some standard pieces of an HTML document. So let's add some more tags to build the basic outline of our page.

Between `<html>` and `</html>`, add the following tags with a line space between them: `<head></head>` and `<body></body>`. Place the opening `<body>` tag above your sentences, "My first web page! Allllll right!" and the closing tag `</body>` below them. These add the **head** and **body** elements to your HTML page—the body of the document is where all the content is displayed, and the head contains information about your page (see "Adding a Head to Your Document" on page 54). We'll focus on content for the **body** for now. Your document should now look like this:

```
<!DOCTYPE html>
<html>
    <head>

    </head>
    <body>

        My first web page! Allllll right!

    </body>
</html>
```

Save your file again, and then try opening *test.html* in a web browser like Chrome. You should see whatever text you added; I see a web page that reads "My first web page! Allllll right!"

This may seem like small potatoes, but if you right-click the page and choose View page source, you should see your handiwork: the HTML that created this web page. When a document's name ends with *.html*, the browser knows to not show the bracketed HTML tags in the page.

Rename the file to *test.txt*. What do you think will happen if you open this file in your browser? Try it, and you'll notice that the HTML tags actually appear within the window this time. This is because the filename ends with *.txt*. Your browser assumes the file does not contain any HTML and simply displays all of the contents of the page, including the HTML tags. Naming the file with the *.html* extension is important for the web browser to understand what to do with the page.

Switch the filename back to *test.html* and then reload it using the refresh button in your browser. As you edit this HTML document, you can save and refresh your browser whenever you want to test that the HTML markup you've added is working.

Using Basic HTML Tags

Now we're ready to start adding more content. The first tag we'll try out is the paragraph tag, `<p>`. Delete your test message, and add `<p>Hello World!</p>` between the `<body>` tags. The `<body>` tag signifies the beginning and ending of the main content area of the page. Any text, including any HTML formatting, placed between the `<body>` and `</body>` tags will appear within the browser window. When you save and then refresh the page, you should see your text but not the `<p>`. Great work!

Now let's add a second paragraph. Try putting `<p>This is a second paragraph.</p>` at the end of that first line. Your file should look like this:

```
<!DOCTYPE html>
<html>
    <head>

    </head>
    <body>
        <p>Hello World!</p><p>This is a second paragraph.</p>
    </body>
</html>
```

When you refresh the page in your web browser, you should see that the paragraphs are separated by a blank space, as shown in Figure 2-1.

test.html
file:///Users/natecooper/Desktop/test.html
Reader
Music
All Music
Apple
Yahoo!
Google Maps
YouTube
Wikipedia
Hello World!
This is a second paragraph.

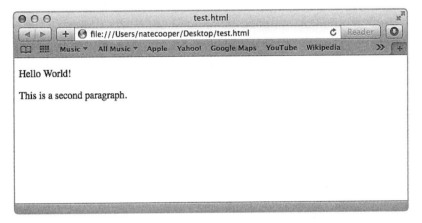

Figure 2-1: This is what your page should look like in a web browser.

Why are the paragraphs separated even though in the HTML code they are on the same line? Remember that HTML doesn't care about whitespace, so the `<p>` tag is what decides where the paragraph goes, not an actual line break.

Although we don't really need returns in our HTML, it is still handy for readability to have a "real" line break in our code. Try writing your HTML document this way:

```
<!DOCTYPE html>
<html>
    <head>

    </head>
    <body>
        <p>Hello World!</p>
        <p>This is a second paragraph.</p>
    </body>
</html>
```

You might notice that I'm indenting my lines. Indents are not recognized or required by HTML; they are there purely for readability. You will often see code written like this; it's an example of a *convention* of HTML. It makes our HTML easier for others to read and helps us ensure that we close all of our tags properly.

Problems can occur if you do not properly close markup in your code. We will see an example of a common mistake after we learn our next two tags. Try applying the `<strong>` tag and `<em>` tag to some new sentences in the second paragraph, shown here in bold:

```
<!DOCTYPE html>
<html>
    <head>

    </head>
    <body>
        <p>Hello World!</p>
        <p>This is a second paragraph. <strong>This is bold text.</strong>
        <em>This is italic.</em></p>
    </body>
</html>
```

Now save the file and refresh your browser. You should see that the sentence **This is bold text.** appears in boldface in the web browser. The `<strong>` tag is typically used to set text in boldface. The sentence *This is italic.* should appear in italic. The `<em>` tag (short for *emphasis*) typically sets your text in italic.

What happens if you don't properly close your tags? Try this: Delete `</strong>` so that the tag isn't closed. Remember to save and refresh your browser. Now the entire rest of the page is bold. This demonstrates why it's important to properly close all of your tags. When your tags aren't closed, the web browser doesn't know when the markup ends, so it continues until the page ends. In the case of a `<strong>` tag, this is pretty inconvenient because it makes all of your paragraphs bold. In a worst-case scenario, forgetting the closing tag might make your content disappear completely from the page. Get in the habit of closing each HTML tag and always double-check before you save your page. Make sure you put back in that `</strong>` tag before we move on!

Some tags are *self-closing*. This means that they stand alone without having to wrap themselves around text—for example, `<br>`. Try putting the `<br>` tag between `<strong>This is bold text.</strong>` and `<em>This is italic.</em>`:

```
<!DOCTYPE html>
<html>
    <head>

    </head>
    <body>
        <p>Hello World!</p>
        <p>This is a second paragraph. <strong>This is bold text.</strong><br>
        <em>This is italic.</em></p>
    </body>
</html>
```

When you save and refresh your browser, you should see a line break. A line break puts the text on a separate line, like <p> but with a smaller gap. This is sometimes called a *soft return* in word processors.

Paragraphs and returns aren't the only dividers within the body of a page. There's also the heading tag. HTML offers six types of headings, with <h1> being the most important and <h6> being the least important. Generally, headings are used to define sections on a page, just like section headings in a book or an article. Let's change the paragraph <p>Hello World!</p> to an <h1>:

```
<!DOCTYPE html>
    <html>
    <head>

    </head>
    <body>
        <h1>Hello World!</h1>
        <p>This is a second paragraph. <strong>This is bold text.</strong><br>
        <em>This is italic.</em></p>
    </body>
</html>
```

When you save your page and reload it in your web browser, you should see that the <h1> tag has made the text *Hello World!* appear larger on the screen. If we had a longer document, we might have subheadings that use smaller heading tags like <h2></h2> or <h3></h3>. Remember that headings go all the way from <h1> to <h6>, so you can use these tags to visually divide sections of your page.

Now we're ready to make links. This tag might seem a little tricky at first. You can think of a link as an *anchor* that has a *reference*. The tag looks like this:

```
<a href="http://website.com">Visitors can click on me!</a>
```

Opening tag	URL	Link text	Closing tag

The a stands for anchor and the **href** stands for hyperlink reference. Notice the angle brackets on either end; that whole thing is the opening tag! The **href** defines the website address, or URL, that will be loaded when someone clicks the link. Between this opening and the closing tag </a>, we have the "clickable" link text.

Try it out with any URL:

```
<!DOCTYPE html>
<html>
    <head>

    </head>
    <body>
        <h1>Hello World!</h1>
        <p>This is a second paragraph. <strong>This is bold text.</strong><br>
        <em>This is italic.</em></p>
```

```
    <p><a href="http://natecooper.co">Click here!</a></p>
  </body>
</html>
```

You should notice when you view the page in your browser that the words *Click here* are blue and underlined, indicating they are a hyperlink. If you click the link, it will take you to my website. Every page on the Web has a corresponding website address (URL) that you can use to link to it directly. You can also link to other pages on your own website.

Knowing how to create paragraphs, headings, italicized and boldface text, and links is invaluable, so take some time to memorize these tags and how they work. Almost every web page in existence will use them. Even when you use more sophisticated systems like WordPress, knowing some basic HTML markup will serve you well.

Embedding Images into Your Web Page

Now let's try to embed an image. There are several ways to do so, as Kim found out while building her portfolio, so we'll want to be careful not to run into any dragons. First, you'll need an image formatted as JPG, GIF, or PNG. You can use the <img> tag to embed an image into your page. Like the <br> tag, <img> doesn't need a closing tag, but it can be a bit tricky because it relies on knowing the exact location of the image file to work properly. A typical image tag looks like this:

```
<img src="path-to-image/image.jpg" alt="description of image">
```

It's the img src="*path-to-image/image*.jpg" part that can be tricky. For an example of an image location, let's take a look at an image hosted on my desktop. If I navigate to this image, I can find the image location in the address bar of my browser, as shown in Figure 2-2.

Figure 2-2: Finding an image's location

The exact address of an image is called the *absolute path* or *absolute URL*. For us, embedding an image using the absolute path isn't ideal, because we're building this web page "locally" (i.e., on your computer). We'll use a *relative path* instead; we'll keep it simple and leave the image in the same folder as our HTML document, which makes the path very easy.

Move your image into the same folder as your web page and rename it *image.jpg* (or *photo.gif* or *photo.png*, depending on your file format). As with our HTML pages, avoid using spaces and uppercase in the name. If the image is in the same folder as your *test.html* page, you can now embed the image using this code:

```
<img src="image.jpg" alt="our first photo">
```

Your document should look like this:

```
<!DOCTYPE html>
<html>
    <head>

    </head>
    <body>
        <h1>Hello World!</h1>
        <p>This is a second paragraph. <strong>This is bold text.</strong><br>
        <em>This is italic.</em></p>
        <p><a href="http://natecooper.co">Click here!</a></p>
        <img src="image.jpg" alt="our first photo">
    </body>
</html>
```

Save and refresh your browser. Is your image there? If not, make sure that you used the exact name of the image and that it's in the same folder as your *test.html* file (in our example, the image is on the desktop).

If you are building a portfolio like Kim and you'd like to put all of your images into a single folder, go back to the folder containing your *test.html* file and create a new folder called *images*. Now move your *image.jpg* file into that folder. As a test, go back and reload your page in the web browser without making any changes to your code. You should get a `broken link` error message, which means the image is no longer visible. To fix the error, we'll need to correct the path in the HTML code. Find your `<img>` tag:

```
<img src="image.jpg" alt="our first photo">
```

and change the file location to this:

```
<img src="images/image.jpg" alt="our first photo">
```

The / represents moving to one folder (or directory) within the current folder. So, for example, if you moved your photo to a folder called *black-and-white*, which was inside a folder called *portfolio*, which was inside a folder called *images*, the path in your HTML code would look like this: `images/portfolio/black-and-white/image.jpg`.

The advantage of using relative paths is that, unlike with absolute paths, there is nothing tying your HTML code to a specific location. So, if you move the entire site (in this case, the *test.html* page and the *images* folder) to a new location or host, the `<img>` paths will still work. If you were using an absolute path instead, even when the files were moved the paths in the code would point to the old address and you'd see a broken image icon.

There's one other way to indicate a relative path that is specific to being on a server: starting the path with a /. When you start with a /, the browser will go all the way to the first folder on the host. This is advantageous if you have an image, like a logo, that you want to use on every page. You might write `<img src="/logo.gif" alt="our company logo">` in your code, for example. This would look for the *logo.gif* file at the *root* of the host—the first folder on your host into which you can place files. Again, this helps if you ever change or move your site.

Adding a Head to Your Document

If you've followed along so far, your HTML page should look like this:

```
<!DOCTYPE html>
<html>
    <head>

    </head>
    <body>
        <h1>Hello World!</h1>
        <p>This is a second paragraph. <strong>This is bold text.</strong><br>
        <em>This is italic.</em></p>
        <p><a href="http://natecooper.co">Click here!</a></p>
        <img src="image.jpg" alt="our first photo">
    </body>
</html>
```

Notice how there is a section at the top that is currently empty?

```
<head>

</head>
```

So far we've avoided putting anything in the `<head>` section of the document because we've been working only on things that are visible in the main window of the web browser.

The `<body>` section of the page contains content that goes into the main window of the web browser. So far, all of the HTML we've seen lives inside these tags. But the `<title>` is one example of a tag that lives in the `<head>` of your document.

Anything we put into the `<head>` of an HTML document will either go outside the main window area or will be completely invisible. Try adding `<title>My Web Page</title>` into the `<head>` of your document:

```
<!DOCTYPE html>
<html>
    <head>
        <title>My Web Page</title>
    </head>
    <body>
        <h1>Hello World!</h1>
        <p>This is a second paragraph. <strong>This is bold text.</strong><br>
        <em>This is italic.</em></p>
        <p><a href="http://natecooper.co">Click here!</a></p>
        <img src="image.jpg" alt="our first photo">
    </body>
</html>
```

Save and reload your page. Did you catch what changed? Depending on your web browser, it might be difficult to see the difference, but you should now see the title at the top of the window (see Figure 2-3) or as the name of your tab.

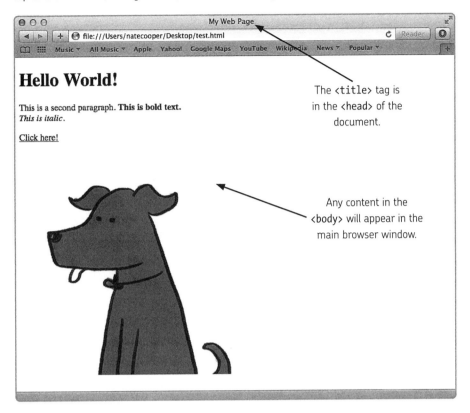

My Web Page
file:///Users/natecooper/Desktop/test.html
Music
All Music
Apple
Yahoo!
Google Maps
YouTube
Wikipedia
News
Popular
Reader
Hello World!
This is a second paragraph. This is bold text.
This is italic.
Click here!
The <title> tag is in the <head> of the document.
Any content in the <body> will appear in the main browser window.

Figure 2-3: Anything you put between the <title> tags appears at the top of the browser window.

What else goes in the `<head>`? In the course of learning to build a website, you may have heard the term *metadata*. Metadata just means information about a document, as opposed to content within the document. The `<title>` is a kind of metadata (namely, the title of your web page). The head of an HTML document can contain `<meta>` tags that we can use to further describe our document. These descriptions don't show up on the page but are used by search engines to learn more about your pages. For example, you can use `<meta name="description" content="`*description goes here*`">` to write a brief description of your page that will show up in search results. Try adding it so that your code looks like this:

```
<!DOCTYPE html>
<html>
    <head>
        <title>My Web Page</title>
        <meta name="description" content="A test page created while learning to
        code using the book Build Your Own Website.">
    </head>
```

```
    <body>
        <h1>Hello World!</h1>
        <p>This is a second paragraph. <strong>This is bold text.</strong><br>
        <em>This is italic.</em></p>
        <p><a href="http://natecooper.co">Click here!</a></p>
        <img src="image.jpg" alt="our first photo">
    </body>
</html>
```

If you save and reload the page, you'll notice that the description doesn't show up anywhere on the page. That's because this metadata is primarily for the benefit of external applications. For example, search engines like Google may use the meta description underneath the link to your site in search results (see Figure 2-4).

Web
News
Images
Videos
Shopping
More
Search tools
About 25,100,000 results (0.54 seconds)
Nate Cooper's Blog
natecooper.net/
Apr 11, 2014 - San Francisco is an eclectic city. Proof of this concept is the breadth of different songs written about it. How can writing about the same thing spur ...
Nate Cooper - Nice Guy
natecooper.co/
by Nate Cooper - in 203 Google+ circles
Author, Coach, edupreneur, Nate helps you remove obstacles to achieving your goals. Specializing in WordPress, Content Strategy & Custom classes.
metadata
A Tech Guru: WordPress - Nate Cooper
natecooper.co/technology-wordpress-blogging-seo/
by Nate Cooper - in 203 Google+ circles
Dec 19, 2012 - Nate thinks technology should be a tool to empower and that's why he is

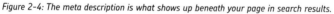

Figure 2-4: The meta description is what shows up beneath your page in search results.

Even though the `<meta>` tags are sometimes used by search engines, it's important to not assume that they can magically increase your search ranking. In the past, `<meta>` tags mattered quite a lot for search engine ranking, but these days they are no longer a major contributing factor. That said, adding a `<meta name="description">` to your pages is considered a good practice.

Now that we have a complete and functional web page, we're ready for CSS. Every web page should have the basic structure we've created here, with a `<head>` section containing metadata and information that's not visible on a page, and a `<body>` section containing information that appears within the main browser window. You might want to memorize some common HTML tags that we used in this chapter. Chances are, you'll need them on your journey.

Some Useful HTML Tags

Here is a list of commonly used HTML tags for your reference:

`<!DOCTYPE html>`   This tells the browser which version of HTML you plan to use. This particular DOCTYPE signifies HTML5. It is not an HTML element, but a declaration that should go at the very top of your page before the opening `<html>` tag.

`<html></html>`   Everything contained within these tags will be processed by the browser as HTML. Every HTML document should contain these tags.

`<head></head>`   Everything that is wrapped within will contain metadata that is used by the browser and doesn't show up within the main browser window.

`<body></body>`   Everything that is wrapped within will be visible in the main browser window. Your page's content will go here.

`<p></p>`   Any text contained within these paragraph tags will be considered part of a single paragraph.

`<strong></strong>`   Text placed between these brackets is important and usually appears larger and with a heavier font weight than the surrounding text.

`<em></em>`   These tags indicate emphasized text. The text contained within these brackets will usually appear in italic.

`<a href="http://website.com">click here</a>`   These are link tags. The link name here is what you'd like the link to be labeled—*click here*, for example. Link text is usually underlined and a different color on the page to indicate that it is clickable. You put the link destination between the quotation marks of the `href`. Use the absolute URL to a page to link to it.

`<h1></h1>`, `<h2></h2>`, `<h3></h3>`, `<h4></h4>`, `<h5></h5>`, `<h6></h6>`   These tags indicate heading text. Like a paragraph, an HTML heading will divide text from surrounding elements. This means that you cannot have a heading within a paragraph. The number indicates the heading's importance; a low number (`h1`) is more important, and a high number (`h6`) is less important. This importance is usually reflected in the size of the text on the finished page. Headings are often bold and large on the screen. You can use CSS to style headings however you like.

`<br>`   This tag signifies a line break. This is a self-closing tag, meaning there is no text to wrap it around. It can be used within a parent element like a paragraph to move text to another line, usually with less space than is found between two paragraphs.

`<img src="path-to-image.jpg" alt="description of image">`   This is a self-closing tag that embeds an image into a page. The `src` can be an absolute or relative path to an image. The `alt` text is a description that is used by search engines to identify what is contained within the image.

`<title>My Web Page</title>`   The `<title>` tag names the HTML document. The title usually shows up at the top of the browser window. Search engines will often use the `<title>` tag to determine what is contained within a page. This tag goes into the `<head>` of your document.

`<meta name="description" content="`*a description of your website goes here*`">`
This description will be displayed in search results from a search engine like Google. The metadata is not visible to visitors of the site but will be visible in the code. This tag goes into the `<head>` of your document.

Of course, there are many more tags, but these are the ones you'll probably use most often. With the basics down, you'll have the context to learn more. Now let's get back to Kim's adventure!

Kim Makes Things
Look Great with CSS

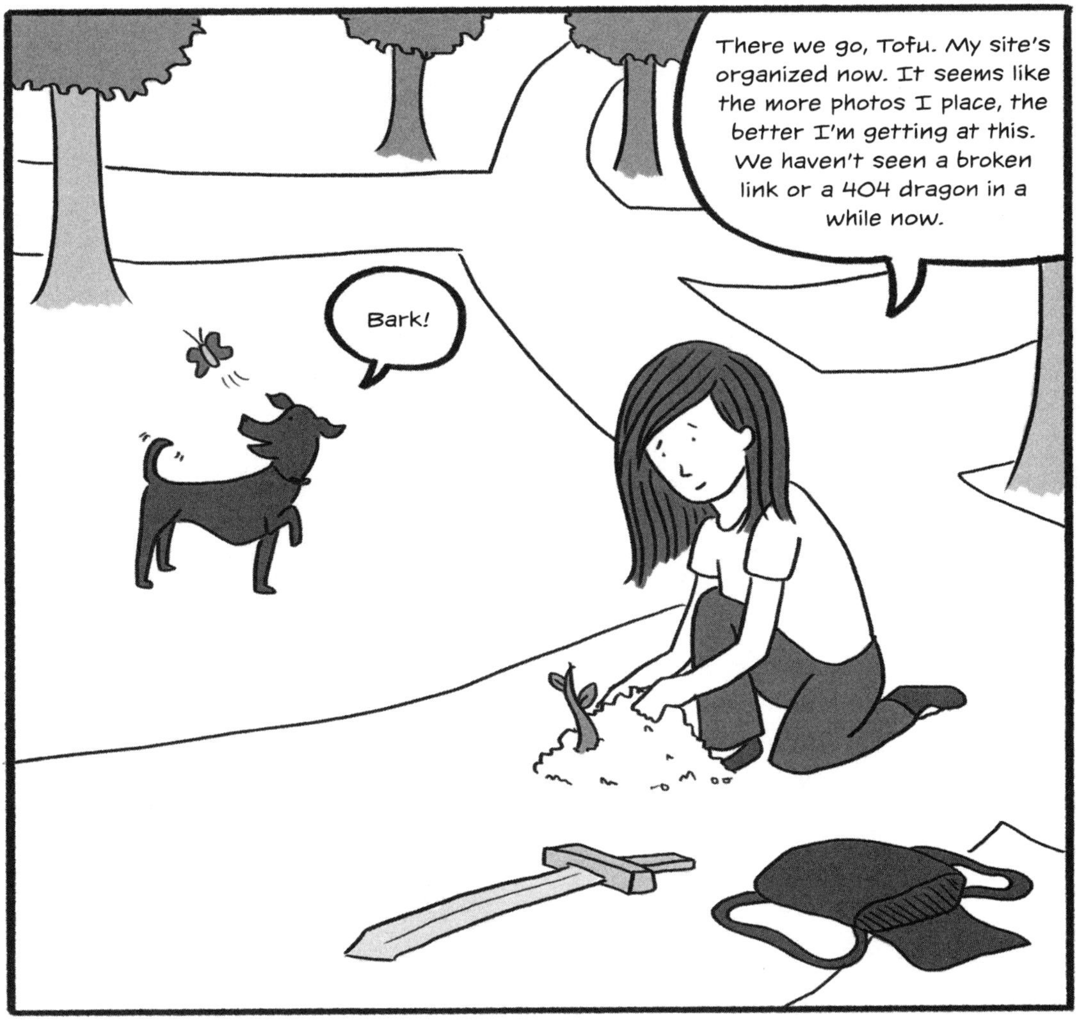
There we go, Tofu. My site's organized now. It seems like the more photos I place, the better I'm getting at this. We haven't seen a broken link or a 404 dragon in a while now.
Bark!

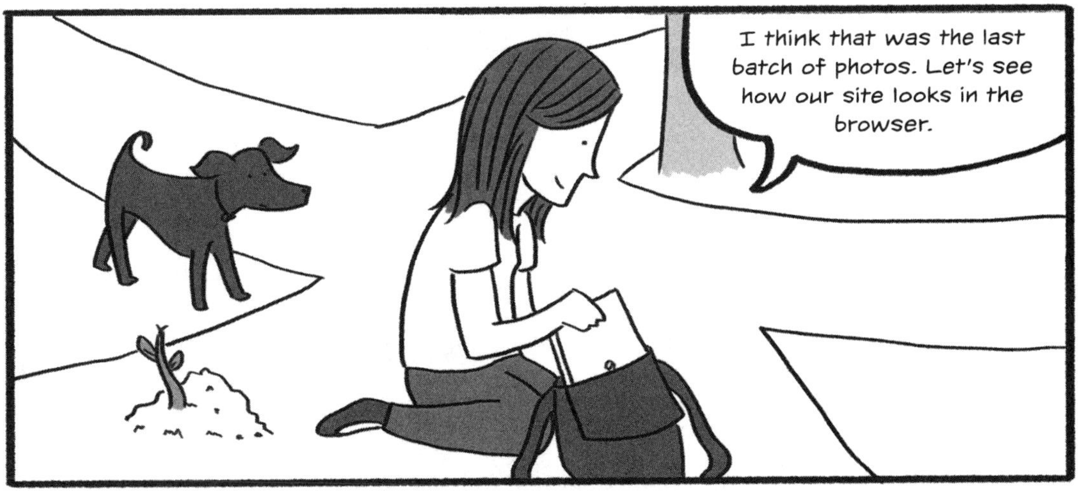
I think that was the last batch of photos. Let's see how our site looks in the browser.

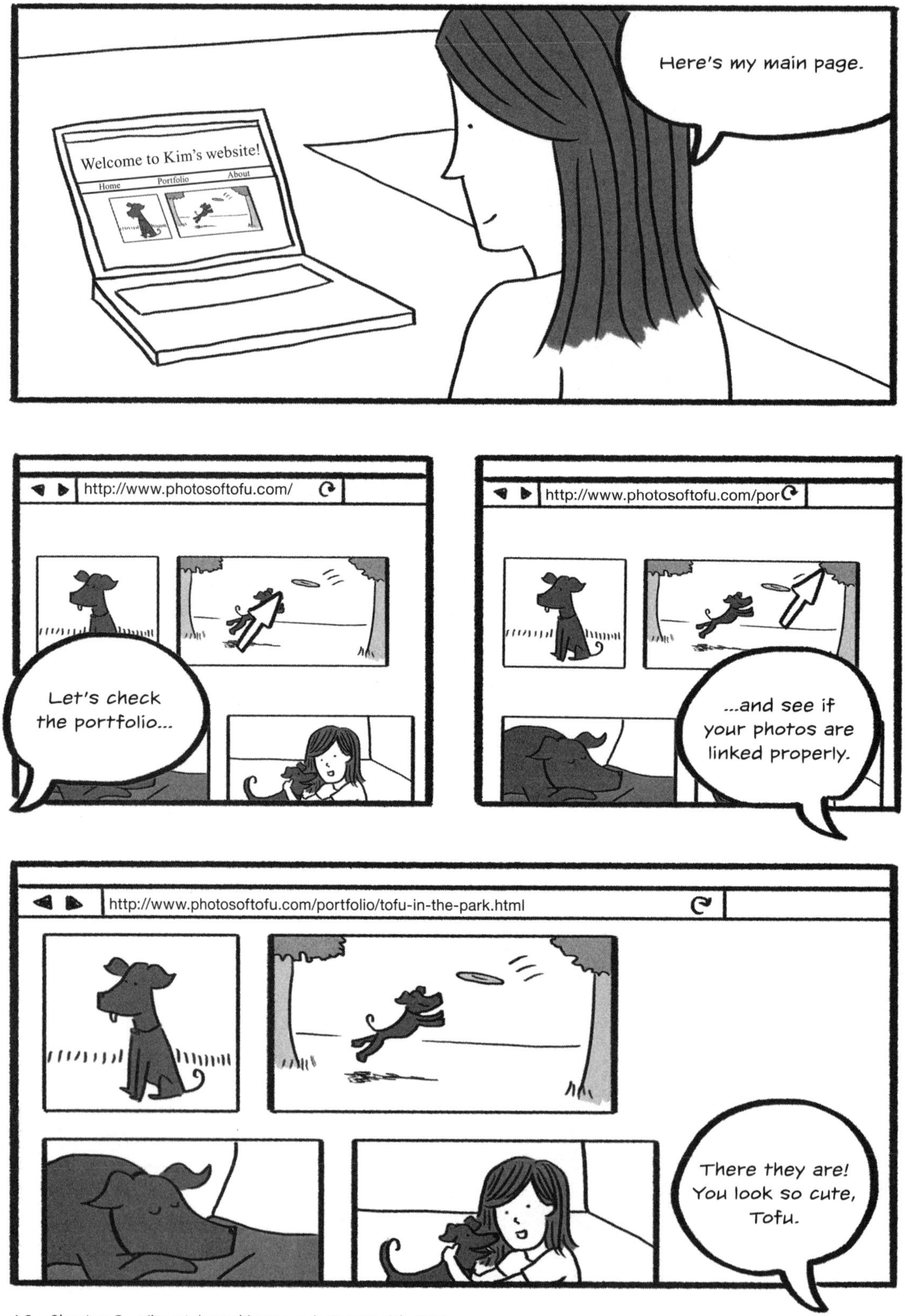
Here's my main page.
Welcome to Kim's website!
Home
Portfolio
About
http://www.photosoftofu.com/
Let's check the portfolio...
http://www.photosoftofu.com/por
...and see if your photos are linked properly.
http://www.photosoftofu.com/portfolio/tofu-in-the-park.html
There they are! You look so cute, Tofu.

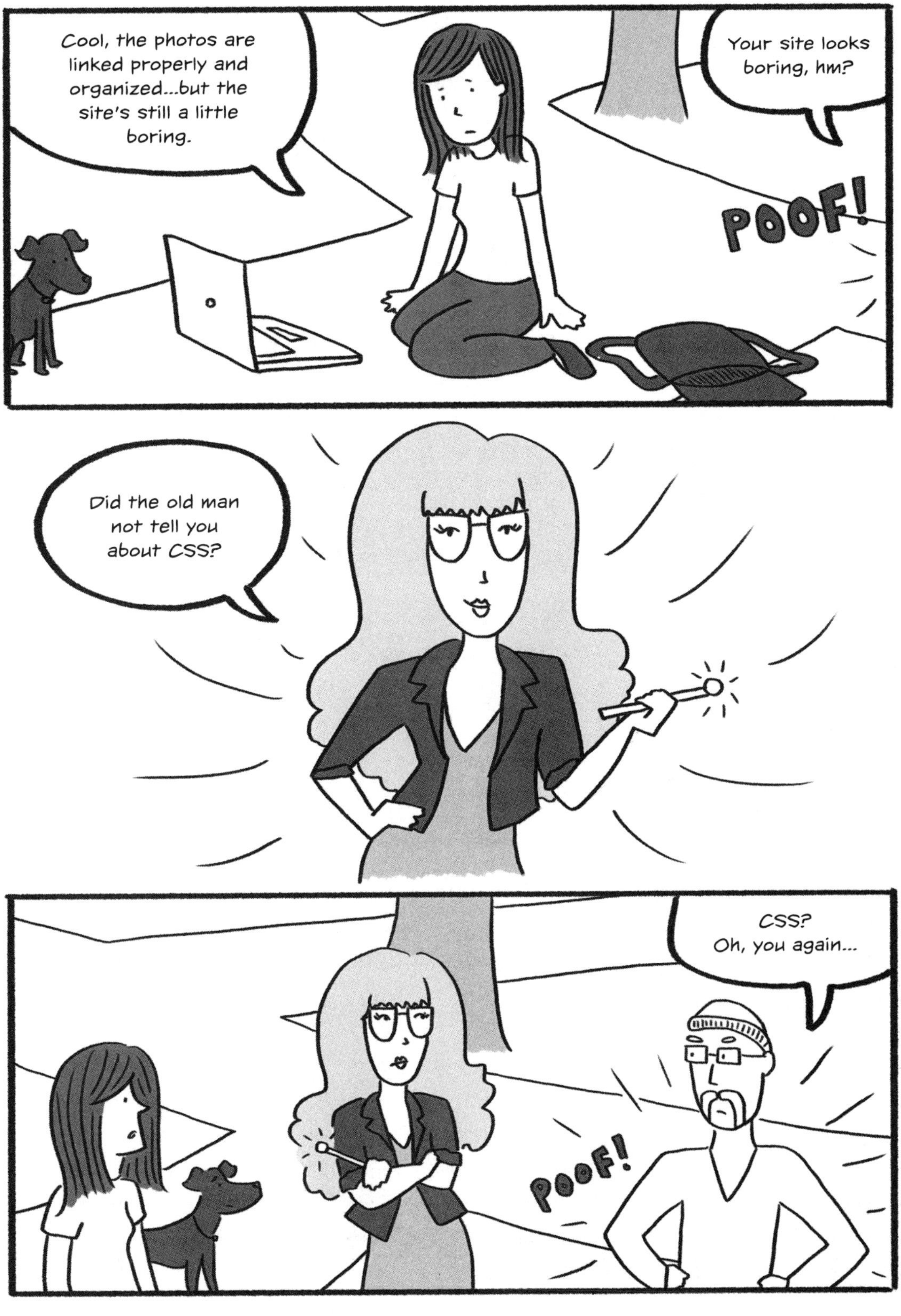
Cool, the photos are linked properly and organized...but the site's still a little boring.
Your site looks boring, hm?
POOF!
Did the old man not tell you about CSS?
CSS?
Oh, you again...
POOF!

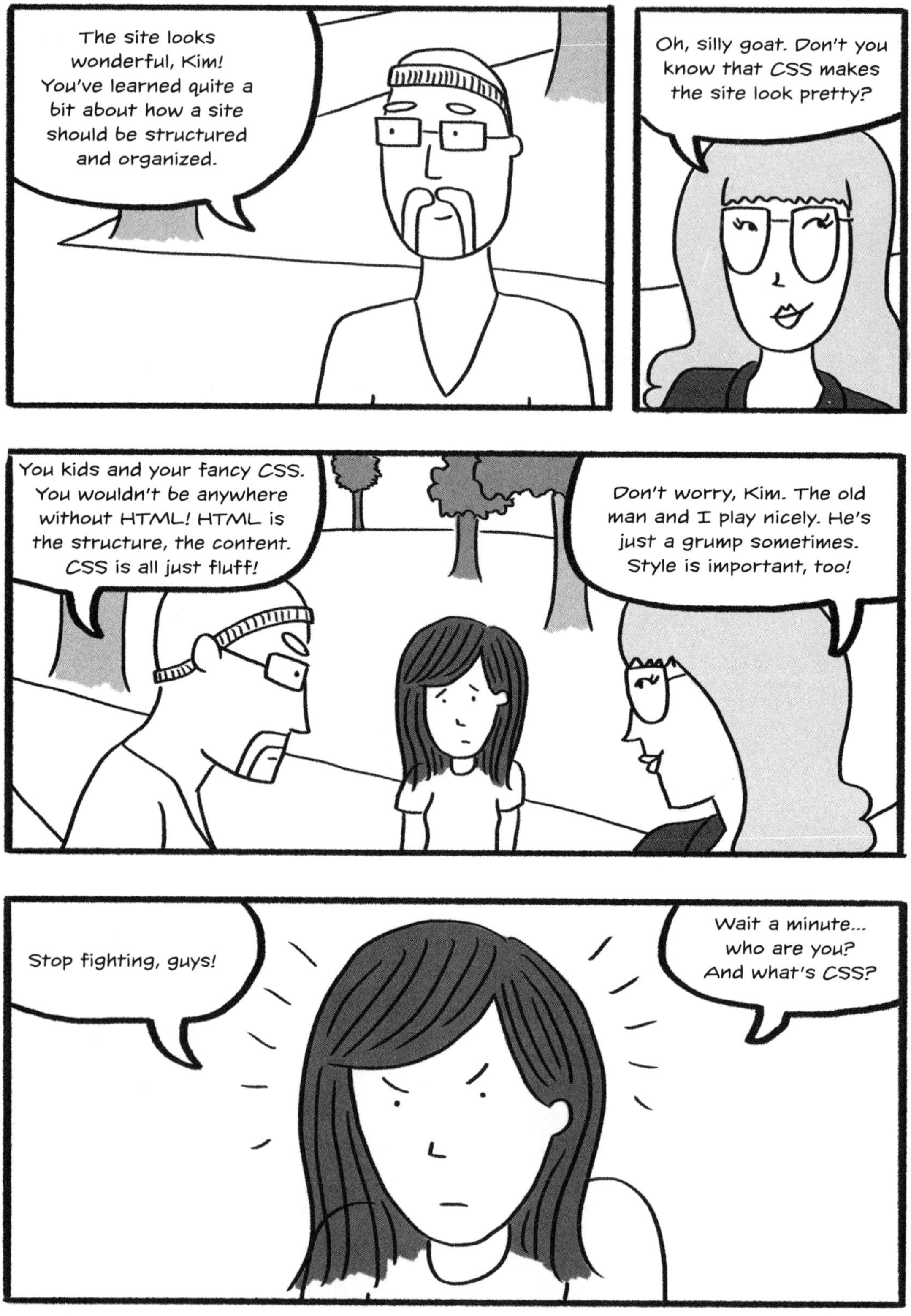
The site looks wonderful, Kim! You've learned quite a bit about how a site should be structured and organized.
Oh, silly goat. Don't you know that CSS makes the site look pretty?
You kids and your fancy CSS. You wouldn't be anywhere without HTML! HTML is the structure, the content. CSS is all just fluff!
Don't worry, Kim. The old man and I play nicely. He's just a grump sometimes. Style is important, too!
Stop fighting, guys!
Wait a minute... who are you? And what's CSS?

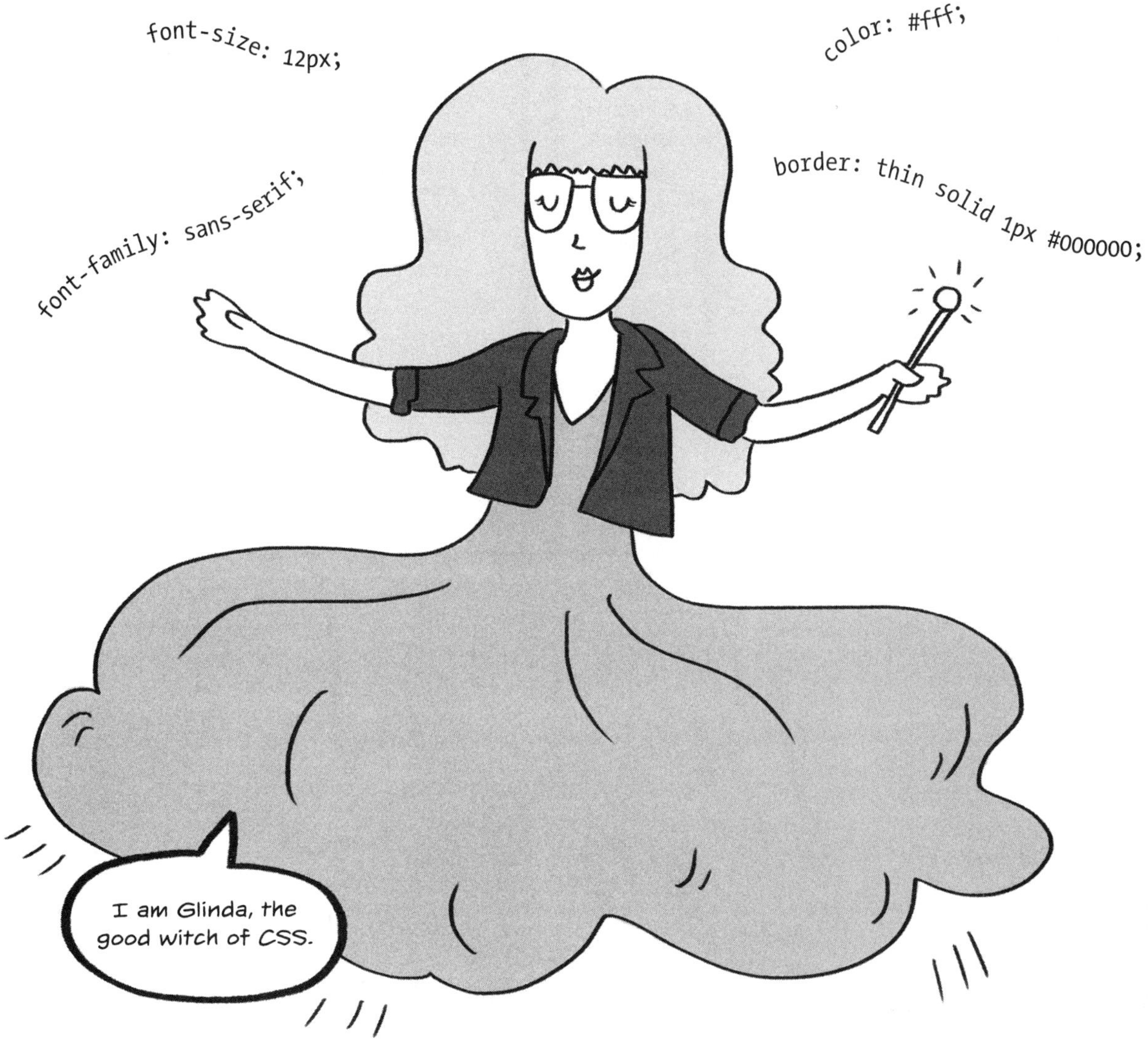
font-size: 12px;
color: #fff;
font-family: sans-serif;
border: thin solid 1px #000000;
I am Glinda, the good witch of CSS.

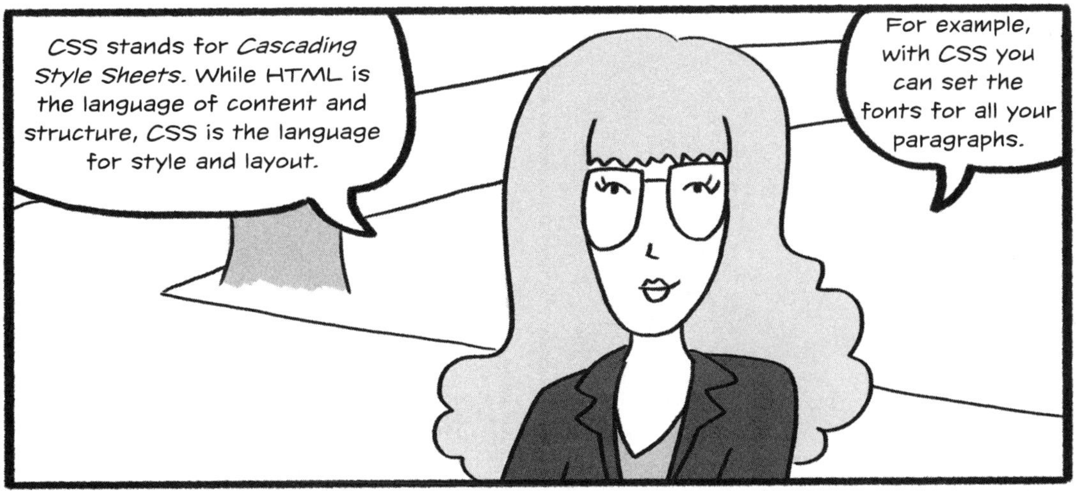
CSS stands for *Cascading Style Sheets*. While HTML is the language of content and structure, CSS is the language for style and layout.
For example, with CSS you can set the fonts for all your paragraphs.

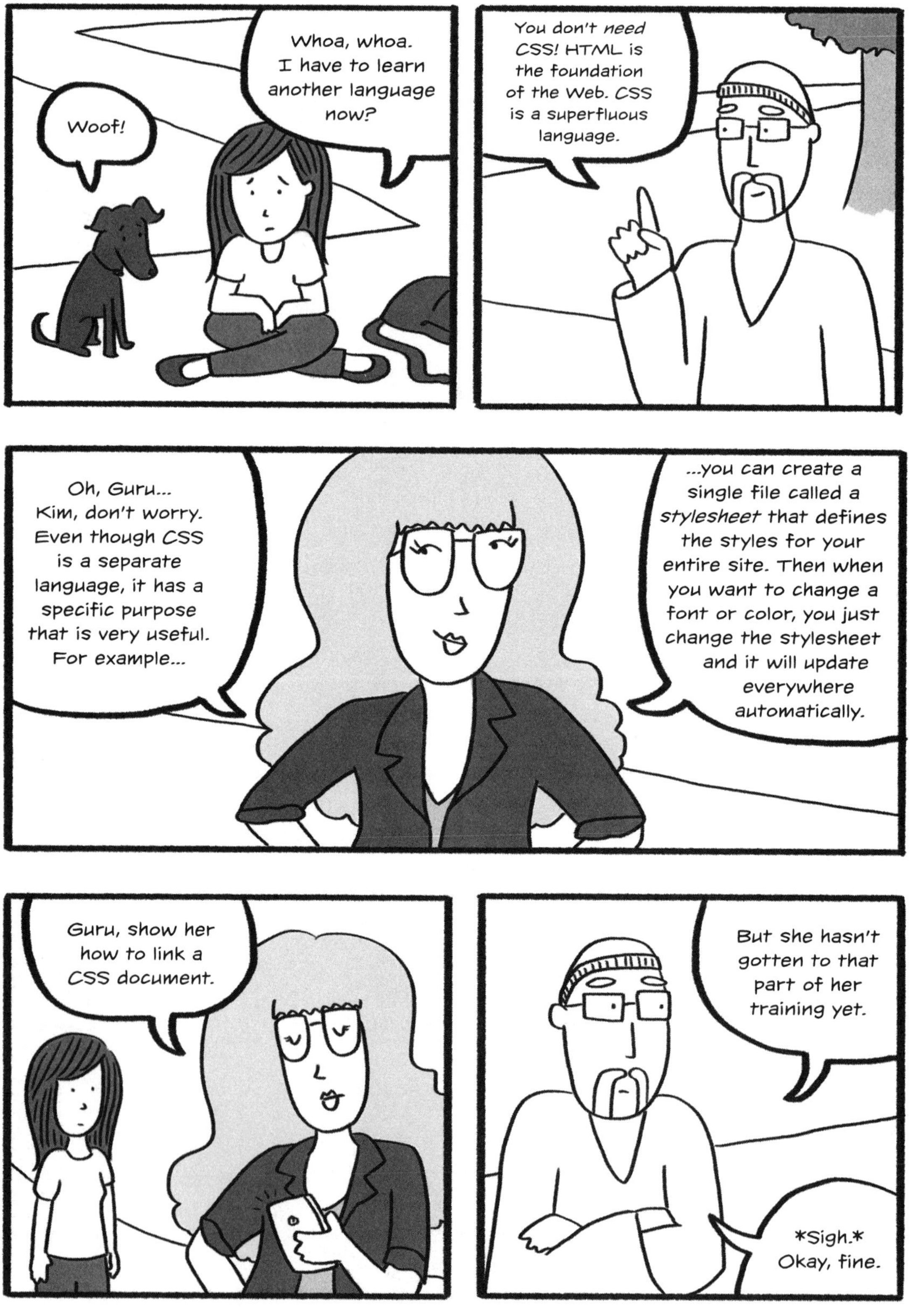
Woof!
Whoa, whoa. I have to learn another language now?
You don't *need* CSS! HTML is the foundation of the Web. CSS is a superfluous language.
Oh, Guru... Kim, don't worry. Even though CSS is a separate language, it has a specific purpose that is very useful. For example...
...you can create a single file called a *stylesheet* that defines the styles for your entire site. Then when you want to change a font or color, you just change the stylesheet and it will update everywhere automatically.
Guru, show her how to link a CSS document.
But she hasn't gotten to that part of her training yet.
Sigh. Okay, fine.

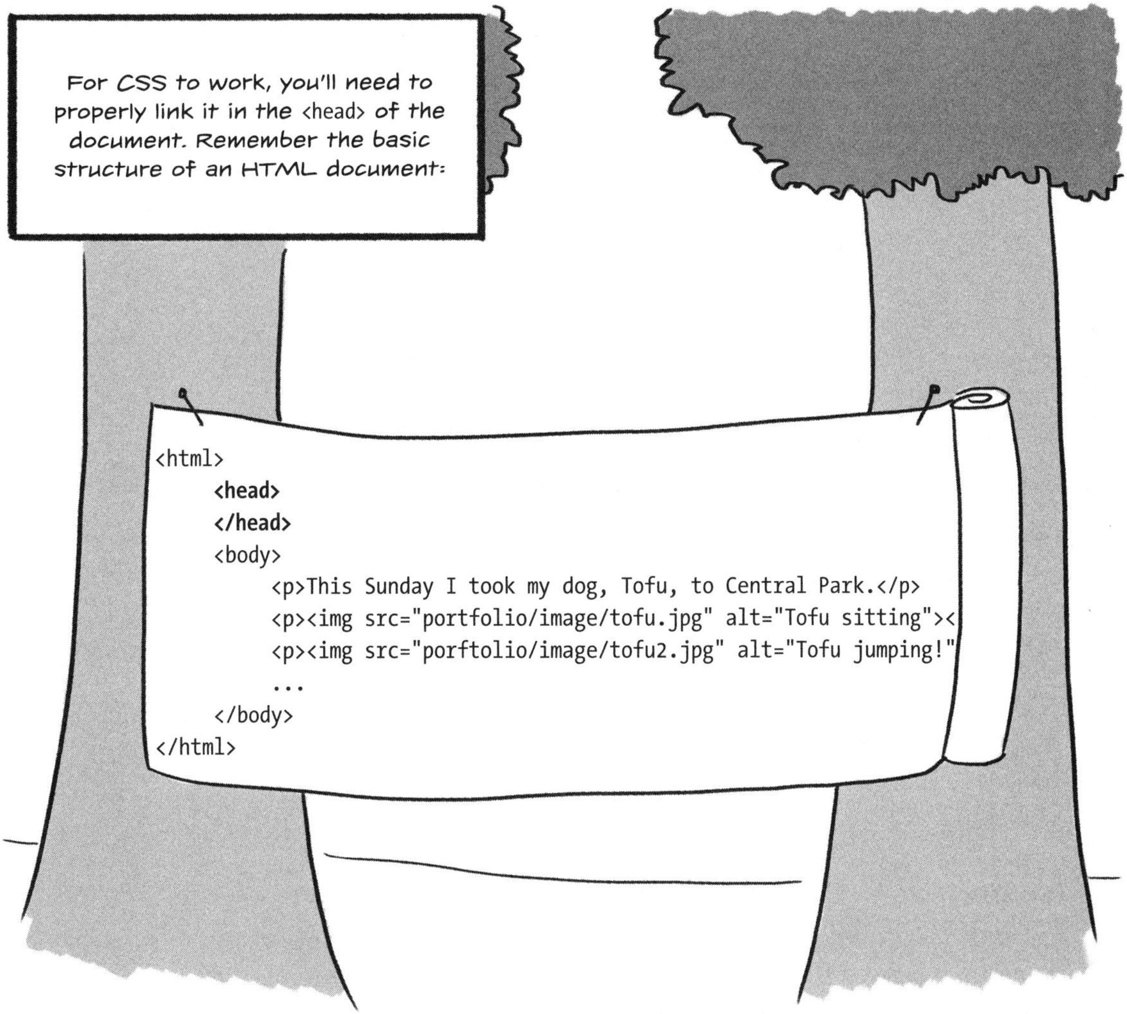
For CSS to work, you'll need to properly link it in the <head> of the document. Remember the basic structure of an HTML document:
<html>
<head>
</head>
<body>
<p>This Sunday I took my dog, Tofu, to Central Park.</p>
<p><img src="portfolio/image/tofu.jpg" alt="Tofu sitting"><
<p><img src="porftolio/image/tofu2.jpg" alt="Tofu jumping!"
...
</body>
</html>

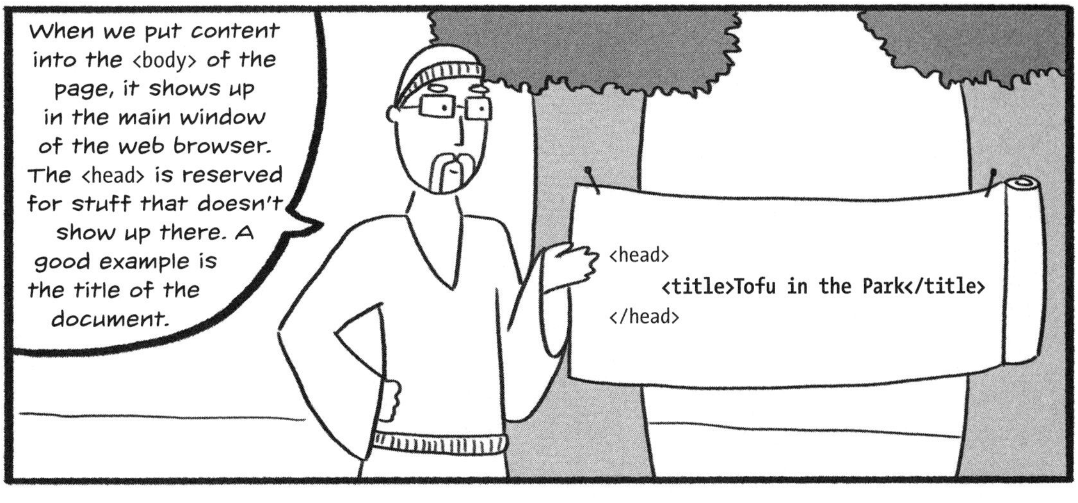
When we put content into the <body> of the page, it shows up in the main window of the web browser. The <head> is reserved for stuff that doesn't show up there. A good example is the title of the document.
<head>
<title>Tofu in the Park</title>
</head>

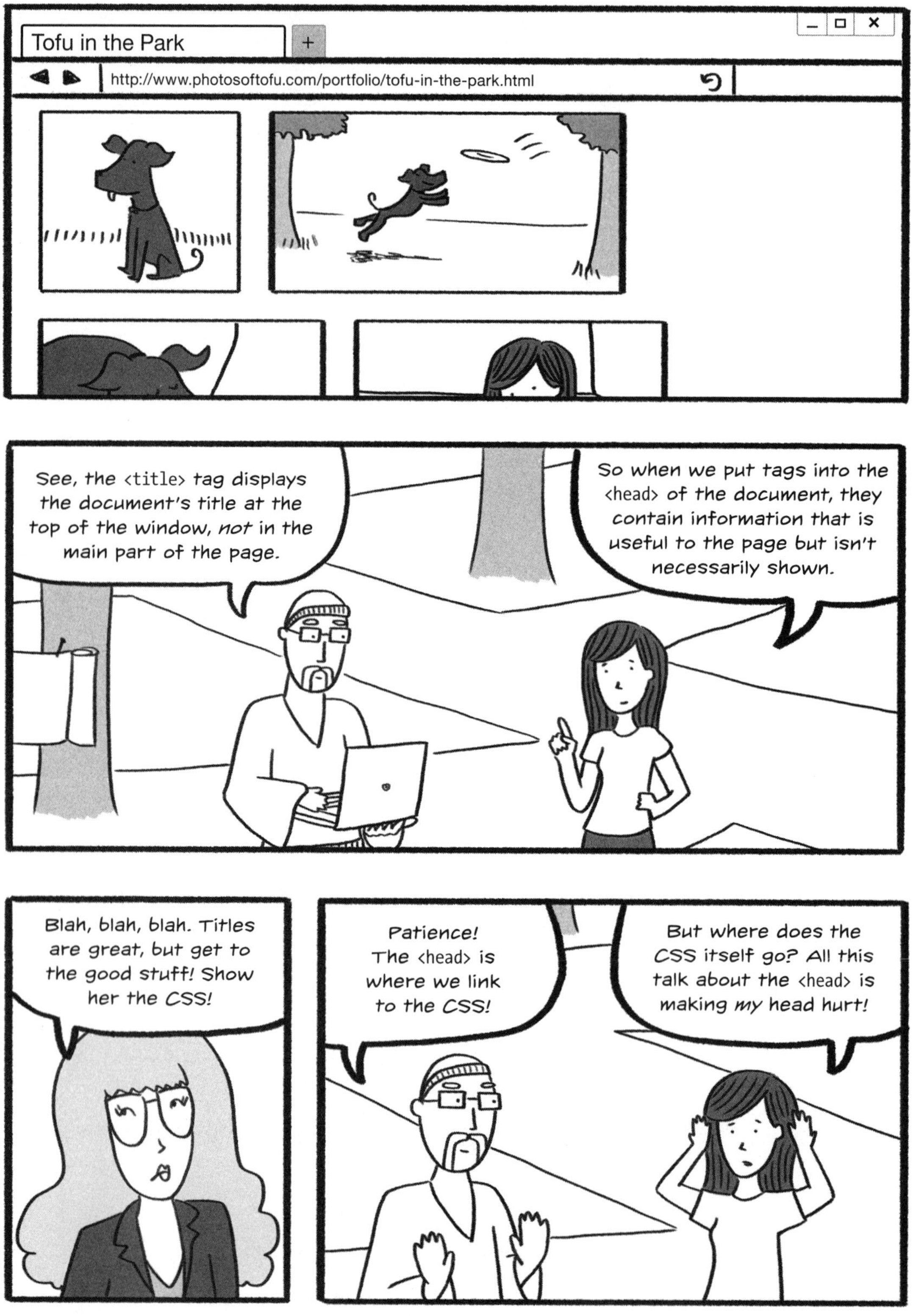
Tofu in the Park
http://www.photosoftofu.com/portfolio/tofu-in-the-park.html
See, the <title> tag displays the document's title at the top of the window, *not* in the main part of the page.
So when we put tags into the <head> of the document, they contain information that is useful to the page but isn't necessarily shown.
Blah, blah, blah. Titles are great, but get to the good stuff! Show her the CSS!
Patience! The <head> is where we link to the CSS!
But where does the CSS itself go? All this talk about the <head> is making *my* head hurt!

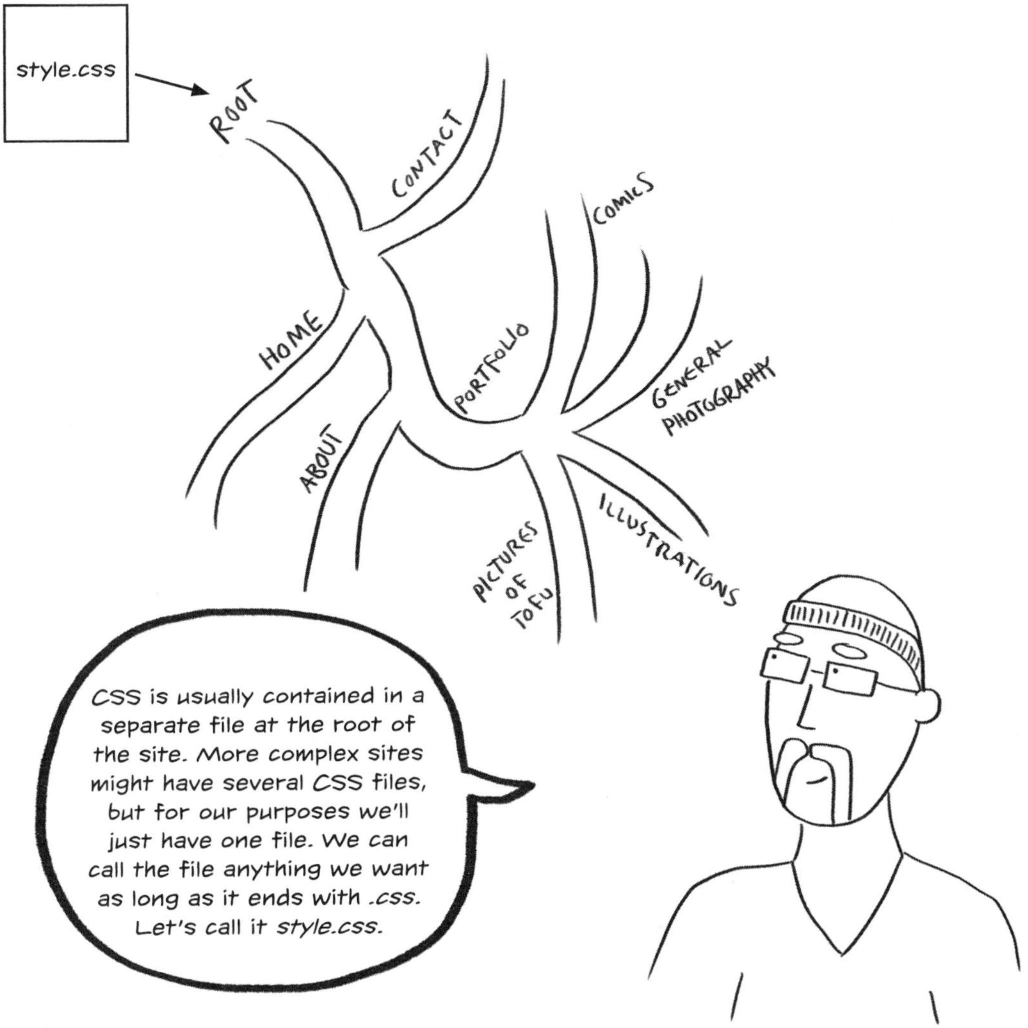
style.css
ROOT
CONTACT
HOME
ABOUT
PORTFOLIO
COMICS
GENERAL PHOTOGRAPHY
ILLUSTRATIONS
PICTURES OF TOFU
CSS is usually contained in a separate file at the root of the site. More complex sites might have several CSS files, but for our purposes we'll just have one file. We can call the file anything we want as long as it ends with *.css*. Let's call it *style.css*.

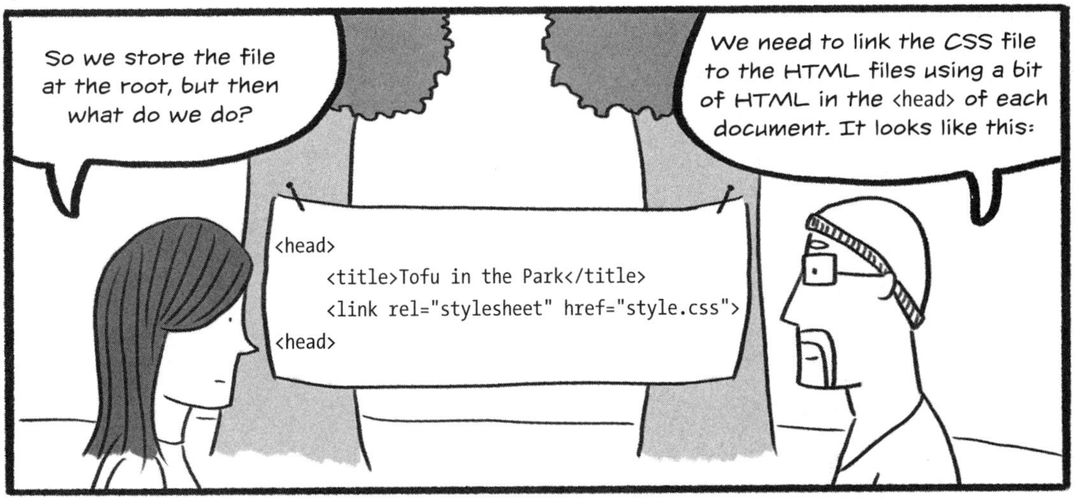
So we store the file at the root, but then what do we do?
We need to link the CSS file to the HTML files using a bit of HTML in the <head> of each document. It looks like this:
<head>
<title>Tofu in the Park</title>
<link rel="stylesheet" href="style.css">
<head>

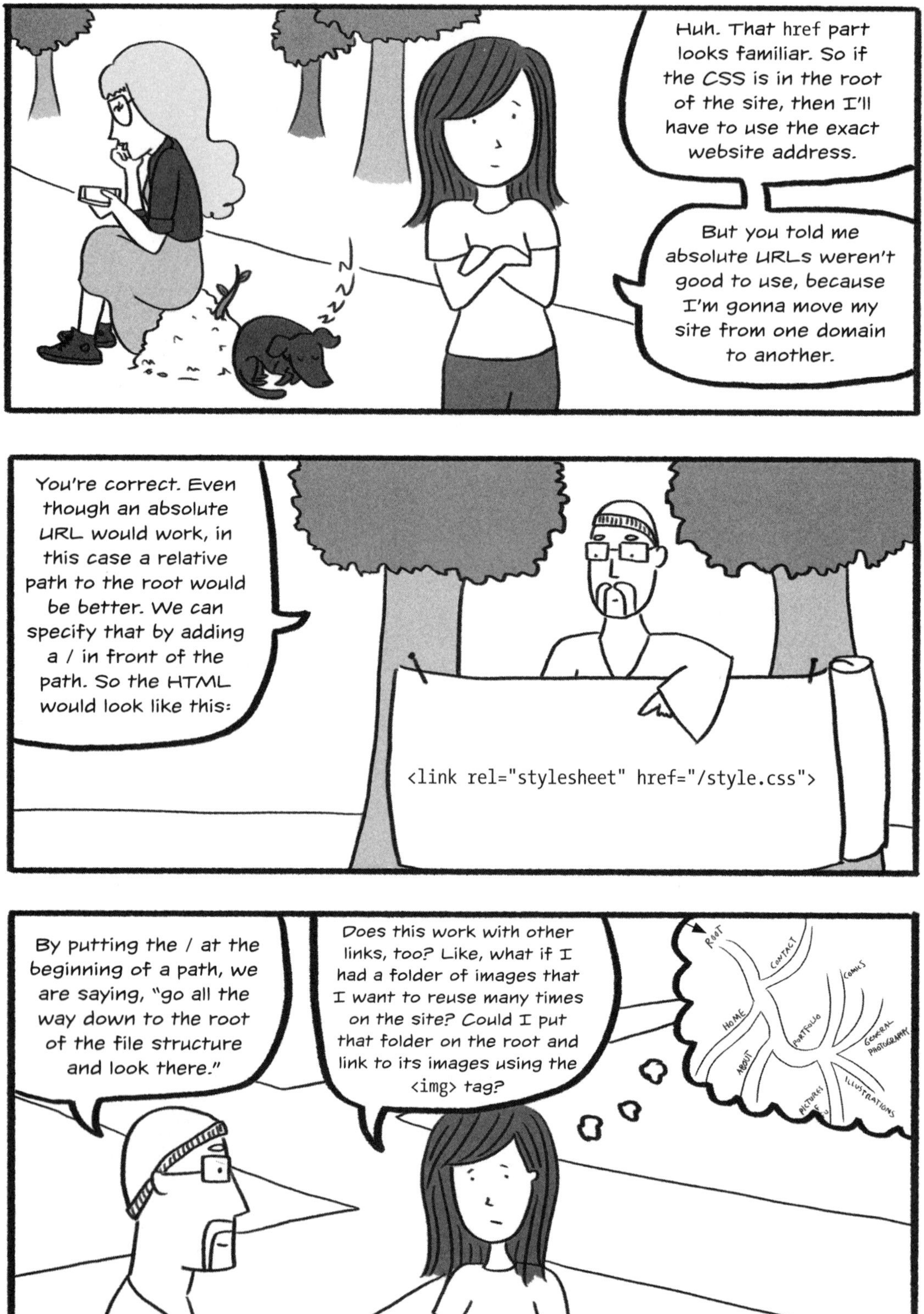
Huh. That href part looks familiar. So if the CSS is in the root of the site, then I'll have to use the exact website address.
But you told me absolute URLs weren't good to use, because I'm gonna move my site from one domain to another.
You're correct. Even though an absolute URL would work, in this case a relative path to the root would be better. We can specify that by adding a / in front of the path. So the HTML would look like this:
<link rel="stylesheet" href="/style.css">
By putting the / at the beginning of a path, we are saying, "go all the way down to the root of the file structure and look there."
Does this work with other links, too? Like, what if I had a folder of images that I want to reuse many times on the site? Could I put that folder on the root and link to its images using the <img> tag?
ROOT
CONTACT
COMICS
HOME
PORTFOLIO
GENERAL PHOTOGRAPHY
ABOUT
ILLUSTRATIONS

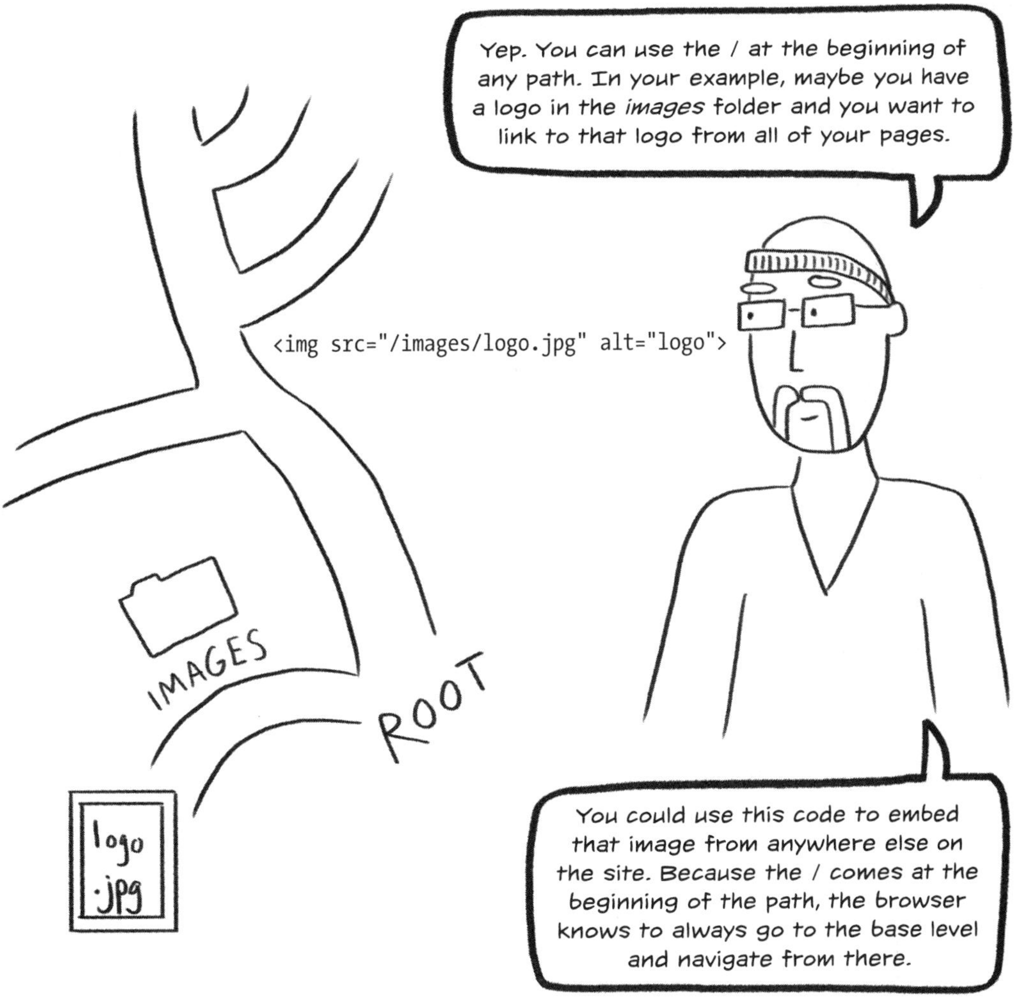
Yep. You can use the / at the beginning of any path. In your example, maybe you have a logo in the *images* folder and you want to link to that logo from all of your pages.
<img src="/images/logo.jpg" alt="logo">
IMAGES
ROOT
logo .jpg
You could use this code to embed that image from anywhere else on the site. Because the / comes at the beginning of the path, the browser knows to always go to the base level and navigate from there.

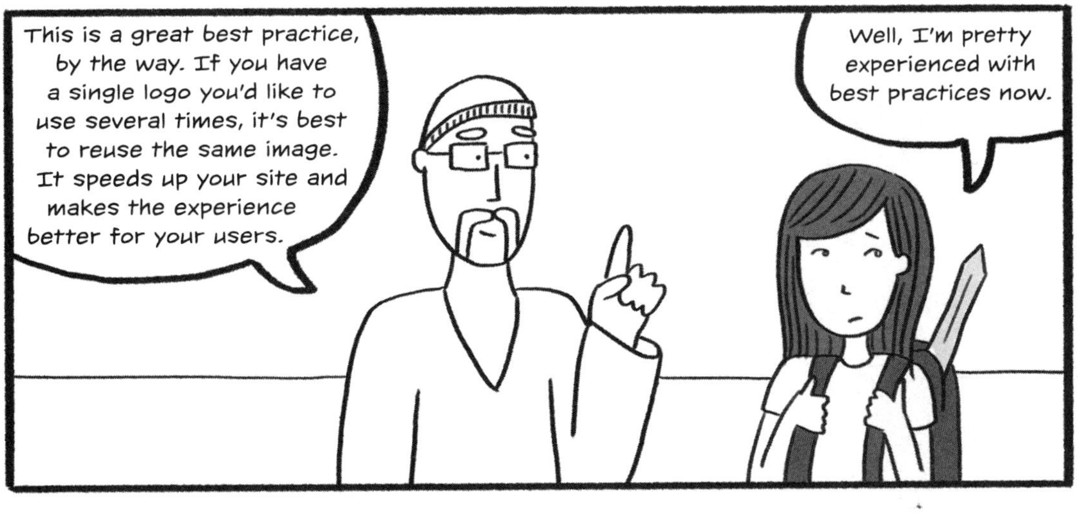
This is a great best practice, by the way. If you have a single logo you'd like to use several times, it's best to reuse the same image. It speeds up your site and makes the experience better for your users.
Well, I'm pretty experienced with best practices now.

Kim Learns Basic CSS

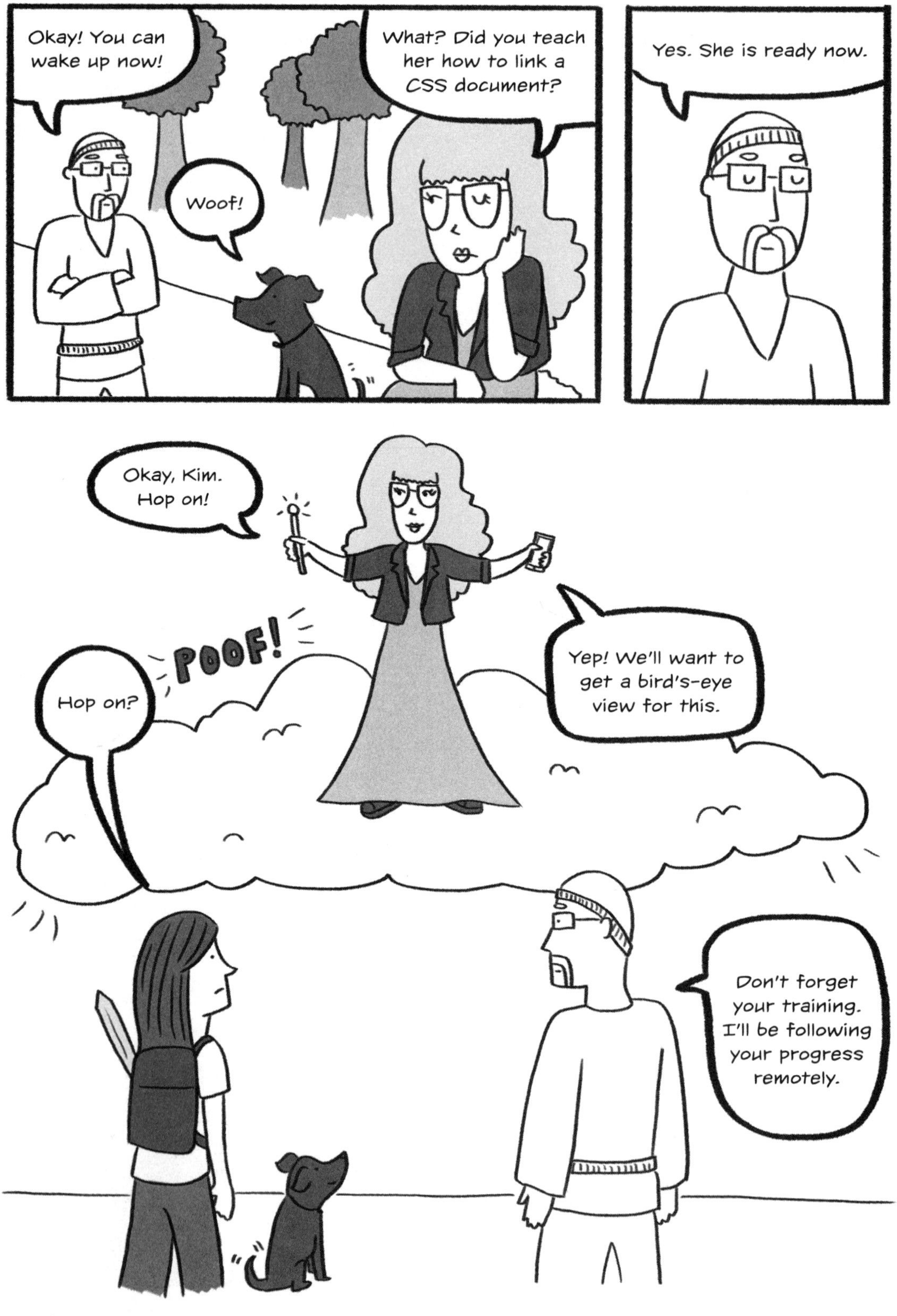

Okay! You can wake up now!
What? Did you teach her how to link a CSS document?
Woof!
Yes. She is ready now.
Okay, Kim. Hop on!
POOF!
Hop on?
Yep! We'll want to get a bird's-eye view for this.
Don't forget your training. I'll be following your progress remotely.

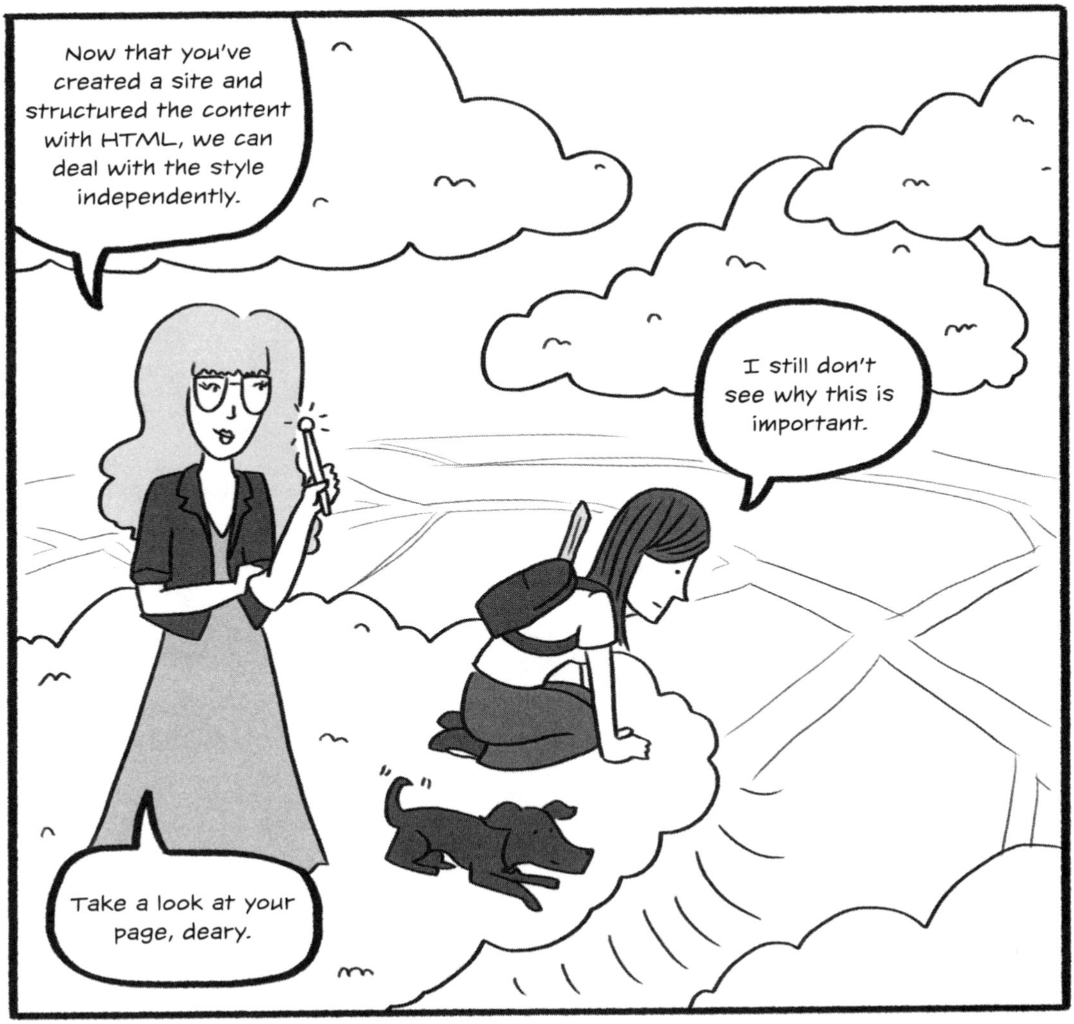
Now that you've created a site and structured the content with HTML, we can deal with the style independently.
I still don't see why this is important.
Take a look at your page, deary.

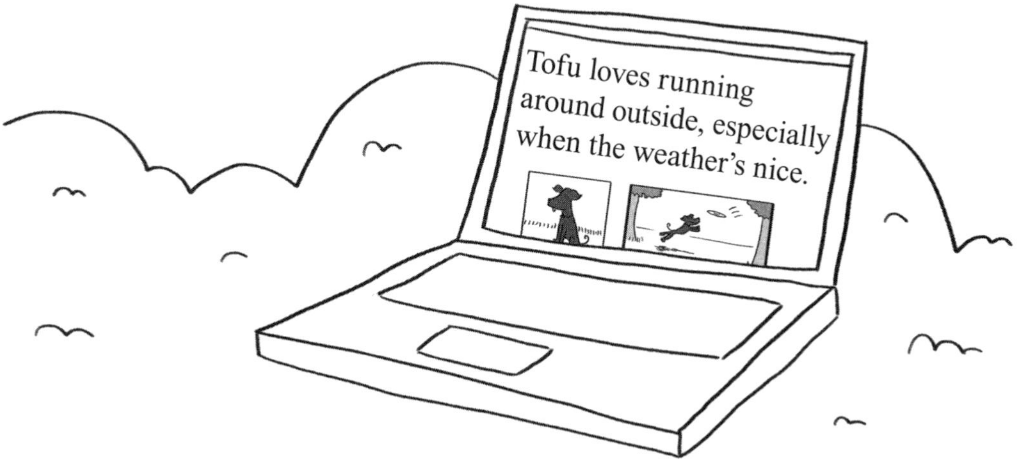
Tofu loves running around outside, especially when the weather's nice.

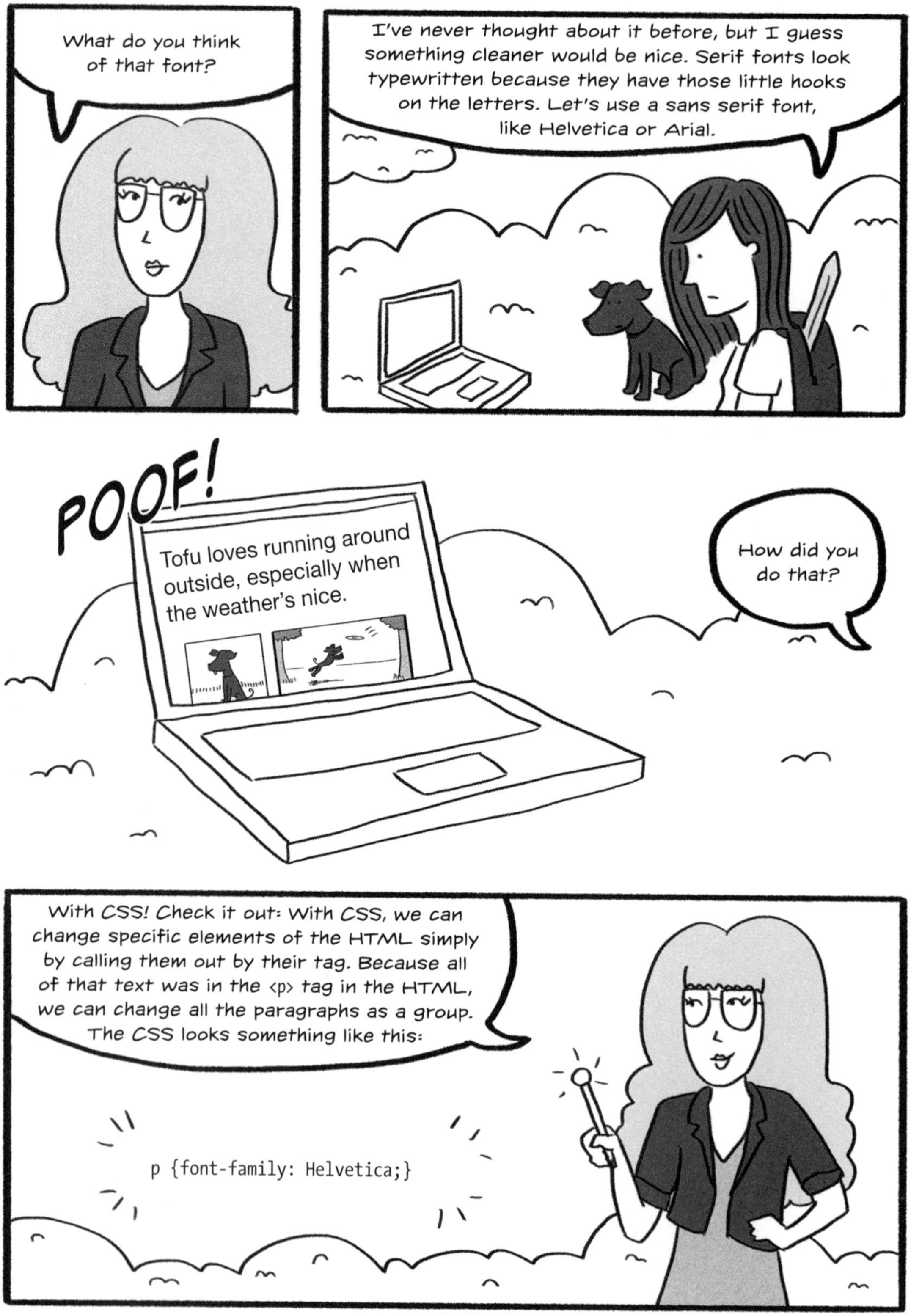
What do you think of that font?
I've never thought about it before, but I guess something cleaner would be nice. Serif fonts look typewritten because they have those little hooks on the letters. Let's use a sans serif font, like Helvetica or Arial.
POOF!
Tofu loves running around outside, especially when the weather's nice.
How did you do that?
With CSS! Check it out: With CSS, we can change specific elements of the HTML simply by calling them out by their tag. Because all of that text was in the <p> tag in the HTML, we can change all the paragraphs as a group. The CSS looks something like this:
p {font-family: Helvetica;}

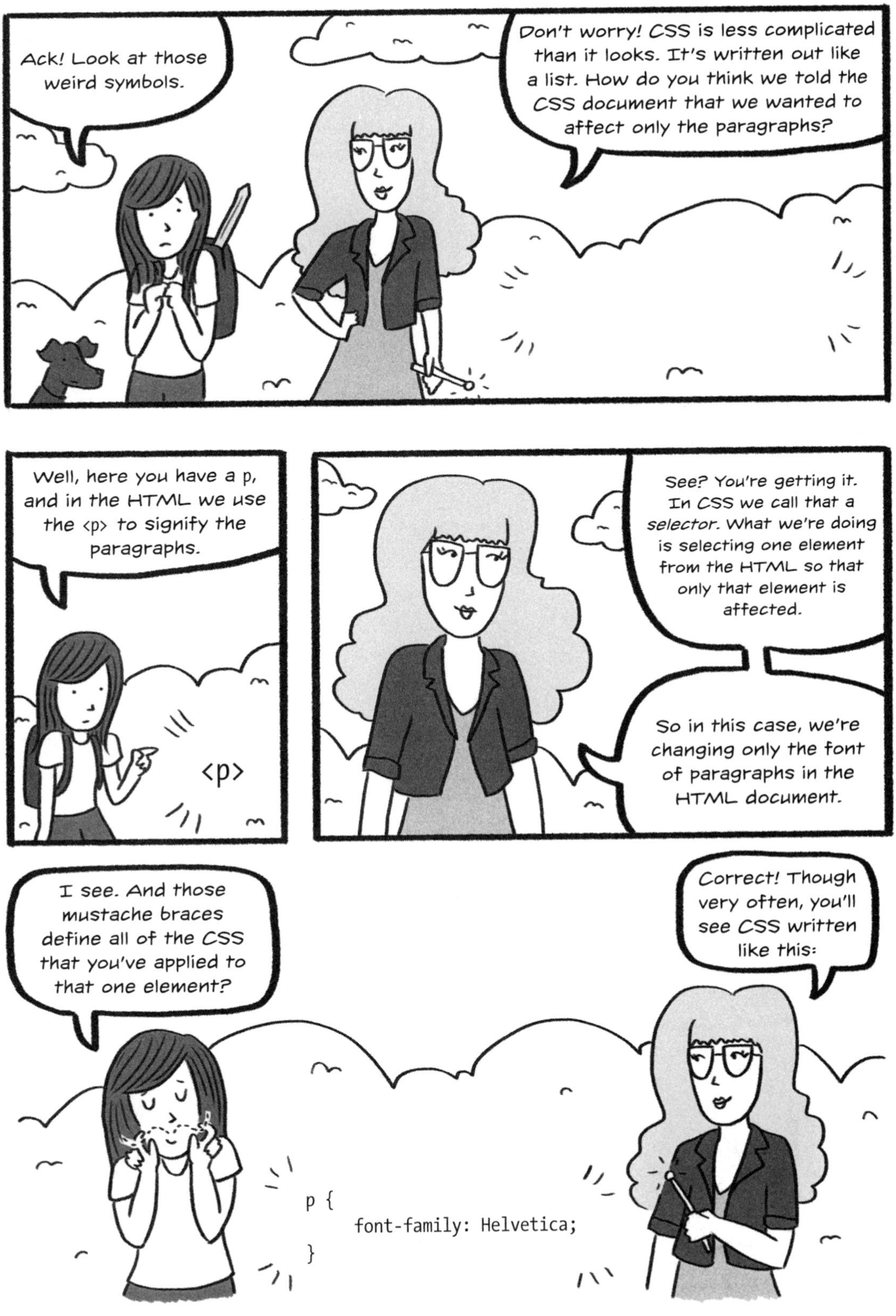
Ack! Look at those weird symbols.
Don't worry! CSS is less complicated than it looks. It's written out like a list. How do you think we told the CSS document that we wanted to affect only the paragraphs?
Well, here you have a p, and in the HTML we use the <p> to signify the paragraphs.
<p>
See? You're getting it. In CSS we call that a *selector*. What we're doing is selecting one element from the HTML so that only that element is affected.
So in this case, we're changing only the font of paragraphs in the HTML document.
I see. And those mustache braces define all of the CSS that you've applied to that one element?
Correct! Though very often, you'll see CSS written like this:
p {
font-family: Helvetica;
}

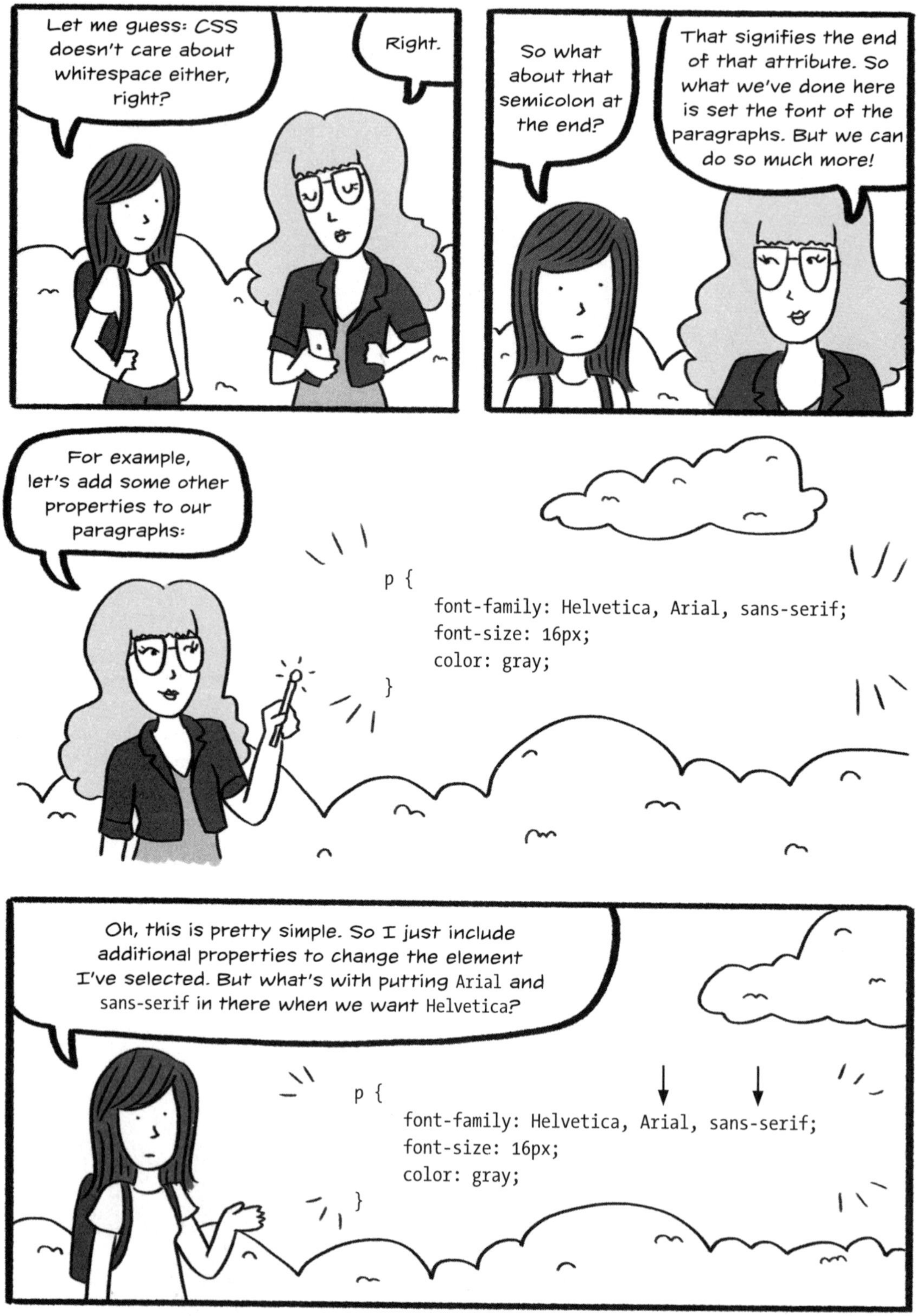
Let me guess: CSS doesn't care about whitespace either, right?
Right.
So what about that semicolon at the end?
That signifies the end of that attribute. So what we've done here is set the font of the paragraphs. But we can do so much more!
For example, let's add some other properties to our paragraphs:
p {
font-family: Helvetica, Arial, sans-serif;
font-size: 16px;
color: gray;
}
Oh, this is pretty simple. So I just include additional properties to change the element I've selected. But what's with putting Arial and sans-serif in there when we want Helvetica?
p {
font-family: Helvetica, Arial, sans-serif;
font-size: 16px;
color: gray;
}

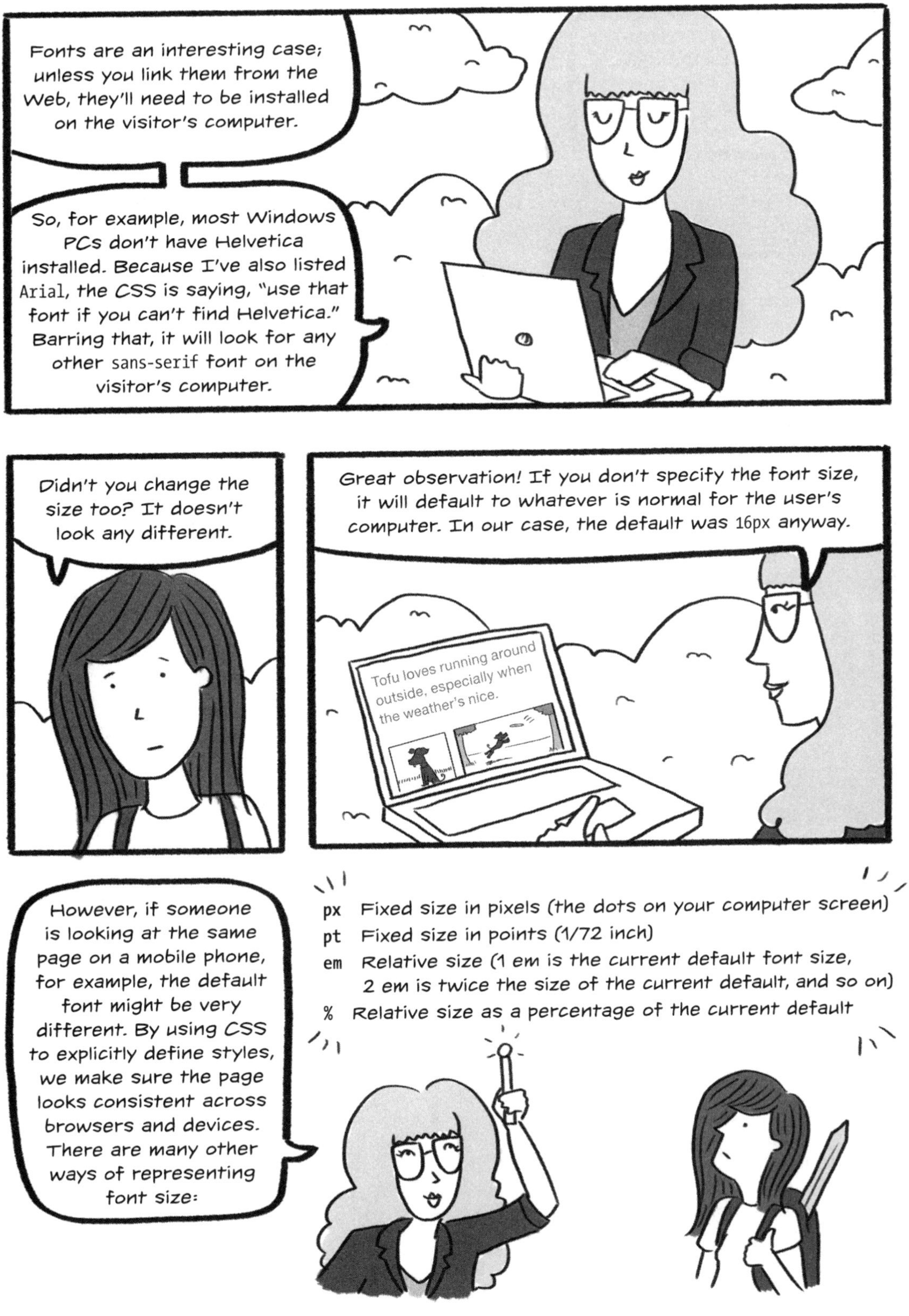
Fonts are an interesting case; unless you link them from the Web, they'll need to be installed on the visitor's computer.
So, for example, most Windows PCs don't have Helvetica installed. Because I've also listed Arial, the CSS is saying, "use that font if you can't find Helvetica." Barring that, it will look for any other sans-serif font on the visitor's computer.
Didn't you change the size too? It doesn't look any different.
Great observation! If you don't specify the font size, it will default to whatever is normal for the user's computer. In our case, the default was 16px anyway.
Tofu loves running around outside, especially when the weather's nice.
However, if someone is looking at the same page on a mobile phone, for example, the default font might be very different. By using CSS to explicitly define styles, we make sure the page looks consistent across browsers and devices. There are many other ways of representing font size:
px Fixed size in pixels (the dots on your computer screen)
pt Fixed size in points (1/72 inch)
em Relative size (1 em is the current default font size, 2 em is twice the size of the current default, and so on)
% Relative size as a percentage of the current default

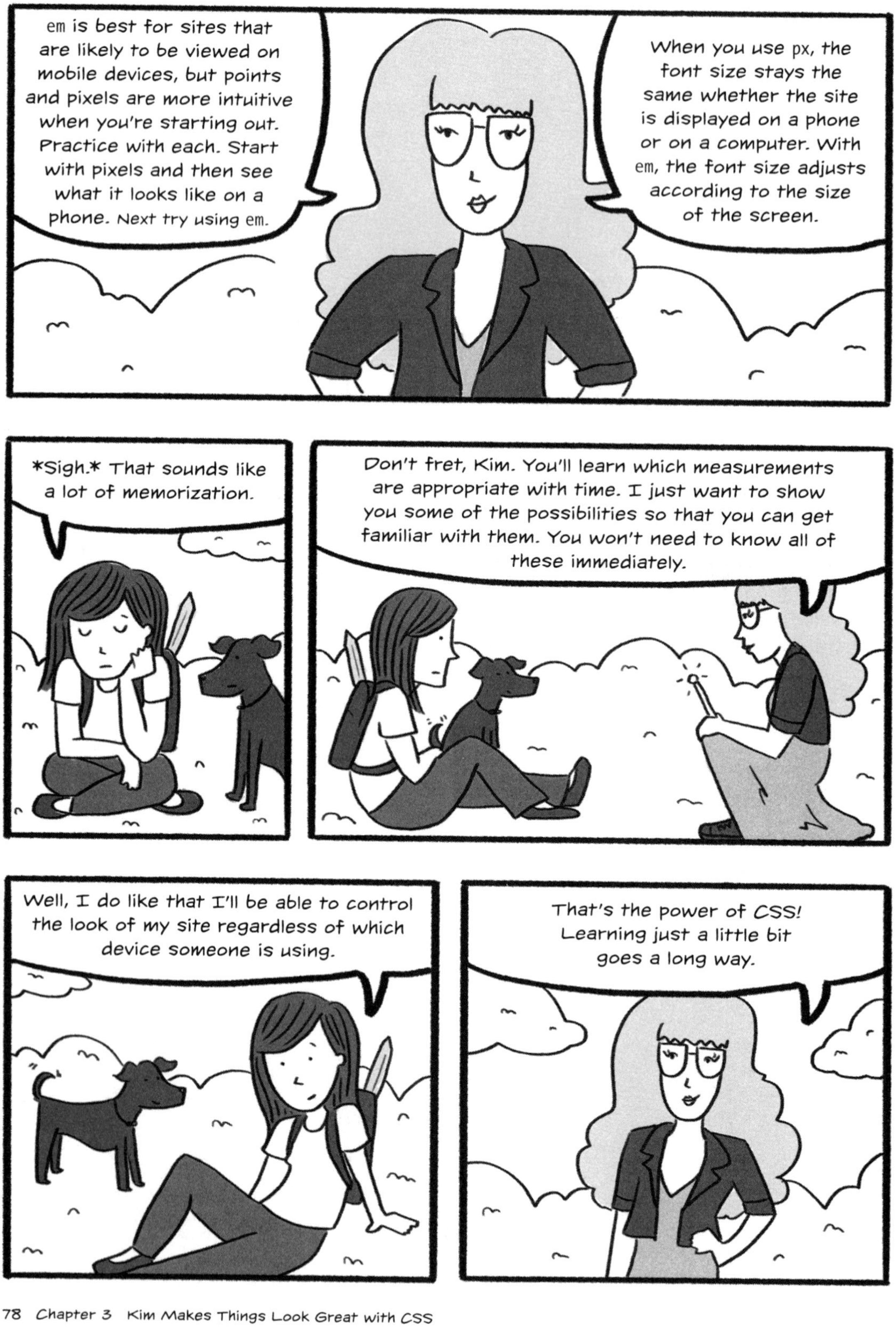
em is best for sites that are likely to be viewed on mobile devices, but points and pixels are more intuitive when you're starting out. Practice with each. Start with pixels and then see what it looks like on a phone. Next try using em.
When you use px, the font size stays the same whether the site is displayed on a phone or on a computer. With em, the font size adjusts according to the size of the screen.
Sigh. That sounds like a lot of memorization.
Don't fret, Kim. You'll learn which measurements are appropriate with time. I just want to show you some of the possibilities so that you can get familiar with them. You won't need to know all of these immediately.
Well, I do like that I'll be able to control the look of my site regardless of which device someone is using.
That's the power of CSS! Learning just a little bit goes a long way.

Digging into CSS

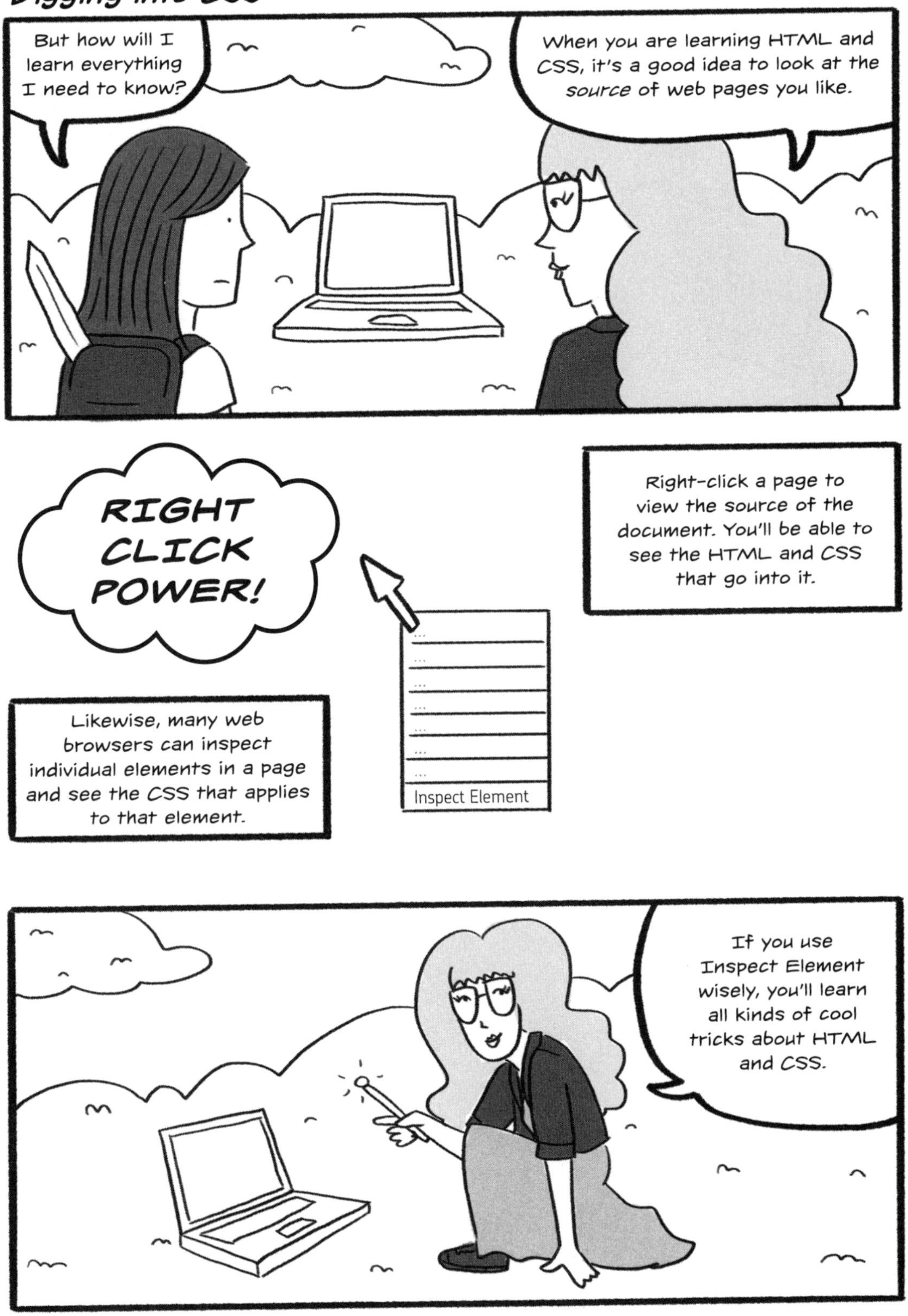
But how will I learn everything I need to know?
When you are learning HTML and CSS, it's a good idea to look at the *source* of web pages you like.
RIGHT CLICK POWER!
Right-click a page to view the source of the document. You'll be able to see the HTML and CSS that go into it.
Likewise, many web browsers can inspect individual elements in a page and see the CSS that applies to that element.
Inspect Element
If you use Inspect Element wisely, you'll learn all kinds of cool tricks about HTML and CSS.

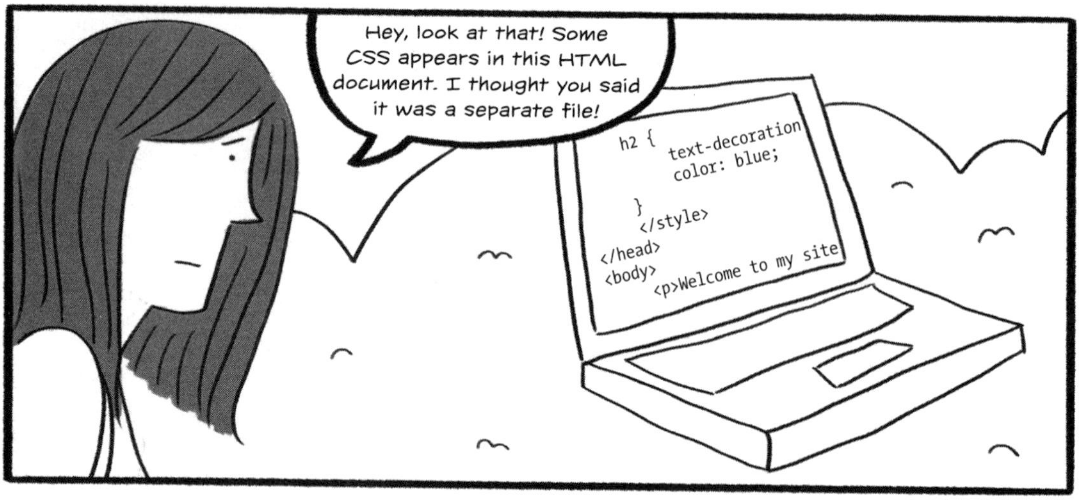
Hey, look at that! Some CSS appears in this HTML document. I thought you said it was a separate file!
h2 {
text-decoration
color: blue;
}
</style>
</head>
<body>
<p>Welcome to my site

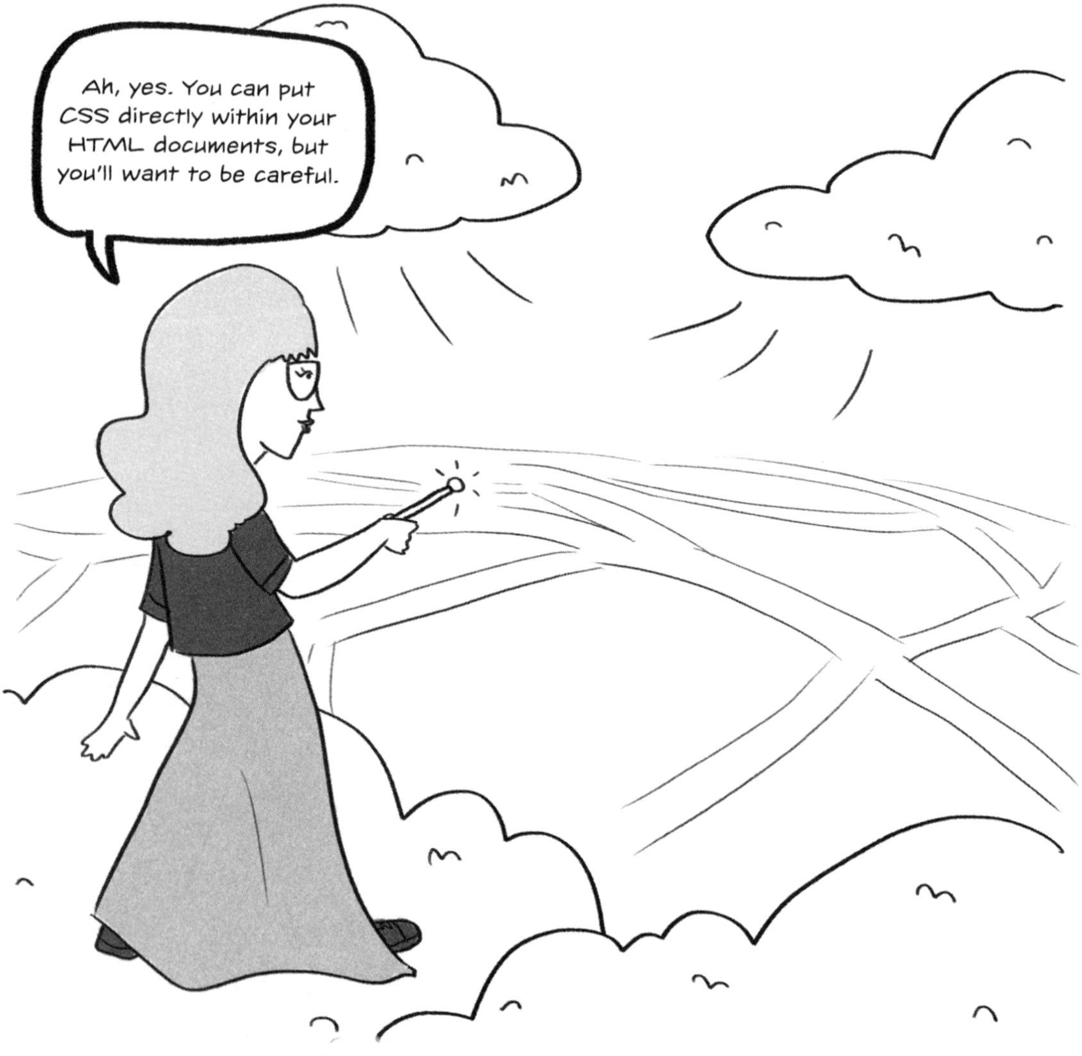
Ah, yes. You can put CSS directly within your HTML documents, but you'll want to be careful.

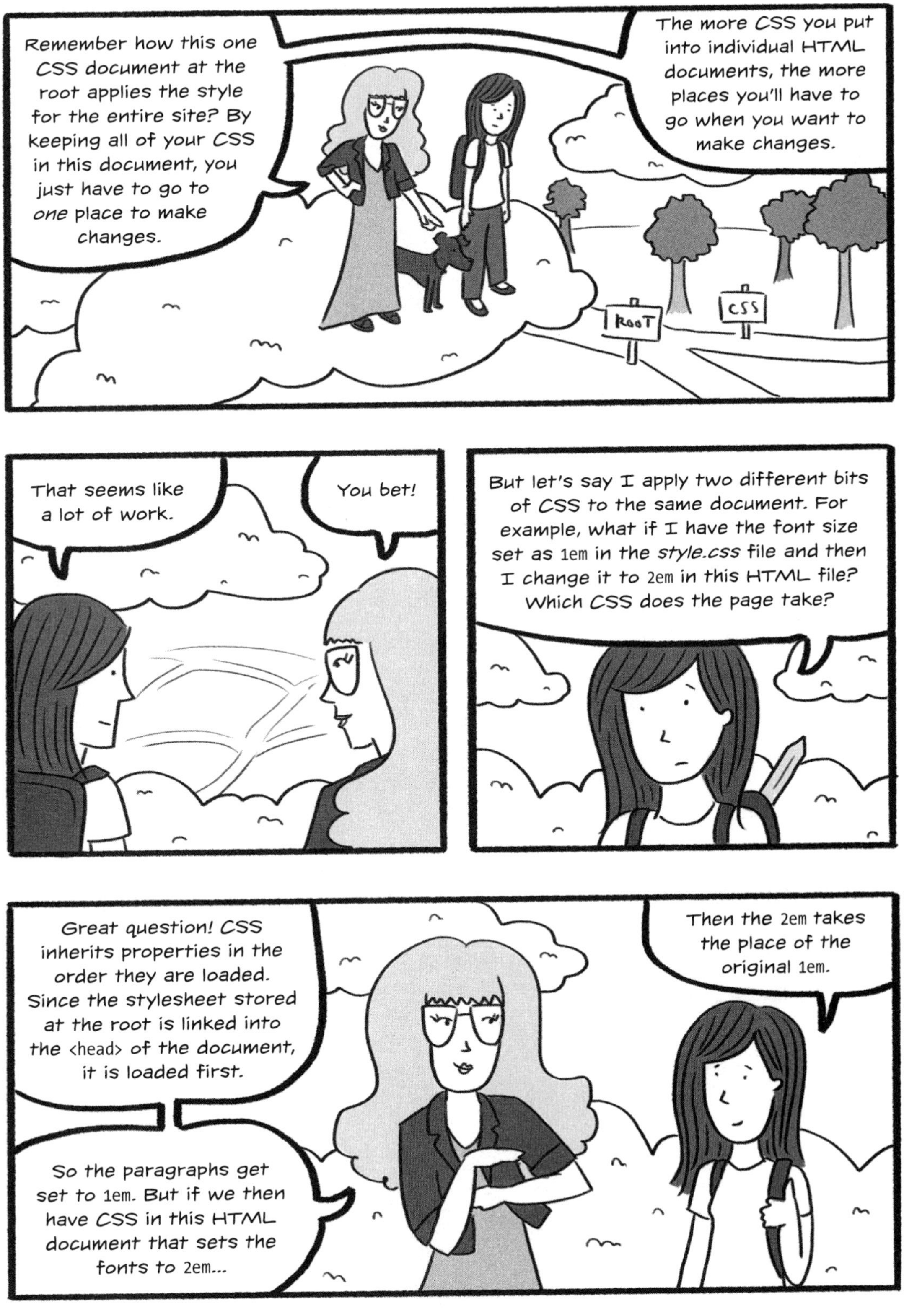
Remember how this one CSS document at the root applies the style for the entire site? By keeping all of your CSS in this document, you just have to go to *one* place to make changes.
The more CSS you put into individual HTML documents, the more places you'll have to go when you want to make changes.
ROOT
CSS
That seems like a lot of work.
You bet!
But let's say I apply two different bits of CSS to the same document. For example, what if I have the font size set as 1em in the *style.css* file and then I change it to 2em in this HTML file? Which CSS does the page take?
Great question! CSS inherits properties in the order they are loaded. Since the stylesheet stored at the root is linked into the <head> of the document, it is loaded first.
So the paragraphs get set to 1em. But if we then have CSS in this HTML document that sets the fonts to 2em...
Then the 2em takes the place of the original 1em.

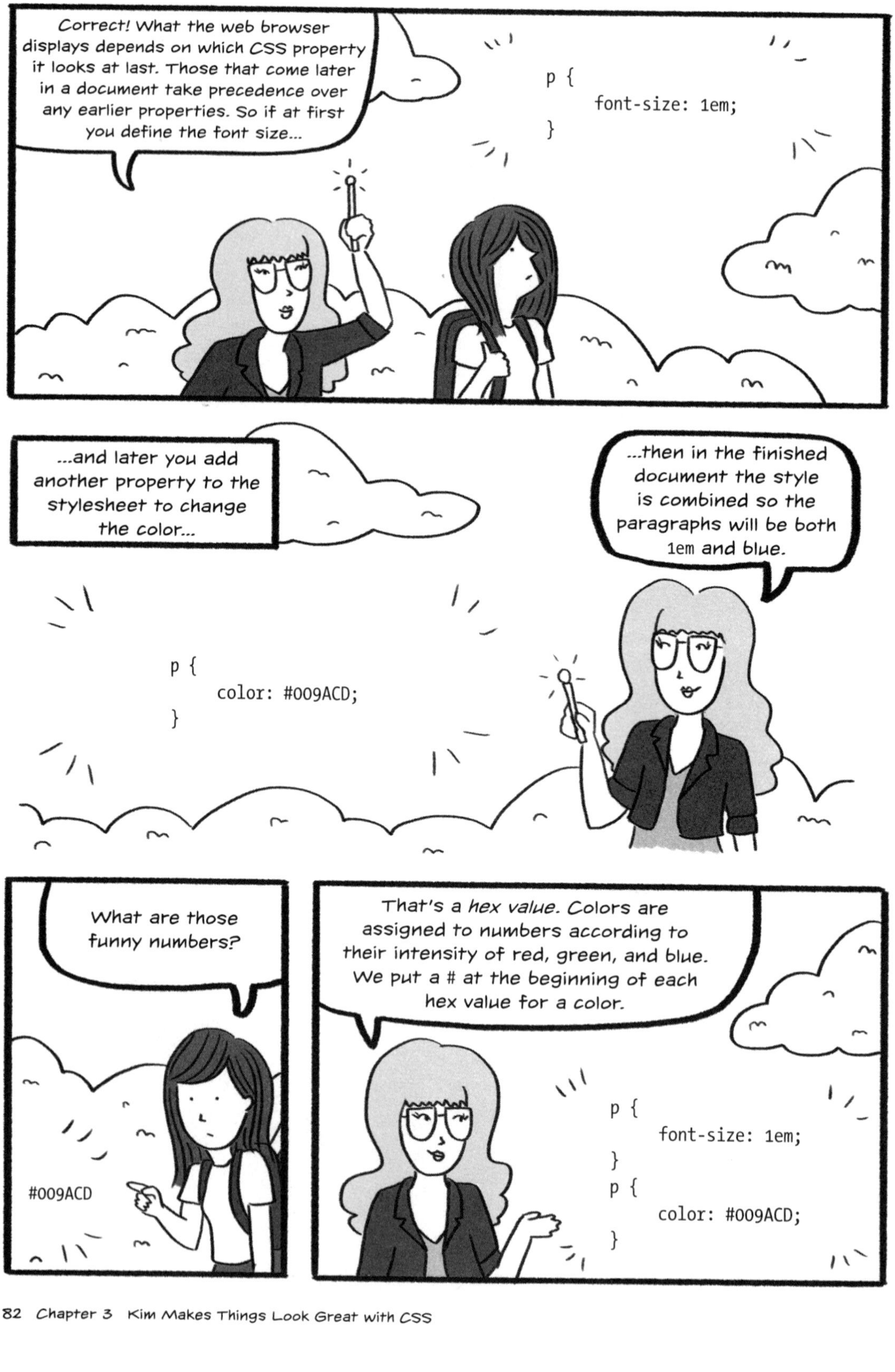
Correct! What the web browser displays depends on which CSS property it looks at last. Those that come later in a document take precedence over any earlier properties. So if at first you define the font size...
p {
font-size: 1em;
}
...and later you add another property to the stylesheet to change the color...
...then in the finished document the style is combined so the paragraphs will be both 1em and blue.
p {
color: #009ACD;
}
What are those funny numbers?
#009ACD
That's a *hex value*. Colors are assigned to numbers according to their intensity of red, green, and blue. We put a # at the beginning of each hex value for a color.
p {
font-size: 1em;
}
p {
color: #009ACD;
}

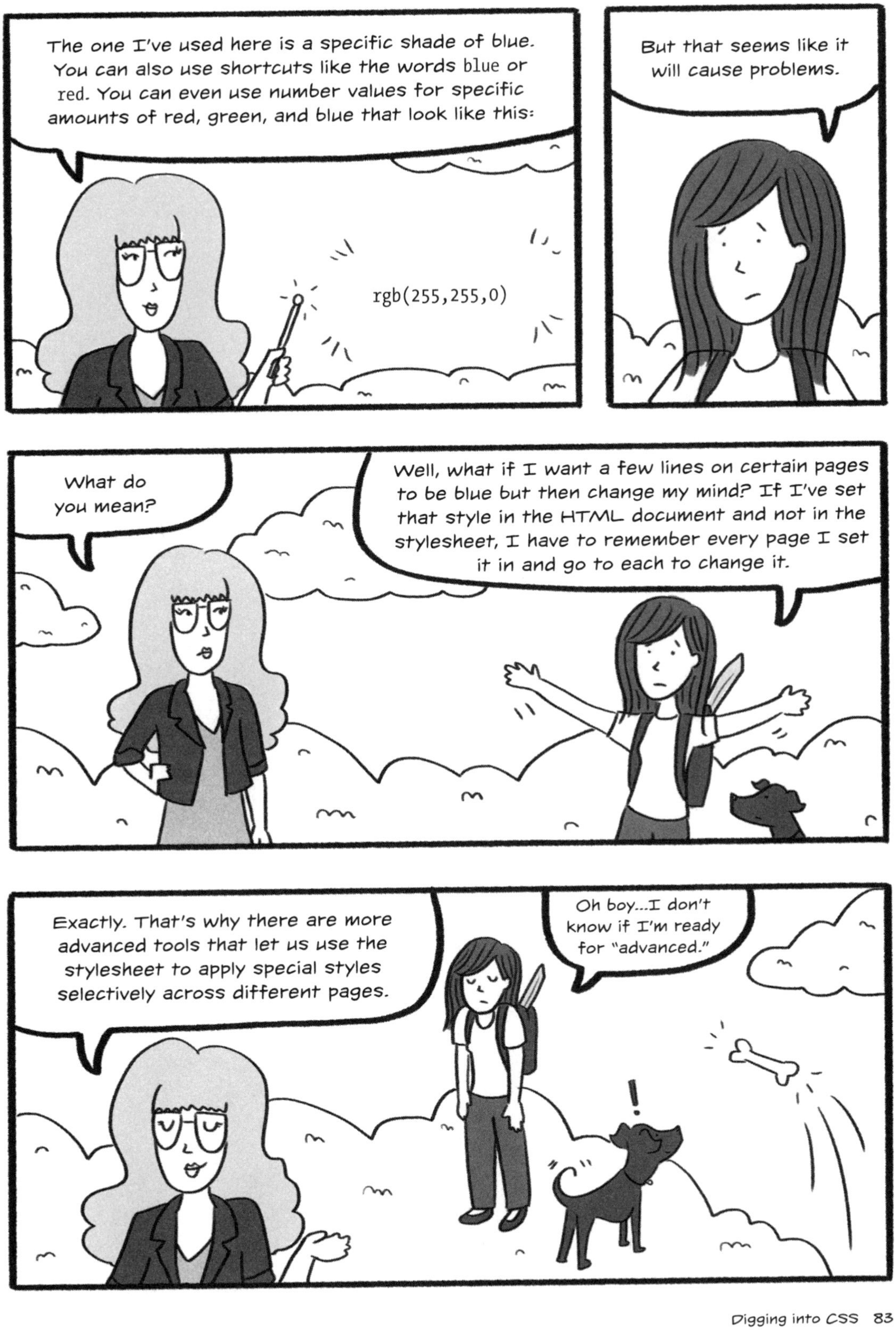
The one I've used here is a specific shade of blue. You can also use shortcuts like the words blue or red. You can even use number values for specific amounts of red, green, and blue that look like this:
rgb(255,255,0)
But that seems like it will cause problems.
What do you mean?
Well, what if I want a few lines on certain pages to be blue but then change my mind? If I've set that style in the HTML document and not in the stylesheet, I have to remember every page I set it in and go to each to change it.
Exactly. That's why there are more advanced tools that let us use the stylesheet to apply special styles selectively across different pages.
Oh boy...I don't know if I'm ready for "advanced."

Kim Learns CSS Classes and IDs

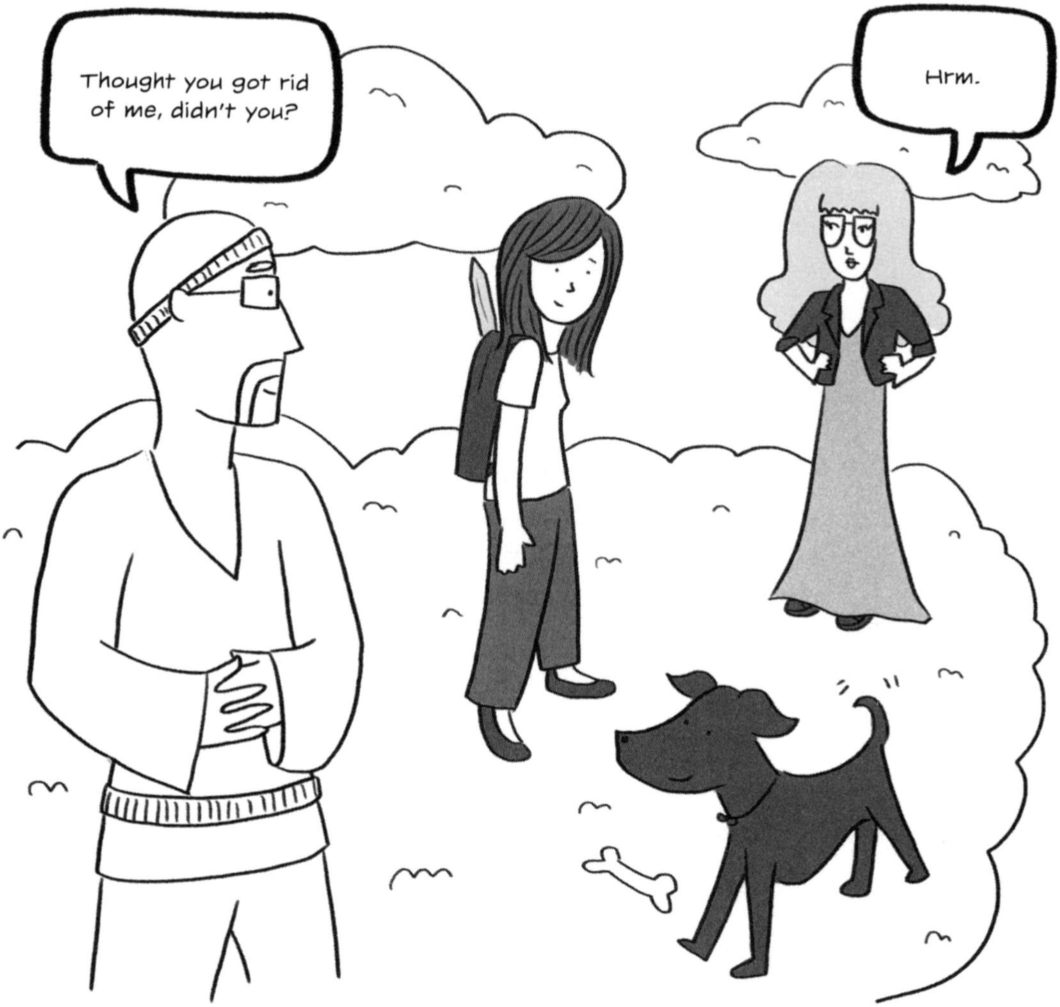

Thought you got rid of me, didn't you?
Hrm.

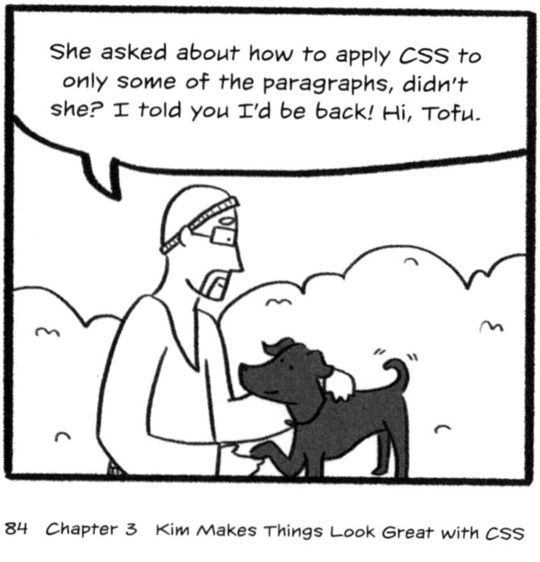

She asked about how to apply CSS to only some of the paragraphs, didn't she? I told you I'd be back! Hi, Tofu.

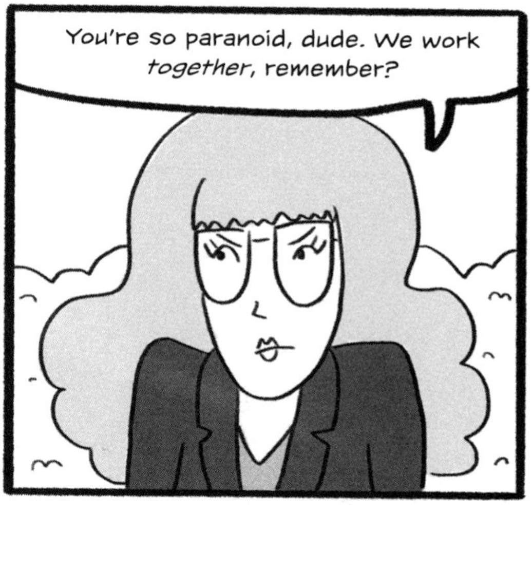

You're so paranoid, dude. We work *together*, remember?

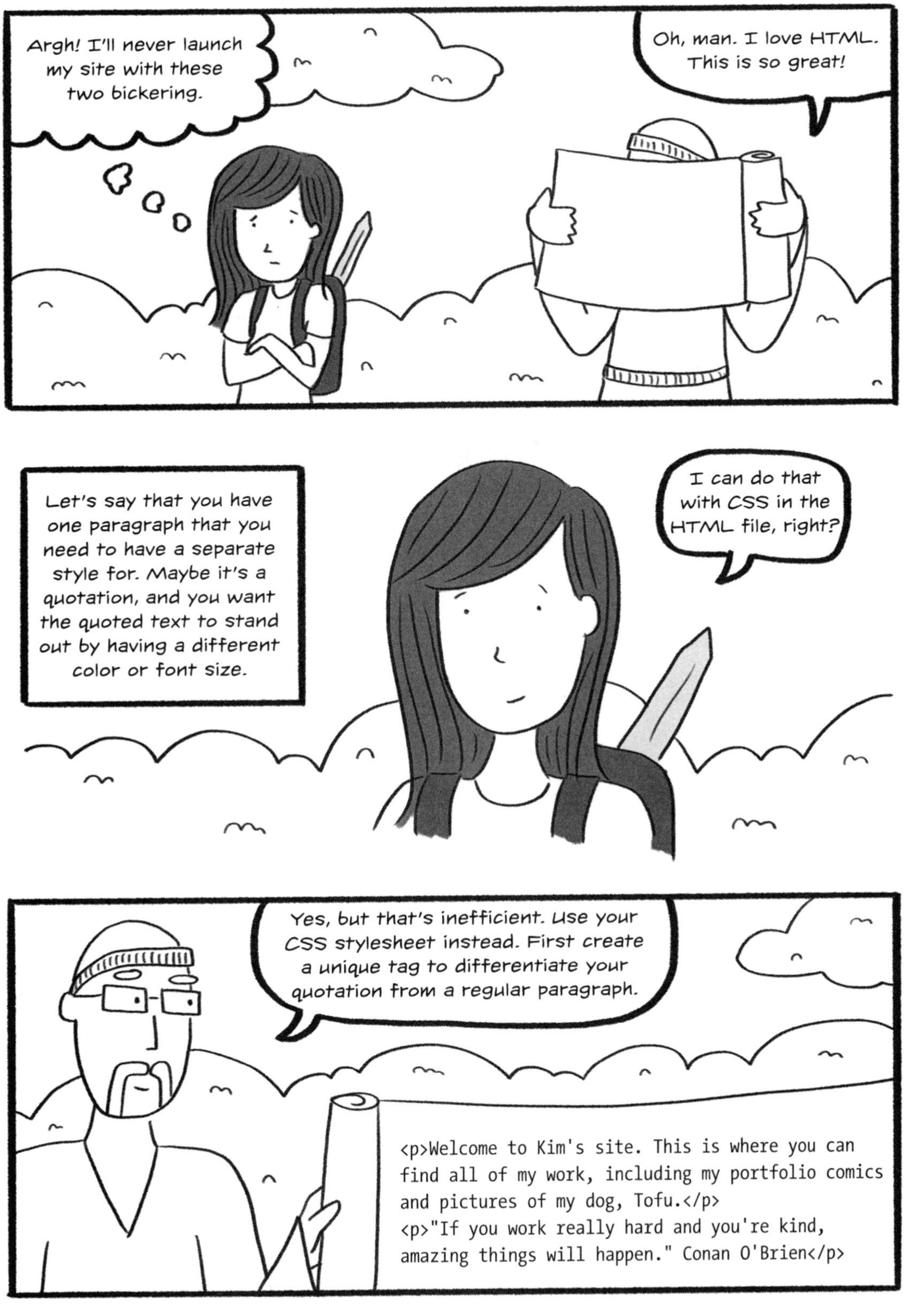
Argh! I'll never launch my site with these two bickering.
Oh, man. I love HTML. This is so great!
Let's say that you have one paragraph that you need to have a separate style for. Maybe it's a quotation, and you want the quoted text to stand out by having a different color or font size.
I can do that with CSS in the HTML file, right?
Yes, but that's inefficient. Use your CSS stylesheet instead. First create a unique tag to differentiate your quotation from a regular paragraph.
<p>Welcome to Kim's site. This is where you can find all of my work, including my portfolio comics and pictures of my dog, Tofu.</p>
<p>"If you work really hard and you're kind, amazing things will happen." Conan O'Brien</p>

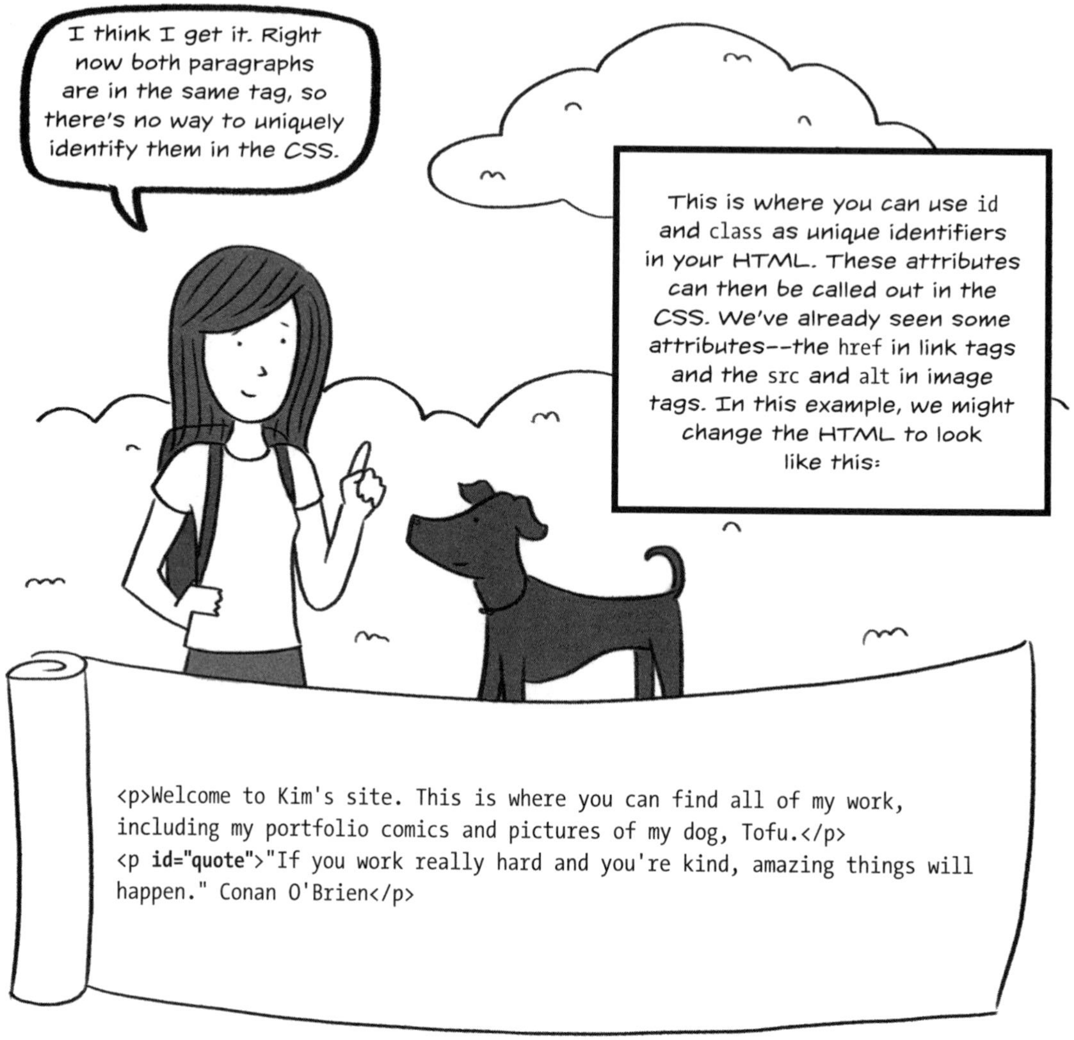
I think I get it. Right now both paragraphs are in the same tag, so there's no way to uniquely identify them in the CSS.
This is where you can use id and class as unique identifiers in your HTML. These attributes can then be called out in the CSS. We've already seen some attributes--the href in link tags and the src and alt in image tags. In this example, we might change the HTML to look like this:
<p>Welcome to Kim's site. This is where you can find all of my work, including my portfolio comics and pictures of my dog, Tofu.</p>
<p **id="quote"**>"If you work really hard and you're kind, amazing things will happen." Conan O'Brien</p>

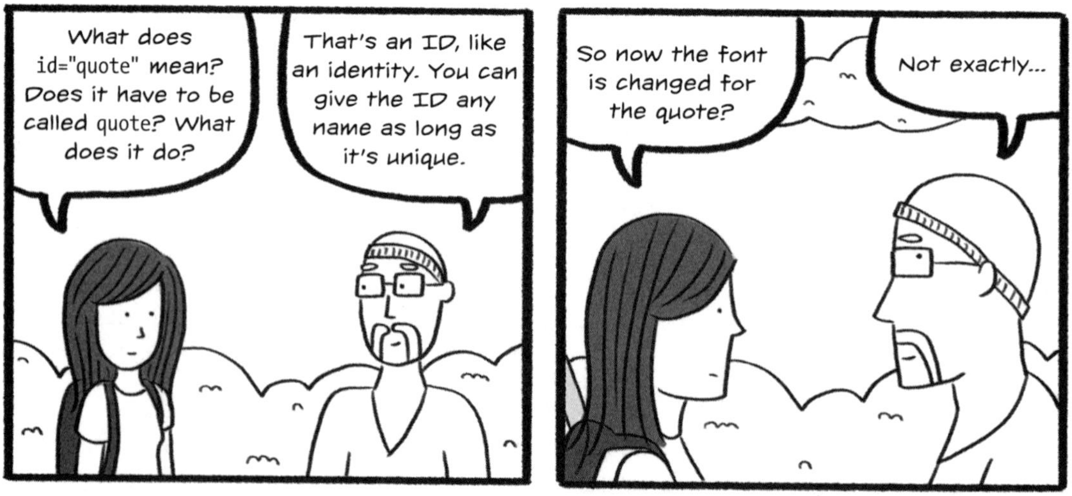
What does id="quote" mean? Does it have to be called quote? What does it do?
That's an ID, like an identity. You can give the ID any name as long as it's unique.
So now the font is changed for the quote?
Not exactly...

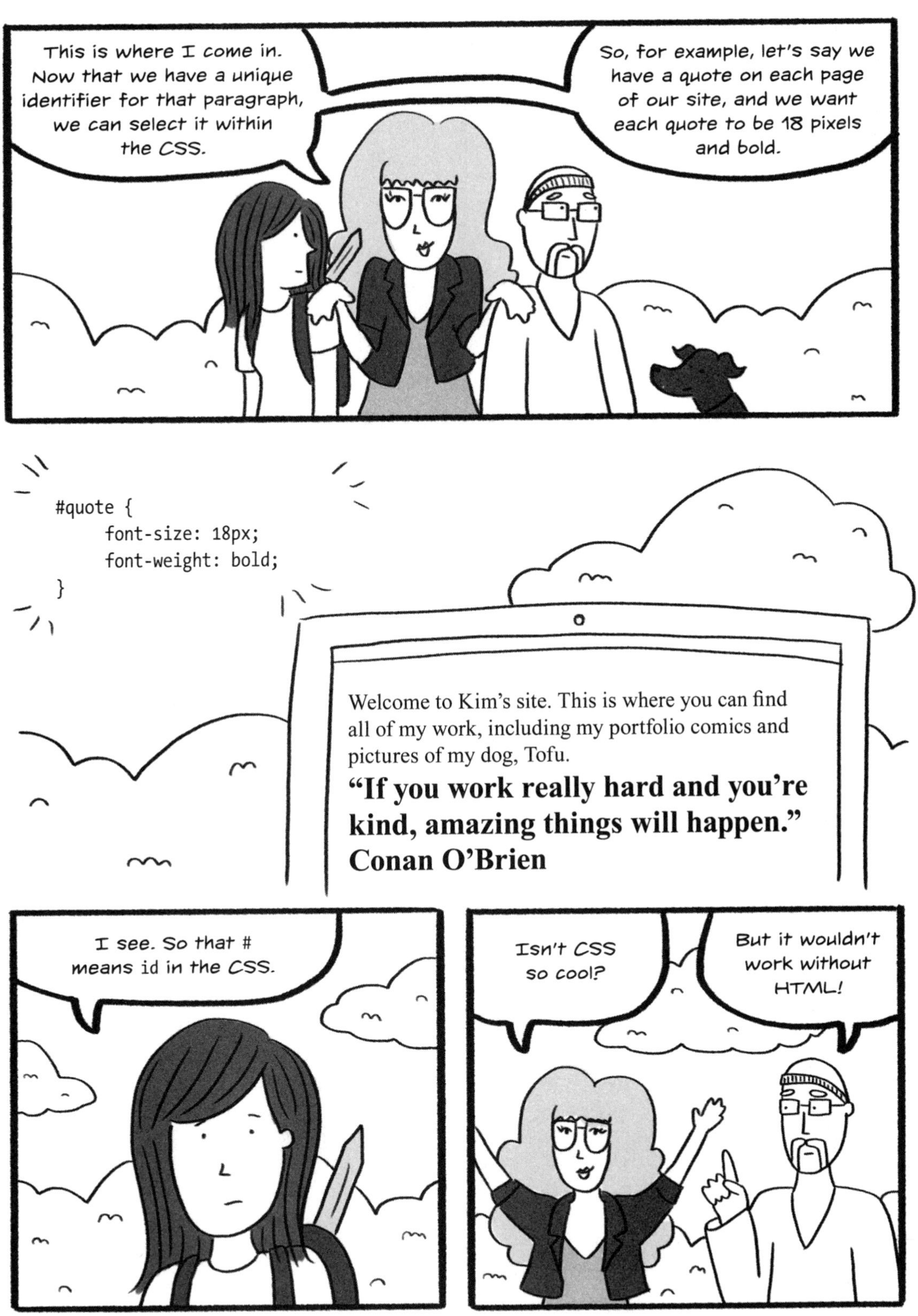
This is where I come in. Now that we have a unique identifier for that paragraph, we can select it within the CSS.
So, for example, let's say we have a quote on each page of our site, and we want each quote to be 18 pixels and bold.
#quote {
font-size: 18px;
font-weight: bold;
}
Welcome to Kim's site. This is where you can find all of my work, including my portfolio comics and pictures of my dog, Tofu.
"If you work really hard and you're kind, amazing things will happen." Conan O'Brien
I see. So that # means id in the CSS.
Isn't CSS so cool?
But it wouldn't work without HTML!

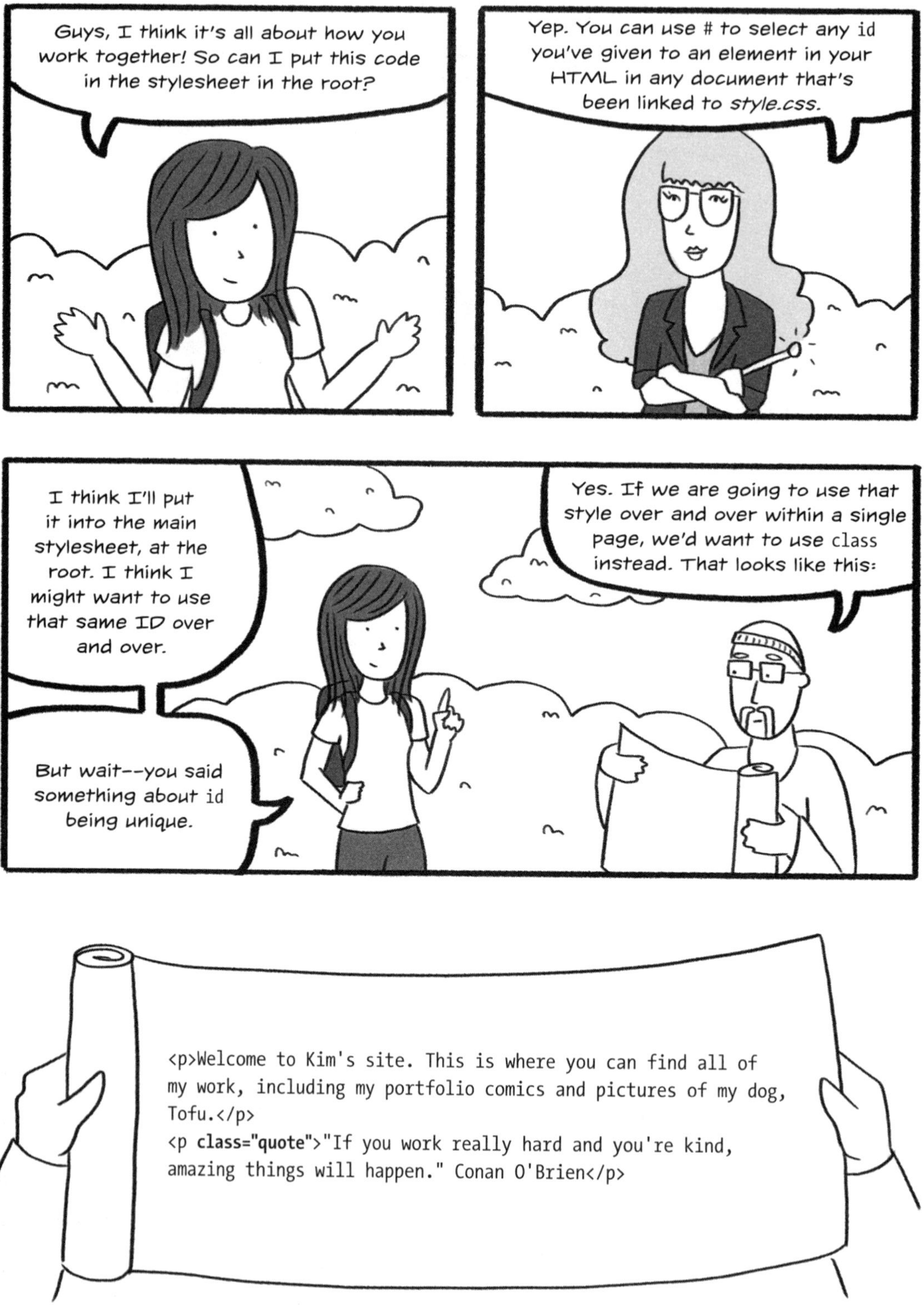
Guys, I think it's all about how you work together! So can I put this code in the stylesheet in the root?
Yep. You can use # to select any id you've given to an element in your HTML in any document that's been linked to *style.css*.
I think I'll put it into the main stylesheet, at the root. I think I might want to use that same ID over and over.
But wait--you said something about id being unique.
Yes. If we are going to use that style over and over within a single page, we'd want to use class instead. That looks like this:
<p>Welcome to Kim's site. This is where you can find all of my work, including my portfolio comics and pictures of my dog, Tofu.</p>
<p **class="quote"**>"If you work really hard and you're kind, amazing things will happen." Conan O'Brien</p>

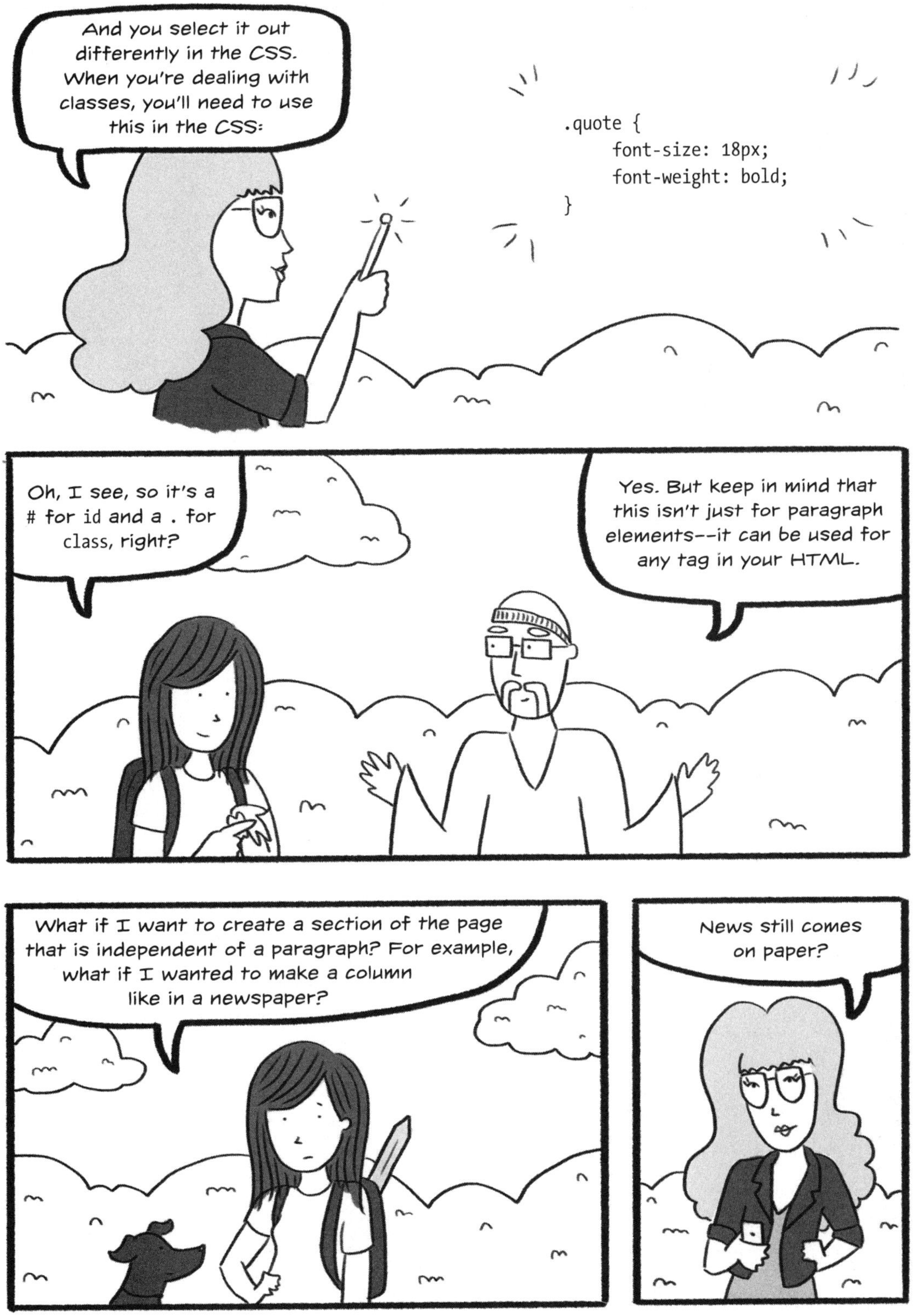
And you select it out differently in the CSS. When you're dealing with classes, you'll need to use this in the CSS:
.quote {
font-size: 18px;
font-weight: bold;
}
Oh, I see, so it's a # for id and a . for class, right?
Yes. But keep in mind that this isn't just for paragraph elements--it can be used for any tag in your HTML.
What if I want to create a section of the page that is independent of a paragraph? For example, what if I wanted to make a column like in a newspaper?
News still comes on paper?

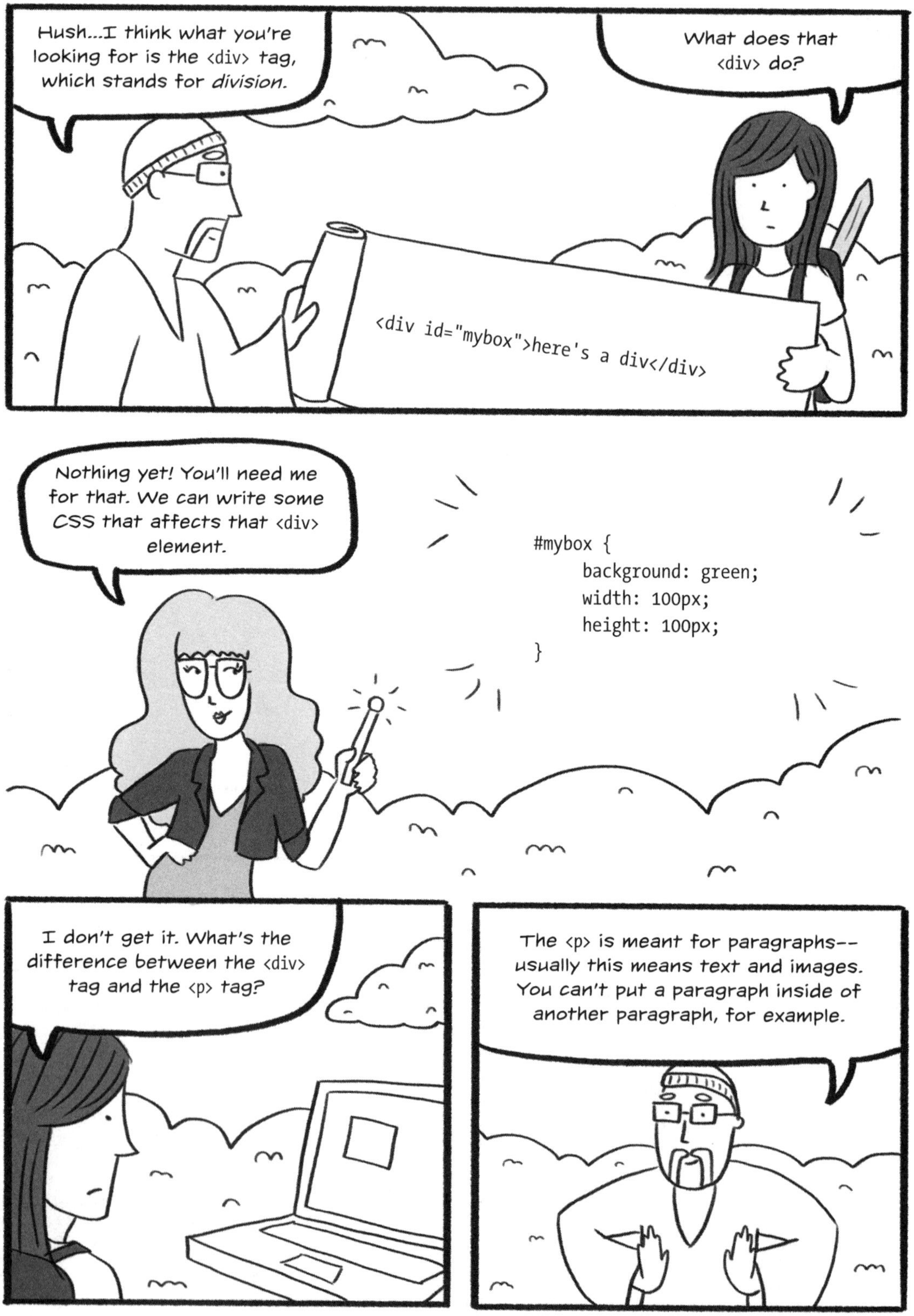

Hush...I think what you're looking for is the <div> tag, which stands for *division.*
What does that <div> do?
<div id="mybox">here's a div</div>
Nothing yet! You'll need me for that. We can write some CSS that affects that <div> element.
#mybox {
background: green;
width: 100px;
height: 100px;
}
I don't get it. What's the difference between the <div> tag and the <p> tag?
The <p> is meant for paragraphs--usually this means text and images. You can't put a paragraph inside of another paragraph, for example.

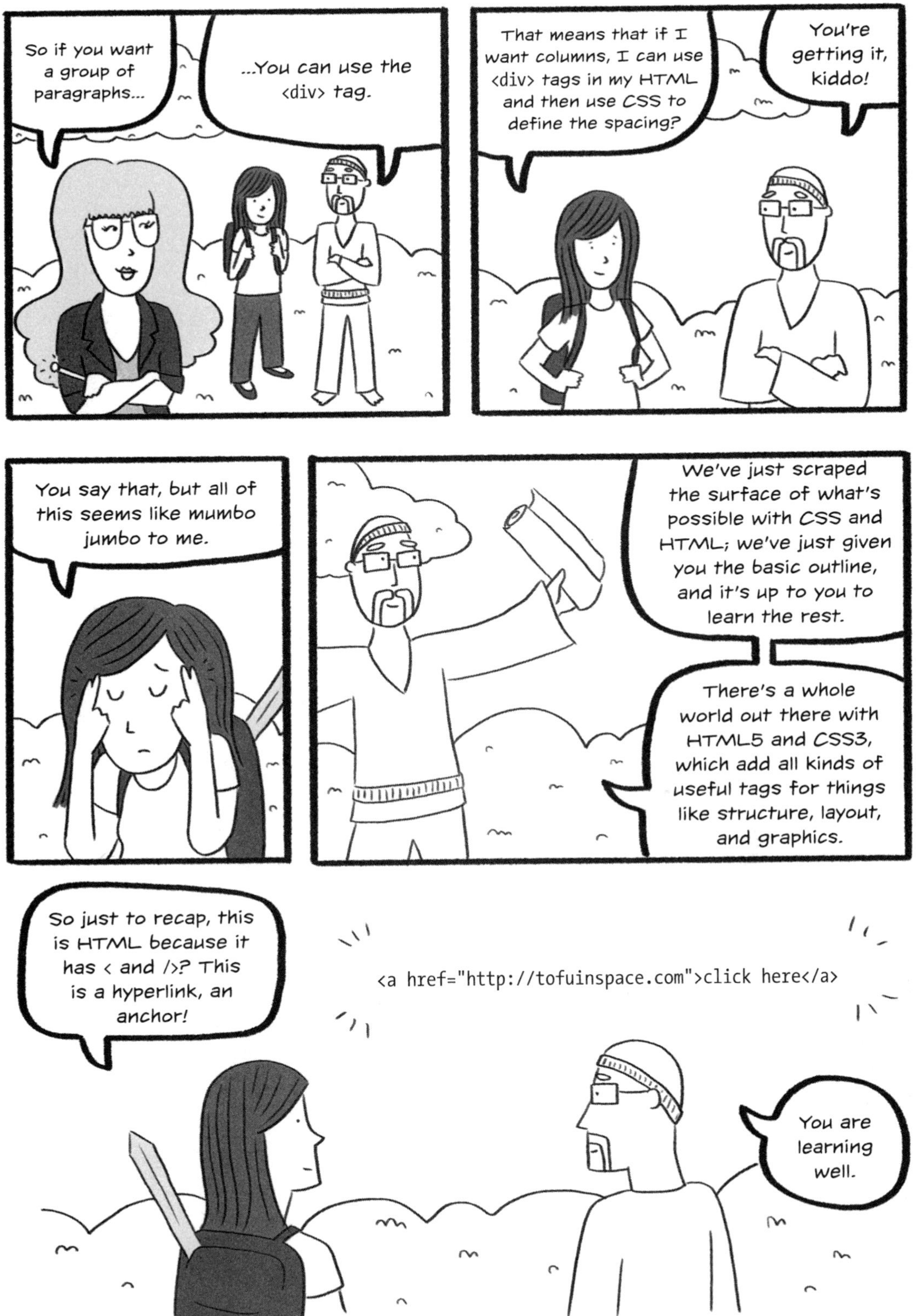
So if you want a group of paragraphs...
...You can use the <div> tag.
That means that if I want columns, I can use <div> tags in my HTML and then use CSS to define the spacing?
You're getting it, kiddo!
You say that, but all of this seems like mumbo jumbo to me.
We've just scraped the surface of what's possible with CSS and HTML; we've just given you the basic outline, and it's up to you to learn the rest.
There's a whole world out there with HTML5 and CSS3, which add all kinds of useful tags for things like structure, layout, and graphics.
So just to recap, this is HTML because it has < and />? This is a hyperlink, an anchor!
<a href="http://tofuinspace.com">click here</a>
You are learning well.

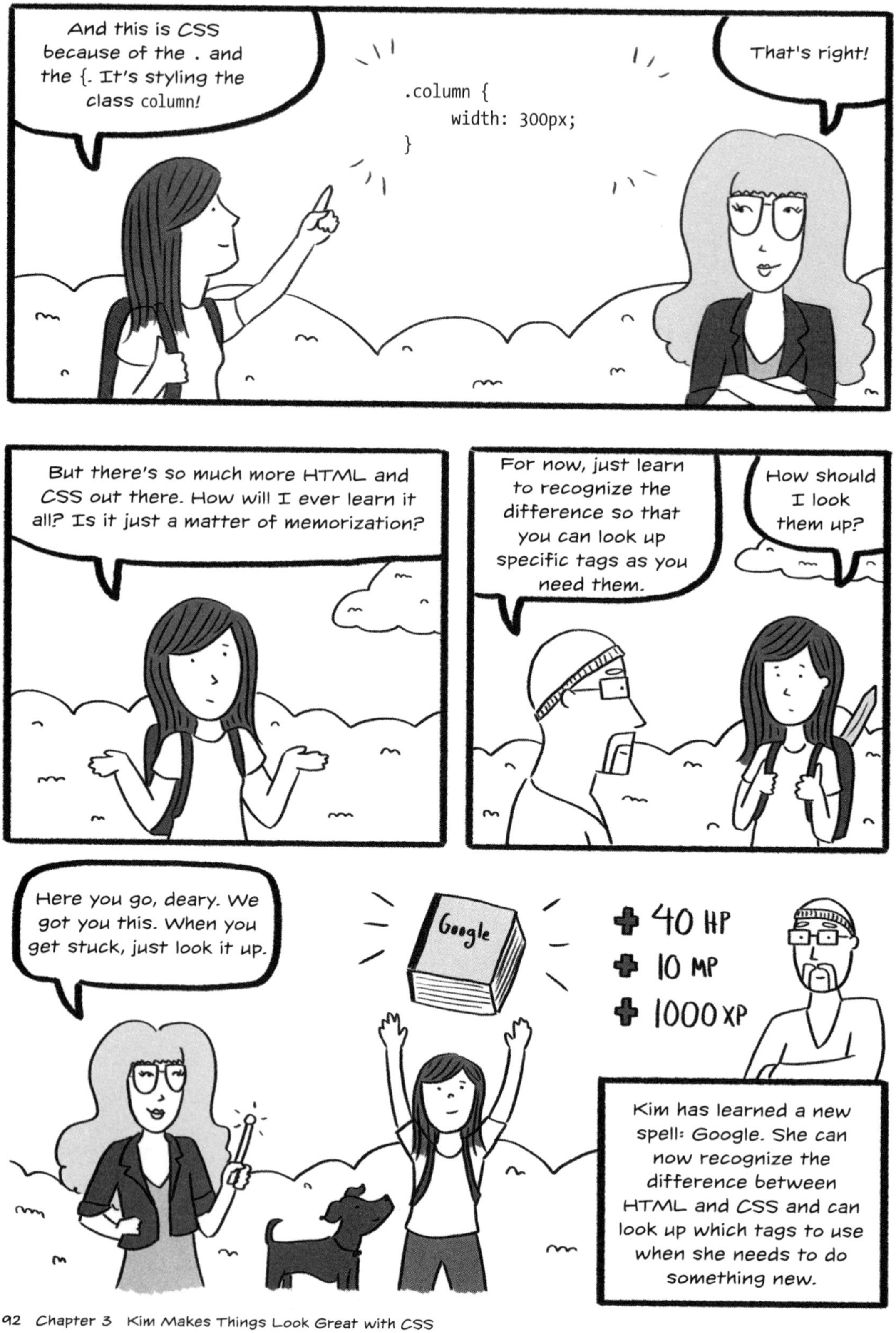
And this is CSS because of the . and the {. It's styling the class column!
.column {
width: 300px;
}
That's right!
But there's so much more HTML and CSS out there. How will I ever learn it all? Is it just a matter of memorization?
For now, just learn to recognize the difference so that you can look up specific tags as you need them.
How should I look them up?
Here you go, deary. We got you this. When you get stuck, just look it up.
Google
+ 40 HP
+ 10 MP
+ 1000 XP
Kim has learned a new spell: Google. She can now recognize the difference between HTML and CSS and can look up which tags to use when she needs to do something new.

Cascading Style Sheets

Before we can dive into learning *Cascading Style Sheets (CSS)*, we'll need to know a little bit about how CSS connects to HTML. CSS and HTML are used together and rely upon each other to work. Think of HTML as an architect who builds the skeleton of a building and gives each web page its basic structure. CSS is more like the interior designer deciding how things look, what color the walls are, and where the furniture goes. In this chapter, we'll see how to build on the bare-bones HTML framework and add some extra flair and finesse with CSS.

CSS can be added to your site in a few different ways. You can use CSS *inline*—that is, written right inside an individual HTML tag—or you can put CSS into the **<head>** of a document. The most common and powerful way of including CSS is to create a separate stylesheet file and link it to each HTML document. That's what we'll be doing in this chapter.

Setting Up Your Stylesheet and Linking It to Your HTML

The name *Cascading Style Sheets* actually comes from the magazine world, where a *stylesheet* is how desktop publishing programs format and present the magazine's pages. It's a single file that dictates things like the font and margins. Any changes that need to apply throughout the entire magazine can be made in a single place, and those edits cascade through the magazine. By creating a separate file for the CSS on your website, you mimic the power of the magazine stylesheet. All you need to do is create a separate CSS file and use the **<head>** section to link each HTML document to that file. The resulting organization might look something like Figure 3-1.

home.html
stylesheet.css
about.html
portfolio.html
portraits.html
landscapes.html

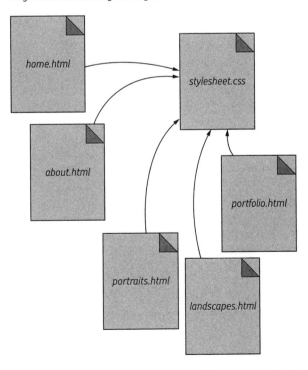

Figure 3-1: You can have all the pages on your website point to a single stylesheet.

Making Your First Stylesheet

In your code editor, create a new document and call it *style.css*. Technically, it doesn't matter what you call the document as long as it ends in *.css*. Like HTML, the contents of the file are just text, but by using the file extension *.css*, you let the web browser and server know to expect CSS and not HTML or text. Save the file in the same folder as your *test.html* file. This is important because you'll need to know the path to connect your stylesheet to your HTML document, just like with linking images.

Next, open your *test.html* document. In the `<head>` of the document, add this line of code: `<link href="style.css" rel="stylesheet">`. It doesn't matter whether you add this above or below the `<title>` and `<meta>` tags, as long as it's between `<head>` and `</head>`, but we'll put it on a line right before the `</head>` tag. Your document should now look like this:

```
<!DOCTYPE html>
<html>
    <head>
        <title>My Web Page</title>
        <meta name="description" content="A test page created while learning to code using
        the book Build Your Own Website.">
        <link href="style.css" rel="stylesheet">
    </head>
    <body>
        <h1>Hello World!</h1>
        <p>This is a second paragraph. <strong>This is bold text.</strong><br>
        <em>This is italic.</em></p>
        <p><a href="http://natecooper.co">Click here!</a></p>
        <img src="image.jpg" alt="our first photo">
    </body>
</html>
```

That little line of code is all we need to link the stylesheet we've created to our HTML document. For every other HTML page in our site, we'll use the same line of code in the `<head>` to link the HTML document to the single stylesheet.

Since a stylesheet is so fundamental to a modern website, it is common practice to place yours in the most important folder of your site, the "top" or so-called *root* directory. We know from the latest part of Kim's adventure that to link to the path to the root of a site, you can simply use the / at the start of your path. For example, if you are working on a web page in a folder called *portfolio*, your `<link>` might look something like this:

```
<link href="/style.css" rel="stylesheet">
```

By including this link in each of the `<head>` sections, you can link many different HTML pages to the same stylesheet, even if they're in different folders.

It might take you some time and practice before you become fully efficient with paths. But don't get intimidated. The main things to remember are that / is used every time there is a new folder, and you always work from the current folder in the case of relative paths. So if a file is in the same folder, you don't need the /; but if it's in a different folder, use / to signify that you are moving up a level. Because we are working off a computer, not a live server, just keep *style.css* in the same folder as *test.html* and link it using just the filename.

CSS: The Language of Style

Now that we have a separate stylesheet in our *style.css* file and a link to *style.css* in *test.html*, we're ready to start doing something with it. Open your blank *style.css* file and type the following text:

```
p {
     font-family: Helvetica, Arial, sans-serif;
}
```

Save your work, and refresh your HTML page, *test.html*. Did you see the difference? The font should have changed for all of the paragraphs on your page. So how did that happen? When we added that `<link>` to the `<head>` of our HTML document, we essentially told the HTML page to behave according to the properties set forth in our *style.css* file. To add a property in CSS, you have to first use a selector. A *selector* is a unique identifier for the segments in the HTML that you want to change. In this example, we used the selector `p`, which corresponds to the HTML tag `<p>`. We then added the property `font-family`—with the values `Helvetica, Arial, sans-serif`—to that selector. By using the `font-family` property, we're indicating that we want to change the font. The values for this property define what to change the font to. In this case, it tells your browser to change the font to Helvetica, but if that font isn't available, then use Arial; and if Arial is also not available, grab the next available sans-serif font. (*Sans-serif* means a font without the little hooks and feet on the letters, like you see in Times New Roman—see Figure 3-2.)

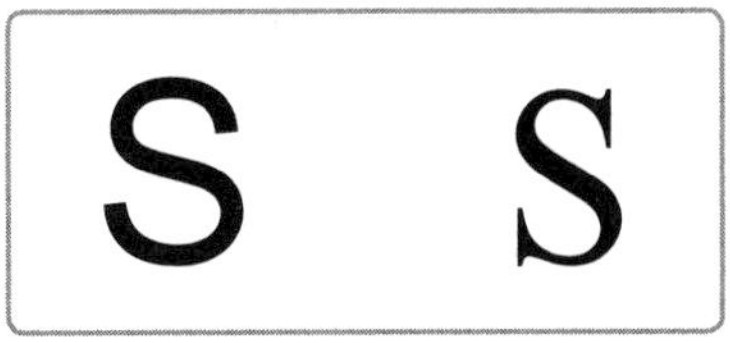
S
S

Figure 3-2: Sans-serif typefaces like Arial (left) are clean and modern-looking; serifed typefaces like Times New Roman (right) have little "feet."

Just like HTML, CSS is not whitespace dependent. That means that the code would have worked the same way had we written it on one line like this:

```
p {font-family: helvetica, arial, sans-serif; }
```

Once again, the extra spacing is just a convention to help make the code easier to read.

What we've done is created a property that must be followed by every paragraph; that is, the `p` in our CSS corresponds to the `<p>` element in any HTML document that links to this stylesheet. You're probably starting to see why CSS is a very powerful tool. Suppose we had 10, 20, 200, or 2,000 pages in our website. If each links to this *style.css* document, we would need to edit only this single file to change all the fonts in all the paragraphs for the entire site.

CSS Syntax

That CSS line looks different from HTML, doesn't it? CSS is a different language from HTML, so when you write CSS you have to follow different properties. The two main components are the selector and the curly brackets ({}) that follow it. The selector tells the CSS which HTML element (such as `<p>` or `<strong>`) you'd like to create a property for. You put the properties between the curly brackets.

Values for a property are defined with a colon (`:`) and separated by commas (where there's more than one). Properties are separated from other properties by a semicolon (`;`). If you forget any of these pieces, your CSS won't work!

Let's define another property to the paragraph selector to see how it works. After the `font-family` line, press RETURN and set the font size to **`10px`**. Your CSS code should look like this:

```
         Selector                 Value     Value     Value
         p {
Property ------ font-family: Helvetica, Arial, sans-serif;
Property ------ font-size: 10px;
         }
                            Value
```

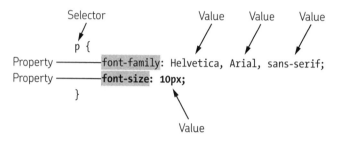

Save your *style.css* document and then reload your *test.html* page in your web browser. Remember that because we linked *test.html* to *style.css*, any changes we make to *style.css* will be automatically reflected in *test.html*. You should see that the paragraphs' font size has decreased.

When changing CSS dimensions like the size of the fonts, you have several ways of measuring. Two commonly used font sizing options are `px` and `em`. In the preceding example, we used `px`, which sizes the font according to a set number of pixels. Since the amount of pixels on a screen can vary depending on its resolution, a font set at 10 pixels might show up slightly larger on a small screen (where there are fewer pixels) but smaller on a huge display (where there are tons of pixels).

If you set the font size with `em`, on the other hand, that font size is relative to the current default font size. Using `em` allows you to adjust the font size proportionally according to the browser it's being viewed on. The default font size for a given browser is 1 em. For a mobile browser, the default font size is usually smaller so you can see more text. On a desktop browser, the default will usually be bigger.

If you set the font size to less than 1 em, the font will appear smaller than the default size; if you set it to more than 1 em, it will appear larger. (For example, a font set to 0.8 em will appear smaller than the default size, while 1.2 em will appear larger.) When you want to have a site that's flexible and adaptable for many different browsers, using `em` is very practical. For starters, though, try sticking with `px` so you can get the hang of sizing.

Don't get overwhelmed. You've already seen that with any technology, you have a couple of different ways of doing the same thing, but with varying results. Imagine painting a canvas. You can use a roller, a sponge, or any of several thousand brush sizes. It all comes down to what's best for the task at hand. You don't become a Rembrandt overnight, but with practice you'll start to understand the advantages and disadvantages of using things like `px` and `em`.

Let's take a look at our web page in the browser (see Figure 3-3).

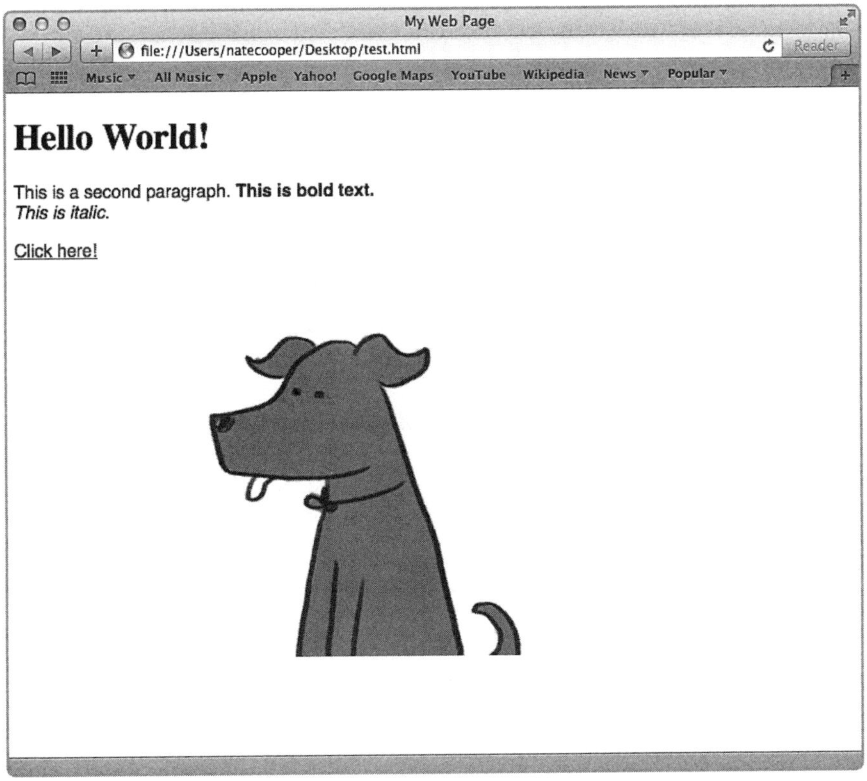
My Web Page
file:///Users/natecooper/Desktop/test.html
Reader
Music
All Music
Apple
Yahoo!
Google Maps
YouTube
Wikipedia
News
Popular
Hello World!
This is a second paragraph. This is bold text.
This is italic.
Click here!

Figure 3-3: The paragraphs have the font properties we applied in the CSS. The headings do not.

So far, we've changed only a single element in our HTML, the `<p>` tag. You may have noticed that the *Hello World!* part hasn't changed. In our code, *Hello World!* is wrapped in the `<h1>` tag. That means that all of the CSS properties we applied under the `p` selector don't apply to it. Let's say we also want to change the font and set the font size for our `<h1>` tags. Open your CSS file and add the properties for the `<h1>` selector, just like we did for the paragraph tag, but set the font size to `1.3em`. Also change the font size in the paragraph tag to `.8em`. Your CSS code should look like this:

```
p {
     font-family: Helvetica, Arial, sans-serif;
     font-size: .8em;
}

h1 {
     font-family: Helvetica, Arial, sans-serif;
     font-size: 1.3em;
}
```

Save your document and reload *test.html* in your web browser. We changed the font, but perhaps you're wondering: Wasn't the <h1> already larger? Why did we add in the font-size if the default setting automatically makes <h1> bigger than <p>? Those are great questions. Anything we don't intentionally take control of in the CSS is left to the browser defaults. While most browsers automatically make <h1> larger than <p>, how *much* bigger can vary from browser to browser. CSS is where *you* get to take control and tell the browser you want something to be exactly a certain size or proportion. By setting up properties in CSS, we're elaborating on the basic structure provided by the HTML page so that the project gets built exactly to our specifications.

Classes, IDs, and Inheritance

We've taken our first steps to define the style of broad elements in the CSS. By now, you should understand that any tagged element in HTML can be selected out in the CSS for modification. What if you want to select out a more specific section, though? Let's say, for example, that you have a quotation that you want to format differently than the rest of the page. Open your HTML document and add the following bolded code:

```
<!DOCTYPE html>
<html>
    <head>
        <title>My Web Page</title>
        <meta name="description" content="A test page created while learning to code using
        the book Build Your Own Website.">
        <link href="style.css" rel="stylesheet">
    </head>
    <body>
        <h1>Hello World!</h1>
        <p>This is a second paragraph. <strong>This is bold text.</strong><br>
        <em>This is italic.</em></p>
        <p><a href="http://natecooper.co">Click here!</a></p>
        <img src="image.jpg" alt="our first photo">
        <p>I have never let my schooling interfere with my education. - Mark Twain</p>
    </body>
</html>
```

It's behaving as we might suspect (see Figure 3-4). We set up the properties for a paragraph to have a certain font and size, and all of our paragraphs are behaving according to those properties.

But we want this quote to have its own properties. There's nothing in the code that makes this paragraph special, so how do we target it in the stylesheet? We'll have to do something to the HTML to give it a special name or qualification—an *attribute*. Open your *test.html* file in your code editor and add this to the paragraph tag:

```
<p id="quote">I have never let my schooling interfere with my education. - Mark Twain</p>
```

My Web Page
file:///Users/natecooper/Desktop/test.html
Reader
Music
All Music
Apple
Yahoo!
Google Maps
YouTube
Wikipedia
News
Popular
Hello World!
This is a second paragraph. This is bold text.
This is italic.
Click here!
I have never let my schooling interfere with my education. - Mark Twain

Figure 3-4: The new paragraph at the bottom of our page behaves by the existing properties from the stylesheet because it is still a paragraph.

ID is a unique identifier you can add to (almost) any tag in HTML to call it out by name in the CSS. In this case, we named it `quote` for simplicity's sake, but when you create an ID you can give it any name you like.

Save and reload, and you should see that, so far, nothing is different. Even though we've given this paragraph a unique ID, it's still a paragraph and it will *inherit* the properties and attributes we've applied to the `<p>` element. But we want to do something special with just this one paragraph, so how do we identify it in the CSS? Any time you want to identify a specific ID in CSS, you use a hash mark (`#`). Instead of specifying `p` in the selector, we'll use a `#quote` selector instead.

Let's add the following into our stylesheet so that we can make some changes to the quote's formatting:

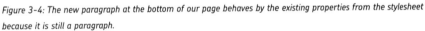

```
#quote {
     text-align: center;
     color: gray;
}
```

After saving and reloading, you should notice that the font color is now gray and the text is centered on the page (see Figure 3-5). The font and size remain the same. This is what's meant by *cascading* (also sometimes called *inheritance*) in CSS: Anything that you don't specifically change will cascade down from the previous property. So in this case, we have a paragraph `#quote` that takes on all of the existing properties of being a paragraph first and then takes on any additional properties we apply to it.

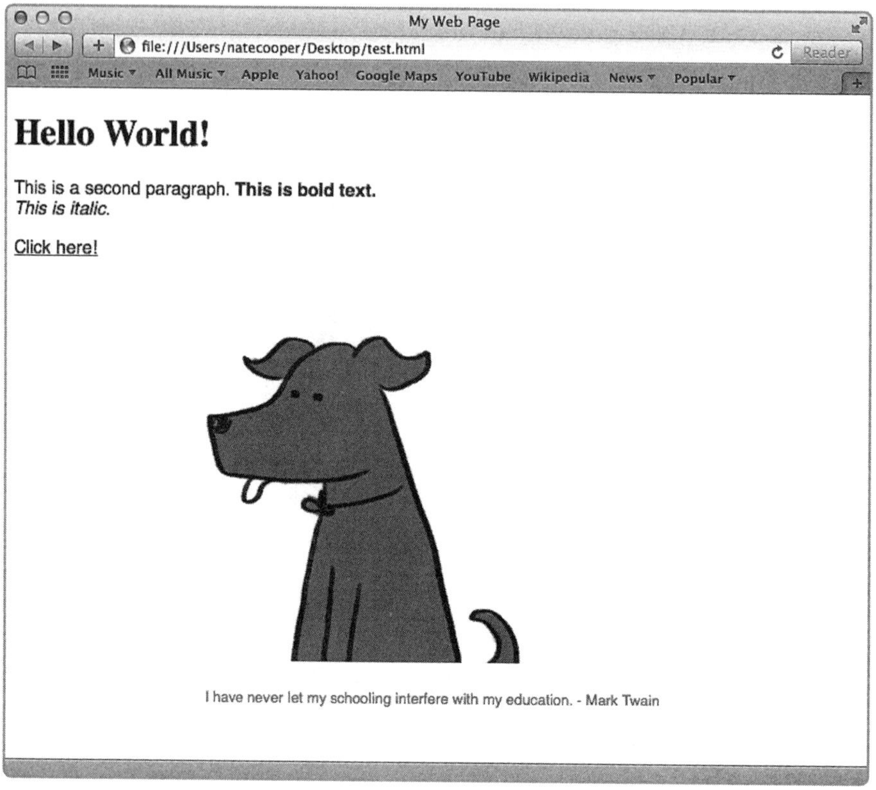
My Web Page
file:///Users/natecooper/Desktop/test.html
Reader
Music
All Music
Apple
Yahoo!
Google Maps
YouTube
Wikipedia
News
Popular
Hello World!
This is a second paragraph. This is bold text.
This is italic.
Click here!
I have never let my schooling interfere with my education. - Mark Twain

Figure 3-5: Because the #quote paragraph is given a unique ID, you can give it different properties to make it centered and gray.

Add `font-family: Times, Courier, serif;` on the next line after `color: gray;`. Your CSS file should look something like this:

```
p {
     font-family: Helvetica, Arial, sans-serif;
     font-size: .8em;
}

h1 {
     font-family: Helvetica, Arial, sans-serif;
     font-size: 1.3em;
}
```

```
#quote {
    text-align: center;
    color: gray;
    font-family: Times, Courier, serif;
}
```

Save and reload. Now you should see that the quote in the browser is in a different font than the other paragraph, while the size remains the same. ID works great if you have only one per page, but what if you want more than one? Class is a better tool to use if you want to style several parts of your page in the same way. In this case, we're looking to style a group of quotes. Let's add another quote into the *test.html* code and see how classes work.

```
<!DOCTYPE html>
<html>
    <head>
        <title>My Web Page</title>
        <meta name="description" content="A test page created while learning to code using
        the book Build Your Own Website.">
        <link href="style.css" rel="stylesheet">
    </head>
    <body>
        <h1>Hello World!</h1>
        <p>This is a second paragraph. <strong>This is bold text.</strong><br>
        <em>This is italic.</em></p>
        <p><a href="http://natecooper.co">Click here!</a></p>
        <img src="image.jpg" alt="our first photo">
        <p class="quote" id="twain">I have never let my schooling interfere with
        my education. - Mark Twain</p>
        <p class="quote" id="einstein">Education is what remains after one has
        forgotten what one has learned in school. - Albert Einstein</p>
    </body>
</html>
```

Notice how we've changed both the original quote and the new quote we've added. In each case, we've given the paragraphs a class of quote, signifying that they are part of a group. A class, unlike an ID, can be used multiple times within a page. You can give an element both a class and an ID, and you can give multiple elements the same class, but you don't want to give the same ID to different elements on the same page. IDs are meant for picking out a single element on a page to style it uniquely, while classes are good for picking out a group of elements on a page to style the same way. As you might imagine, classes and IDs are targeted separately via your CSS document. You can see the code here:

```
p {
    font-family: Helvetica, Arial, sans-serif;
    font-size: .8em;
}
```

```
h1 {
    font-family: Helvetica, Arial, sans-serif;
    font-size: 1.3em;
}

.quote {
    text-align: center;
    color: gray;
    font-family: Times, Courier, serif;
}

#twain {
    color: blue;
}

#einstein {
    color: red;
}
```

Notice how in the CSS we use a *dot* (.) to signify class. The `<p class="quote">` in HTML is selected with `.quote` in the CSS. Knowing when you would use class and when it's better to use ID can seem tricky at first, but you'll get the hang of it with some practice. The main takeaway here is that both class and ID can be applied to any HTML elements that you need to separate from the general CSS properties for an element. Class can be applied as often as needed within a page or across pages, while ID can be used only once per page. Class defines styles that you might want to use again and again; in this case, `quote` is a `class` because we are going to have more than one quote on the page. Since ID is narrower and more specific, the style within it can trump styles set by class, as shown in Figure 3-6. Here we're applying class and ID to the `<p>` tag, but you can apply them to any tag that you want to distinguish from the rest of the page.

Colors

In the previous example, we changed the color of our paragraphs using the words blue, red, and gray. This is one of several ways to set the color of elements in CSS. For many colors, you can use English words to change them in CSS (even weird ones like azure and salmon), but another way to assign colors is by using a *hex value*. What does that look like? For example, #FFFFFF is white and #000000 is black. You can also represent colors using red, green, and blue (RGB) values. That looks like rgb(0,0,0) for black, or rgb(255,255,255) for white. Hex values, RGB values, and color names are just different ways of expressing the same concept. Unlike px and em, though, you get the same results no matter what you use.

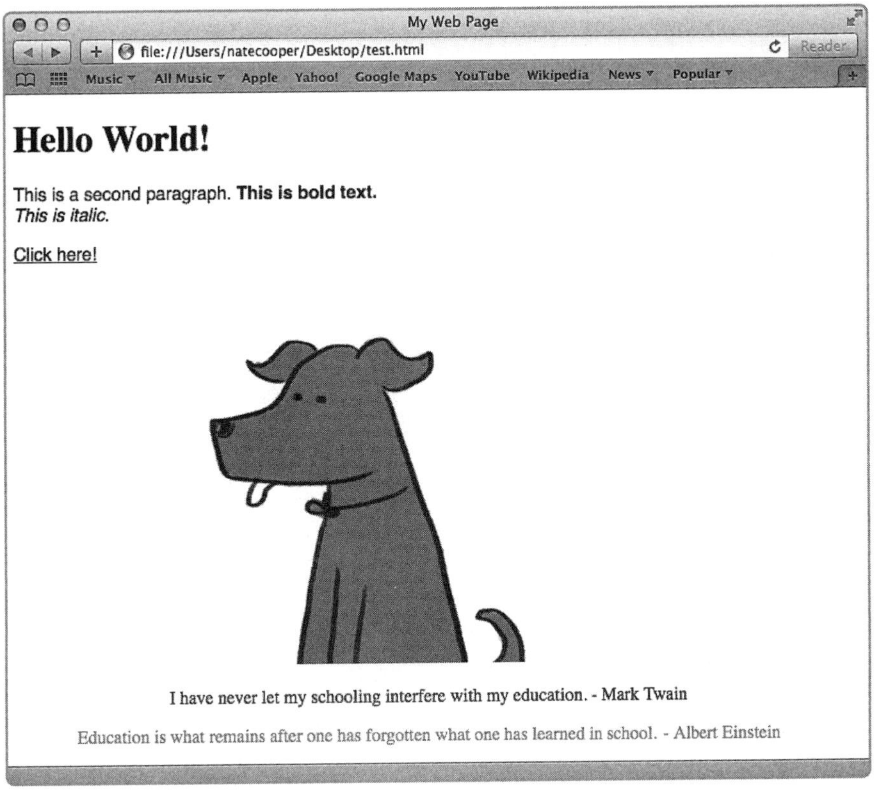
My Web Page
file:///Users/natecooper/Desktop/test.html
Reader
Music
All Music
Apple
Yahoo!
Google Maps
YouTube
Wikipedia
News
Popular
Hello World!
This is a second paragraph. This is bold text.
This is italic.
Click here!
I have never let my schooling interfere with my education. - Mark Twain
Education is what remains after one has forgotten what one has learned in school. - Albert Einstein

Figure 3-6: Class defines characteristics for both quote paragraphs. ID specifies the color for each uniquely.

For example, any one of these will give you the exact same color for your `#twain`:

```
#twain {
     color: rgb(0,0,255);
}

#twain {
     color: #0000FF;
}

#twain {
     color: blue;
}
```

For your reference, Table 3-1 lists common colors you might want to use in CSS. You can learn whichever color system makes the most sense to you.

Table 3-1: Common Colors

Color	Hex value	RGB
black	#000000	rgb(0,0,0)
gray	#C0C0C0	rgb(192,192,192)
white	#FFFFFF	rgb(255,255,255)
yellow	#FFFF00	rgb(255,255,0)
red	#FF0000	rgb(255,0,0)
green	#00FF00	rgb(0,255,0)
blue	#0000FF	rgb(0,0,255)

The <div> Tag and Alignment with CSS

Every HTML element we've discussed so far has some basic default styling. The <p> tag, for example, separates one paragraph from another with a space. The <h1> tag automatically makes the text bold and larger. Next we'll look at the <div> tag. This tag has no inherent properties, which makes it especially handy for custom CSS. Go back to your HTML document and add the following code:

```
<!DOCTYPE html>
<html>
    <head>
        <title>My Web Page</title>
        <meta name="description" content="A test page created while learning to code using
        the book Build Your Own Website.">
        <link href="style.css" rel="stylesheet">
    </head>
    <body>
        <h1>Hello World!</h1>
        <p>This is a second paragraph. <strong>This is bold text.</strong><br>
        <em>This is italic.</em></p>
        <p><a href="http://natecooper.co">Click here!</a></p>
        <img src="image.jpg" alt="our first photo">
        <p class="quote" id="twain">I have never let my schooling interfere with my
        education. - Mark Twain</p>
        <p class="quote" id="einstein">Education is what remains after one has forgotten
        what one has learned in school. - Albert Einstein</p>
        <div>This is The Guru's div.</div><div>This is Glinda's div.</div>
    </body>
</html>
```

Save the document and refresh your browser. You should notice a few things. One is that the `<div>`s are not using the Helvetica font that your paragraphs use. That should make sense because when we applied that CSS property, we applied it only to the `<p>` tag. Another interesting thing to note is that the spacing between the two `<div>`s is different than the spacing between paragraphs; it's more like what you get with a `<br>` than a `<p>`. `<div>` is short for *division*, and it's a kind of code separator that has little or no inherent qualities until we add them with CSS. Let's do that now. We'll need to create a unique identifier for each of our two `<div>`s in the HTML first so that we can style them differently in the CSS. We can do that with IDs. Go back to the line of HTML code and label each `<div>` like so:

```
<div id="guru">This is The Guru's div</div>
<div id="glinda">This is Glinda's div</div>
```

Now that we have unique IDs on each `<div>`, we can select them out in the CSS.

```
#guru {
    height: 100px;
    width: 100px;
    background-color: blue;
    float: left;
}

#glinda {
    height: 100px;
    width: 100px;
    background-color: green;
    float: left;
}
```

Save and reload your page. If all works well, you'll see something that looks like Figure 3-7.

We applied a couple of CSS properties there, so let's look at each of them. First, we set the `width` and `height` of each `<div>`. `<div>`s have no inherent dimensions. If we hadn't added text and set the width and height, our `<div>`s wouldn't be visible on the page at all. By setting each `<div>` to 100px by 100px, we're making a small box. We also set the color of the background with the `background-color` properties. The property `color`, which we used earlier, is for setting the color of fonts, while `background-color` sets the *container* background color. A container is what we might call an element that holds something between its start and end tags. In this case, the container is a `<div>`, but you could also set the `background-color` of a `<p>` or a `<a href="">`</a>`. The last property we apply is `float: left`. `float` is a positioning property that can help us with alignment; it adds a kind of gravity to the left or the right side of the browser window. When we add `float: left` to each `<div>`, they fall together as if gravity is pulling them to the left side of the window.

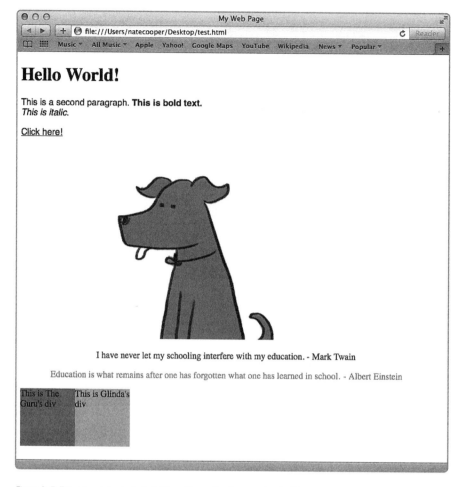

Figure 3-7: The `<div>` is basically invisible until you give it properties. In this case, we've changed the color and shape.

Let's look at our CSS code again:

```
#guru {
    height: 100px;
    width: 100px;
    background-color: blue;
    float: left;
}

#glinda {
    height: 100px;
    width: 100px;
    background-color: green;
    float: left;
}
```

There is a lot of overlap with the properties for our boxes. There must be a cleaner way we can add CSS. What about adding an attribute to the HTML? Open your HTML document and add a class="box" to each <div>.

```
<div class="box" id="guru">This is The Guru's div</div>
<div class="box" id="glinda">This is Glinda's div</div>
```

Now we can open our CSS file and attach a lot of our common properties to the class and leave the unique properties to the IDs, like so:

```
.box {
    height: 100px;
    width: 100px;
    float: left;
}

#guru {
    background-color: blue;
}

#glinda {
    background-color: green;
}
```

In this case, we've taken all of our alignment and sizing properties and attached them to the class and left only the colors (the unique properties) attached to the IDs. This will leave us in good shape to add common properties that apply to both boxes. Let's add a text alignment property to .box in our CSS file.

```
.box {
    height: 100px;
    width: 100px;
    float: left;
    text-align: center;
}
```

Once you save *style.css* and reload your HTML document, you should see that the text within the boxes is centered, but the boxes themselves are still floating to the left. The float property is applied to the container in this case, while the text-align property is applied to the text within the container. You'll notice this kind of thing happening a lot with CSS; the inner and outer parts of a container are affected differently depending on which properties you use.

Margins and Padding

Margins and padding provide a good example of the difference between a property that affects the inner part of a container and one that affects the outer part. Open your CSS file and add the following to the `.box`:

```
.box {
     height: 100px;
     width: 100px;
     float: left;
     text-align: center;
     margin: 5px;
}
```

When you save and reload your page, you should see something like Figure 3-8.

My Web Page
file:///Users/natecooper/Desktop/test.html
Reader
Music
All Music
Apple
Yahoo!
Google Maps
YouTube
Wikipedia
News
Popular
Hello World!
This is a second paragraph. This is bold text.
This is italic.
Click here!
I have never let my schooling interfere with my education. - Mark Twain
Education is what remains after one has forgotten what one has learned in school. - Albert Einstein
This is The Guru's div
This is Glinda's div

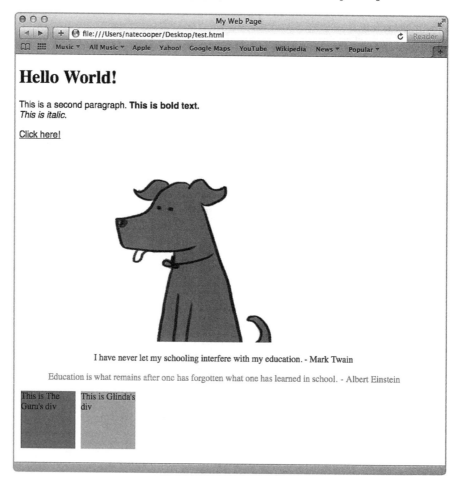

Figure 3-8: The `margin` *property creates space between objects.*

Space was created all around the boxes, which pushes them apart. Now go back to your CSS file and change the margin to padding, like this:

```
.box {
    height: 100px;
    width: 100px;
    float: left;
    text-align: center;
    padding: 10px;
}
```

Now you have something like Figure 3-9.

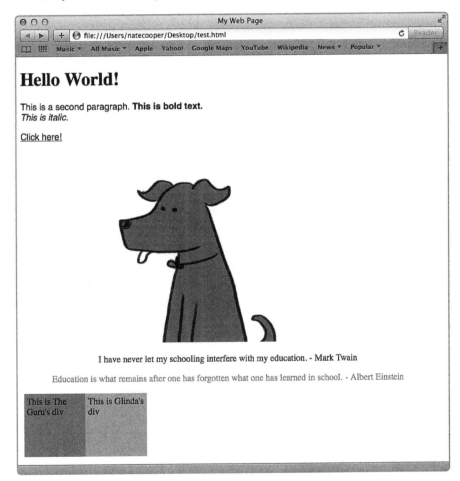

Figure 3-9: The padding property creates space within the <div>s.

The boxes are squished together again, but there is some space between the text and the outer edges of the boxes. `margin` is space *between* elements, and `padding` is spacing *within* an element, as illustrated in Figure 3-10.

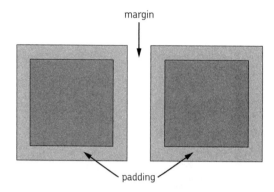

Figure 3-10: Notice the difference between margin, which separates two containers, and padding, which separates the edge of the container from its contents. It's a subtle but important difference.

Go back to your CSS file, and restore `margin` and adjust your `padding` to 5px. Your code should look like this:

```
.box {
    height: 100px;
    width: 100px;
    float: left;
    text-align: center;
    padding: 5px;
    margin: 5px;
}
```

This should leave a little room between your text and the edge of an element and also some space between the boxes. Deciding when to use `padding` and when to use `margin` can be tricky at first. The important thing is to practice, and don't worry too much initially about things looking a bit wonky. That's part of learning.

Using <div>s for Structure

If you'd like to see how CSS can be used for structuring a document, here is an example you can try. Create an HTML document, save it as *columns.html*, and type the following code into it:

```
<!DOCTYPE html>
<html>
    <head>
        <title>Columns Example</title>
        <link rel="stylesheet" href="columns.css">
    </head>
```

```
<body>
    <div class="main">
        <div class="header">Header</div>
        <div class="column" id="leftcolumn">left column</div>
        <div class="column" id="rightcolumn">right column</div>
    </div>
</body>
</html>
```

Next, create and save a CSS file called *columns.css*. Type the following code in it:

```
.main {
    margin: 0 auto;
    width: 80%;
}

.main:after {
    display: block;
    clear: both;
    content: "";
}

.column {
    width: 50%;
    min-height: 500px;
    margin-bottom: 20px;
    float: left;
    display: block;
}

#leftcolumn {
    background-color: blue
}

#rightcolumn {
    background-color: red;
}

.header {
    width: 100%;
    height: 100px;
    background-color: yellow;
    clear: both;
}
```

You should see something like Figure 3-11.

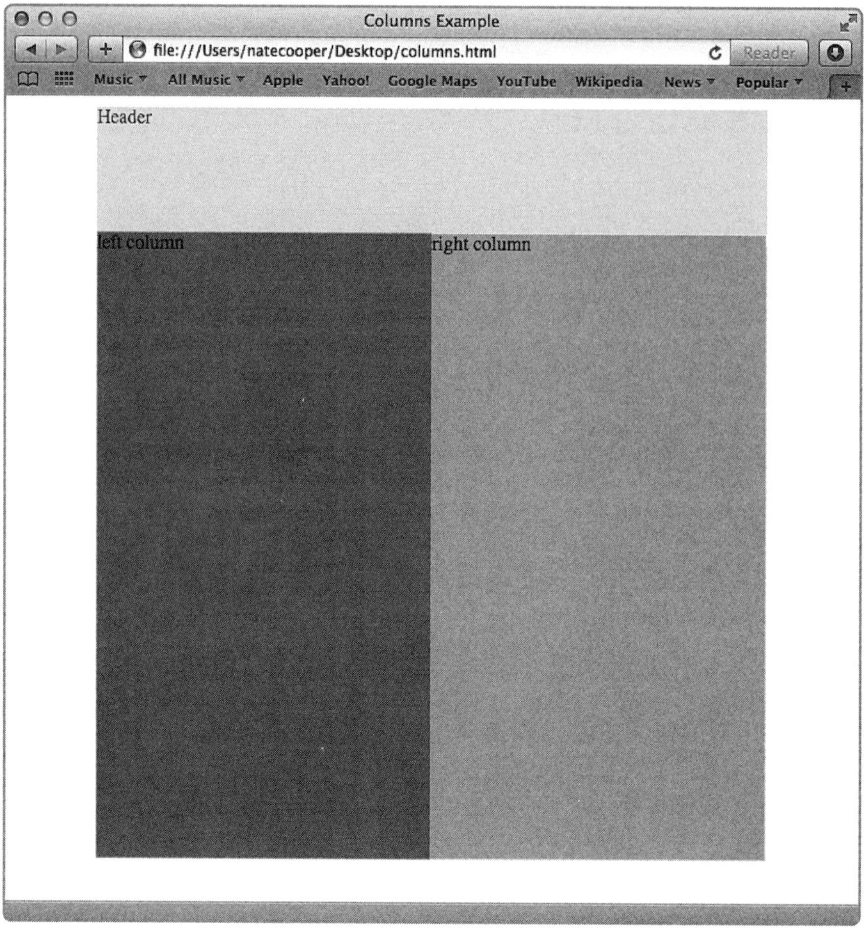
Columns Example
file:///Users/natecooper/Desktop/columns.html
Reader
Music
All Music
Apple
Yahoo!
Google Maps
YouTube
Wikipedia
News
Popular
Header
left column
right column

Figure 3-11: In this example, we've created two columns using <div>s and placed a third <div> on top as a kind of header.

As you can see from this example, CSS isn't just for fonts. You can use it to scaffold complex layouts that scale and change according to the browser. In this case, we've used `<div>`s to structure our page.

First, we've got one large `<div>` called `main` that wraps all of our content together. We've given it some properties: `margin: 0 auto; width: 80%;`. These center the `<div>` and set its width to a fraction of the overall page.

Inside of the main `<div>` we have a header `<div>` and two `<div>`s with a class `column`. We want the header to be the full width of the `<div>`, so we add `width: 100%;`. We want it only on the top, so we set the height dimensions in pixels: `height: 100px;`. Below the header, we want the two columns. Since the columns will be equal in width and height, we'll use `class` to define the properties that are shared among them: `width: 50%; min-height: 500px;`. Each column takes up half of the main `<div>`, so its width is `50%`. We want the height to be a little shorter than the `<body>` so we use `margin-bottom: 20px;` to add some space at the bottom.

NOTE   *In CSS, nesting HTML elements inside of each other—as we've nested our header and column elements inside the main <div>—is called the* box model.

Now the header, the left column, and the right column are set up correctly with the right dimensions; however, until you add the *float*, they are going to stack vertically on the page. Floats are often used to wrap elements around each other. For example, if you put a `float: left;` property on an image, the image will hug the left side of its container element and text will wrap to the right. Here, the `float: left;` property tells the column `<div>`s to cling to the left side of the page.

Be careful, though—floats can be tricky. Once you add a float to one element, the browser expects to wrap it around all the others. In our case, the header might not work right without accounting for the floats. We use the `clear: both;` property on the header to help with this. `clear` tells an element to ignore a float happening on its left, right, or both left and right. We also have to add a `clear` float to the main `<div>` using what's called a *pseudo-element*: `main: after;`. However, this will work only if we add the `display` and `content` properties as shown. A pseudo-element creates a dynamic within HTML, most commonly before or after a paragraph. This is a workaround that should give you a nice structured document that you can actually use and play around with.

As you start to master some of the more advanced properties in CSS, you can make columns and sidebars, and even hide and show elements on a page.

Ready for even more CSS? Try out the properties in Table 3-2.

Table 3-2: Common CSS Properties

Property	Value(s)	Description
background-color	*hexvalue, rgb, color name*	Sets the background color of a container (like a `<p>` or `<div>`).
background-image	*url("http://address-to-image")*	Sets the background of a container to be an image located at a specific address.
border-color	*hexvalue, rgb, color name*	Sets the color of a border on an element.
border-style	dotted, solid, double dashed	Sets the look of the border line.
border-width	thin, thick, medium	Places a border around an element and sets the thickness.
border	*(shorthand)*	Rather than listing border properties individually, you can group the values under the single **border** property (e.g., `border: thin solid black;`).
clear	left, right, none, both	Tells an element to ignore a float.
color	*hexvalue, rgb, color name*	Sets the color of text within a container.
float	left, right, none	Makes elements cling toward one direction or another.
font-family	*font names separated by commas*	Sets the fonts for a container element.
font-size	px, pt, in, cm, em	Sets the size of a font in a container in pixels, points, inches, centimeters, or ems.

(continued)

Table 3-2: Common CSS Properties (continued)

Property	Value(s)	Description
font-weight	light, lighter, normal, bold, bolder	Changes the thickness of a font.
height	px, in, cm, %	Sets the height of an element.
margin	px, in, cm, %	Sets the margin between two elements.
margin-bottom	px, in, cm, %	Sets the bottom margin.
margin-left	px, in, cm, %	Sets the left margin.
margin-right	px, in, cm, %	Sets the right margin.
margin-top	px, in, cm, %	Sets the top margin.
overflow	hidden, scroll, visible	Sets what happens when the contents of a container are larger than the size of the container.
padding	px, in, cm, %	Sets the spacing between a container element and its contents.
padding-bottom	px, in, cm, %	Sets the bottom spacing between a container element and its contents.
padding-left	px, in, cm, %	Sets the left spacing between a container element and its contents.
padding-right	px, in, cm, %	Sets the right spacing between a container element and its contents.
padding-top	px, in, cm, %	Sets the top spacing between a container element and its contents.
text-align	left, right, center, justify	Aligns the text within a container element.
text-decoration	underline, line-through, none	Styles the text.
width	px, in, cm, %	Sets the width of an element.

Kim Explores WordPress City

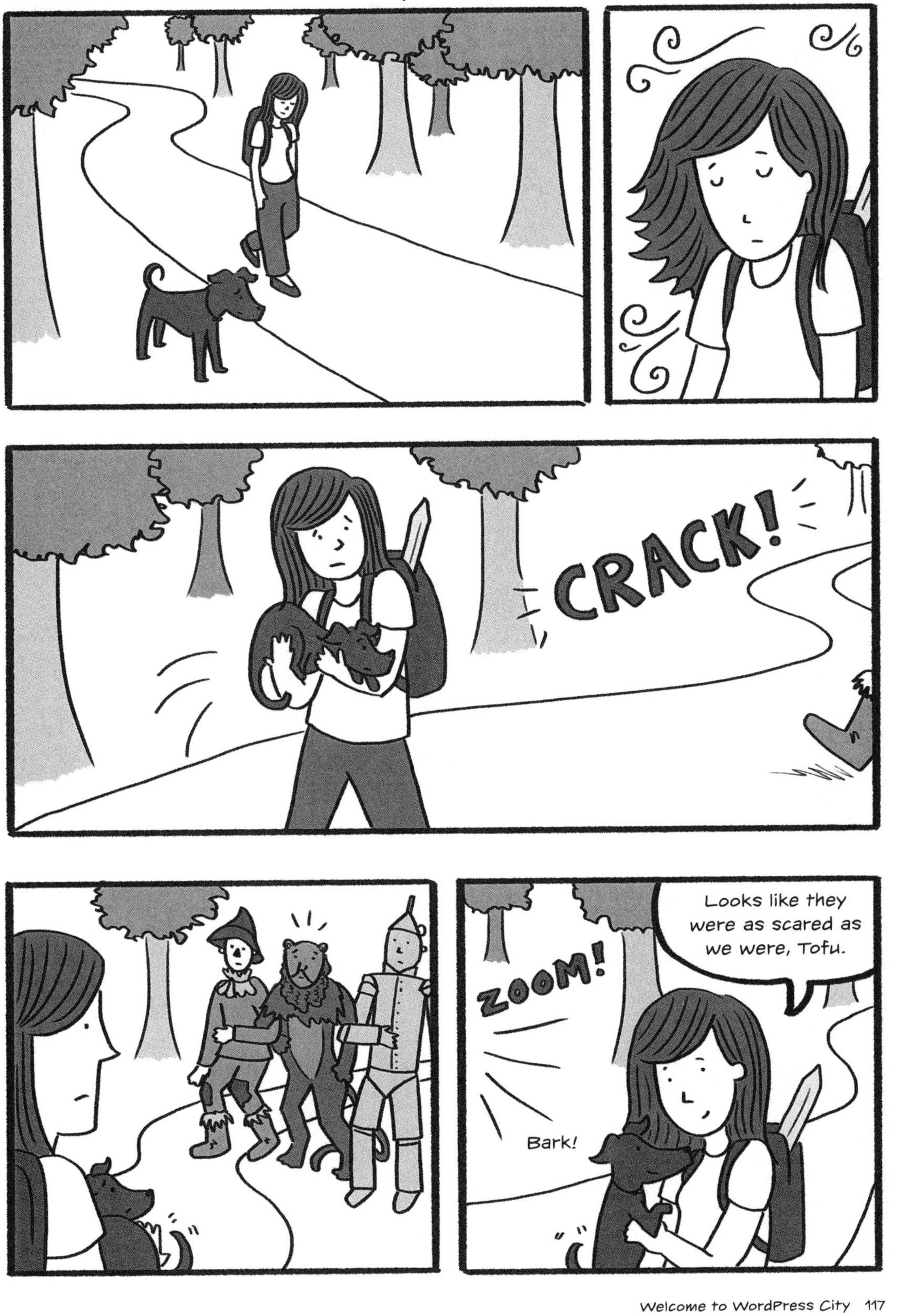
CRACK!
ZOOM!
Looks like they were as scared as we were, Tofu.
Bark!

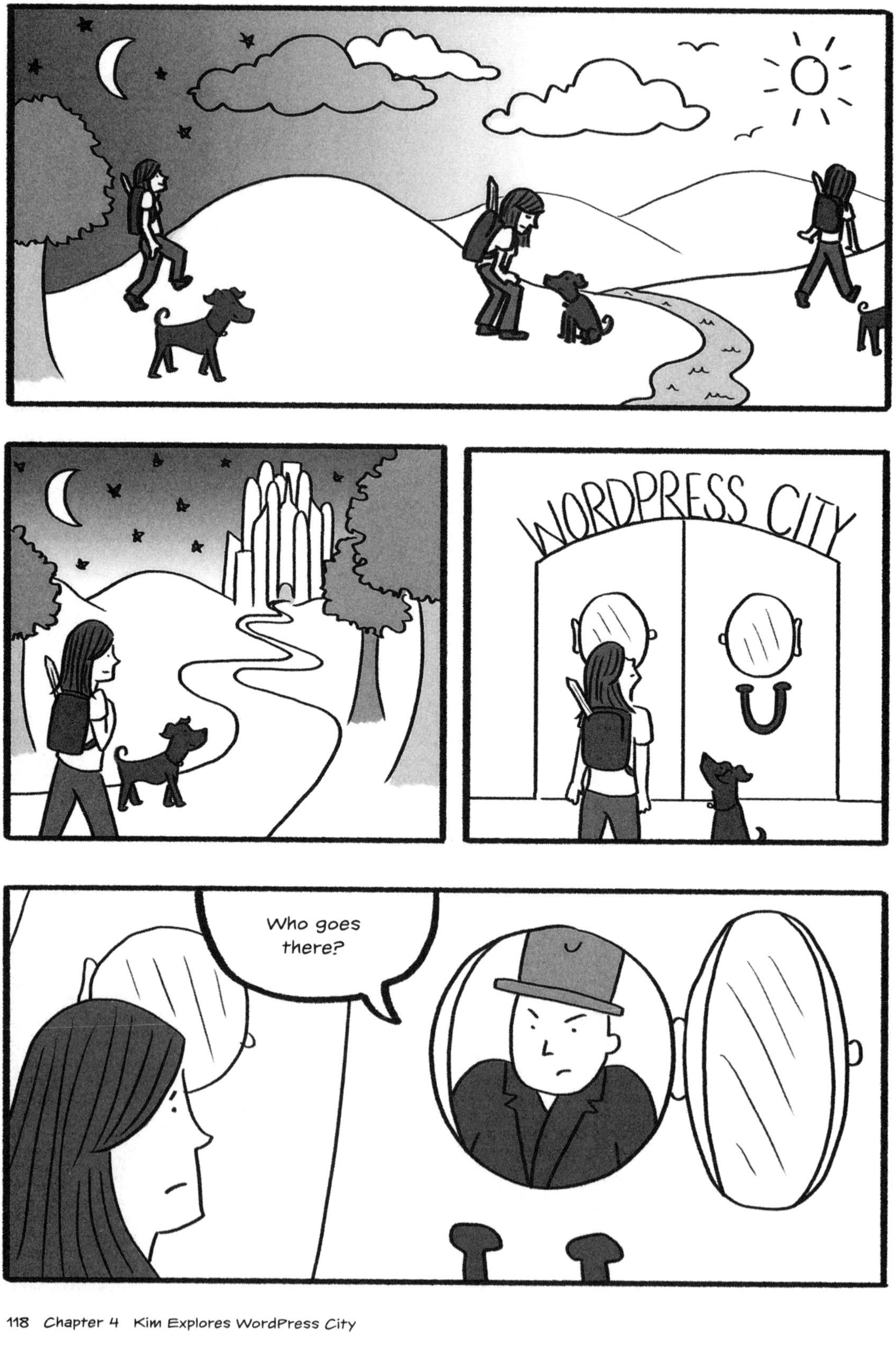
WORDPRESS CITY
Who goes there?

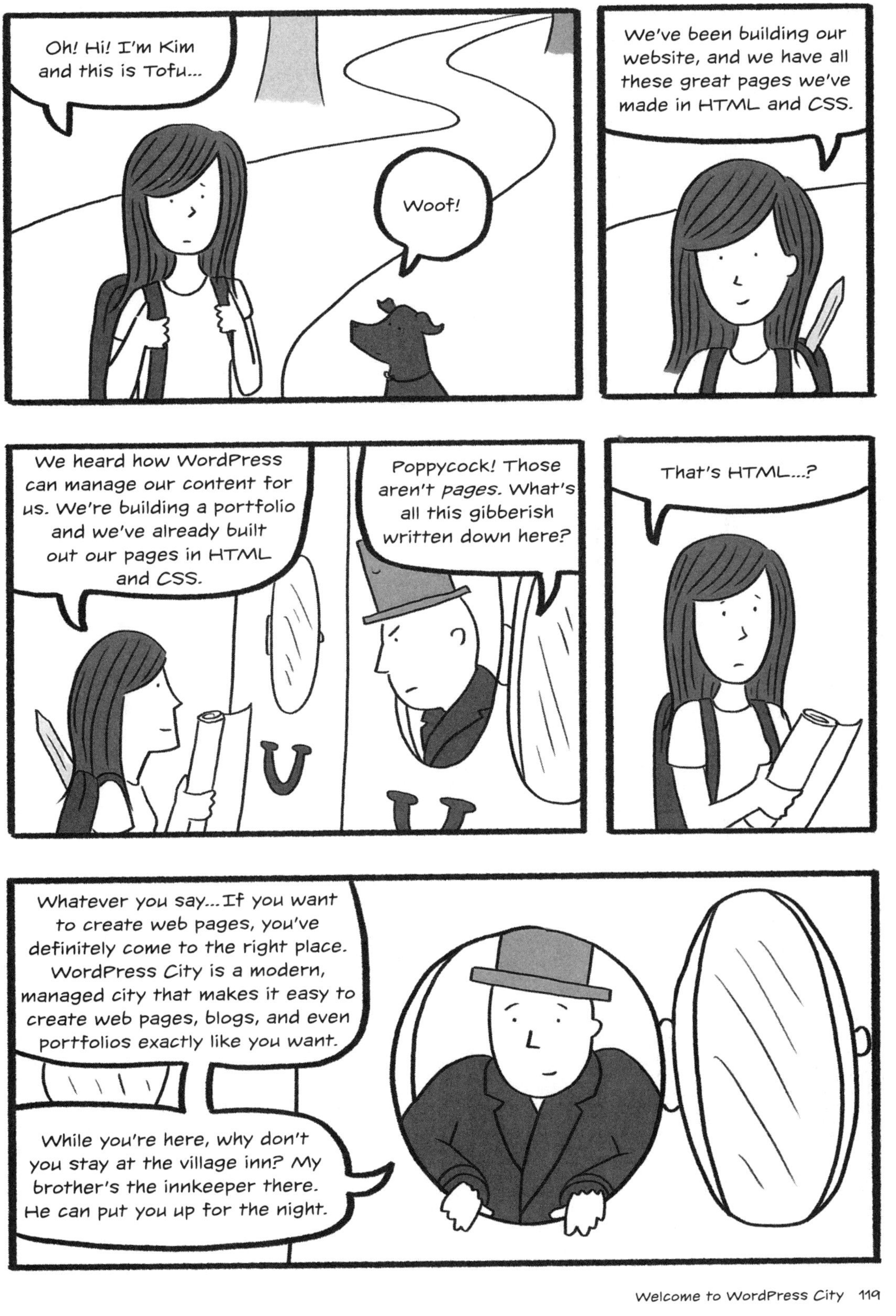
Oh! Hi! I'm Kim and this is Tofu...
Woof!
We've been building our website, and we have all these great pages we've made in HTML and CSS.
We heard how WordPress can manage our content for us. We're building a portfolio and we've already built out our pages in HTML and CSS.
Poppycock! Those aren't *pages*. What's all this gibberish written down here?
That's HTML...?
Whatever you say...If you want to create web pages, you've definitely come to the right place. WordPress City is a modern, managed city that makes it easy to create web pages, blogs, and even portfolios exactly like you want.
While you're here, why don't you stay at the village inn? My brother's the innkeeper there. He can put you up for the night.

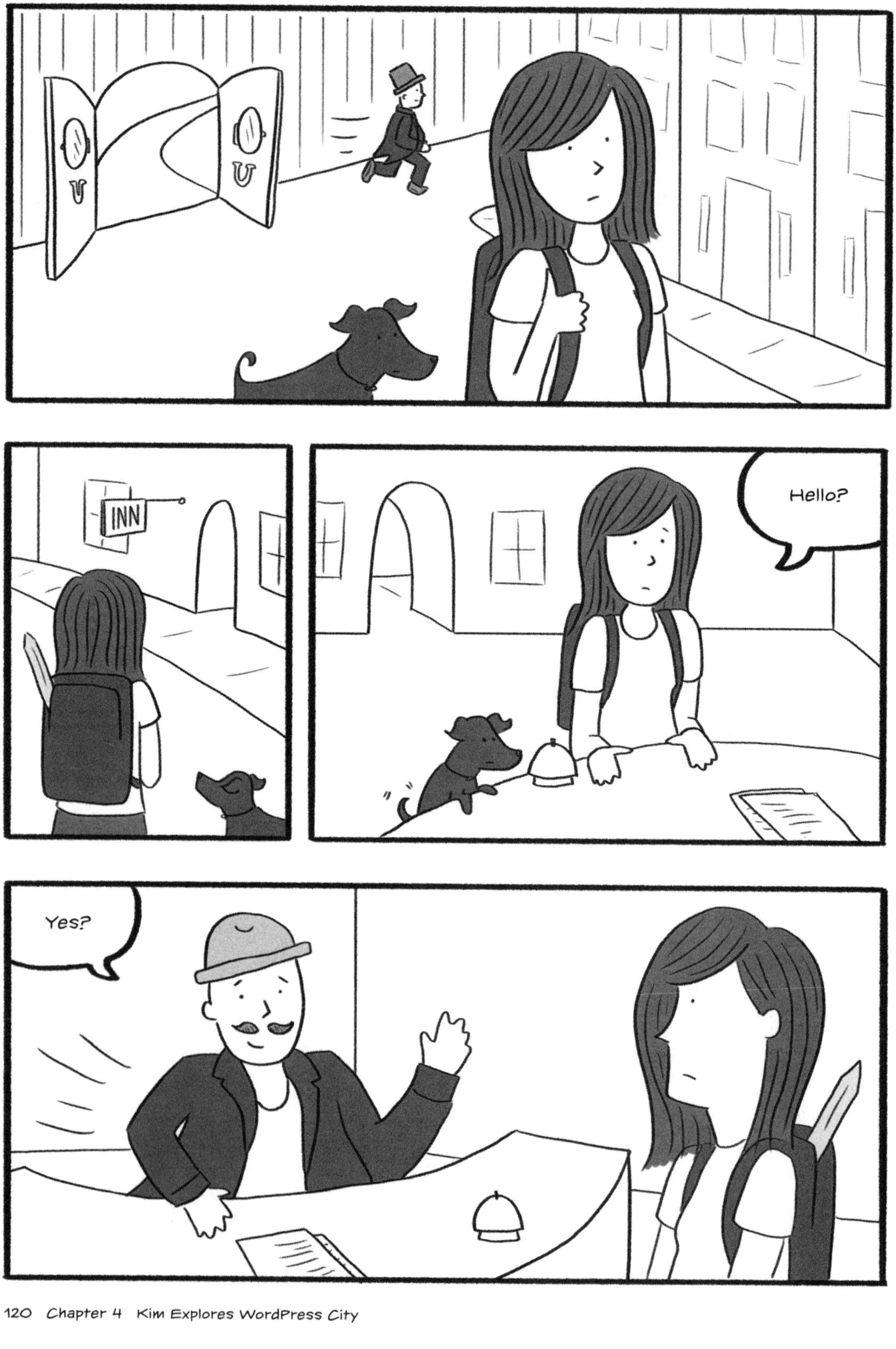
INN
Hello?
Yes?

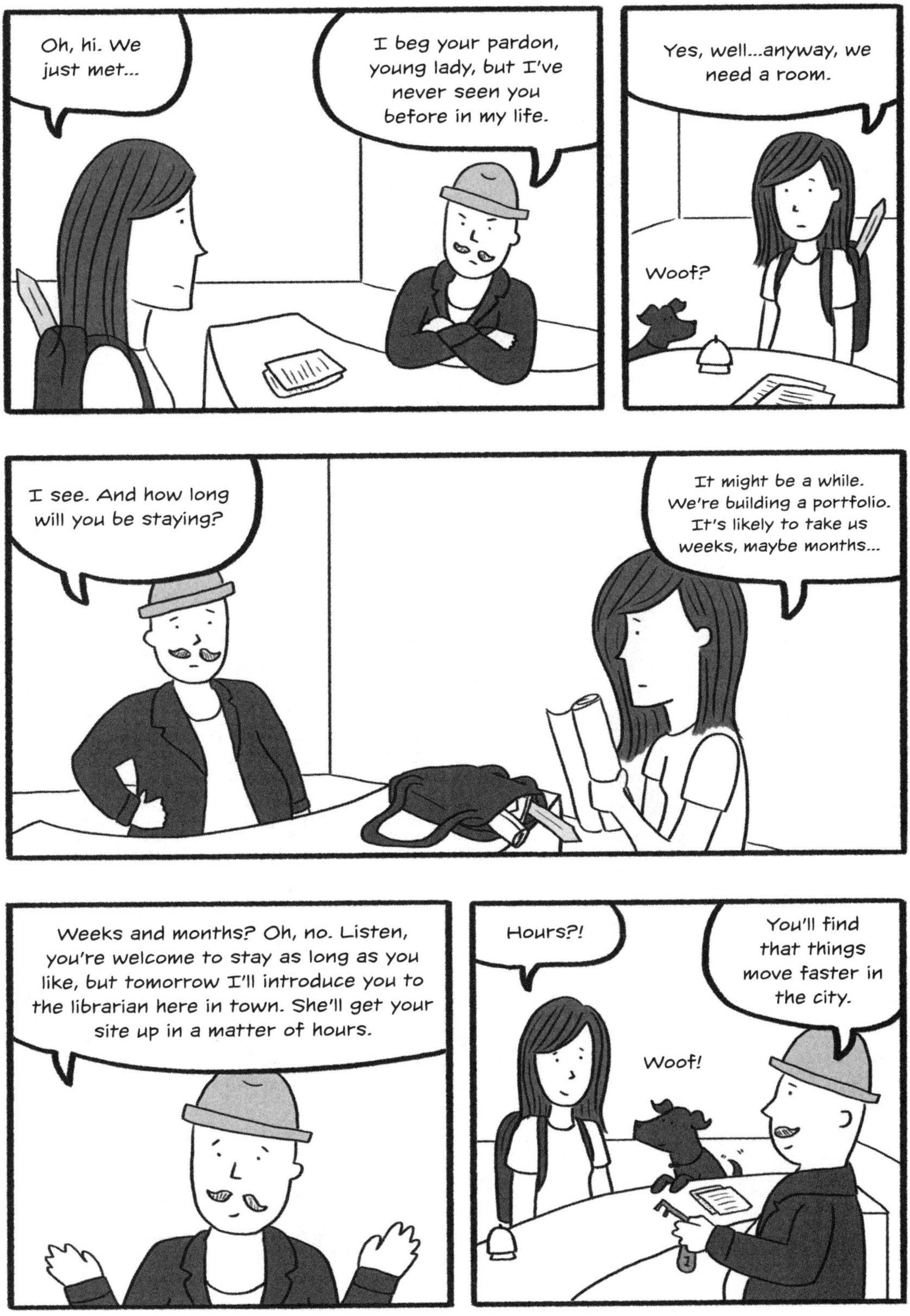
Oh, hi. We just met...
I beg your pardon, young lady, but I've never seen you before in my life.
Yes, well...anyway, we need a room.
Woof?
I see. And how long will you be staying?
It might be a while. We're building a portfolio. It's likely to take us weeks, maybe months...
Weeks and months? Oh, no. Listen, you're welcome to stay as long as you like, but tomorrow I'll introduce you to the librarian here in town. She'll get your site up in a matter of hours.
Hours?!
You'll find that things move faster in the city.
Woof!

Kim Learns Her Way Around WordPress

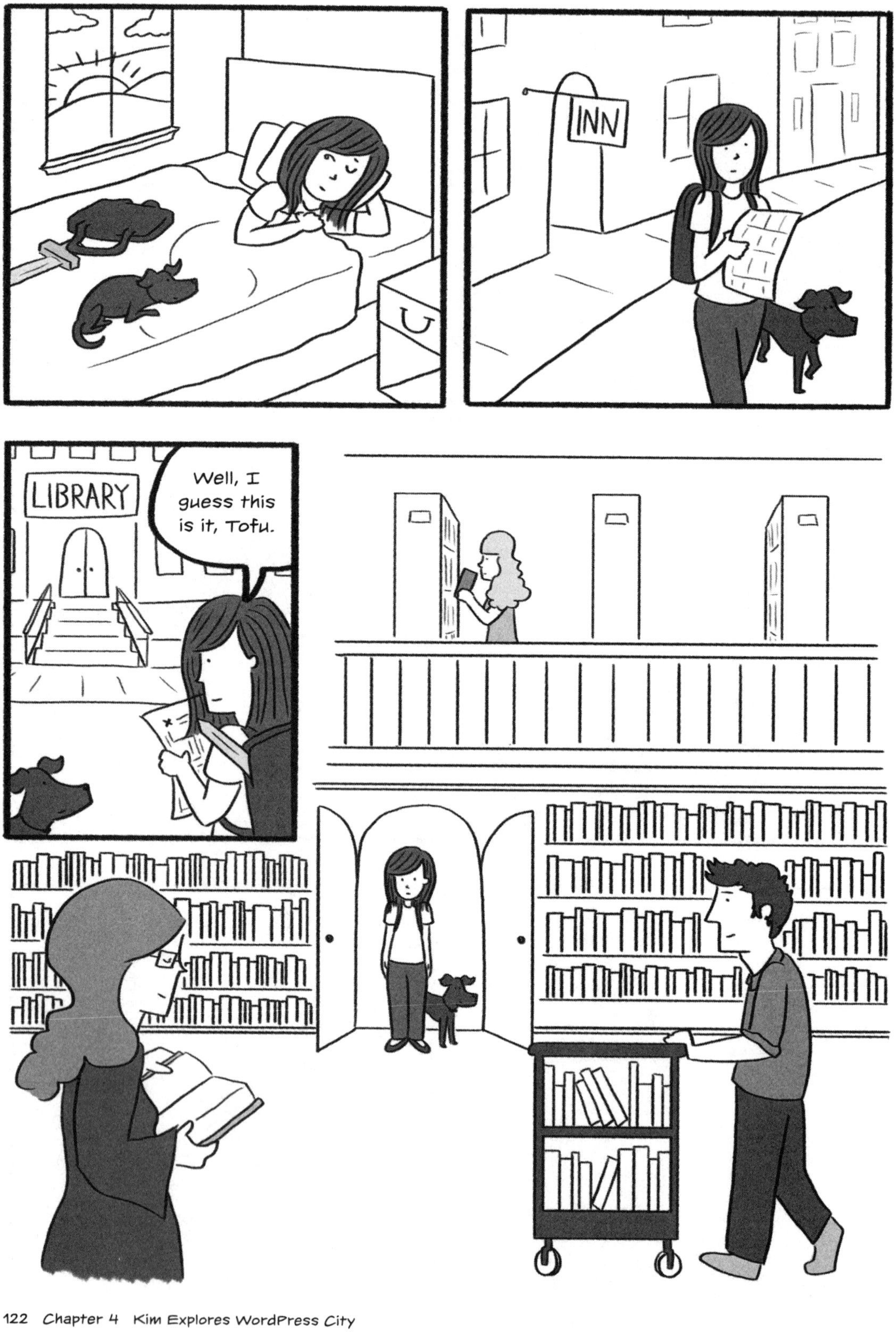
INN
LIBRARY
Well, I guess this is it, Tofu.

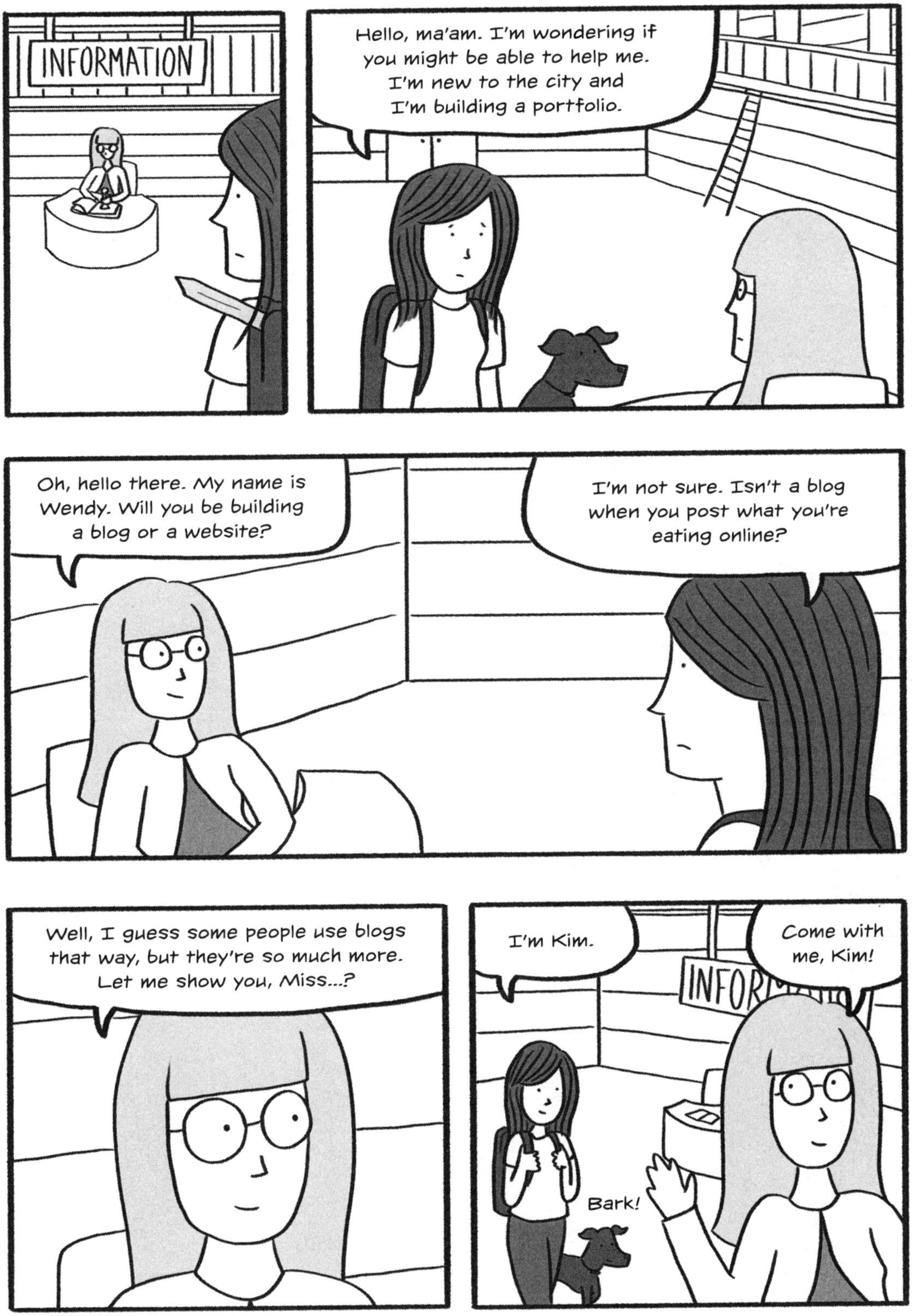
INFORMATION
Hello, ma'am. I'm wondering if you might be able to help me. I'm new to the city and I'm building a portfolio.
Oh, hello there. My name is Wendy. Will you be building a blog or a website?
I'm not sure. Isn't a blog when you post what you're eating online?
Well, I guess some people use blogs that way, but they're so much more. Let me show you, Miss...?
I'm Kim.
Come with me, Kim!
Bark!

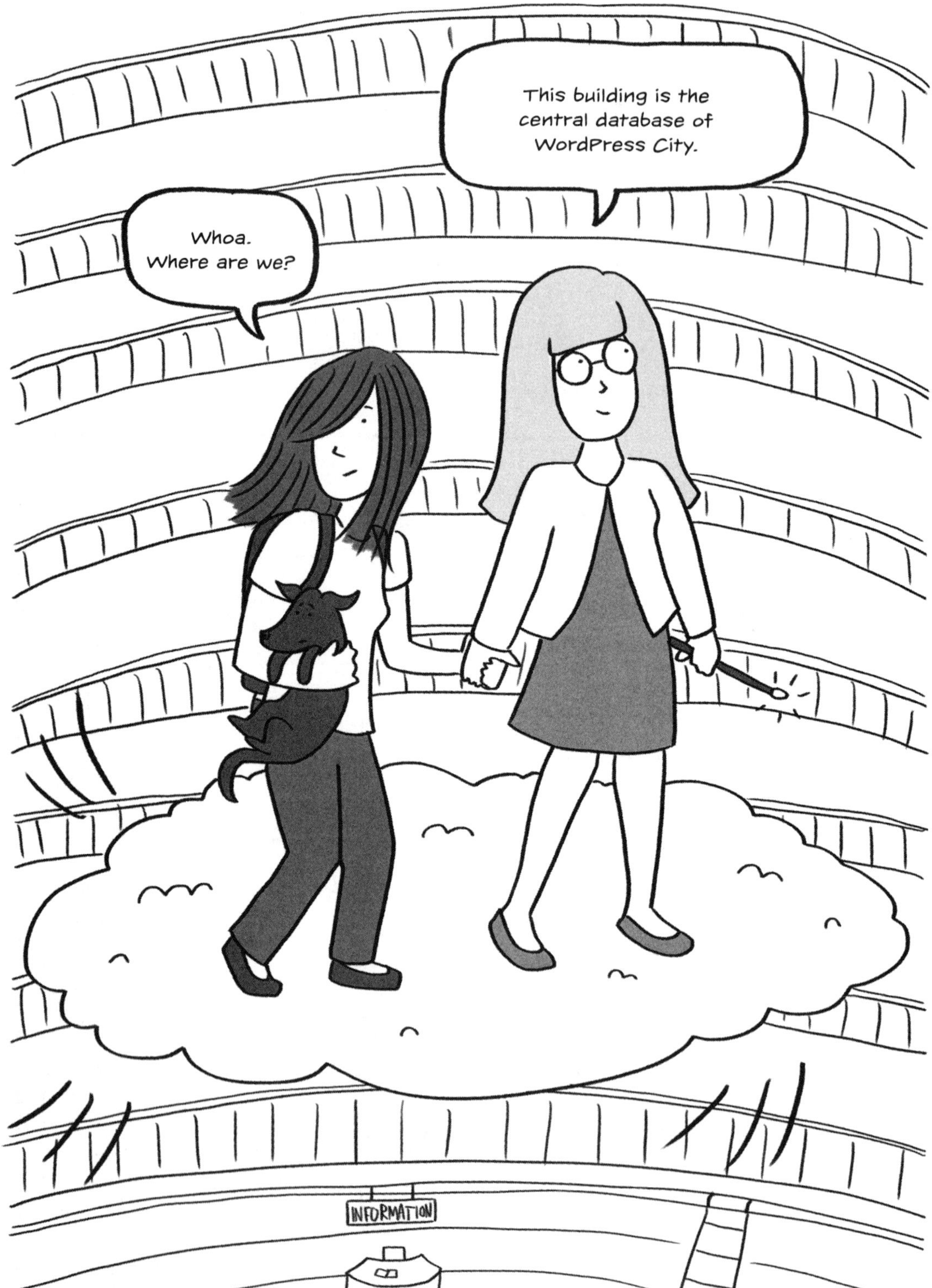
Whoa.
Where are we?
This building is the central database of WordPress City.
INFORMATION

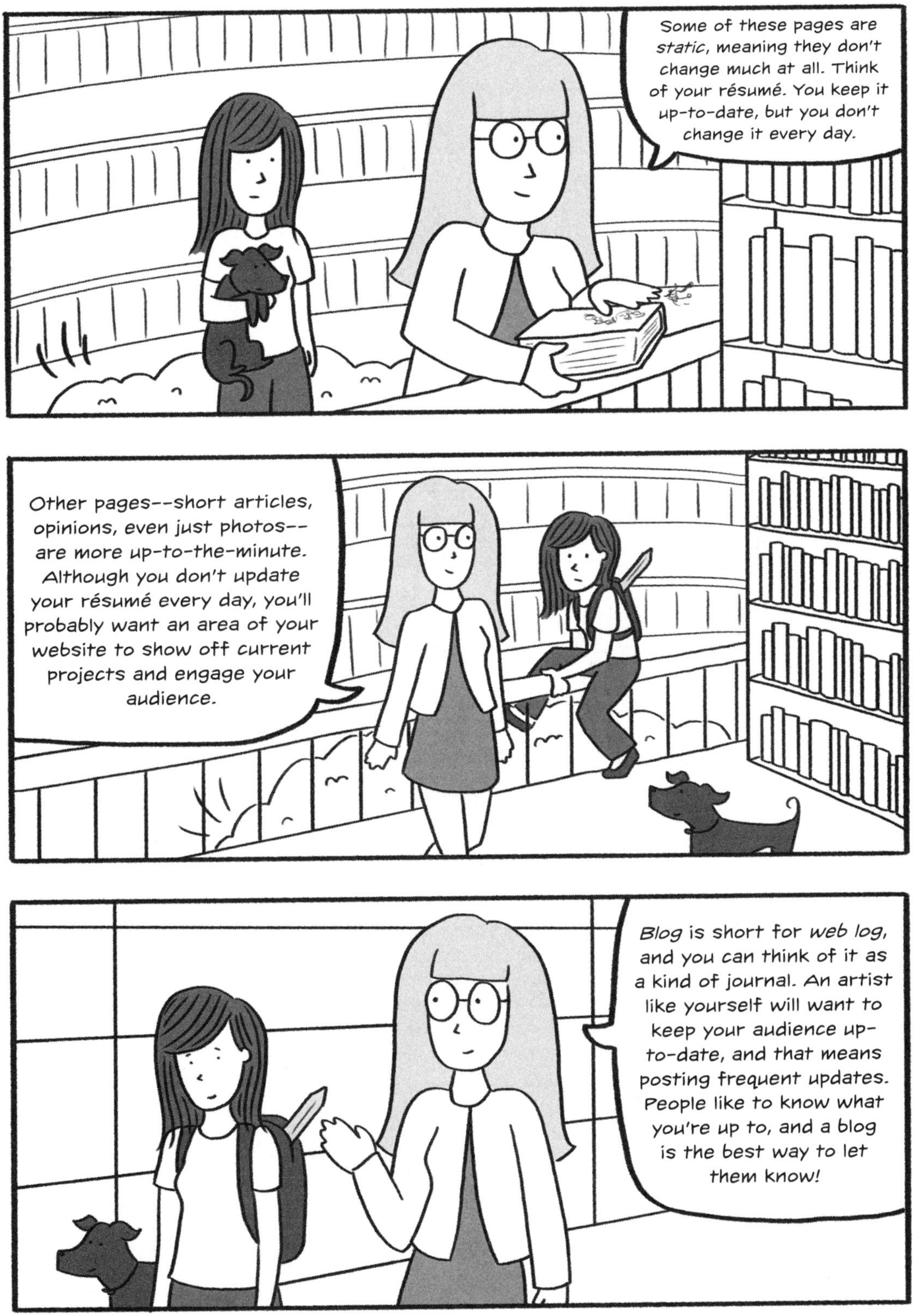
Some of these pages are *static*, meaning they don't change much at all. Think of your résumé. You keep it up-to-date, but you don't change it every day.
Other pages--short articles, opinions, even just photos--are more up-to-the-minute. Although you don't update your résumé every day, you'll probably want an area of your website to show off current projects and engage your audience.
Blog is short for *web log*, and you can think of it as a kind of journal. An artist like yourself will want to keep your audience up-to-date, and that means posting frequent updates. People like to know what you're up to, and a blog is the best way to let them know!

An article written for a blog is called a *post*.

POSTS

This one has today's date on it!

Yep. Thousands of bloggers write millions of blog posts every day. It's up-to-the-minute content, created by people just like you.

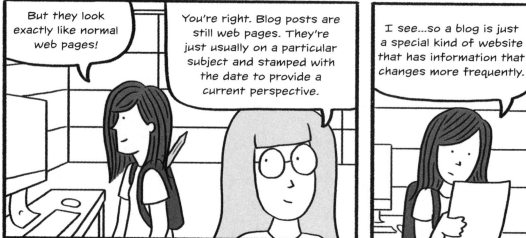

But they look exactly like normal web pages!

You're right. Blog posts are still web pages. They're just usually on a particular subject and stamped with the date to provide a current perspective.

I see...so a blog is just a special kind of website that has information that changes more frequently.

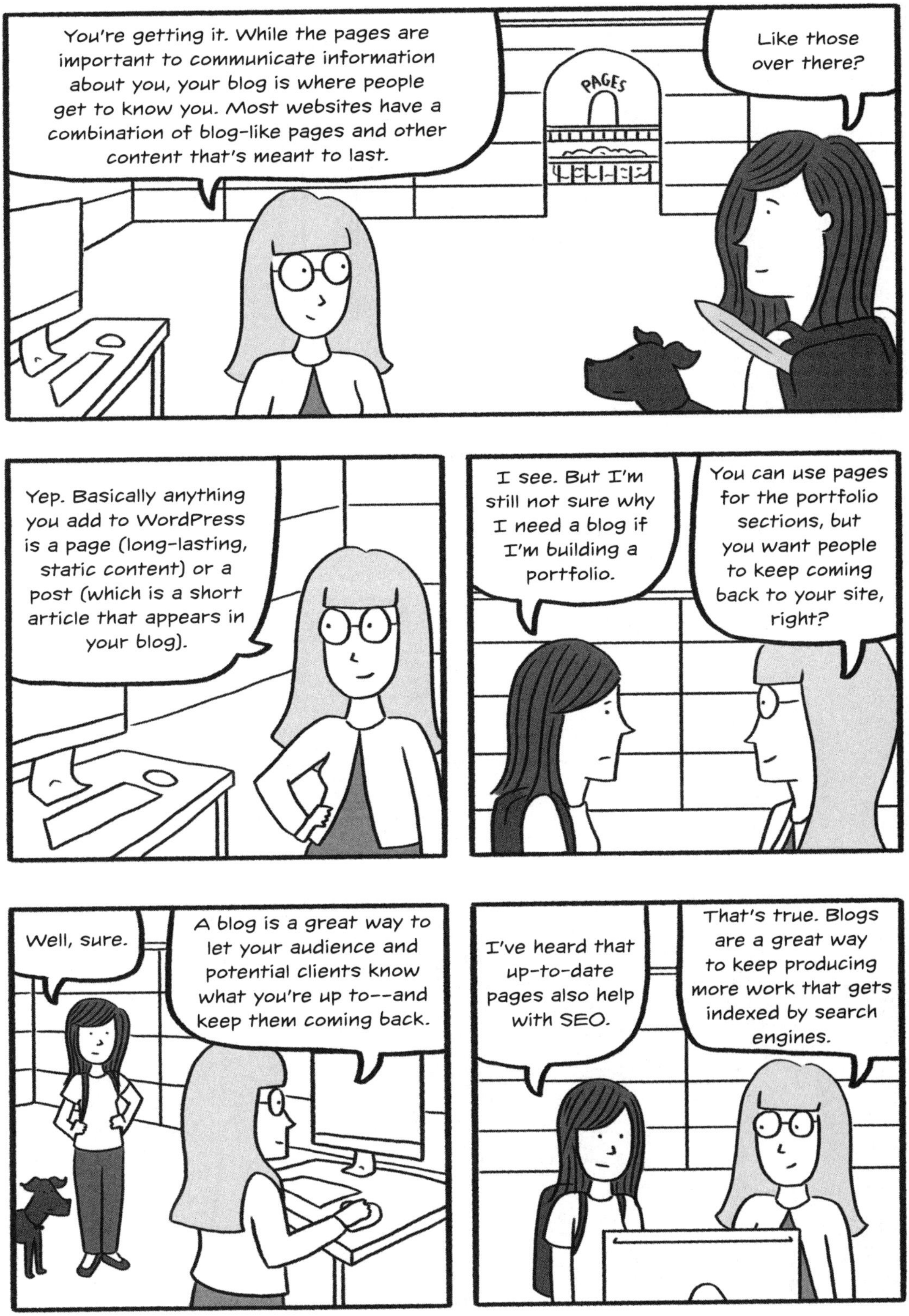
You're getting it. While the pages are important to communicate information about you, your blog is where people get to know you. Most websites have a combination of blog-like pages and other content that's meant to last.
PAGES
Like those over there?
Yep. Basically anything you add to WordPress is a page (long-lasting, static content) or a post (which is a short article that appears in your blog).
I see. But I'm still not sure why I need a blog if I'm building a portfolio.
You can use pages for the portfolio sections, but you want people to keep coming back to your site, right?
Well, sure.
A blog is a great way to let your audience and potential clients know what you're up to--and keep them coming back.
I've heard that up-to-date pages also help with SEO.
That's true. Blogs are a great way to keep producing more work that gets indexed by search engines.

Kim Builds Her First Page in WordPress

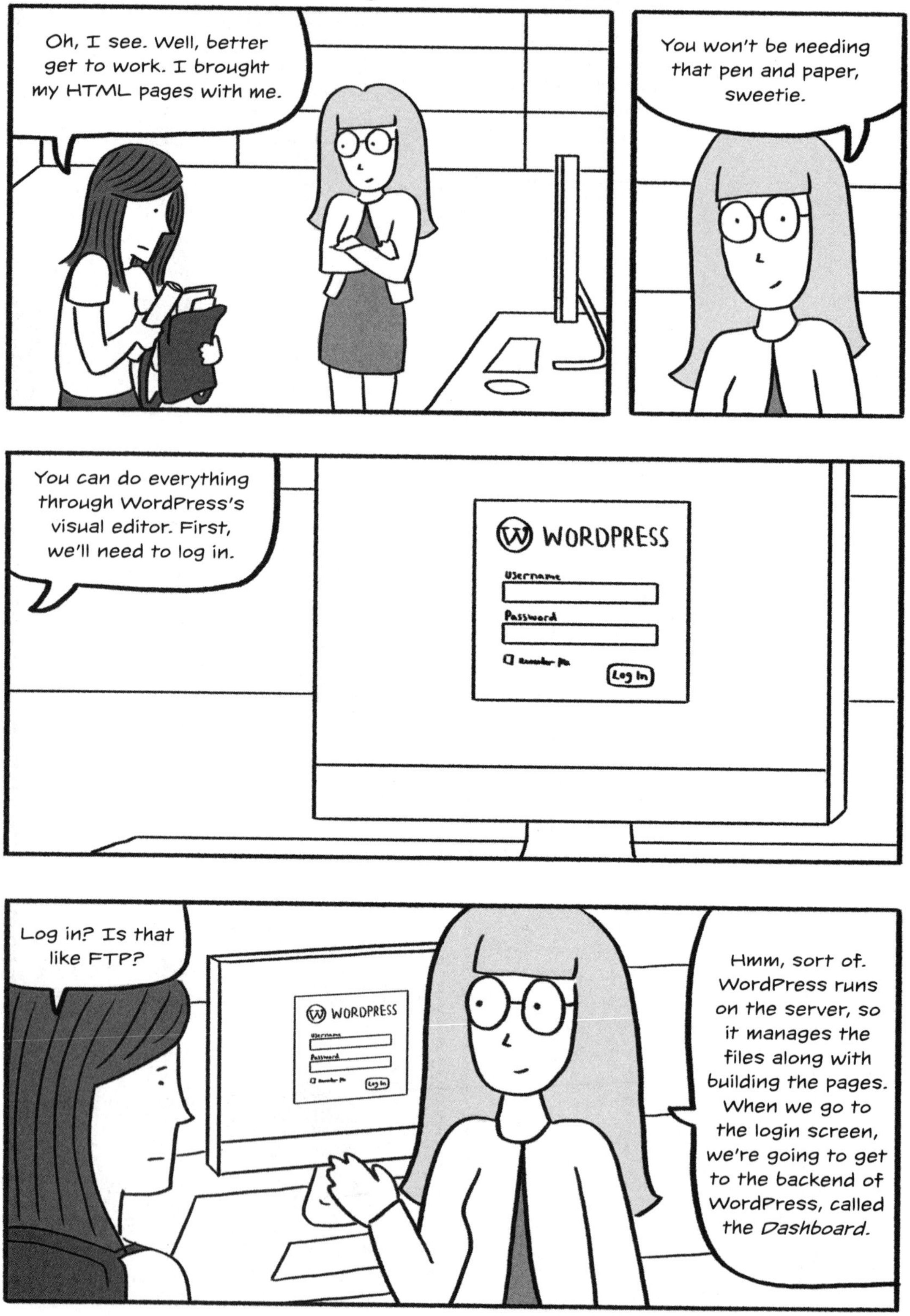
Oh, I see. Well, better get to work. I brought my HTML pages with me.
You won't be needing that pen and paper, sweetie.
You can do everything through WordPress's visual editor. First, we'll need to log in.
WORDPRESS
Username
Password
Log In
Log in? Is that like FTP?
Hmm, sort of. WordPress runs on the server, so it manages the files along with building the pages. When we go to the login screen, we're going to get to the backend of WordPress, called the *Dashboard*.

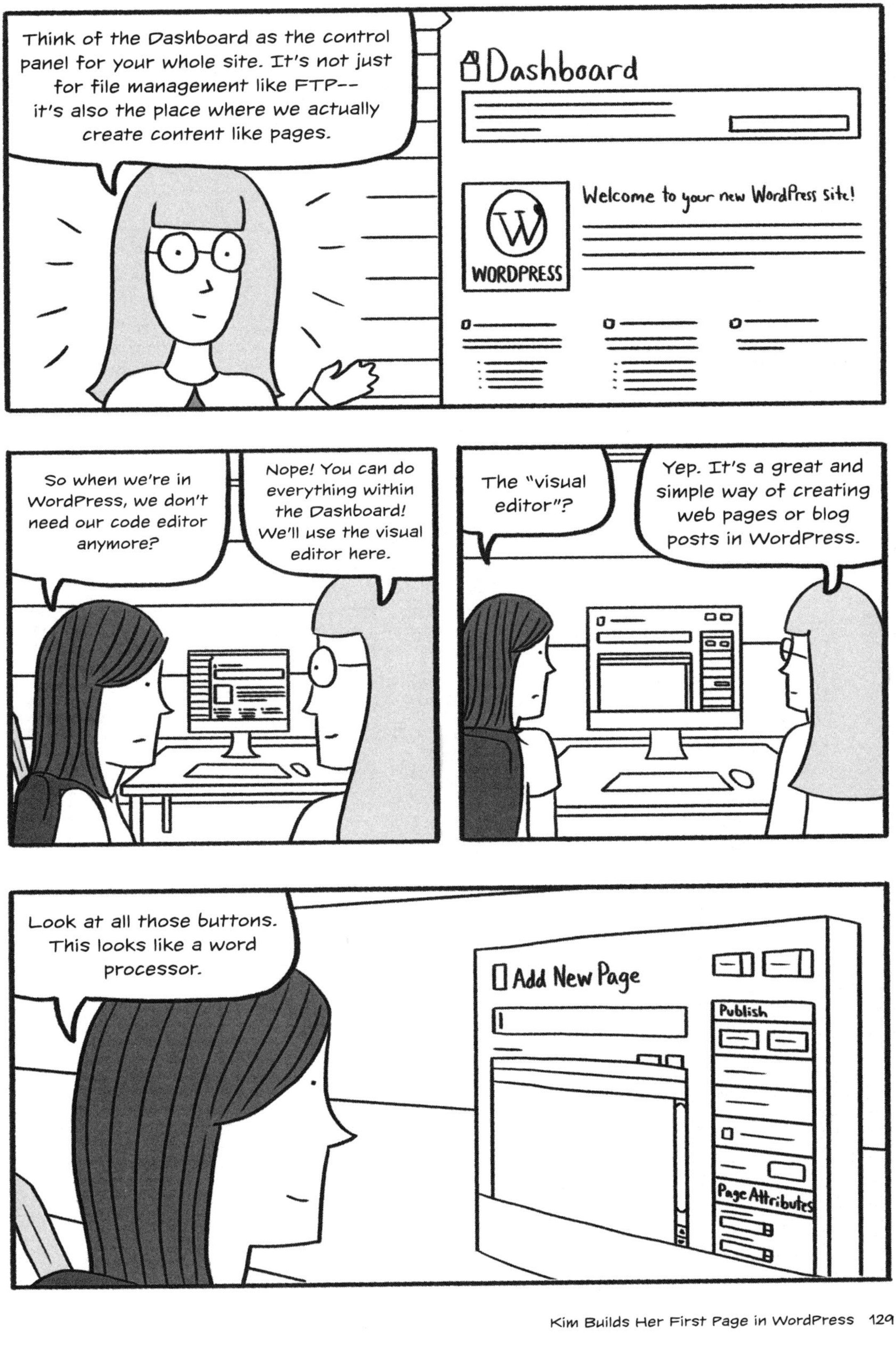
Think of the Dashboard as the control panel for your whole site. It's not just for file management like FTP-- it's also the place where we actually create content like pages.
Dashboard
Welcome to your new WordPress site!
WORDPRESS
So when we're in WordPress, we don't need our code editor anymore?
Nope! You can do everything within the Dashboard! We'll use the visual editor here.
The "visual editor"?
Yep. It's a great and simple way of creating web pages or blog posts in WordPress.
Look at all those buttons. This looks like a word processor.
Add New Page
Publish
Page Attributes

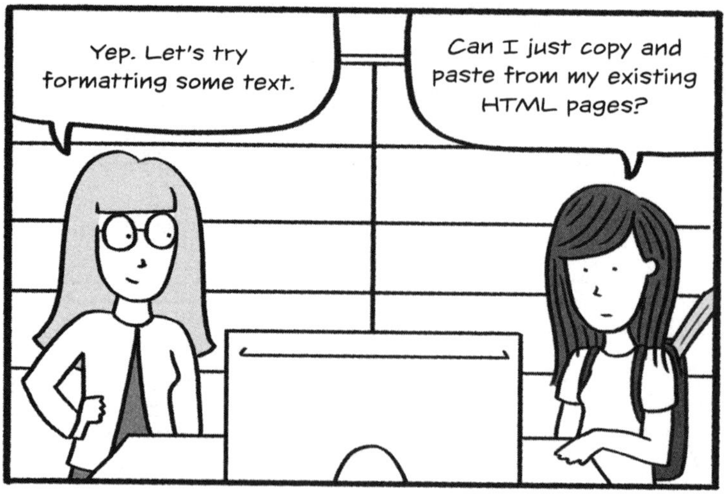
Yep. Let's try formatting some text.
Can I just copy and paste from my existing HTML pages?

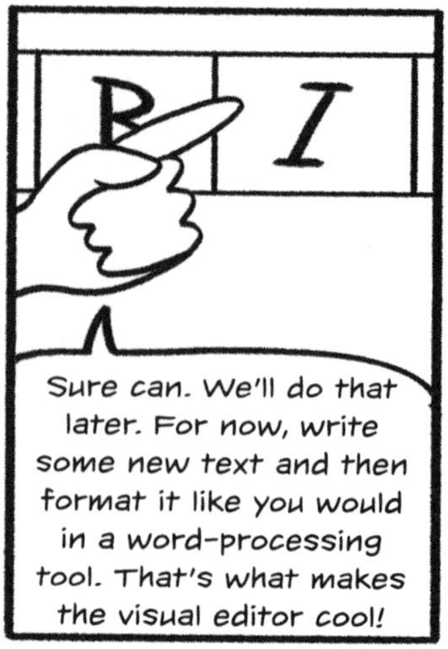
B I
Sure can. We'll do that later. For now, write some new text and then format it like you would in a word-processing tool. That's what makes the visual editor cool!

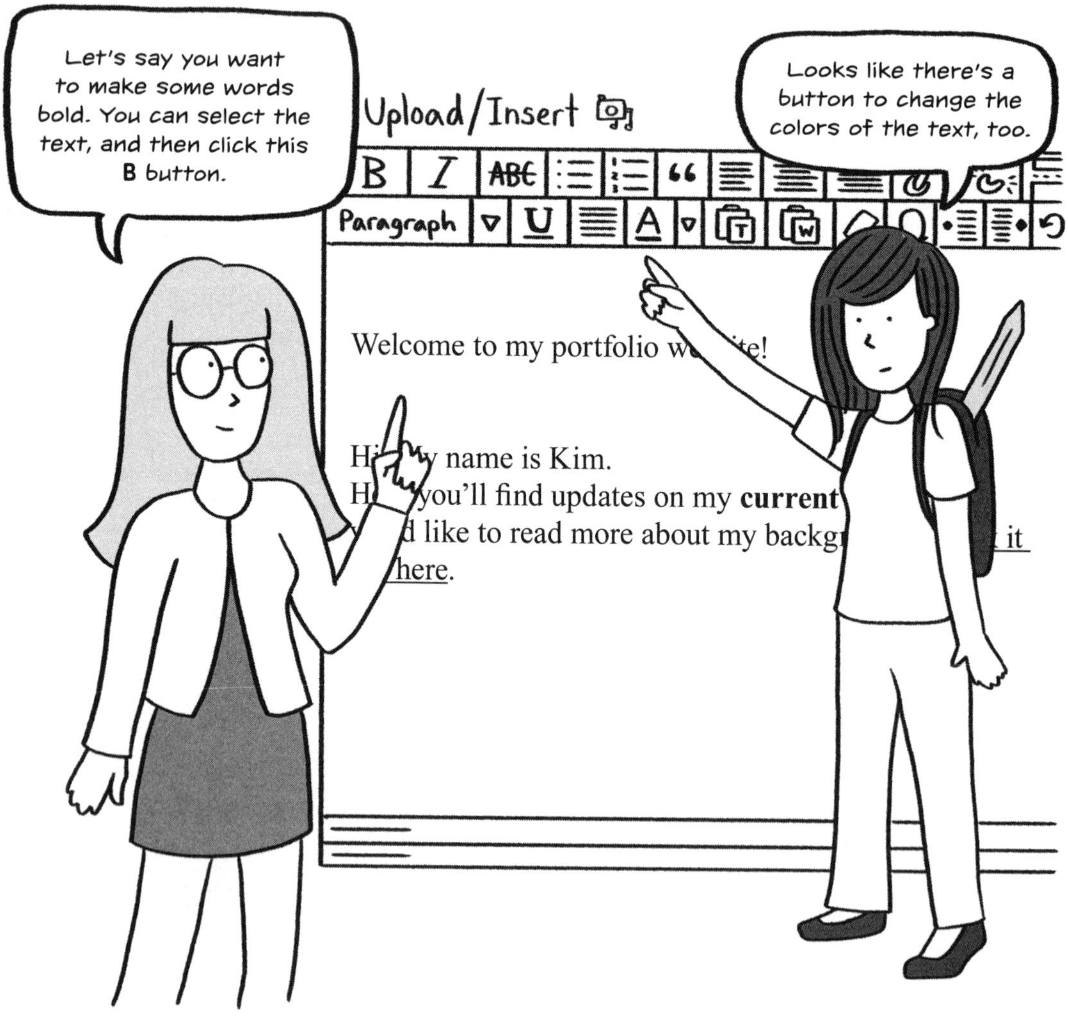
Let's say you want to make some words bold. You can select the text, and then click this **B** button.
Looks like there's a button to change the colors of the text, too.
Upload/Insert
Paragraph

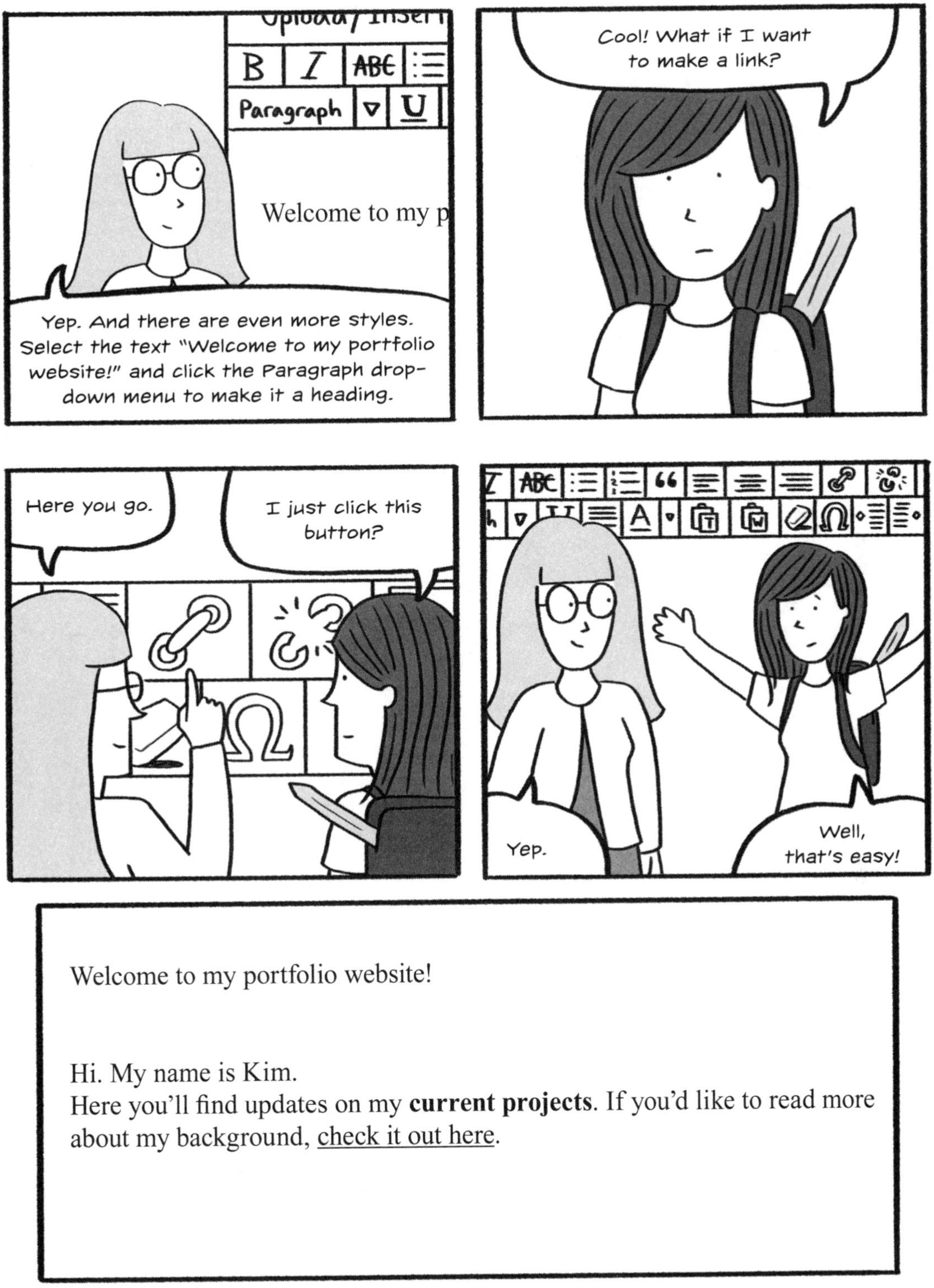
Paragraph
Yep. And there are even more styles. Select the text "Welcome to my portfolio website!" and click the Paragraph drop-down menu to make it a heading.
Cool! What if I want to make a link?
Here you go.
I just click this button?
Yep.
Well, that's easy!
Welcome to my portfolio website!
Hi. My name is Kim.
Here you'll find updates on my **current projects**. If you'd like to read more about my background, check it out here.

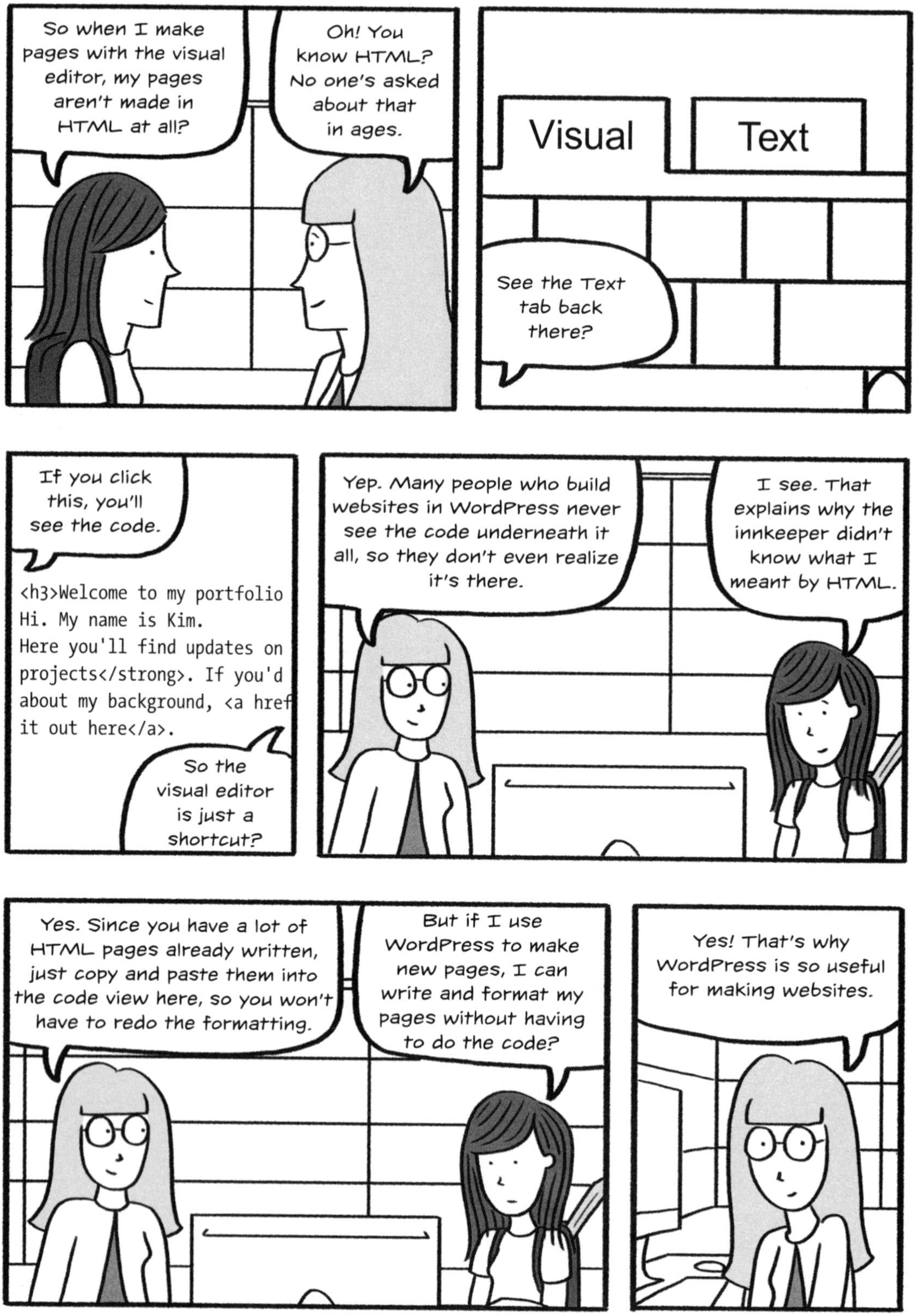
So when I make pages with the visual editor, my pages aren't made in HTML at all?
Oh! You know HTML? No one's asked about that in ages.
Visual
Text
See the Text tab back there?
If you click this, you'll see the code.
<h3>Welcome to my portfolio
Hi. My name is Kim.
Here you'll find updates on
projects</strong>. If you'd
about my background, <a href
it out here</a>.
So the visual editor is just a shortcut?
Yep. Many people who build websites in WordPress never see the code underneath it all, so they don't even realize it's there.
I see. That explains why the innkeeper didn't know what I meant by HTML.
Yes. Since you have a lot of HTML pages already written, just copy and paste them into the code view here, so you won't have to redo the formatting.
But if I use WordPress to make new pages, I can write and format my pages without having to do the code?
Yes! That's why WordPress is so useful for making websites.

Kim Organizes Her Site

So how do I get started, then? Do I want to write a page or a post? I guess I'm still confused about how WordPress organizes them.

Oh, don't worry! It's a little confusing at first. Remember, your portfolio pages will be "pages" within WordPress and not "posts," which are part of the blog.

POSTS

These are all pages, because they won't change over time. We'll organize them to branch off, just like you've done on the paper, right in WordPress.

PAGES

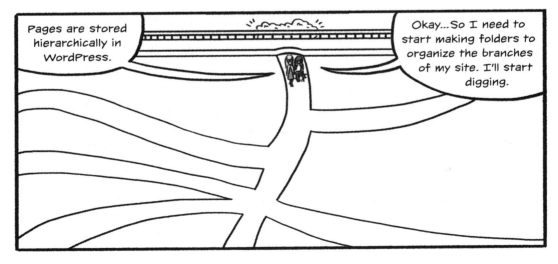

Pages are stored hierarchically in WordPress.

Okay...So I need to start making folders to organize the branches of my site. I'll start digging.

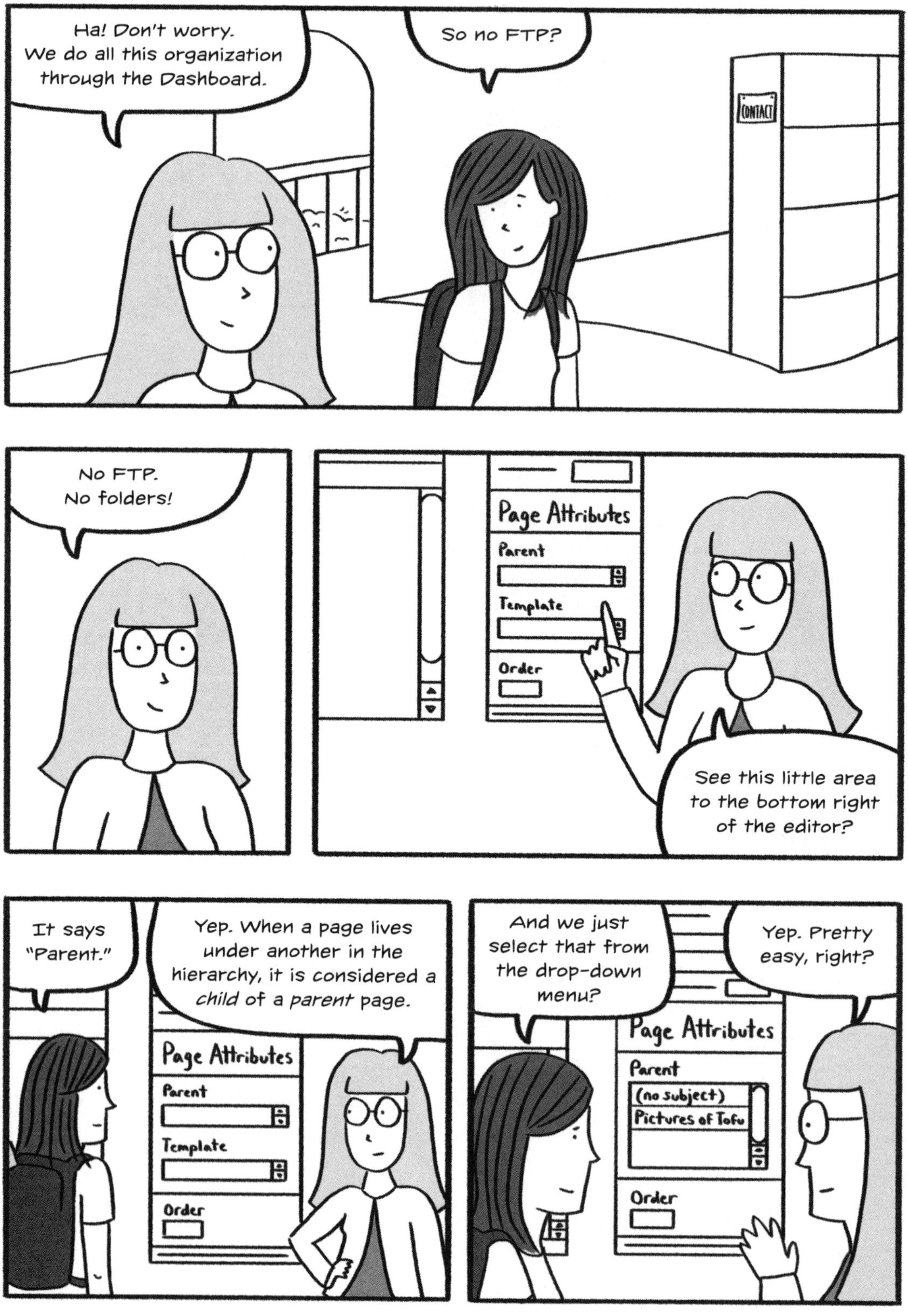
Ha! Don't worry. We do all this organization through the Dashboard.
So no FTP?
CONTACT
No FTP. No folders!
Page Attributes
Parent
Template
Order
See this little area to the bottom right of the editor?
It says "Parent."
Yep. When a page lives under another in the hierarchy, it is considered a *child* of a *parent* page.
Page Attributes
Parent
Template
Order
And we just select that from the drop-down menu?
Yep. Pretty easy, right?
Page Attributes
Parent
(no subject)
Pictures of Tofu
Order

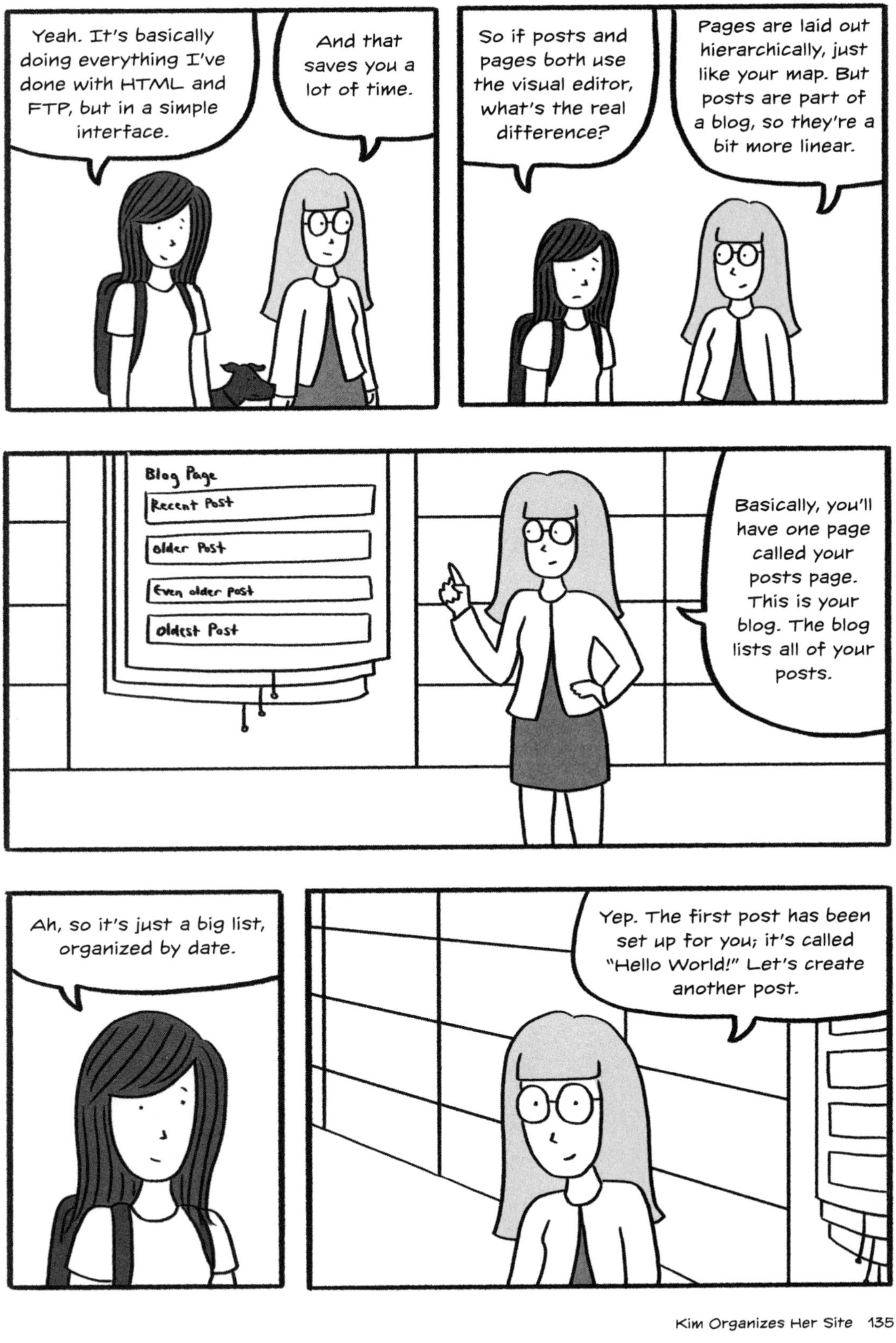
Yeah. It's basically doing everything I've done with HTML and FTP, but in a simple interface.
And that saves you a lot of time.
So if posts and pages both use the visual editor, what's the real difference?
Pages are laid out hierarchically, just like your map. But posts are part of a blog, so they're a bit more linear.
Blog Page
Recent Post
Older Post
Even older post
Oldest Post
Basically, you'll have one page called your posts page. This is your blog. The blog lists all of your posts.
Ah, so it's just a big list, organized by date.
Yep. The first post has been set up for you; it's called "Hello World!" Let's create another post.

There's no Parent section here.

Right. That's because posts aren't stored hierarchically. They are usually organized by subject. See where it says "Categories"?

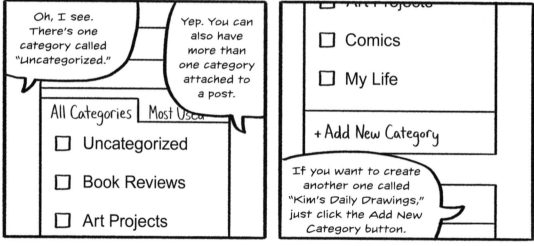

Oh, I see. There's one category called "Uncategorized."

Yep. You can also have more than one category attached to a post.

All Categories | Most Used

☐ Uncategorized

☐ Book Reviews

☐ Art Projects

☐ Art Projects

☐ Comics

☐ My Life

+ Add New Category

If you want to create another one called "Kim's Daily Drawings," just click the Add New Category button.

I'm starting to get it. So I could also create a category called "Upcoming Projects" for posts about what I'm working on.

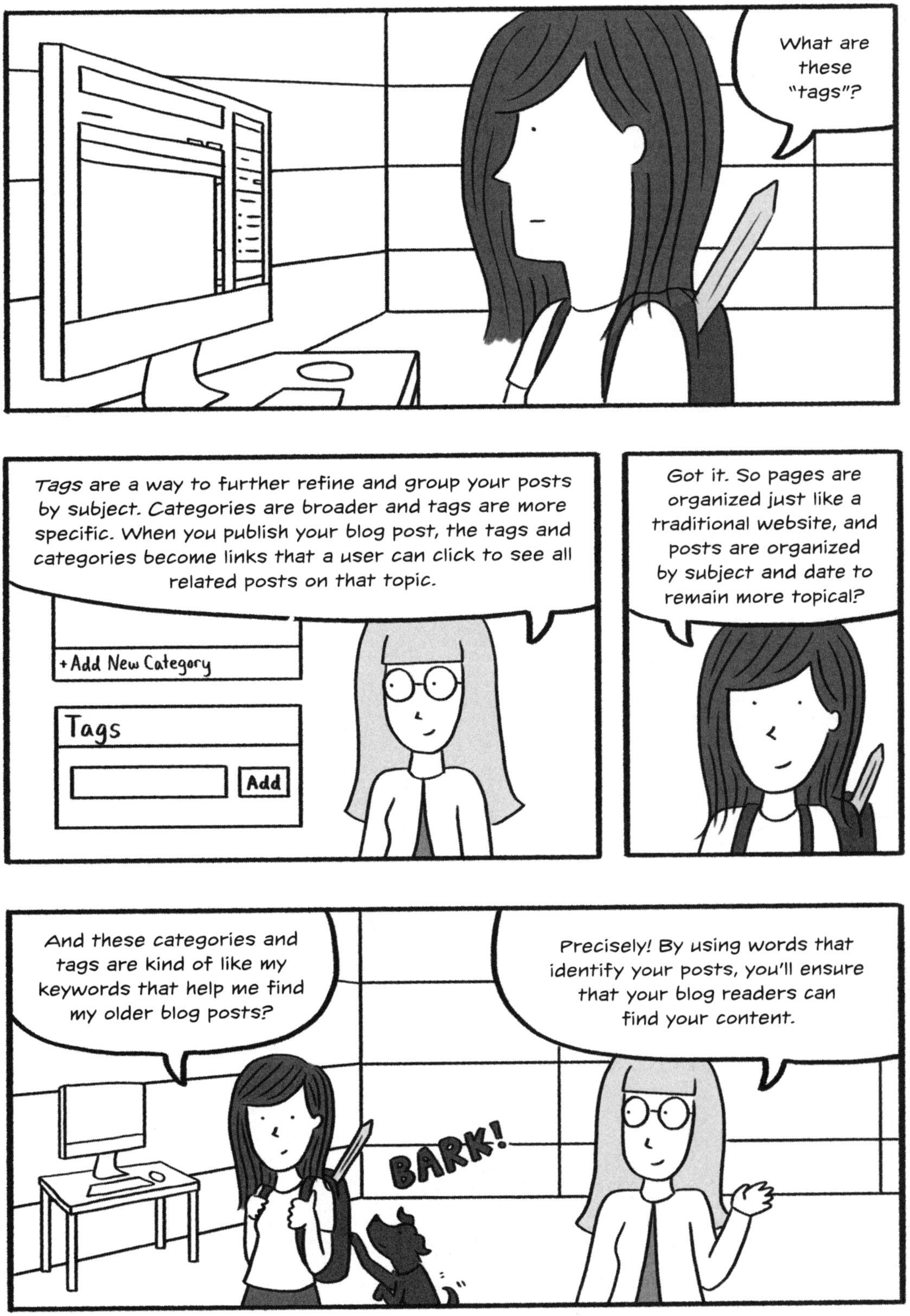

What are these "tags"?
Tags are a way to further refine and group your posts by subject. Categories are broader and tags are more specific. When you publish your blog post, the tags and categories become links that a user can click to see all related posts on that topic.
+ Add New Category
Tags
Add
Got it. So pages are organized just like a traditional website, and posts are organized by subject and date to remain more topical?
And these categories and tags are kind of like my keywords that help me find my older blog posts?
Precisely! By using words that identify your posts, you'll ensure that your blog readers can find your content.
BARK!

Kim Adds Photos and Other Media to Her Site

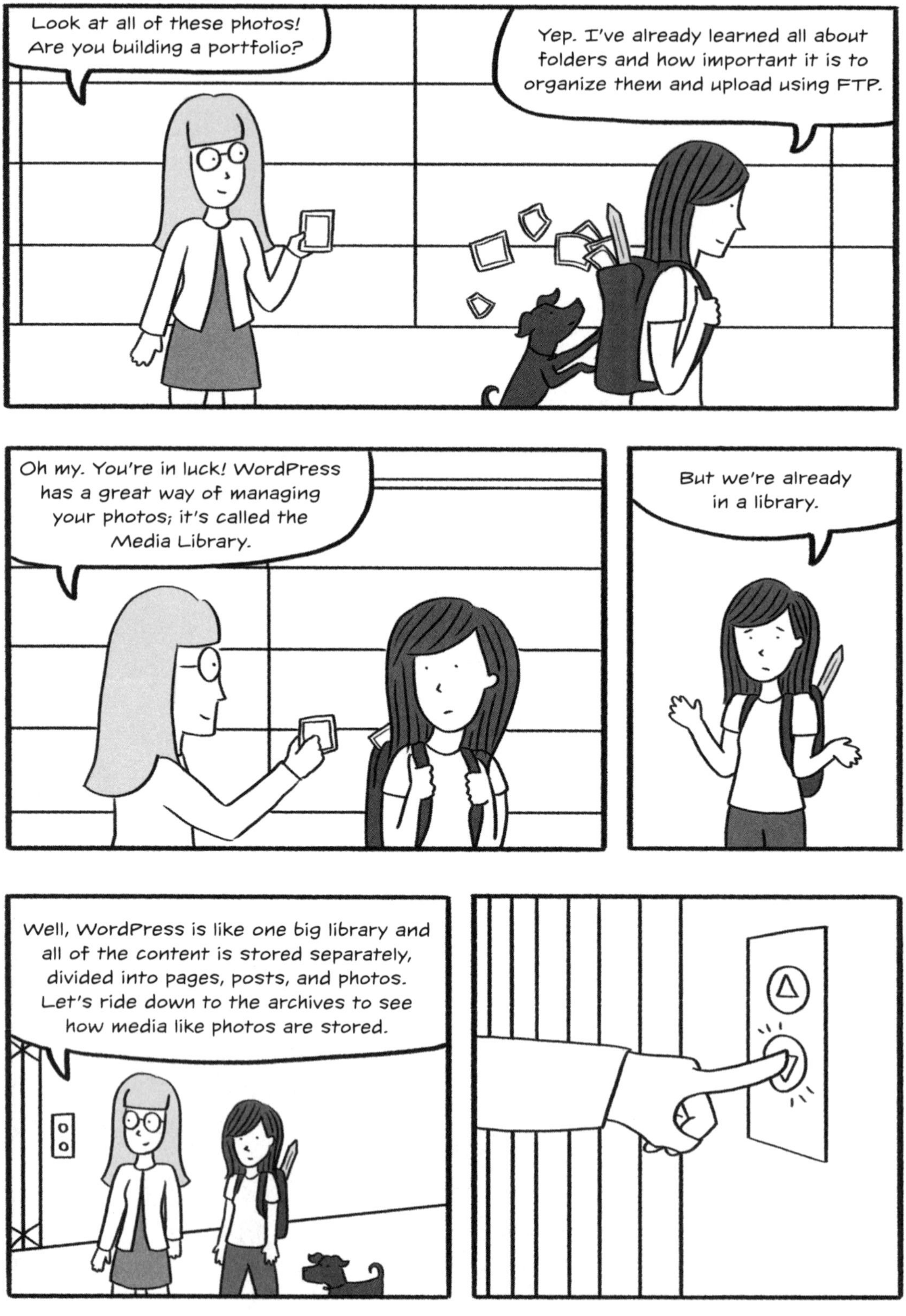
Look at all of these photos! Are you building a portfolio?
Yep. I've already learned all about folders and how important it is to organize them and upload using FTP.
Oh my. You're in luck! WordPress has a great way of managing your photos; it's called the Media Library.
But we're already in a library.
Well, WordPress is like one big library and all of the content is stored separately, divided into pages, posts, and photos. Let's ride down to the archives to see how media like photos are stored.

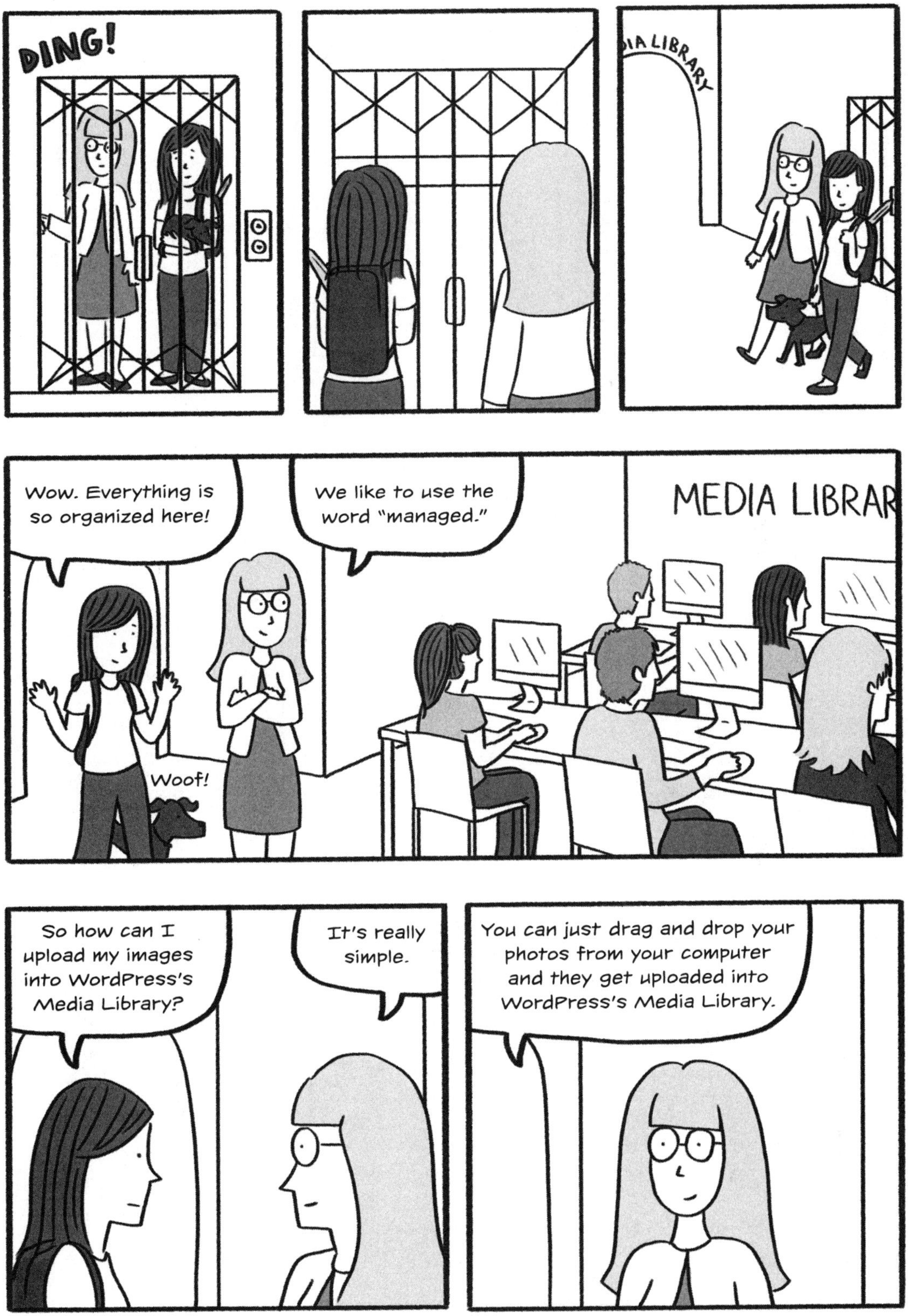
DING!
IA LIBRARY
Wow. Everything is so organized here!
We like to use the word "managed."
MEDIA LIBRAR
Woof!
So how can I upload my images into WordPress's Media Library?
It's really simple.
You can just drag and drop your photos from your computer and they get uploaded into WordPress's Media Library.

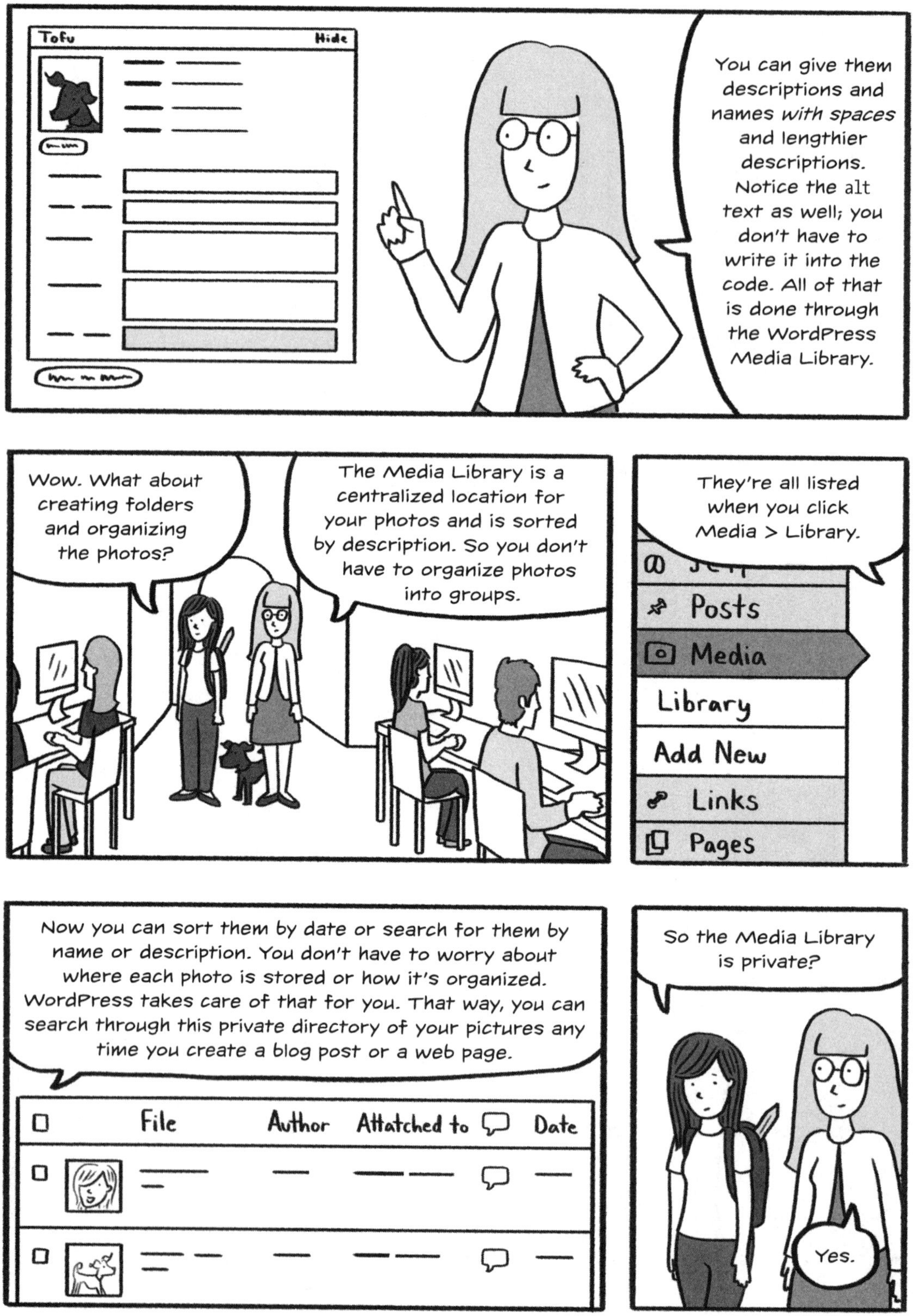
Tofu
Hide
You can give them descriptions and names *with spaces* and lengthier descriptions. Notice the alt text as well; you don't have to write it into the code. All of that is done through the WordPress Media Library.
Wow. What about creating folders and organizing the photos?
The Media Library is a centralized location for your photos and is sorted by description. So you don't have to organize photos into groups.
They're all listed when you click Media > Library.
Posts
Media
Library
Add New
Links
Pages
Now you can sort them by date or search for them by name or description. You don't have to worry about where each photo is stored or how it's organized. WordPress takes care of that for you. That way, you can search through this private directory of your pictures any time you create a blog post or a web page.
File
Author
Attatched to
Date
So the Media Library is private?
Yes.

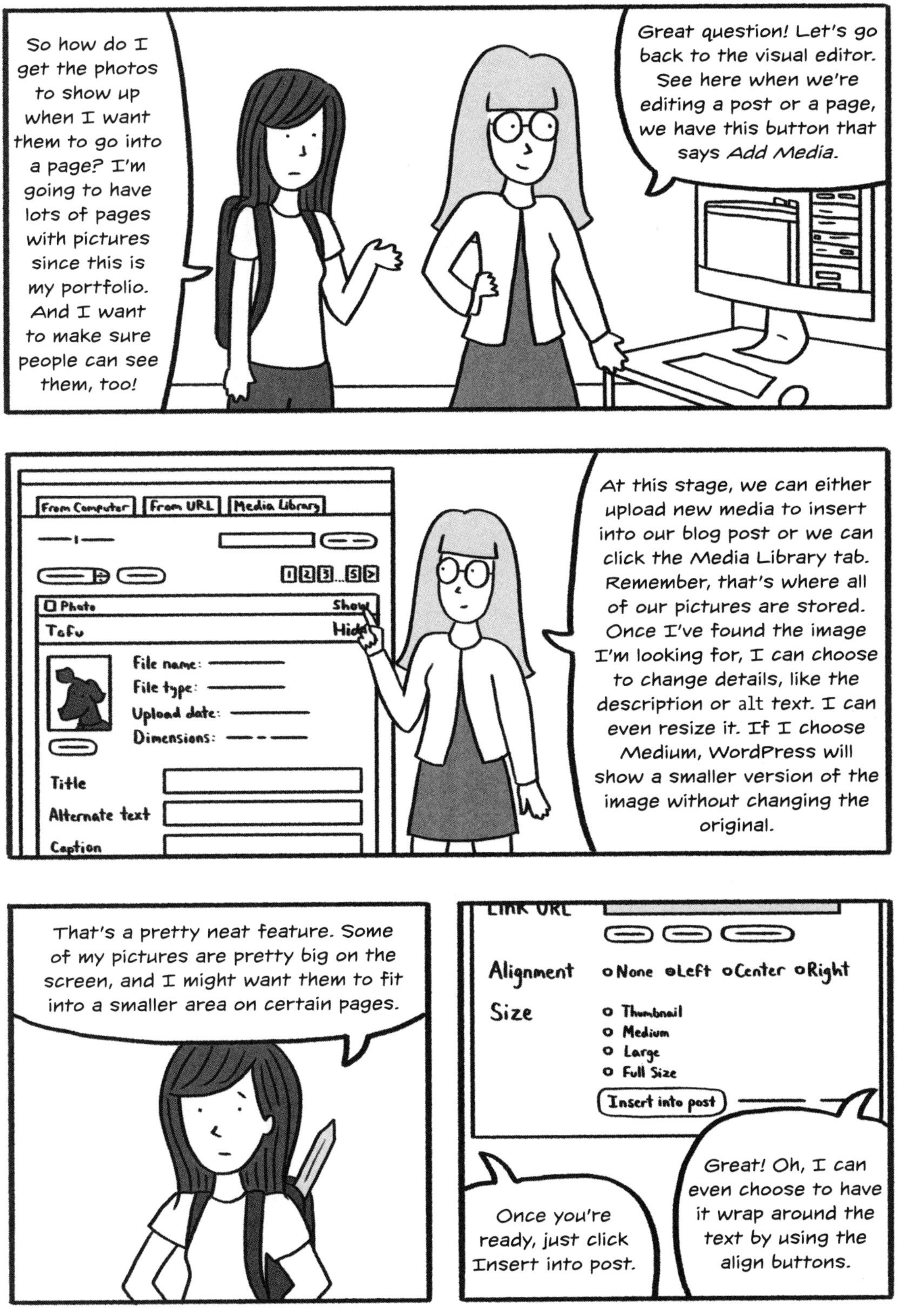
So how do I get the photos to show up when I want them to go into a page? I'm going to have lots of pages with pictures since this is my portfolio. And I want to make sure people can see them, too!
Great question! Let's go back to the visual editor. See here when we're editing a post or a page, we have this button that says *Add Media*.
From Computer
From URL
Media Library
Photo
Show
Tofu
File name:
File type:
Upload date:
Dimensions:
Title
Alternate text
Caption
At this stage, we can either upload new media to insert into our blog post or we can click the Media Library tab. Remember, that's where all of our pictures are stored. Once I've found the image I'm looking for, I can choose to change details, like the description or alt text. I can even resize it. If I choose Medium, WordPress will show a smaller version of the image without changing the original.
That's a pretty neat feature. Some of my pictures are pretty big on the screen, and I might want them to fit into a smaller area on certain pages.
Alignment
None
Left
Center
Right
Size
Thumbnail
Medium
Large
Full Size
Insert into post
Once you're ready, just click Insert into post.
Great! Oh, I can even choose to have it wrap around the text by using the align buttons.

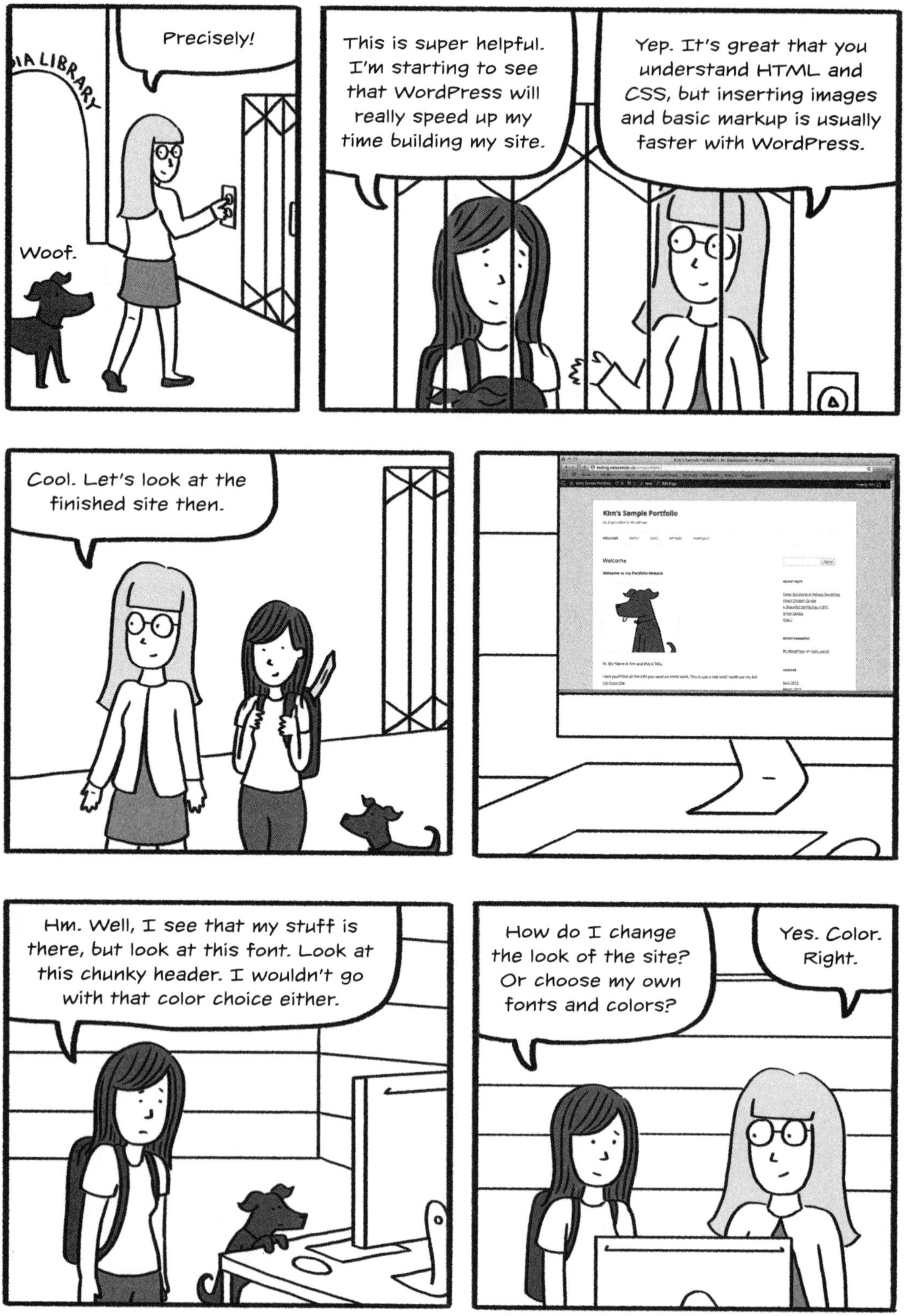
Precisely!
Woof.
This is super helpful. I'm starting to see that WordPress will really speed up my time building my site.
Yep. It's great that you understand HTML and CSS, but inserting images and basic markup is usually faster with WordPress.
Cool. Let's look at the finished site then.
Kim's Sample Portfolio
Welcome
Hm. Well, I see that my stuff is there, but look at this font. Look at this chunky header. I wouldn't go with that color choice either.
How do I change the look of the site? Or choose my own fonts and colors?
Yes. Color. Right.

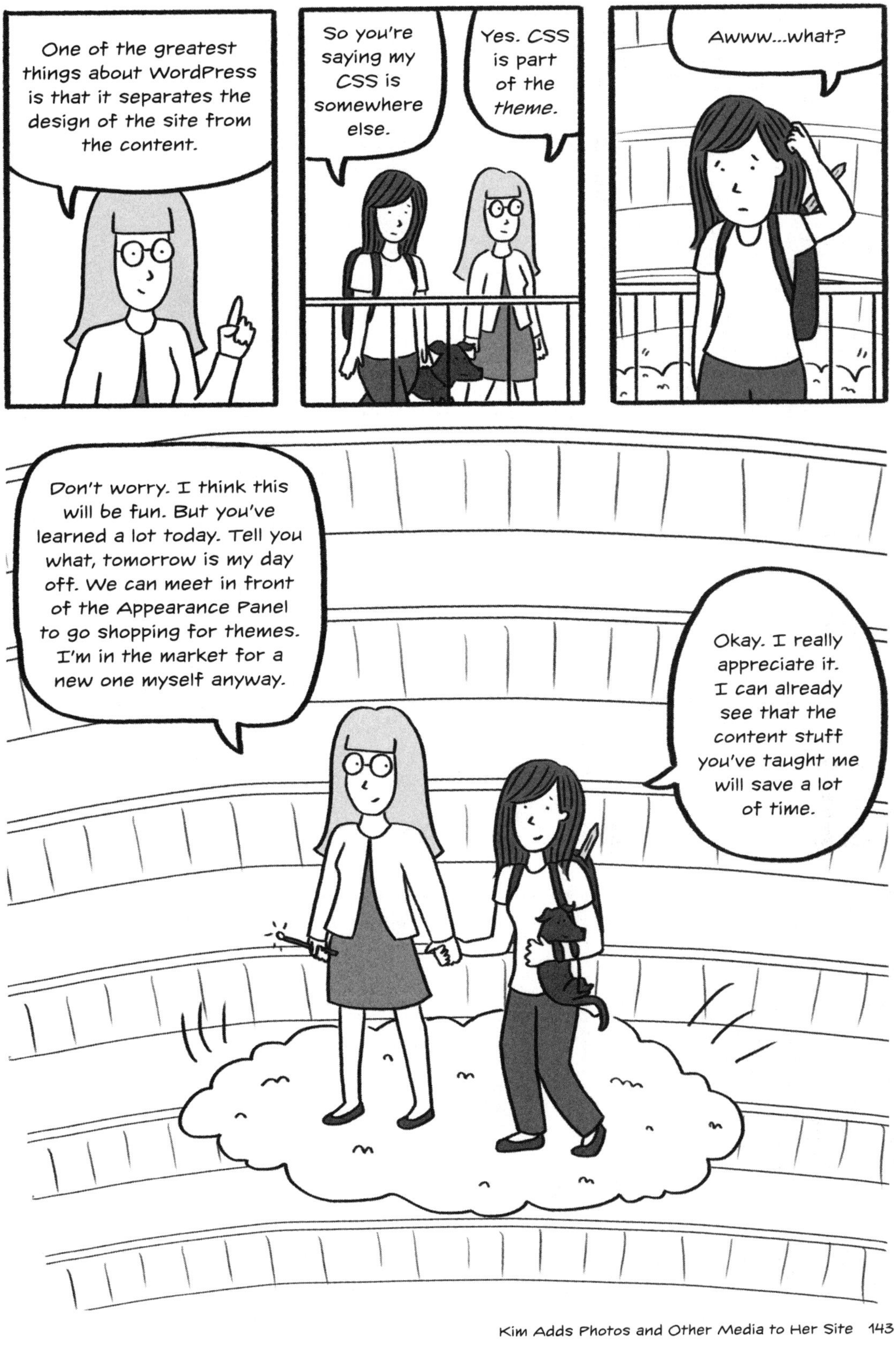
One of the greatest things about WordPress is that it separates the design of the site from the content.
So you're saying my CSS is somewhere else.
Yes. CSS is part of the *theme.*
Awww...what?
Don't worry. I think this will be fun. But you've learned a lot today. Tell you what, tomorrow is my day off. We can meet in front of the Appearance Panel to go shopping for themes. I'm in the market for a new one myself anyway.
Okay. I really appreciate it. I can already see that the content stuff you've taught me will save a lot of time.

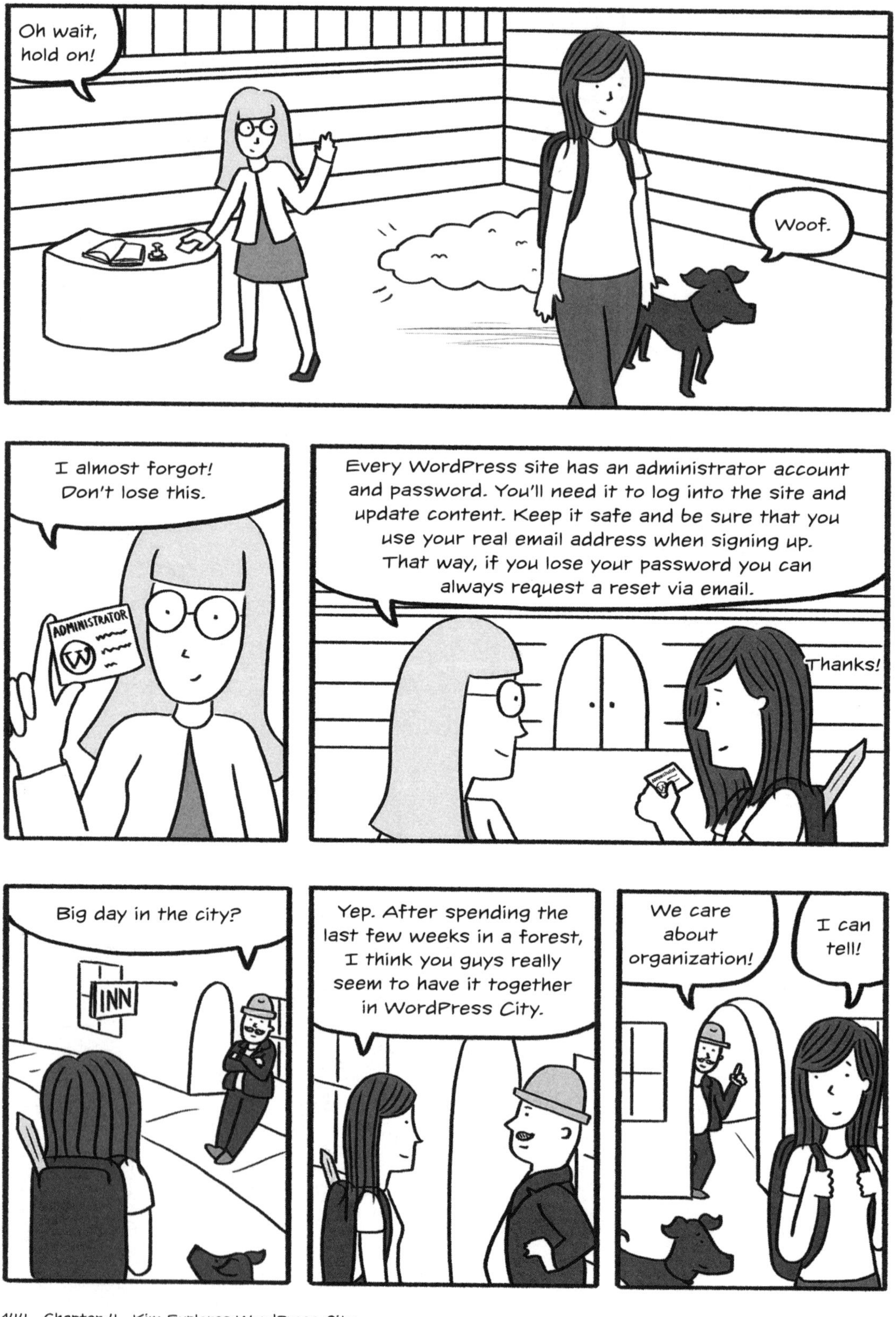
Oh wait, hold on!
Woof.
I almost forgot! Don't lose this.
ADMINISTRATOR
Every WordPress site has an administrator account and password. You'll need it to log into the site and update content. Keep it safe and be sure that you use your real email address when signing up. That way, if you lose your password you can always request a reset via email.
Thanks!
Big day in the city?
INN
Yep. After spending the last few weeks in a forest, I think you guys really seem to have it together in WordPress City.
We care about organization!
I can tell!

Getting Started with WordPress

WordPress is a powerful blogging tool and *content management system*, or *CMS*. A CMS like WordPress automates a lot of the work in creating web pages, like uploading photos and organizing content. WordPress also eliminates the need to hand code individual web pages or blog entries!

Unlike in Chapters 2 and 3—where you could test out your HTML and CSS pages on your computer—to start building your own WordPress site and follow along with this chapter, you'll first need a *host* (discussed in Chapter 5) or you can register on WordPress.com for a free site. Of course, there's no such thing as a free lunch. The free account on WordPress.com has limited functionality, and you won't have your own domain name, either: You'll have to choose a domain like *<yourname>.wordpress.com*. There are some upgrade options for WordPress.com that allow you greater flexibility (like adding a custom domain) for an additional cost.

For our purposes, we'll focus on using a self-hosted version of WordPress (sometimes called WordPress.org). This will allow us to work with some more advanced features, like installing themes and plugins, with no limitations. If you want to set up WordPress on your host in order to follow along exactly with this chapter, just hop ahead to "A Note on Buying WordPress Hosts" on page 243, and follow the steps there. Don't worry, we'll wait here.

One big advantage of using WordPress is that it separates the content from the structure *and* the style of the site. Think back to when we created web pages using HTML. All of the content (the words on the page) and the markup (the various `<tags>`) were in a single document. This means that if you wanted to make a change to the words on your page, you'd have to navigate through a document full of `<tags>`. WordPress makes editing the words and media on a page a lot simpler because it shows you just the content, and hides all of the markup. And if you want to make changes to the style of your website, there's a whole separate feature for doing that, called a *theme*. That's something like the CSS for an HTML page.

All of these conveniences let you focus on the really hard part of making a cool website—writing interesting content without worrying about markup! It's really no wonder that WordPress is so popular. Let's dig in.

Logging In and Out of WordPress

When you install WordPress (or sign up for a WordPress.com account), you'll need to create an administrator username and password. These are the keys to the kingdom. An administrator has full access to edit any content, post new pages, or delete the whole site. Every WordPress site needs at least one administrator, though you can have more than one, too.

Once you've gotten this information, log into the WordPress Dashboard (see Figure 4-1). You can access your Dashboard by going to *http://<your-wordpress-address>/wp-admin/*. To save some time, bookmark your Dashboard in your favorite web browser so that you can log in again easily. You'll be using it a lot!

Figure 4-1: The Login screen

The WordPress Dashboard, which looks something like Figure 4-2, is the *backend* for your new WordPress website. This is the management tool—how you'll add something to your site or make changes. Only you, and others you've created accounts for, can see the backend of the site.

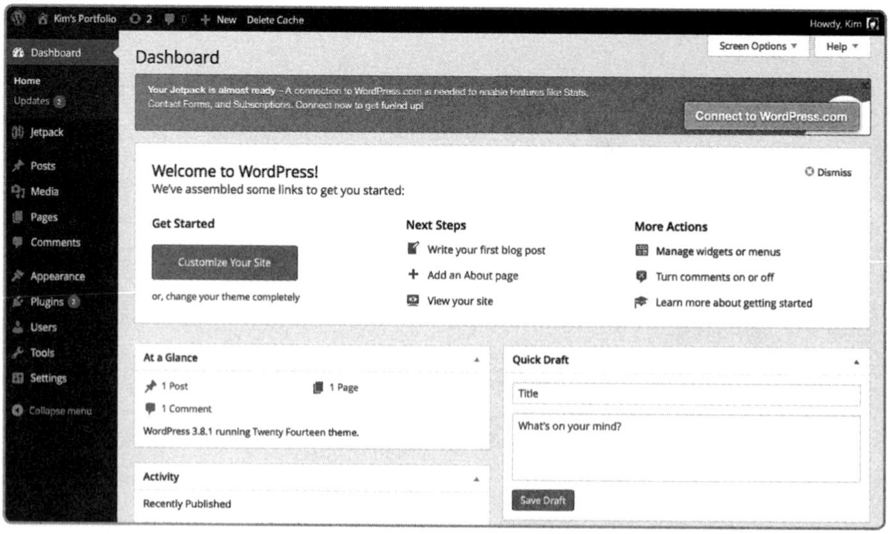

Figure 4-2: The WordPress Dashboard. Use the tabs on the left to manage different areas of your site.

Everyone else visiting your site sees the *frontend*, which will have blog posts as well as other content on it. For now, that probably looks something like Figure 4-3.

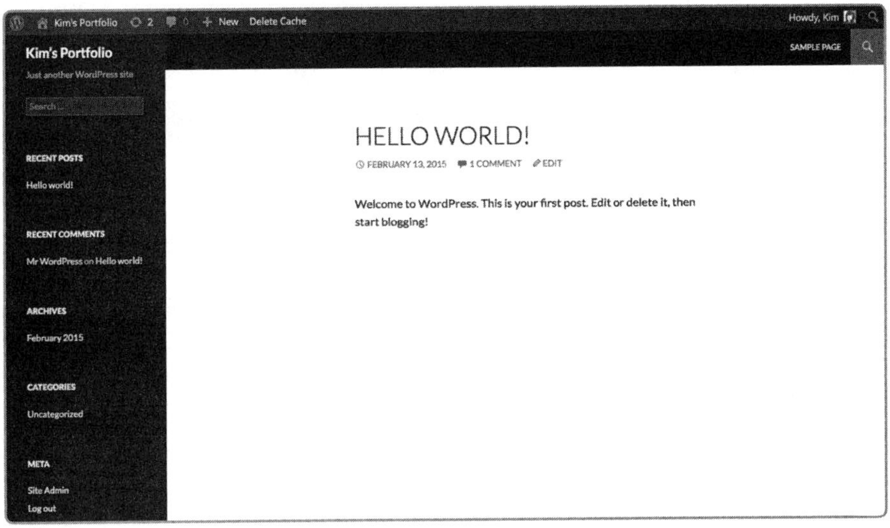
Kim's Portfolio
2
0
New
Delete Cache
Howdy, Kim
Kim's Portfolio
Just another WordPress site
SAMPLE PAGE
Search ...
HELLO WORLD!
FEBRUARY 13, 2015
1 COMMENT
EDIT
Welcome to WordPress. This is your first post. Edit or delete it, then start blogging!
RECENT POSTS
Hello world!
RECENT COMMENTS
Mr WordPress on Hello world!
ARCHIVES
February 2015
CATEGORIES
Uncategorized
META
Site Admin
Log out

Figure 4-3: The frontend of your site. This is what visitors see. As you make changes in the Dashboard (the backend of WordPress), those changes will be reflected here in the finished site. Your blog will look different depending on which WordPress theme is active. This figure shows the Twenty Fourteen theme.

NOTE *One thing to keep in mind is that once a WordPress site is set up, it is immediately accessible to anyone who has the address. While you can create draft posts that aren't public in WordPress, some of the activities in this chapter involve posting to the Internet. Even though the site is "live" on the Web, don't be too concerned about privacy at this stage. It's pretty unlikely that someone will find the site without your providing the exact address. It's quite easy to delete all the test pages we'll be creating.*

Forget Where to Log In?

If you forget the URL where you log into your site, try adding */wp-admin* at the end of the site and then visiting that page. So, for example, if you installed WordPress at *http://<your-site>/*, to log in you'd go to the address *http://<your-site>/wp-admin/*.

Check Your Work as You Go

As you make pages and create content on the backend, you'll probably want to see how things appear to regular visitors of your site. While you're logged in as an administrator, you should see the WordPress admin bar across the top of the window (see Figure 4-4).

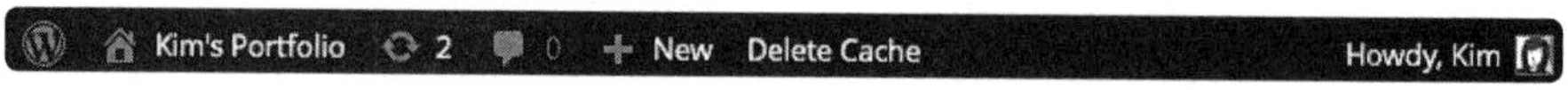

Kim's Portfolio
2
0
New
Delete Cache
Howdy, Kim

Figure 4-4: The admin bar

In the Dashboard, click the site's name to switch to the frontend. Our site is called *Kim's Portfolio*, so we'd just click that. Our current username is *Kim*. If you're on the frontend and want to start adding content, just use the drop-down menu and select **Dashboard** to switch back to the backend (see Figure 4-5).

On the right side of the admin bar is a menu that will allow you to log out of the site (Figure 4-6). Logging out is super important if you're using a public computer! You don't want anyone else editing your site.

Kim's Portfolio
2
Dashboard
Themes
Customize
Widgets
Menus
Background
Header
Hello world!

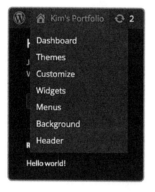

Figure 4-5: Use the drop-down menu on the left to switch between the frontend of the site and the backend (Dashboard).

Howdy, Kim
Kim
Edit My Profile
Log Out

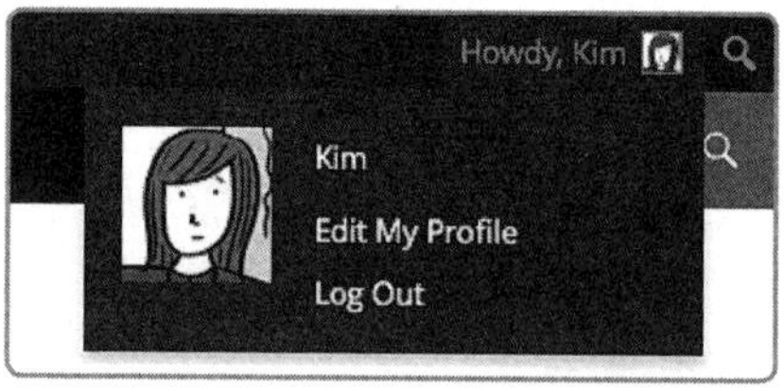

Figure 4-6: The drop-down menu on the right allows you to edit your profile or log out of the site.

Enough flipping and flopping between frontend and backend; let's actually create some new stuff on our site! Let's enable the Twenty Fourteen theme for now so that your experience will mirror what you see in the book. Go to your Dashboard and click **Appearance and Themes** from the left-hand side. You should see the Theme Chooser, which we'll cover in "Changing the Appearance: Theme Basics" on page 193. For now, just make sure that Twenty Fourteen is the active theme. If it is not, scroll down to the Twenty Fourteen theme and click the **Activate** button.

WordPress Content: Posts and Pages

WordPress has two basic types of content: *blog posts* (or just *posts*) and *pages*. They both can handle the same kinds of content: text, links, images, video, and so forth. Because WordPress was designed as a blogging tool, the first thing you see, by default, when you visit a WordPress site is a list of all of the blog posts. Posts are organized by date, just like entries in a journal.

On the other hand, when you add a new *page* to your site, like an "About the Author" or "Contact Us" page, it stands alone and stays put. It wouldn't make too much sense for that kind of information to be a blog post, buried under the latest news.

In fact, pages are more important than blog posts in another way: When you create a page, a link to that page usually gets added to the *navigation menu*—in the Twenty Fourteen theme, that's the horizontal bar with links that shows up near the top of every page (see Figure 4-7).

Howdy, Kim
ABOUT
PORTFOLIO
SAMPLE PAGE

Figure 4-7: The navigation menu is where pages show up when you create them. It lets visitors navigate the most important sections of your website. You can always remove these links later.

Blog posts are just a series of short entries accessible from the posts page (see Figure 4-8).

Kim's Portfolio
New
Delete Cache
Howdy, Kim
ABOUT
PORTFOLIO
SAMPLE PAGE
Kim's Portfolio
RECENT POSTS
Posts 3
Post 2
Hello world!
RECENT COMMENTS
Mr WordPress on Hello world!
ARCHIVES
March 2015
February 2015
CATEGORIES
Uncategorized
META
Site Admin
Log out
POSTS 3
MARCH 31, 2015
EDIT
Yet another riveting post.
POST 2
MARCH 31, 2015
EDIT
This is my second post.
HELLO WORLD!
FEBRUARY 13, 2015
1 COMMENT
EDIT
Welcome to WordPress. This is your first post. Edit or delete it, then

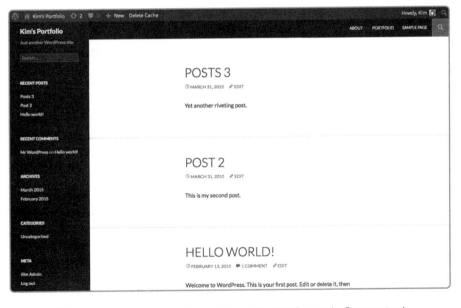

Figure 4-8: Unlike pages, your blog posts usually aren't shown in the menu for your site. Posts are stored chronologically on your posts page. By default, the posts page is the first page on your site.

The difference between posts and pages is one of the simplest yet most important things to understand about building a site using WordPress. Remember that pages are for standalone content, and posts are for blog articles.

Plan Your Site

While you don't need a good plan when you're just getting started and experimenting with WordPress, it's a good idea to map out the structure of your website when you start adding content. Begin by thinking about making a good first impression—which page do you want visitors to see first? WordPress calls this the *front page* of your site. It can either be a blog page or a landing page (see "Customized Settings" on page 203). (You don't even have to use WordPress's blogging features at all!)

Then, how do you organize the other pages? A good plan will lay out the structure of your pages and show you how the blog fits into the site. If you plan on creating a simple blog, you might have a very simple structure that has one blog page and one About page (like Figure 4-9).

Home
(blog)
About

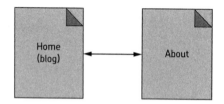

Figure 4-9: A very simple organizational scheme

If you have a portfolio site—like Kim—you'll likely have more pages, so a written plan will be more important (see Figure 4-10).

Home
(blog)
About
Portfolio
Photos
Comics
Pictures
of Tofu
Art Photos

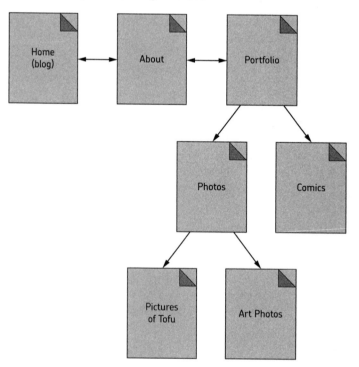

Figure 4-10: A plan for your site will guide you as you create your content. Make one before you build your site, and your content will be more organized.

Once you have created a site map, you should be ready to start creating pages in earnest. I'll remind you to create a plan at the end of this chapter, once you have a better idea of how all the different pieces of WordPress fit together. For now, you'll just get used to how WordPress works and start creating content.

Creating Your First Page

Let's make a page. Log into the Dashboard and navigate to the Pages tab on the left-hand sidebar. Next, select **Add New**, as shown in Figure 4-11.

This will take you to the *visual editor* (see Figure 4-12), where you'll write and edit all your pages and posts.

Let's create a simple web page now using the WordPress visual editor. First we'll want to give it a title. Click the text **Enter title here**, and enter **My Page**. Next, click the **Save Draft** button in the Publish box to the right. Saving a draft means we keep things private while we're working on them. Try clicking the **Preview** button next. This will open a new window or new tab in your browser and show you a view of what the page will look like with your current theme, as shown in Figure 4-13. (You can preview a draft post or page at any time, but it won't go public until you press the big blue Publish button.)

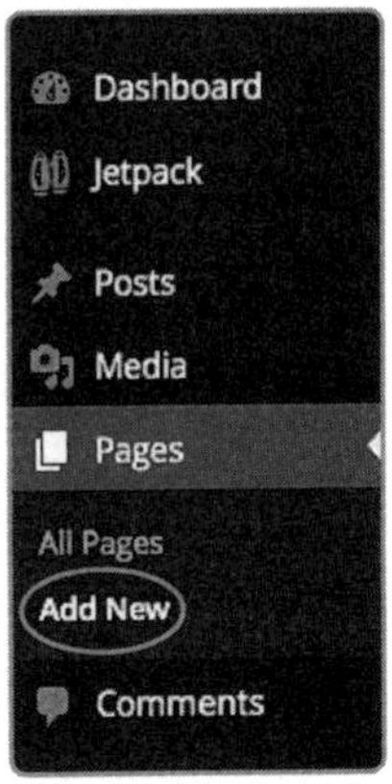
Dashboard
Jetpack
Posts
Media
Pages
All Pages
Add New
Comments

Figure 4-11: On the left side of the Dashboard, you'll see the Pages tab. Here you can create a new page by clicking Add New.

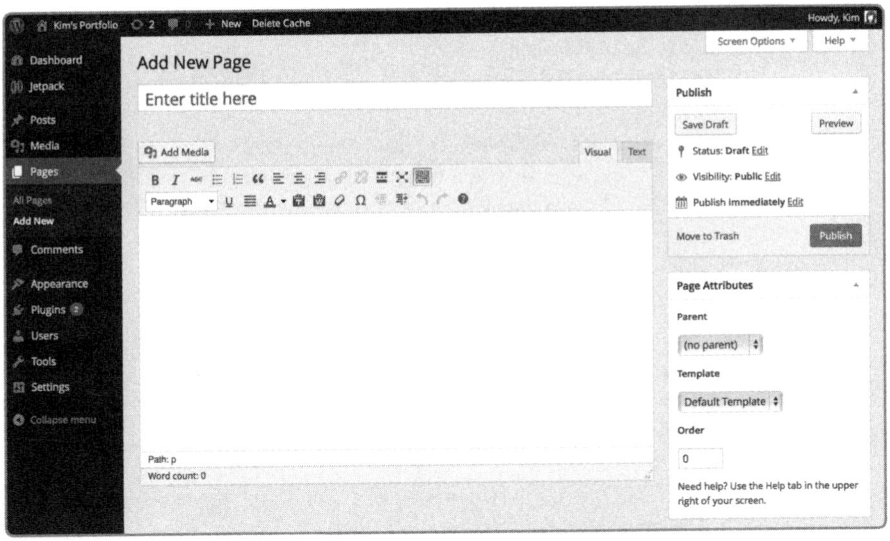
Kim's Portfolio
New
Delete Cache
Howdy, Kim
Screen Options
Help
Add New Page
Enter title here
Add Media
Visual
Text
Paragraph
Path: p
Word count: 0
Dashboard
Jetpack
Posts
Media
Pages
All Pages
Add New
Comments
Appearance
Plugins
Users
Tools
Settings
Collapse menu
Publish
Save Draft
Preview
Status: Draft Edit
Visibility: Public Edit
Publish immediately Edit
Move to Trash
Publish
Page Attributes
Parent
(no parent)
Template
Default Template
Order
0
Need help? Use the Help tab in the upper right of your screen.

Figure 4-12: The visual editor for pages. On the right are publication and organization settings. In the middle is the editor itself, where you'll write posts, add images, and so on. You use the title field to name the page.

Kim's Portfolio
Just another WordPress site
ABOUT
PORTFOLIO
SAMPLE PAGE
MY PAGE
EDIT
RECENT POSTS
Posts 3
Post 2
Hello world!
RECENT COMMENTS
Mr WordPress on Hello world!
ARCHIVES
March 2015
February 2015

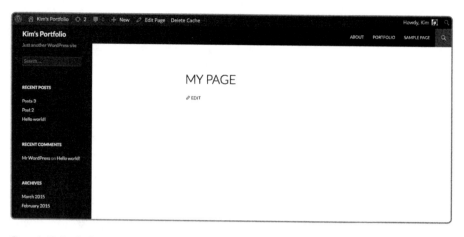

Figure 4-13: Previewing a page shows you the changes you've made before you make the page public.

You should already be seeing how much easier it is to write web pages using WordPress—no `<title>` tag, no upfront CSS work to style the fonts or headers. WordPress separates the content from the structure and the style, so when we're working on a page in the Dashboard we don't have to worry about those things. We just write the content we want and WordPress does the remaining work for us.

Go back to the Dashboard by closing this new window or tab. Let's complete the rest of our test page using the visual editor. Enter the following text:

```
This is bold text.
This is italic text.
```

Now let's format this text using the *formatting bar* (see Figure 4-14). Select the first line and click the **B** button to bold the selected text. Select the second line and click the **I** button to make it italic.

Add Media
Visual
Text

Figure 4-14: The formatting bar in the visual editor lets you do basic text formatting like bold or italic without writing HTML.

Save the draft and preview your page again. You should see something like Figure 4-15.

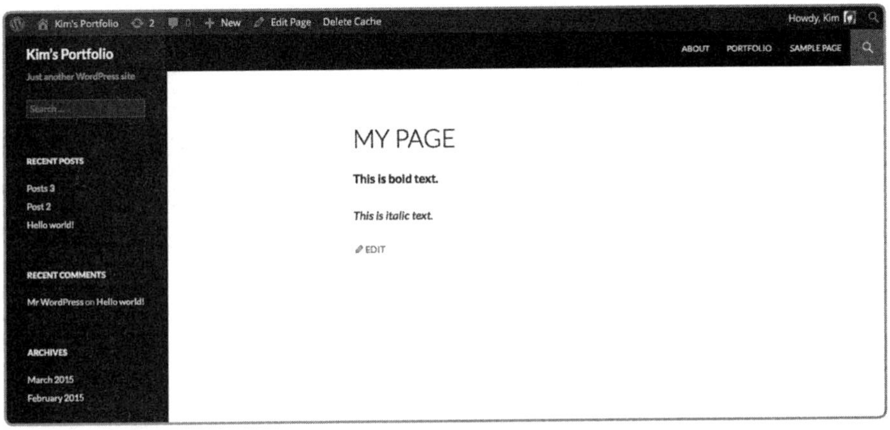
Kim's Portfolio
New
Edit Page
Delete Cache
Howdy, Kim
Kim's Portfolio
Just another WordPress site
ABOUT
PORTFOLIO
SAMPLE PAGE
MY PAGE
This is bold text.
This is italic text.
EDIT
RECENT POSTS
Posts 3
Post 2
Hello world!
RECENT COMMENTS
Mr WordPress on Hello world!
ARCHIVES
March 2015
February 2015

Figure 4-15: After you use the visual editor to format your text, the preview will show the finished version of your page.

WordPress formatted the text for you, and you got to skip typing the `<strong>` and `<em>` tags. Also, notice in the preview that WordPress puts each paragraph on its own line, even though we didn't insert any `<p>` tags. This is another time saver when you're writing content into WordPress. The visual editor is a *WYSIWYG* tool, which is computer-geek speak for *what you see is what you get* and is typically a lot more user-friendly than HTML. Let's add more content to our page using the visual editor. Add another line:

```
Click here
```

Let's turn that *Click here* text into a link. Select the text and then click the **Link** button in the visual editor, as shown in Figure 4-16.

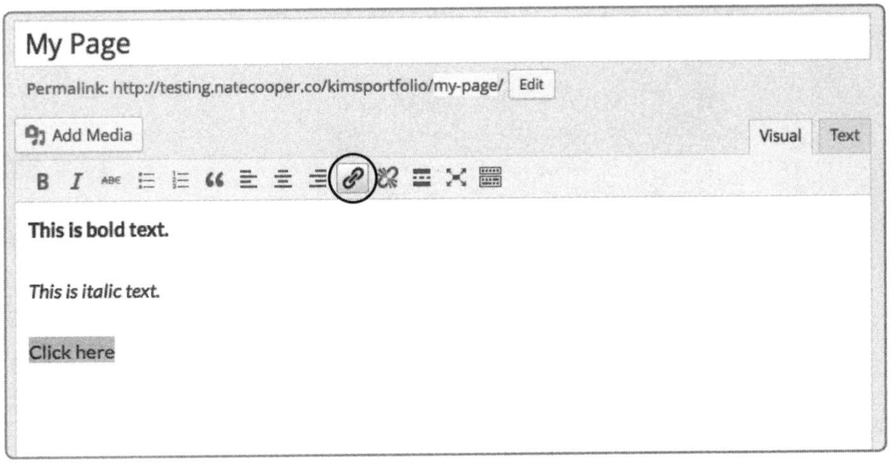
My Page
Permalink: http://testing.natecooper.co/kimsportfolio/my-page/
Edit
Add Media
Visual
Text
This is bold text.
This is italic text.
Click here

Figure 4-16: Adding a link to content is as simple as highlighting text and clicking the Link button.

A little box pops up where you can type your URL (see Figure 4-17). Go ahead and type ***http://natecooper.co***, and then click **Add Link**. Notice that it looks like a link even in the visual editor. Pretty easy, right?

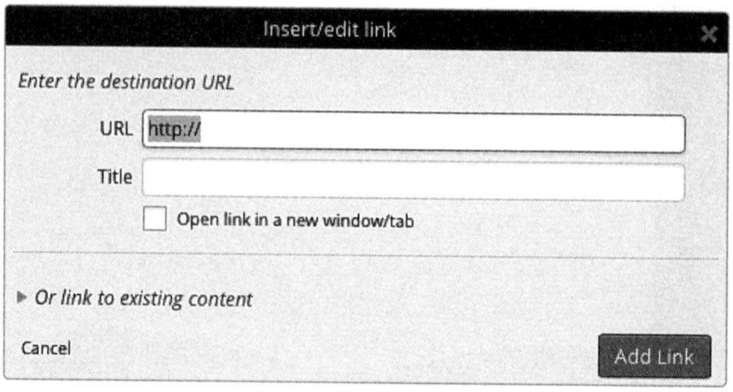
Insert/edit link
Enter the destination URL
URL
http://
Title
Open link in a new window/tab
Or link to existing content
Cancel
Add Link

Figure 4-17: Clicking the Link button brings up a pop-up that asks for the link's destination URL.

Next, let's add a first line to our page that reads "Hello World." We want this line to be a heading. But in the visual editor's toolbar, there's no obvious button to make text into a heading. What gives? Maybe you've noticed a strange little button on the far right of the toolbar. This is the Toolbar Toggle button (see Figure 4-18). If you click it, you'll get another whole row of options for formatting our text. One of those options is a Paragraph drop-down menu. Type **Hello World**, select the text, click the **Paragraph** drop-down menu, and select **Heading 1**. Now we have a heading on our page.

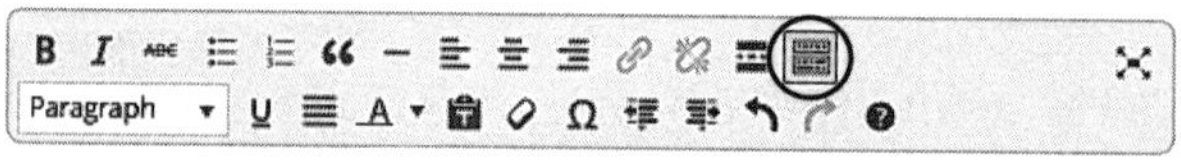
Paragraph

Figure 4-18: Clicking the Toolbar Toggle button enables a second row of formatting options that was previously hidden.

Save the draft and then preview your document. It should look like Figure 4-19.

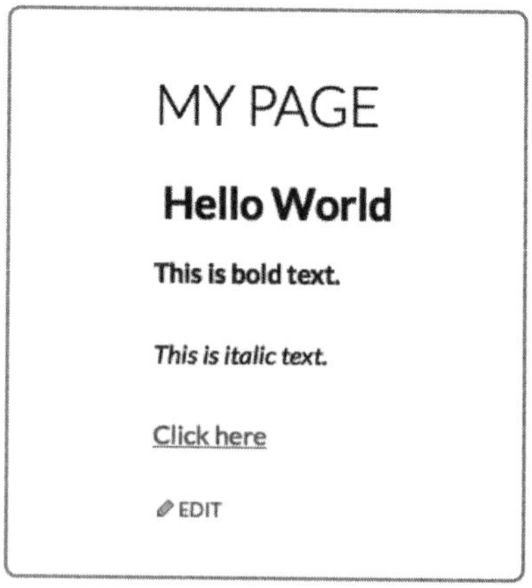
MY PAGE
Hello World
This is bold text.
This is italic text.
Click here
EDIT

Figure 4-19: Now that you've changed the text "Hello World" into a heading, it stands out more on the page.

We've built a functional web page in a few minutes using WordPress. The visual editor replaces the need to type HTML tags to format a website. So there's no need to learn to code, right? Yeah, right! There is no such thing as knowing too much HTML or CSS. WordPress's visual editor is doing the coding for you and that can help speed things up, but the HTML is still there. Close the preview to return to your page in the Dashboard. Click the **Text** tab at the top of the visual editor. You should see *almost* all of the HTML code for your page, as shown in Figure 4-20.

Edit Page
Add New
My Page
Permalink: http://testing.natecooper.co/kimsportfolio/my-page/
Edit
View Page
Get Shortlink
Add Media
Add slider
Visual
Text
b
i
link
b-quote
del
ins
img
ul
ol
li
code
more
close tags
<h1>Hello World</h1>
<strong>This is bold text.</strong>
<em>This is italic text.</em>
<a href="http://natecooper.co">Click here</a>
Word count: 12
Draft saved at 9:06:10 pm. Last edited by Kim on May 8, 2015 at 1:00 pm

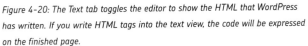

Figure 4-20: The Text tab toggles the editor to show the HTML that WordPress has written. If you write HTML tags into the text view, the code will be expressed on the finished page.

The page is still built in HTML; you've just used WordPress to automate the process. There are a couple of things to note here. One is that the CSS is not contained within this page. Just like when we built our site using our code editor, the CSS file is stored in a separate place. Second, another somewhat particular quirk about the WordPress editor is that there are still no `<p></p>` tags. Interestingly, WordPress filters them out in this text view. However, if you include `<p></p>` or `<br>` tags while writing in the text tab, WordPress will recognize them and format your text accordingly.

The beauty of knowing what's happening in the code is that you're never stuck with the formatting that WordPress does for you automatically. If you're comfortable looking at the HTML in the text editor, you're that much closer to manually editing it and tweaking it when you need to make a change.

Millions of people use WordPress every day without ever learning HTML, but they can get stuck trying to make sure they've gotten the paragraphs, spacing, and formatting just right. *You*, however, won't get stuck. The more familiar you get with HTML and CSS, the more you'll be able to customize these pages to your exact specifications and the less limited you'll be.

Adding Media to Your Page

Now let's add a picture to our page. Go ahead and choose the same image that you embedded in your sample web page from Chapter 2. Here's where things get really exciting, because WordPress streamlines how you organize your pictures through its built-in Media Library. In the visual editor for your page, highlight the text *Hello World* and press DELETE. This is where we'll insert our image. Click the **Add Media** button (shown in Figure 4-21), and you'll see a screen like Figure 4-22, prompting you to insert media.

Add Media

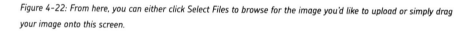

Figure 4-21: The Add Media button

Insert Media
Create Gallery
Set Featured Image
Insert from URL
Insert Media
Upload Files
Media Library
Drop files anywhere to upload
Select Files
Maximum upload file size: 64MB.

Figure 4-22: From here, you can either click Select Files to browse for the image you'd like to upload or simply drag your image onto this screen.

Alternatively, you can just drag an image into the visual editor, which takes you to a screen like the one shown in Figure 4-23.

Insert Media
Create Gallery
Set Featured Image
Insert from URL
Insert Media
Upload Files
Media Library
All media items
Search
ATTACHMENT DETAILS
IMG_8454.jpg
April 1, 2014
576 × 600
Edit Image
Delete Permanently
Title
IMG_8454
Caption
Alt Text
Description
1 selected
Clear
Insert into page

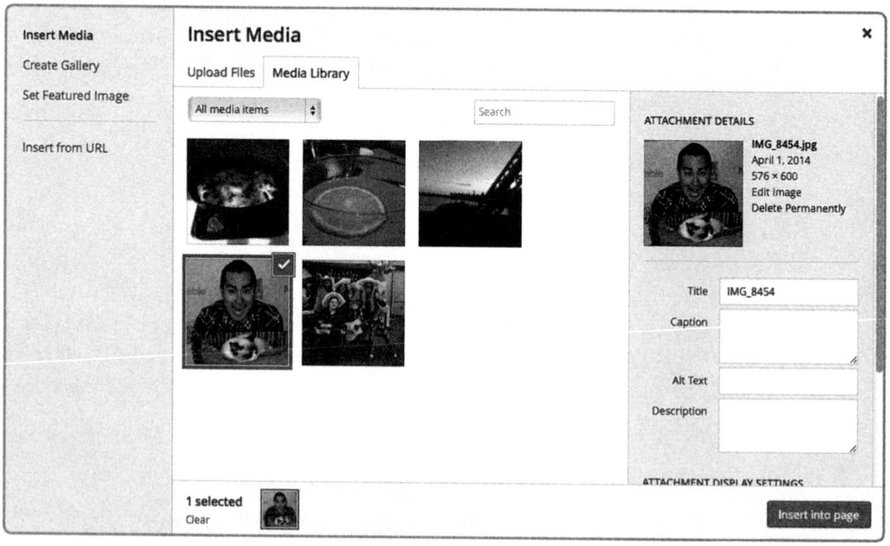

Figure 4-23: The Media Library in WordPress shows all of the images ever uploaded. It can also be used to store video, PDFs, Word docs, and other files.

WordPress will immediately upload that photo. You'll see a progress bar while the image is uploading, and then once it's finished, in your Media Library you'll see a blue border around your image and a checkmark in its upper-right corner (Figure 4-23). This means that the image has been uploaded and is ready to be inserted into your page. Pretty slick, right?

Now that the photo is on WordPress, we can insert it into our page. You might have already noticed that Insert into page button at the bottom right, but before we get trigger-happy, there are some options we need to set.

To the right of the selected image, you'll see some details about it (see Figure 4-24). Remember when we used the <img src> tag in our HTML document that we added alt="description" so that search engines could more easily understand what's in the picture? In WordPress, we can add the alt text similarly. The Title and Description fields are optional descriptions that usually don't show up on the public view of the page, but they may make finding the image in the Dashboard easier later. For example, you might put a couple of words in the Description field that will remind you what's in the image so you can search for those words later. The Caption field will show up within the page and is also optional. If nothing else, you should get in the habit of at least putting something in the Alt Text field because it's so important for SEO. It's also used by screen-reading software for blind or visually impaired individuals.

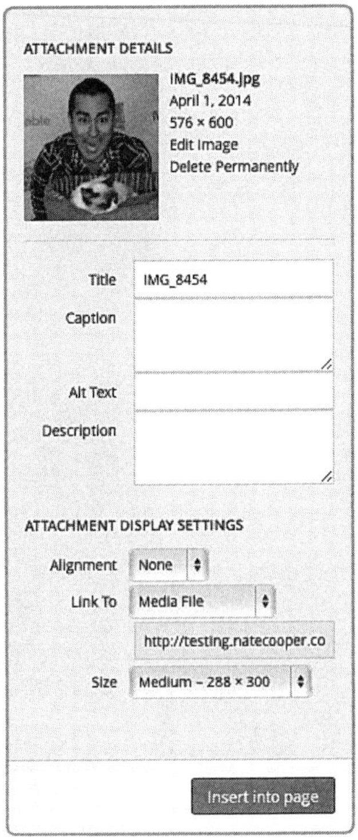
ATTACHMENT DETAILS
IMG_8454.jpg
April 1, 2014
576 × 600
Edit Image
Delete Permanently
Title
IMG_8454
Caption
Alt Text
Description
ATTACHMENT DISPLAY SETTINGS
Alignment
None
Link To
Media File
http://testing.natecooper.co
Size
Medium – 288 × 300
Insert into page

Figure 4-24: WordPress has a lot of options for organizing images, including adding captions and `alt` *text and even resizing the image to fit within the current page.*

For now, let's skip the Alignment drop-down menu but set the **Link To** setting to **None**. Remember, images can be links! By default, WordPress sets the image to link to itself. This is great when you want to see a thumbnail version of an image on a page and then let users click to see the larger version. But right now we just want the image. By setting the link to None, we'll have the image embedded but not link to anything. WordPress can also automatically resize the image within the page. If your photo is large enough, you should be presented with four choices: Thumbnail, Medium, Large, and Full Size. Let's select **Medium** if that's an option (Figure 4-25). Now go ahead and click **Insert into page**, and you'll see something like Figure 4-26.

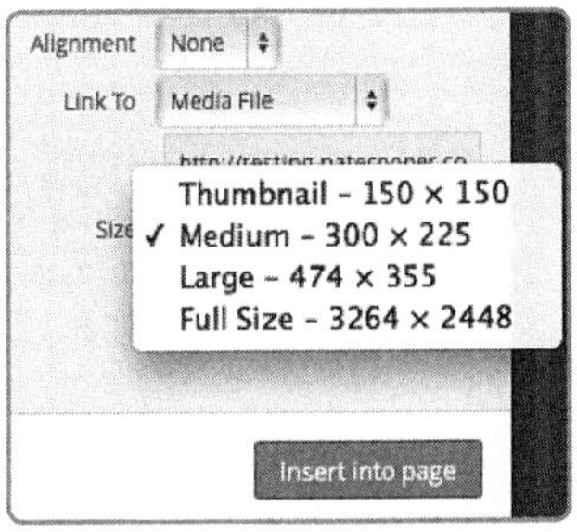
Alignment
None
Link To
Media File
Thumbnail – 150 × 150
✓ Medium – 300 × 225
Large – 474 × 355
Full Size – 3264 × 2448
Insert into page

Figure 4-25: Whenever an image is uploaded to WordPress, Thumbnail, Medium, and Large size versions will also be created. If the image is too small, then only the Thumbnail or Medium sizes may be available.

NOTE *WordPress will not stretch a small image up to fit into the Thumbnail, Medium, or Large sizes. If your image isn't at least as large as the Thumbnail, Medium, or Large sizes, you won't see those options.*

Edit Page
Add New
My Page
Permalink: http://testing.natecooper.co/kimsportfolio/my-page/
Edit
View Page
Add Media
Add slider
Visual
Text
Paragraph
This is bold text.
This is italic text.

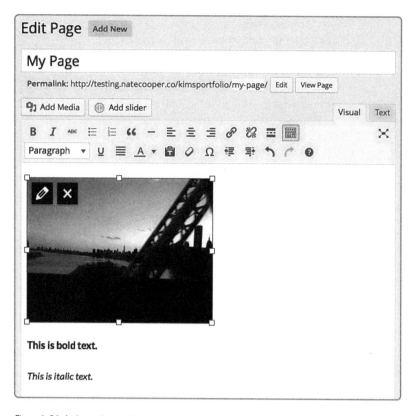

Figure 4-26: An image inserted into the visual editor shows up as an image, not as source code as it does when you're writing HTML.

Click the image to highlight it. You should see eight dots that you can drag out to resize the image. If you want to delete the image from this page, just click the X icon. Don't worry, that only deletes the image from the page; it'll still be in your Media Library in case you want to use it again later. You can also click the image to go back and edit the description, caption, or `alt` text. While the image is highlighted, you can align it using the alignment buttons or even make the image a link to something just like you would with text. The preview you see here appears in the visual editor as it will on the finished page. Click **Save Draft** and **Preview** to see the full effect in the finished page (see Figure 4-27).

Now go back to your visual editor. Click the image and then click the **Left Align** button in the toolbar, as shown in Figure 4-28.

Click **Save** and **Preview**, and you should see that the text is now to the right of the image. If this hasn't blown your mind yet, you haven't spent enough time using HTML to try to get alignment just right with images in a web page. When the left or right alignment buttons are clicked, WordPress assigns a class to the image that is referenced in the CSS of the theme. This class has a rule to float either to the left or right, causing the text to wrap around the object on the opposite side.

MY PAGE

This is bold text.

This is italic text.

<u>Click here</u>

✏ EDIT

Figure 4-27: The finished page is almost identical to what's shown in the visual editor.

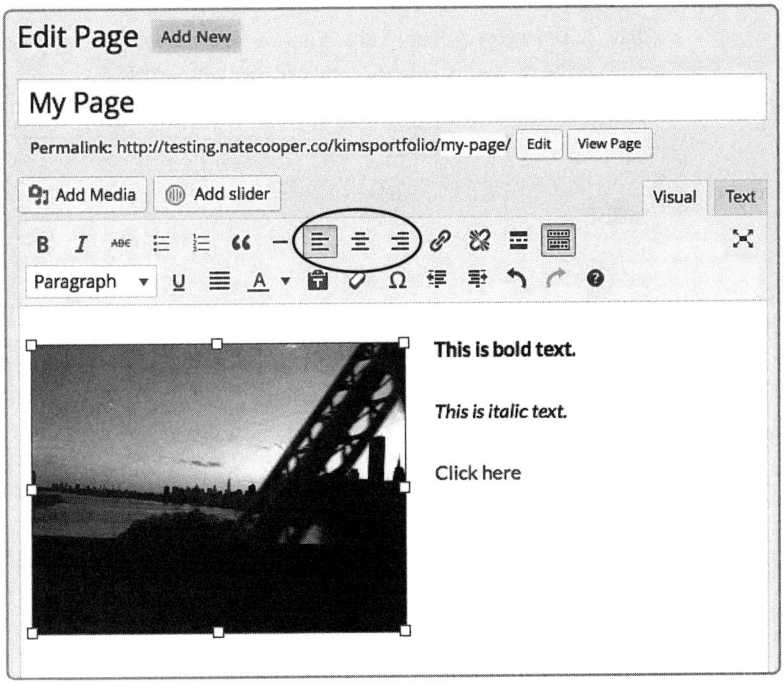

Edit Page   Add New

My Page

Permalink: http://testing.natecooper.co/kimsportfolio/my-page/ | Edit | View Page

📷 Add Media   ⦿ Add slider   Visual | Text

B | *I* | ABC | ☰ | ☷ | 66 | — | ☰ ☰ ☰ | 🔗 | ✂ | ▭ | ▦   ⤢

Paragraph ▼ | U | ☰ | A ▼ | 📋 | ⌀ | Ω | ⇥ | ⇤ | ↶ | ↷ | ❓

This is bold text.

This is italic text.

Click here

Figure 4-28: When an image is selected, the alignment buttons can move the image to the left or the right of text, causing the text to wrap around the image just like in a word processor.

Publishing Your Page

Now that we've added all of the content into our page, we're ready to make it live to the world. In the Publish box in the upper-right corner of your page, click the big blue **Publish** button (see Figure 4-29). Publishing makes your WordPress page live.

Once you've clicked Publish on a page, go to the frontend of the site to see how it looks. You should see that your page appears in the navigation menu (see Figure 4-30).

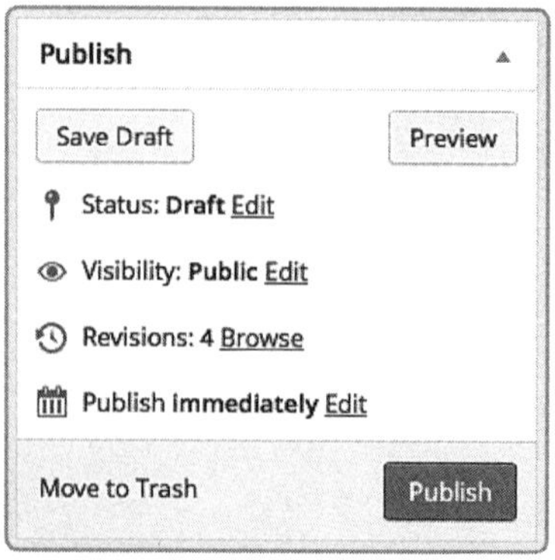
Publish
Save Draft
Preview
Status: Draft Edit
Visibility: Public Edit
Revisions: 4 Browse
Publish immediately Edit
Move to Trash
Publish

Figure 4-29: The Publish box is where you set when a page will be published or save it as a draft to return to later.

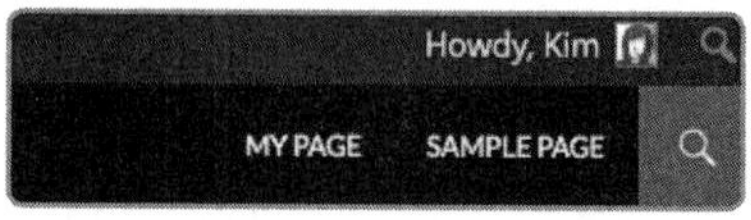
Howdy, Kim
MY PAGE
SAMPLE PAGE

Figure 4-30: The published pages on a site show up in this menu on the frontend.

That's it. Once you click the Publish button, your page is live for all to see. Want to take it back? WordPress has many flexible options for that as well. Go back to the Dashboard and select the Pages tab from the sidebar on the left. This will show you all of the pages on your site (see Figure 4-31).

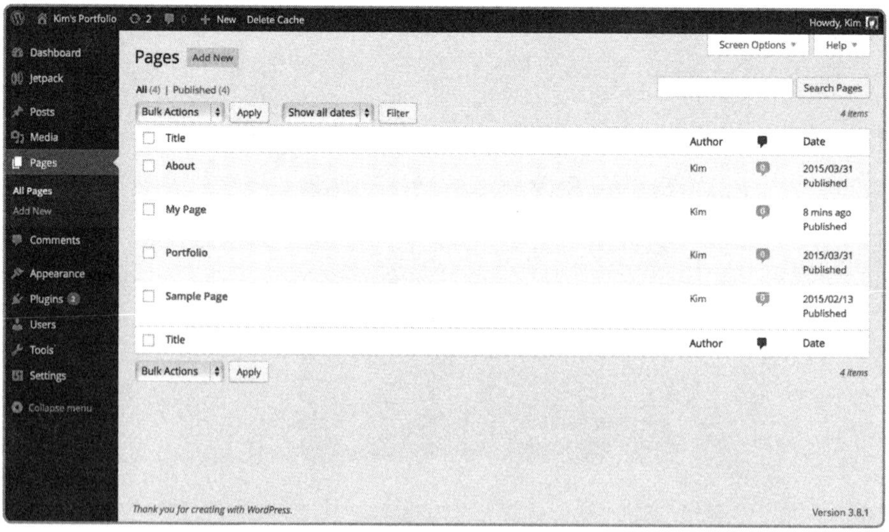
Kim's Portfolio
New
Delete Cache
Howdy, Kim
Dashboard
Jetpack
Posts
Media
Pages
All Pages
Add New
Comments
Appearance
Plugins
Users
Tools
Settings
Collapse menu
Pages
Add New
Screen Options
Help
All (4) | Published (4)
Search Pages
Bulk Actions
Apply
Show all dates
Filter
4 items
Title
Author
Date
About
Kim
2015/03/31
Published
My Page
Kim
8 mins ago
Published
Portfolio
Kim
2015/03/31
Published
Sample Page
Kim
2015/02/13
Published
Title
Author
Date
Bulk Actions
Apply
4 items
Thank you for creating with WordPress.
Version 3.8.1

Figure 4-31: The pages within a site show up under the All Pages section of the Pages tab.

Click the name **My Page**. This will bring you back to the visual editor. Under Status in the Publish box, click **Edit** and then select **Draft** from the drop-down menu. Click **OK** and then **Update** (see Figure 4-32).

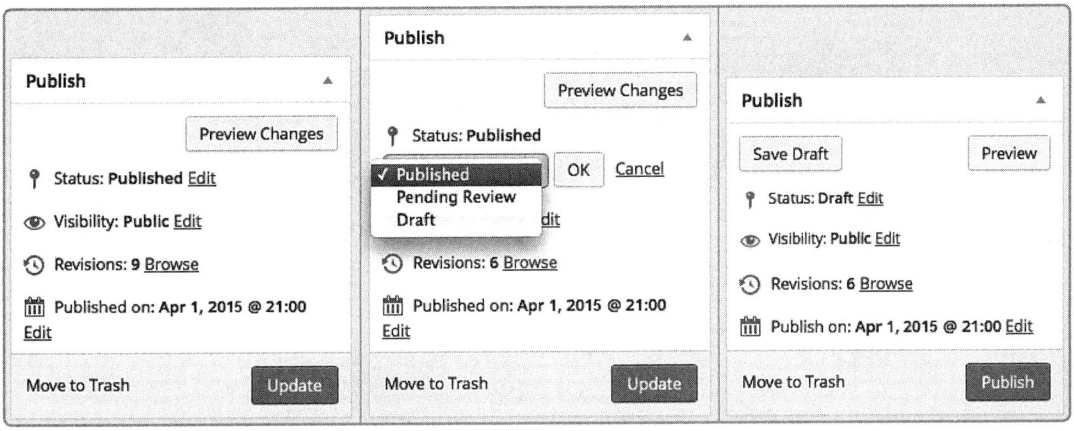

Publish
Preview Changes
Status: Published Edit
Visibility: Public Edit
Revisions: 9 Browse
Published on: Apr 1, 2015 @ 21:00 Edit
Move to Trash
Update
Publish
Preview Changes
Status: Published
✓ Published
Pending Review
Draft
OK
Cancel
Revisions: 6 Browse
Published on: Apr 1, 2015 @ 21:00 Edit
Move to Trash
Update
Publish
Save Draft
Preview
Status: Draft Edit
Visibility: Public Edit
Revisions: 6 Browse
Publish on: Apr 1, 2015 @ 21:00 Edit
Move to Trash
Publish

Figure 4-32: Even if a page has already been published, it can be moved back into drafts. This keeps it in the WordPress Dashboard so you can see and edit it, but removes it from the frontend of the site so that it won't be visible to visitors.

Congrats, you've just *un*published your page from your website! The information is still stored, and you can always republish it. It's just been placed back into draft mode, which means that you can see it in the Dashboard, but it's not publicly visible to the world. WordPress also has a section for Visibility that allows you to keep posts private or password-protected (see Figure 4-33).

One of the nicest features of the Publish box is that it enables you to set the publish date to a specified time in the past or the future. If you set it for the past, it will look like the page was actually written and published on that date. If you set it into the future, the page will remain visible only to you until that date, and then it will be automatically published publicly by WordPress. Pretty cool, right? These publishing options even work the same for Posts as they do for Pages.

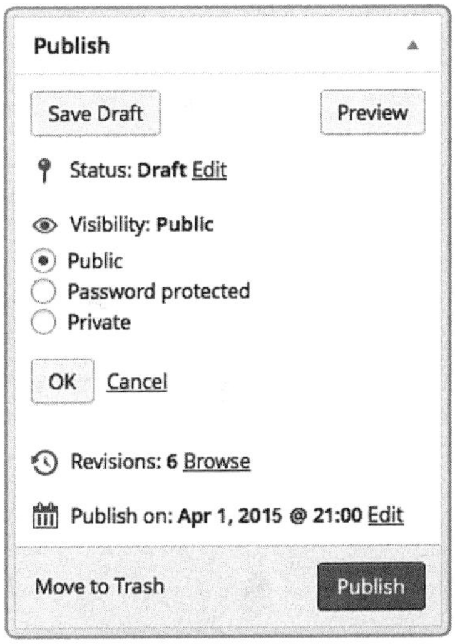

Publish
Save Draft
Preview
Status: Draft Edit
Visibility: Public
Public
Password protected
Private
OK
Cancel
Revisions: 6 Browse
Publish on: Apr 1, 2015 @ 21:00 Edit
Move to Trash
Publish

Figure 4-33: A public page can be set to private (viewable only by the creator) or password-protected (viewable only with a password).

Organizing Your Pages

What if you wanted to do something a bit fancier with your pages? Kim wanted to build Portfolio pages, but she had Drawings and Photos below that Portfolio page. With WordPress, organizing a site like that is easy (see Figure 4-34).

sting.natecooper.co/kimsportfolio/porfolio/drawings/
Reader
All Music Apple Yahoo! Google Maps YouTube Wikipedia News Popular
olio 2 0 New Edit Page Delete Cache
Howdy, Kim
io
ABOUT
PORTFOLIO
SAMPLE PAGE
DRAWINGS
PHOTOS
DRAWINGS
Coming Soon

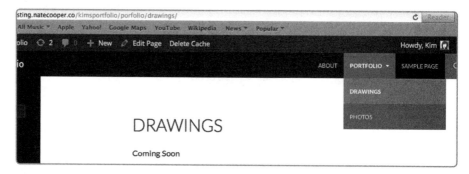

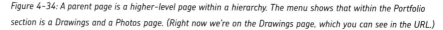

Figure 4-34: A parent page is a higher-level page within a hierarchy. The menu shows that within the Portfolio section is a Drawings and a Photos page. (Right now we're on the Drawings page, which you can see in the URL.)

Pages at the top of the hierarchy (like Kim's portfolio) are called *top-level* or *parent* pages. Pages that live on the second level and below are called *child* pages. You can see the relationship between parent and child pages right in the navigation bar, which makes organizing your site that much more useful for visitors.

Let's flesh out our site by creating a Portfolio section. Click **Dashboard** and then click **Pages** from the sidebar on the left. This will give us our list of pages.

We'll start with three pages. First we'll create the Portfolio page, then the Photos page, and finally the Drawings page. Then we'll want to make sure Photos and Drawings are nested underneath Portfolio. For now, we'll just populate each of these pages with the text *Coming Soon*.

Click **Add New**, title your first page **Portfolio**, and then click **Publish**, as shown in Figure 4-35.

Now that you have a Portfolio page published, it's time to add the two pages, Photos and Drawings, that will appear on the Portfolio page. Click the **Add New** button at the top of the page, as shown in Figure 4-36.

Let's make this our Photos page. Title the page **Photos** and type **Coming Soon** on the page. Before you click Publish, however, scroll down to the lower-right side of the page (see Figure 4-37). There you should see the Page Attributes section, where you'll see a Parent drop-down menu, a Template drop-down menu, and an Order number. Right now the Parent is set to (no parent). Change the **Parent** to **Portfolio**.

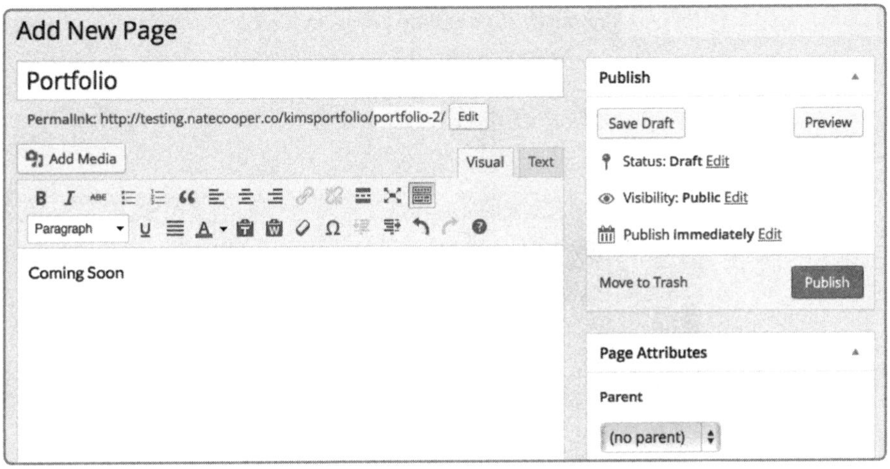

Figure 4-35: To understand how pages are organized hierarchically within WordPress, create a dummy page called Portfolio. In the content box, type Coming Soon.

Figure 4-36: Once a page has been published, an Add New button appears at the top of the window.

Figure 4-37: The page editor has a special section called Page Attributes where a page's parent can be set.

Click **Publish**. You can then click **Add New** and repeat the same process for the Drawings page. When you've finished, revisit your site's frontend. Notice that the menu lists the
Portfolio page, and the two subpages appear in a drop-down menu. Child pages will have
dashes next to them in the Dashboard to indicate that they are not top-level pages (see
Figure 4-38).

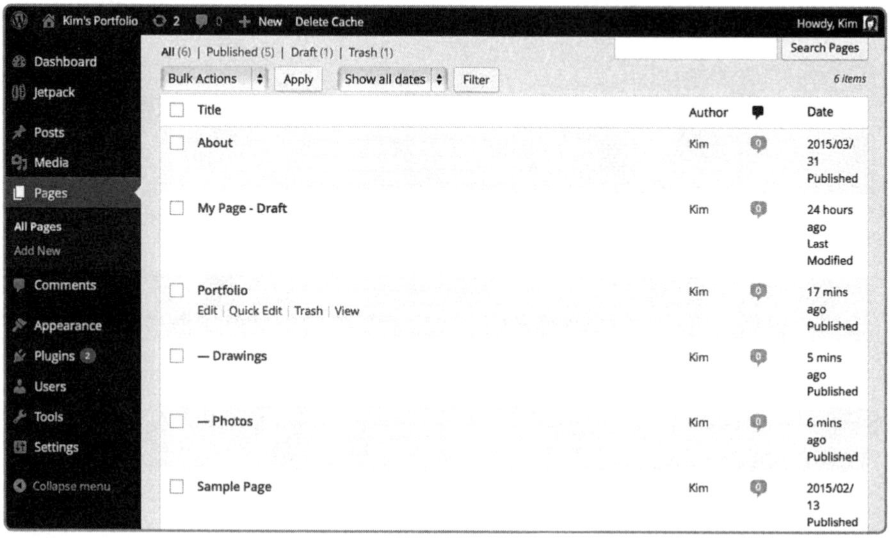

Figure 4-38: Child pages have dashes next to them in the Dashboard to distinguish them from top-level pages.

Creating a Blog Post

Now let's create a blog post. Go to your Dashboard and select **Posts ▸ Add New**. You'll see
the visual editor again, as shown in Figure 4-39.

Go ahead and enter **Post 2** as the title, and in the visual editor type **This is my second
post**. Then click **Publish**. Add another couple of blog posts if you like, to get the hang of
things. When you're ready, click the site name in the upper-left corner to switch to the
frontend of the site.

Remember, blog posts appear on the posts page on a WordPress site. Click **Home** or
your site title to get there. You should see your newest post at the top of the page and any
existing posts further down the page (see Figure 4-40). By default, the post order is sorted
by descending date.

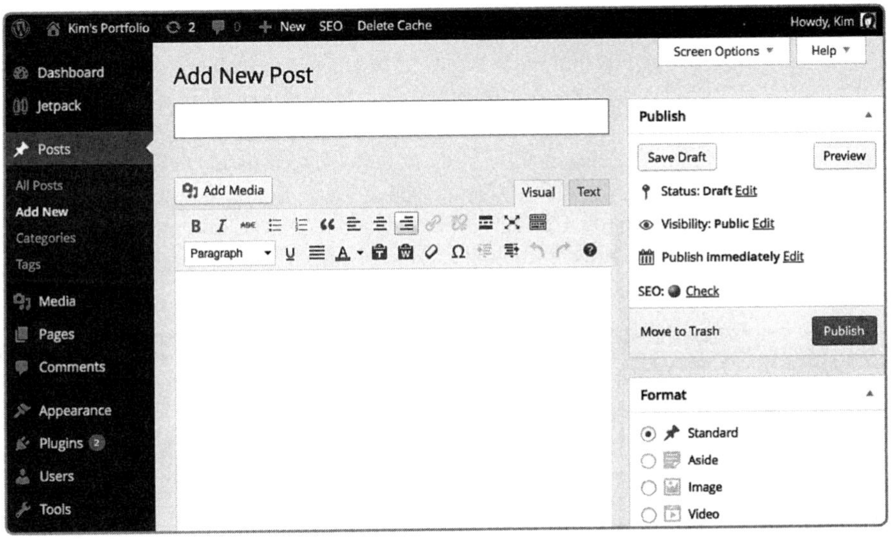
Kim's Portfolio
New
SEO
Delete Cache
Howdy, Kim
Screen Options
Help
Dashboard
Jetpack
Posts
All Posts
Add New
Categories
Tags
Media
Pages
Comments
Appearance
Plugins
Users
Tools
Add New Post
Add Media
Visual
Text
Paragraph
Publish
Save Draft
Preview
Status: Draft Edit
Visibility: Public Edit
Publish immediately Edit
SEO: Check
Move to Trash
Publish
Format
Standard
Aside
Image
Video

Figure 4-39: The visual editor for posts is nearly identical to the editor for pages. All of the same content—pictures, links, and formatted text—can go into the content box.

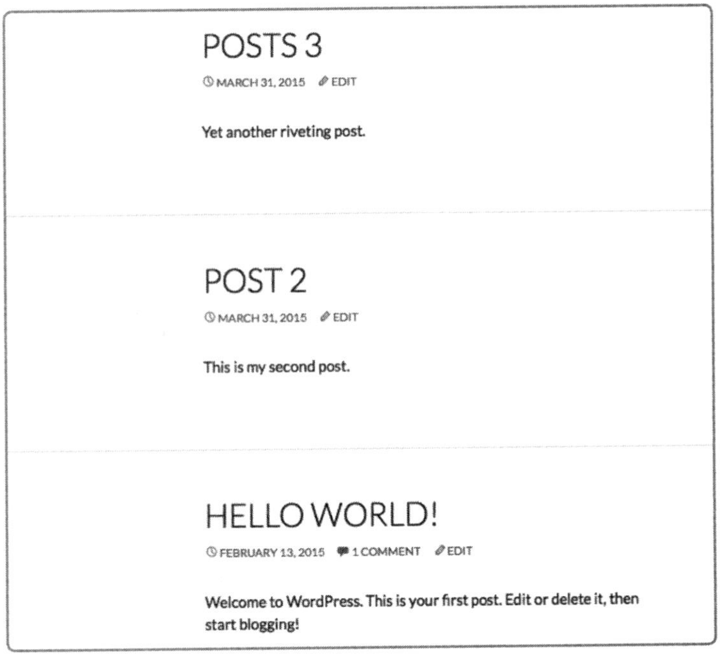
POSTS 3
MARCH 31, 2015
EDIT
Yet another riveting post.
POST 2
MARCH 31, 2015
EDIT
This is my second post.
HELLO WORLD!
FEBRUARY 13, 2015
1 COMMENT
EDIT
Welcome to WordPress. This is your first post. Edit or delete it, then start blogging!

Figure 4-40: The posts page is where blog posts get aggregated. Unlike with pages, which stand alone, each post goes into the single posts page and is organized by date, with the newest posts on top.

Getting Organized: Post Categories and Tags

Another tool for organizing your blog posts is using tags and categories. Go back to your Dashboard and click **Posts** to bring up all of your existing posts, as shown in Figure 4-41. You should see a list of all of your existing posts.

As an example, let's say we're going to be writing book reviews on our blog. We'll want to group these particular blog posts together so that any readers on our site can easily pull them up. Click **Add New** to create a new post. Give the blog post the title **The Great Gatsby**. In the lower-right corner of your window, you should see the Categories and Tags sections.

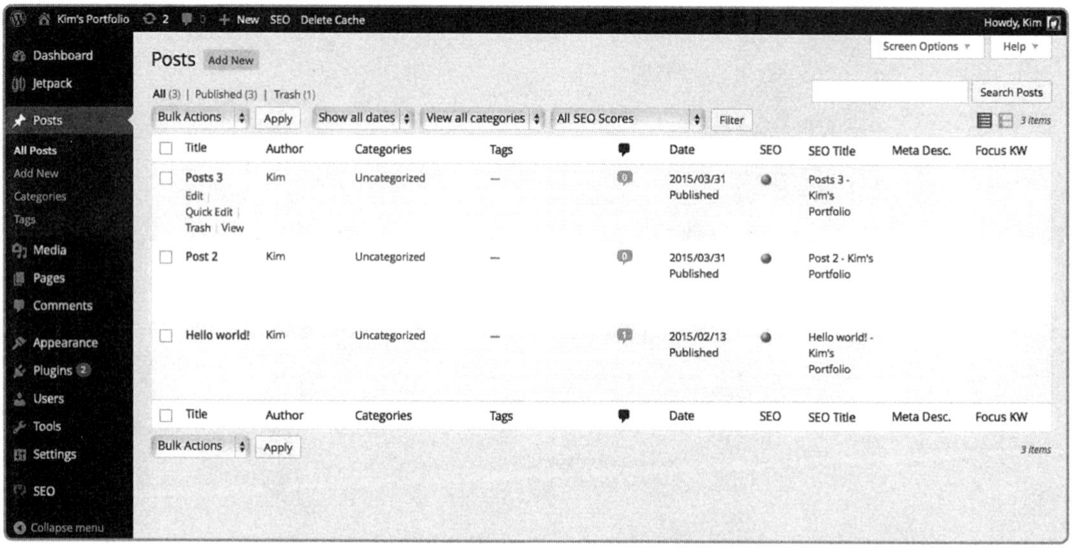

Figure 4-41: The Posts tab displays all of the posts within your blog, whether they're drafts or published.

These are qualifiers you create to group your posts together, which will make it easier for people visiting your website to find posts on the same subject. *Categories* are broad groupings, and *tags* are more specific. For this Gatsby post, we might create a category called *Book Reviews* in case we are planning to write more reviews in the future. We don't currently have a Book Reviews category, so we'll have to make one. Click the **Add New Category** link. Enter **Book Reviews** and click the **Add New Category** button. Now your category will show up in the list, and you can select it for your post (see Figure 4-42).

For tags, we can be more specific. In the Tags field, type **Fitzgerald, bootlegging, Jazz Age** (including the commas) and then click the **Add** button (shown in Figure 4-43).

A post can live in more than one category and tag, but generally speaking posts usually have more tags than categories, since categories are broad subjects and tags are narrower. This isn't a rule so much as a convention.

Type **Coming Soon** into the body of the post and then click **Publish**. A shortcut to the post should appear at the top of the screen, as shown in Figure 4-44. Click **View Post** to be taken to the post on the frontend.

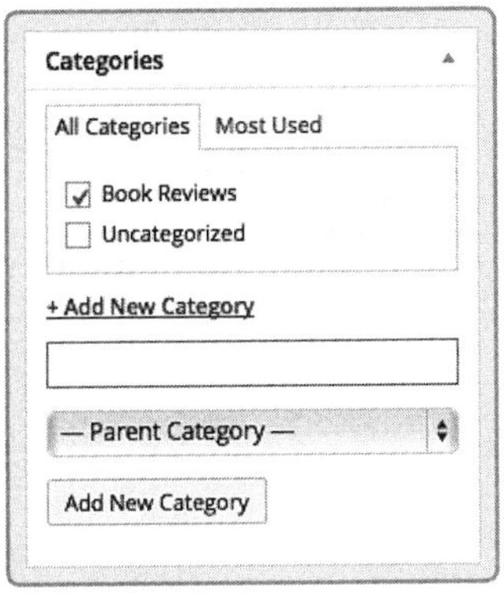

Figure 4-42: Creating categories is as simple as typing a category name and clicking the Add New Category button. All posts will have at least one category attached to them. Once a category has been created, it will be available for any new posts added to the blog.

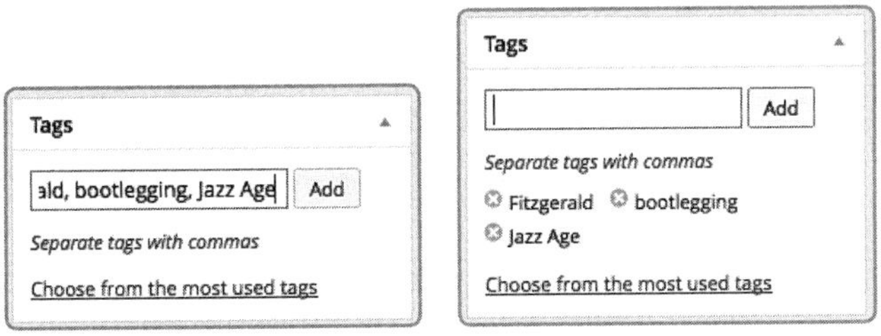

Figure 4-43: Tags are a way to get more specific about what's in a post. Once you add tags to a post, they'll show up in WordPress when you're writing a new post so you can use them again.

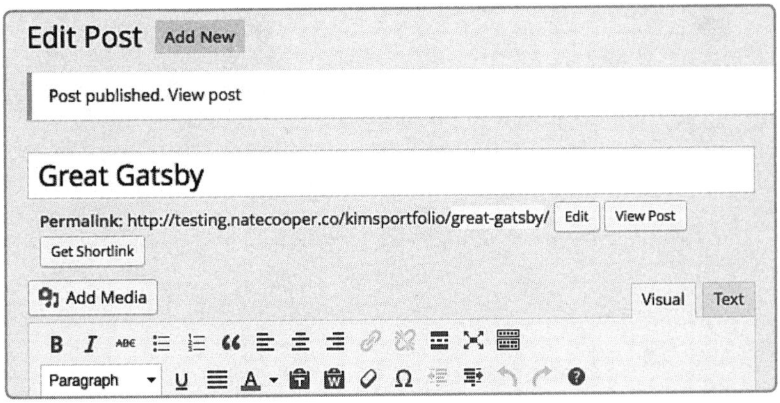

Figure 4-44: After a post has been published, a link to View Post appears at the top of the page.

WordPress automatically creates links out of your categories and tags and displays them under each post, as shown in Figure 4-45. These are clickable links, which allow readers to easily find any posts that might be on the same subject.

The more consistently you tag or categorize your posts, the more useful these conventions will be on your site. It may not seem that important when you are starting out, but once you have many posts in your blog, your readers will value having a way to access related content at the click of a mouse.

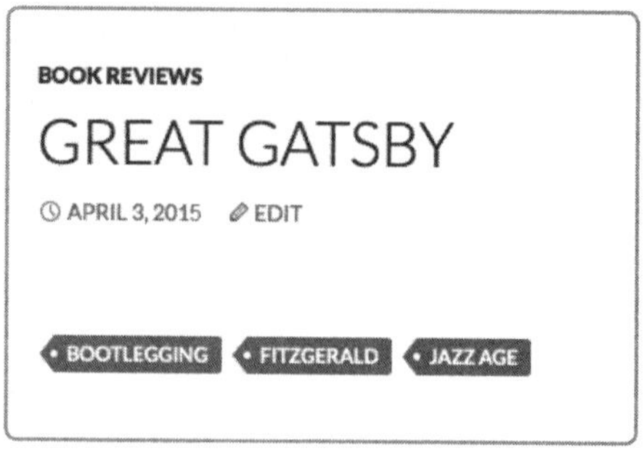

BOOK REVIEWS
GREAT GATSBY
APRIL 3, 2015
EDIT
BOOTLEGGING
FITZGERALD
JAZZ AGE

Figure 4-45: In the Twenty Fourteen theme, categories appear at the top, while tags appear at the bottom. Both will be links in WordPress.

Featured Images

Some themes use a *featured image* to display for each blog post (see Figure 4-46). A featured image is often a panorama-style image that lives at the top of the page or post, as in Figure 4-47, or a thumbnail image that lives next to the post. This can make your blog look quite appealing. Since we've enabled Twenty Fourteen, which supports featured images, you'll see another box below the tags, called Featured Image. To add a featured image, click the link and then select an image you'd like to be associated with the post. You won't have to choose the size because the theme will choose that for you.

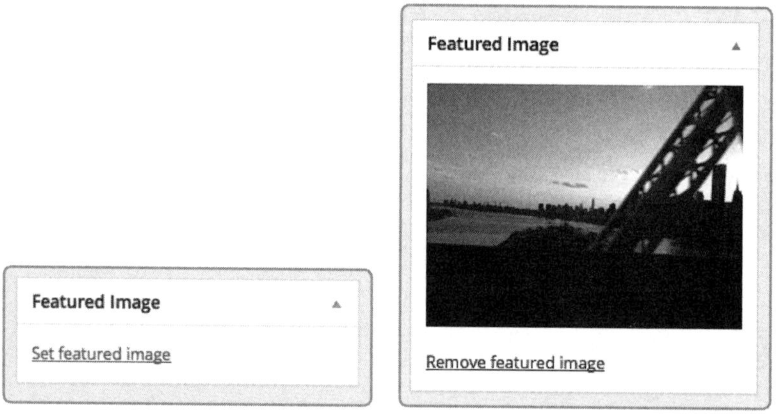

Featured Image
Set featured image
Featured Image
Remove featured image

Figure 4-46: Some themes support featured images on posts, which enhance your site's content.

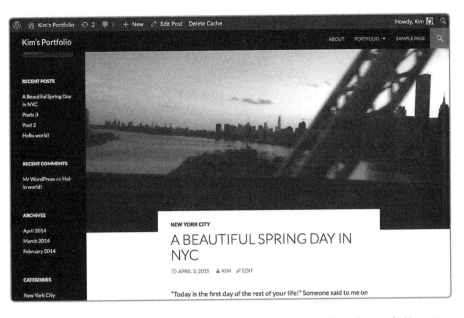

Figure 4-47: A featured image in the Twenty Fourteen theme. Many themes support featured images for blog posts.

Using Video, Photos, and Quotes with Post Formats

Another theme-specific feature, supported by the Twenty Fourteen theme is *post formats*. What does that mean? Particular kinds of media, like photos, videos, and quotes, might have their own unique look in some "magazine-style" themes. For example, if you have a post that is *just* a quote you can choose Quote as the format, and the theme will make the text larger so that the words stand out more. Conversely, a video post might be styled to focus on the video content. You'll see the Format box above the Categories box in your post editor (see Figure 4-48). Themes that support formats help you display your content in the style that best fits its type.

Each format looks a little different (see Figure 4-49).

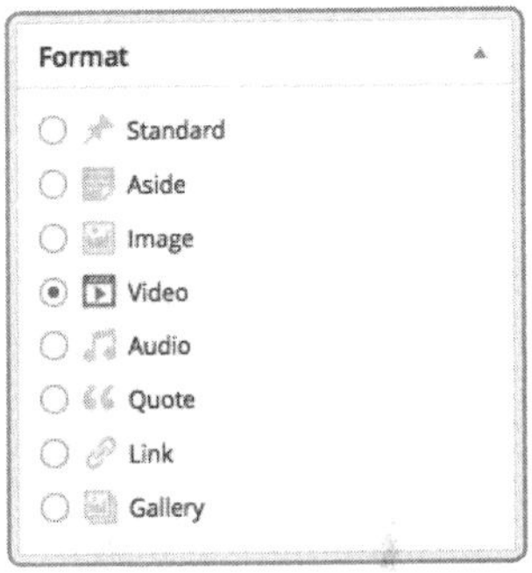

Format	▲
○ ✈ Standard	
○ ▦ Aside	
○ ▦ Image	
◉ ▶ Video	
○ ♫ Audio	
○ ❝❝ Quote	
○ ⟋ Link	
○ ▦ Gallery	

Figure 4-48: Setting a format in the Dashboard allows post content to stand out on your blog.

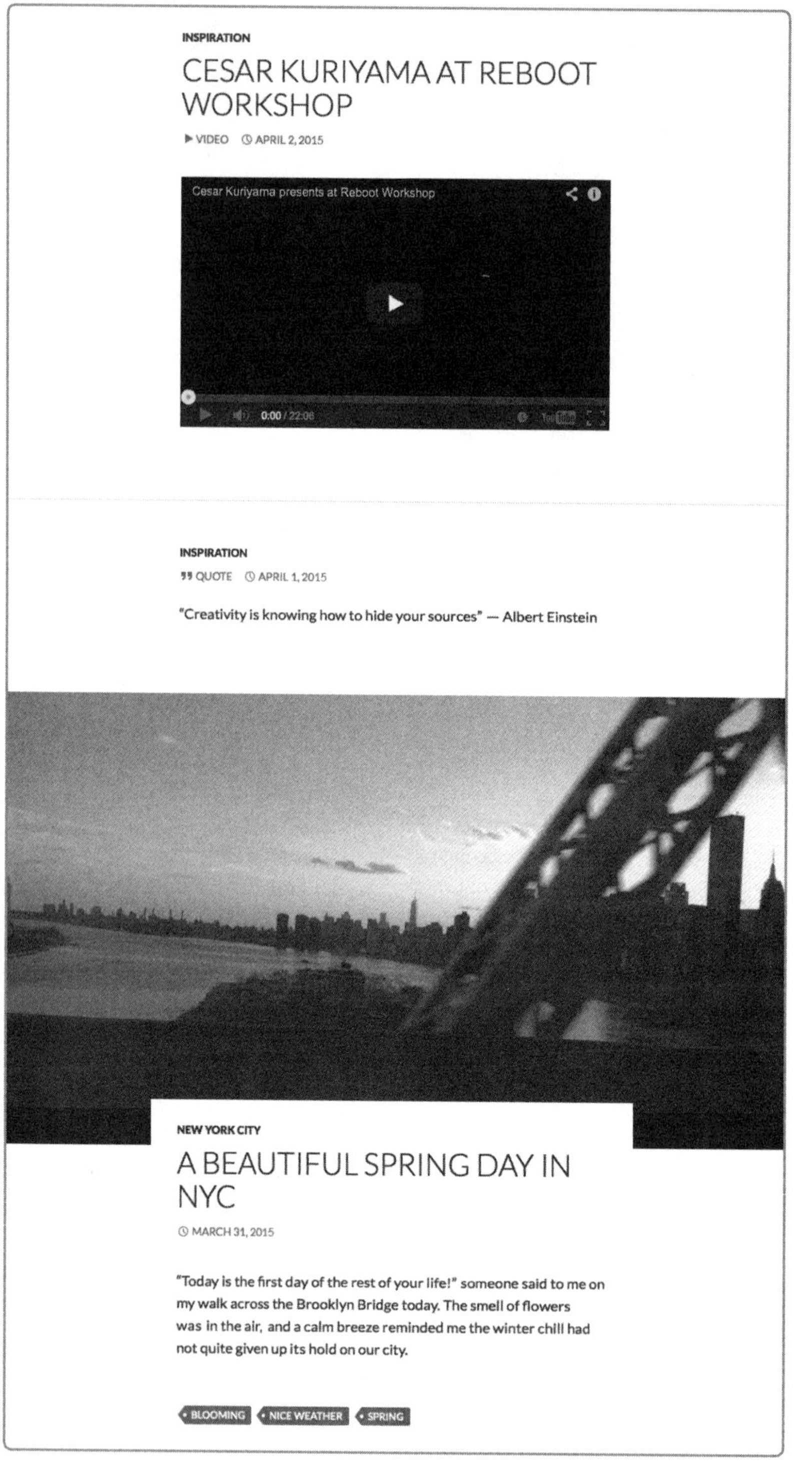
INSPIRATION
CESAR KURIYAMA AT REBOOT WORKSHOP
VIDEO
APRIL 2, 2015
Cesar Kuriyama presents at Reboot Workshop
0:00 / 22:06
INSPIRATION
QUOTE
APRIL 1, 2015
"Creativity is knowing how to hide your sources" — Albert Einstein
NEW YORK CITY
A BEAUTIFUL SPRING DAY IN NYC
MARCH 31, 2015
"Today is the first day of the rest of your life!" someone said to me on my walk across the Brooklyn Bridge today. The smell of flowers was in the air, and a calm breeze reminded me the winter chill had not quite given up its hold on our city.
BLOOMING
NICE WEATHER
SPRING

Figure 4-49: From top to bottom: a video post, a quote post, and an unformatted post in the Twenty Fourteen theme

Managing and Deleting Content

If you've been worried about all these blank pages we've been creating, don't fret. WordPress gives you the ability to update or delete pages on the fly in the Dashboard. It also has some nice options for managing other content, including photos and posts. Go to the Dashboard and click **Posts**. You should see the list of all your posts in your blog, as shown in Figure 4-50.

Kim's Portfolio
New
Delete Cache
Howdy, Kim
Screen Options
Help
Dashboard
Jetpack
Posts
Add New
All (4) | Published (4) | Trash (1)
Search Posts
Bulk Actions
Apply
Show all dates
View all categories
Filter
4 items
All Posts
Add New
Categories
Tags
Title
Author
Categories
Tags
Date
Great Gatsby
Edit | Quick Edit | Trash | View
Kim
Book Reviews
bootlegging, Fitzgerald, Jazz Age
4 mins ago
Published
Posts 3
Kim
Uncategorized
2015/03/31
Published
Post 2
Kim
Uncategorized
2015/03/31
Published
Hello world!
Kim
Uncategorized
2015/02/13
Published
Media
Pages
Comments
Appearance
Plugins
Users
Tools
Settings
Collapse menu
Thank you for creating with WordPress.
Version 3.8.1

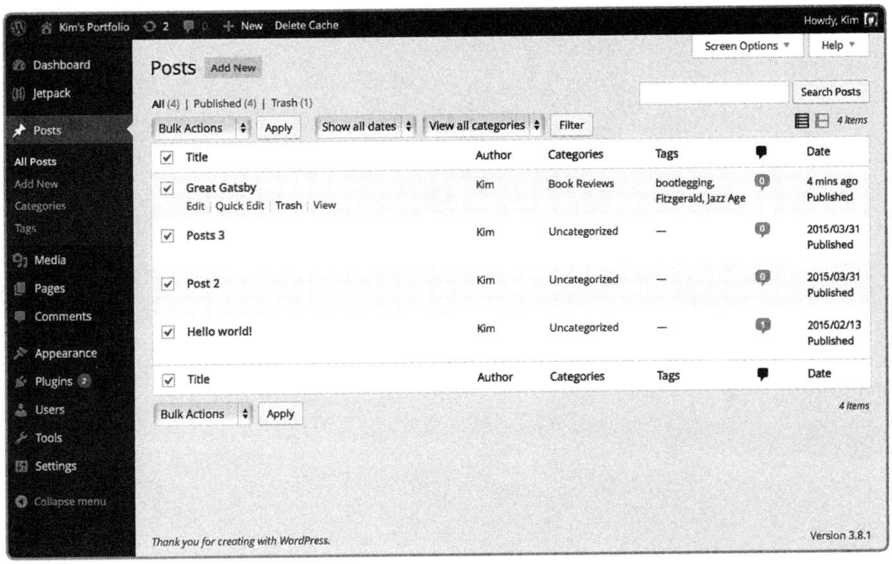

Figure 4-50: The All Posts section on the Posts tab displays each post that's been created within the WordPress blog. Checking the box to the left of the post name allows for bulk changes.

The little menus at the top of the page give you some options for managing or finding posts. You'll see the Bulk Action drop-down menu in each list in WordPress. It allows you to edit or delete your pages and media; just check the boxes next to the items you want to change and choose what you'd like to do with them from the drop-down menu. If you wanted to delete all of the sample pages we've created in order to start working on your own site, you'd just highlight all of the pages and select Move to Trash, as shown in Figure 4-51. As with the trash on your computer, you'll need to empty it. Click **Trash** and then **Empty Trash** to completely erase the pages we've created.

All (4) | Published (4) | Trash (1)
✓ Bulk Actions
Edit
Move to Trash
Apply
Great Gatsby

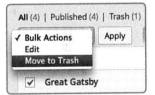

Figure 4-51: After checking the box to the left of each post you'd like to change, you can click the Bulk Actions drop-down menu to either edit all of the checked posts or delete them.

You can also, of course, delete a page or post by editing it individually. Use the **Move to Trash** link while in the visual editor to delete an individual post or page.

In this chapter we've learned how to organize and manage our content, including pages, posts, and media. But we haven't seen how to change fonts, colors, structure, or functions in WordPress. Let's see where Kim goes next in her adventure!

5

Customizing WordPress

BIG & TALL themes
HUGE SAL
THEM R US

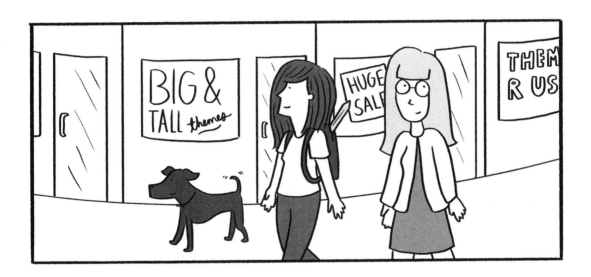

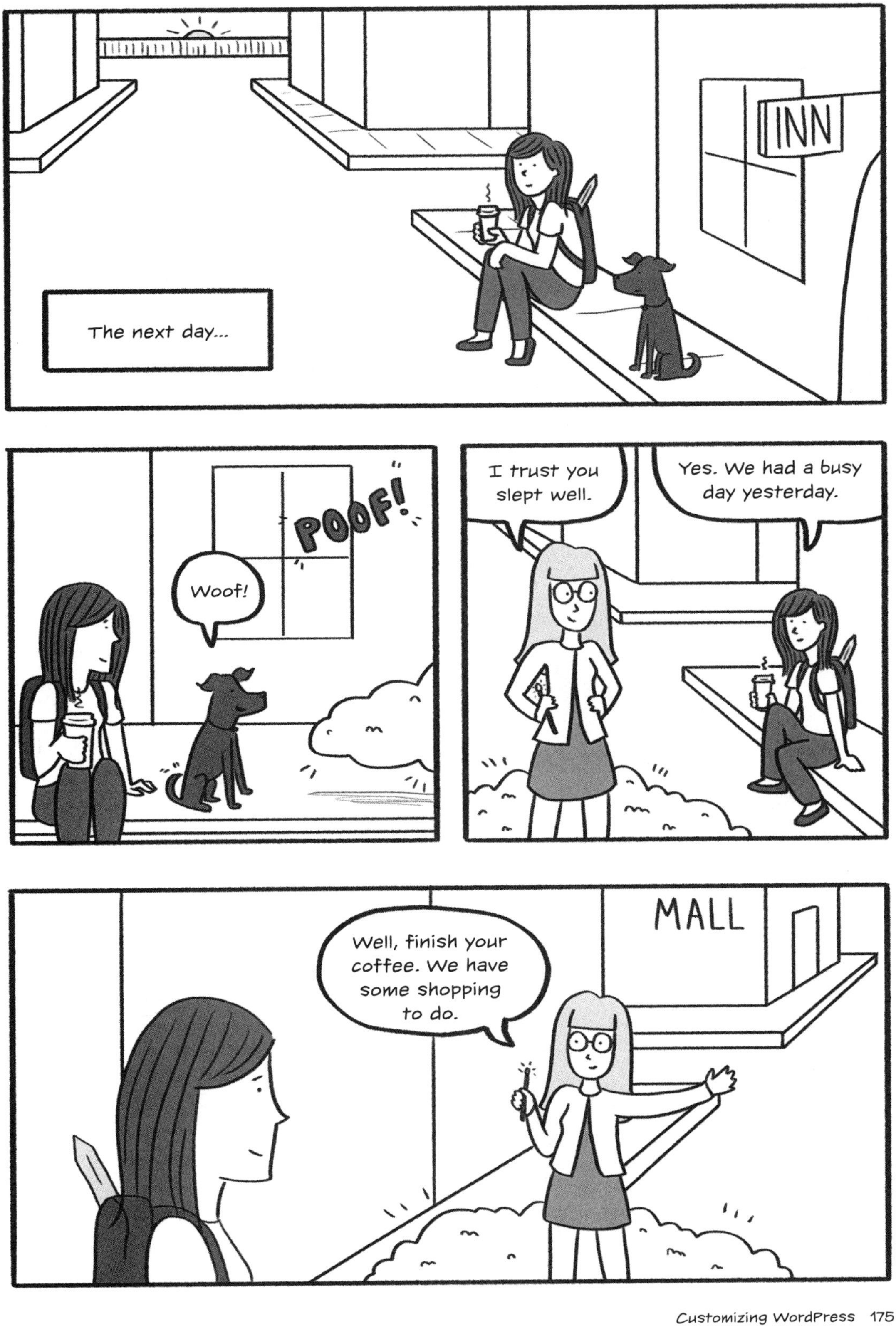
The next day...
INN
Woof!
POOF!
I trust you slept well.
Yes. We had a busy day yesterday.
MALL
Well, finish your coffee. We have some shopping to do.

The Appearance Panel

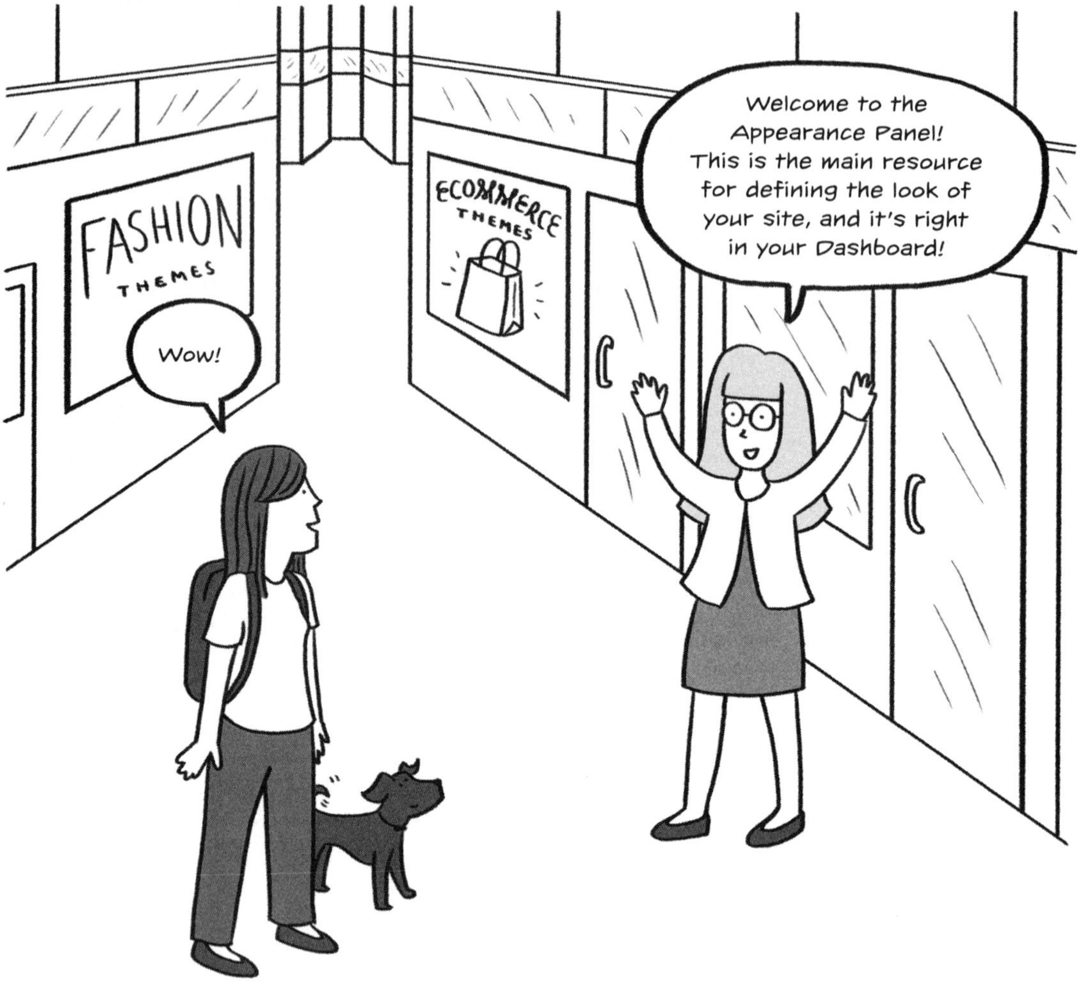
FASHION
THEMES
ECOMMERCE
THEMES
Wow!
Welcome to the Appearance Panel! This is the main resource for defining the look of your site, and it's right in your Dashboard!

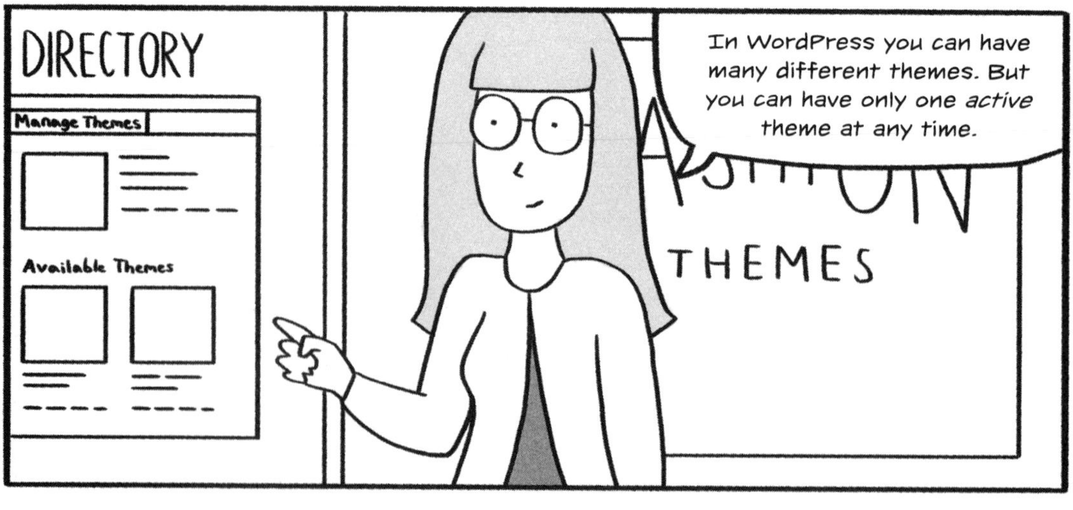
DIRECTORY
Manage Themes
Available Themes
THEMES
In WordPress you can have many different themes. But you can have only one *active* theme at any time.

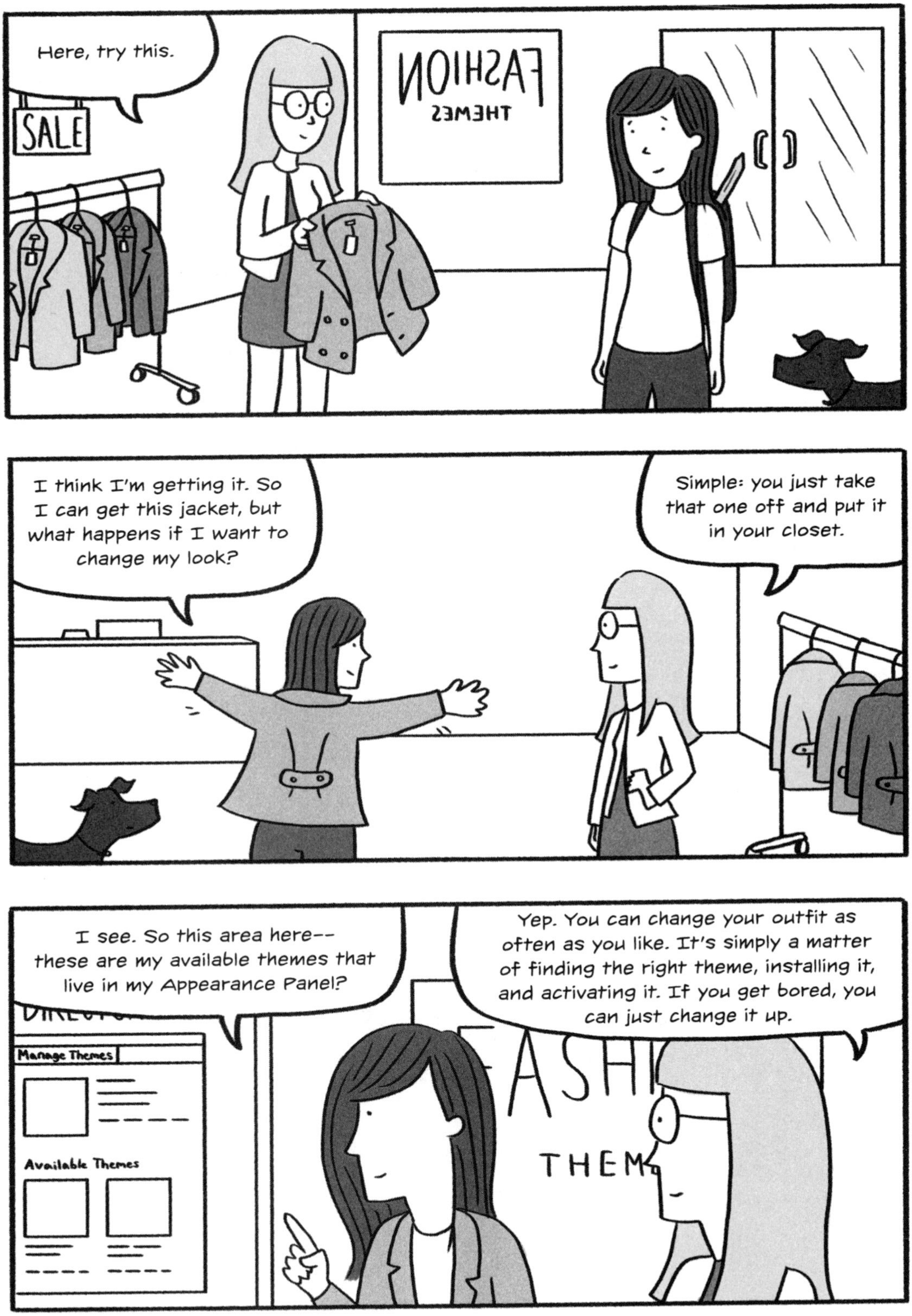
Here, try this.
SALE
FASHION
THEMES
I think I'm getting it. So I can get this jacket, but what happens if I want to change my look?
Simple: you just take that one off and put it in your closet.
I see. So this area here--these are my available themes that live in my Appearance Panel?
Yep. You can change your outfit as often as you like. It's simply a matter of finding the right theme, installing it, and activating it. If you get bored, you can just change it up.
Manage Themes
Available Themes
THEM

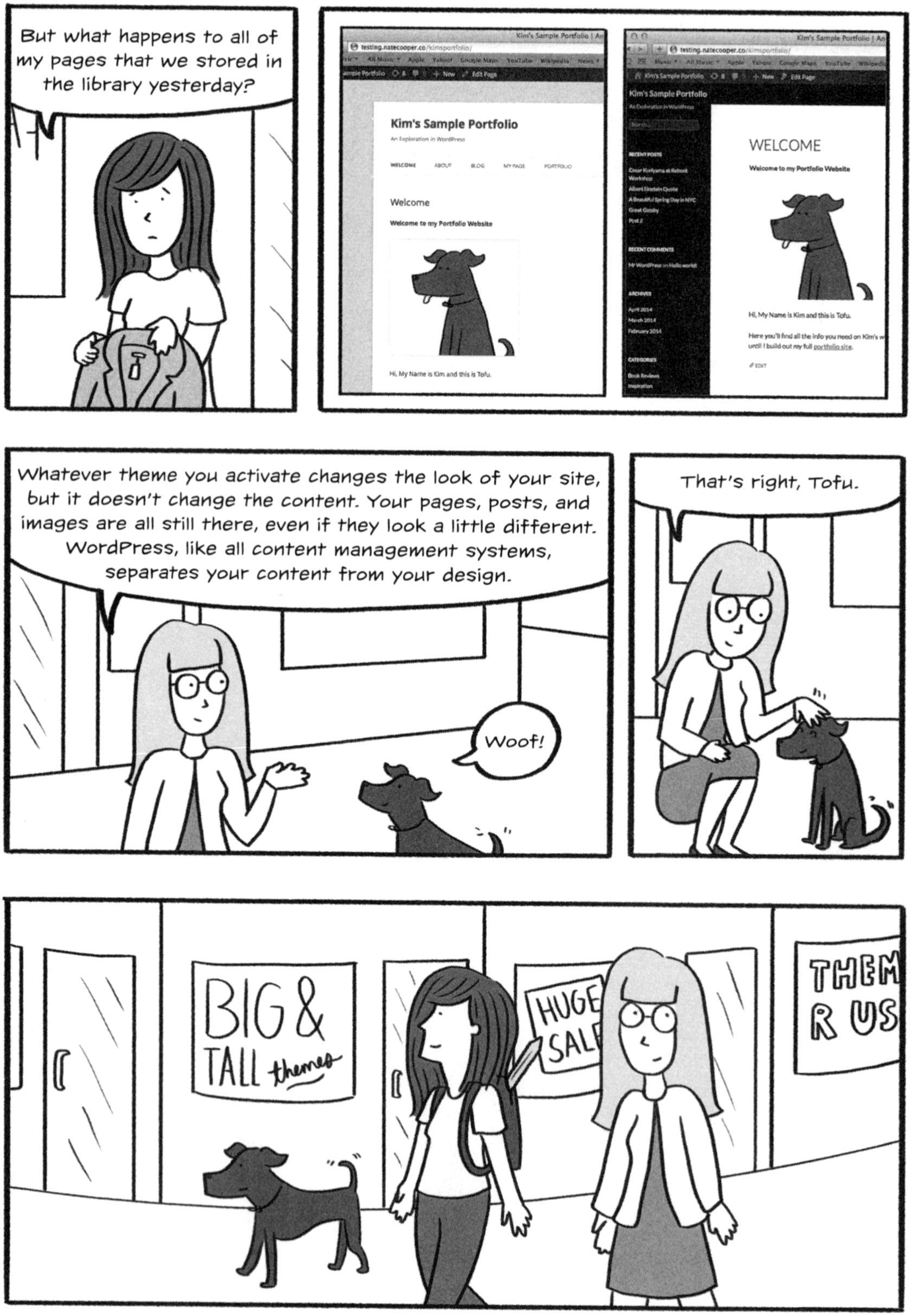
But what happens to all of my pages that we stored in the library yesterday?
Kim's Sample Portfolio
An Exploration in WordPress
Welcome
Welcome to my Portfolio Website
Hi, My Name is Kim and this is Tofu.
Kim's Sample Portfolio
WELCOME
Welcome to my Portfolio Website
Hi, My Name is Kim and this is Tofu.
Whatever theme you activate changes the look of your site, but it doesn't change the content. Your pages, posts, and images are all still there, even if they look a little different. WordPress, like all content management systems, separates your content from your design.
Woof!
That's right, Tofu.
BIG & TALL themes
HUGE SAL
THEM R US

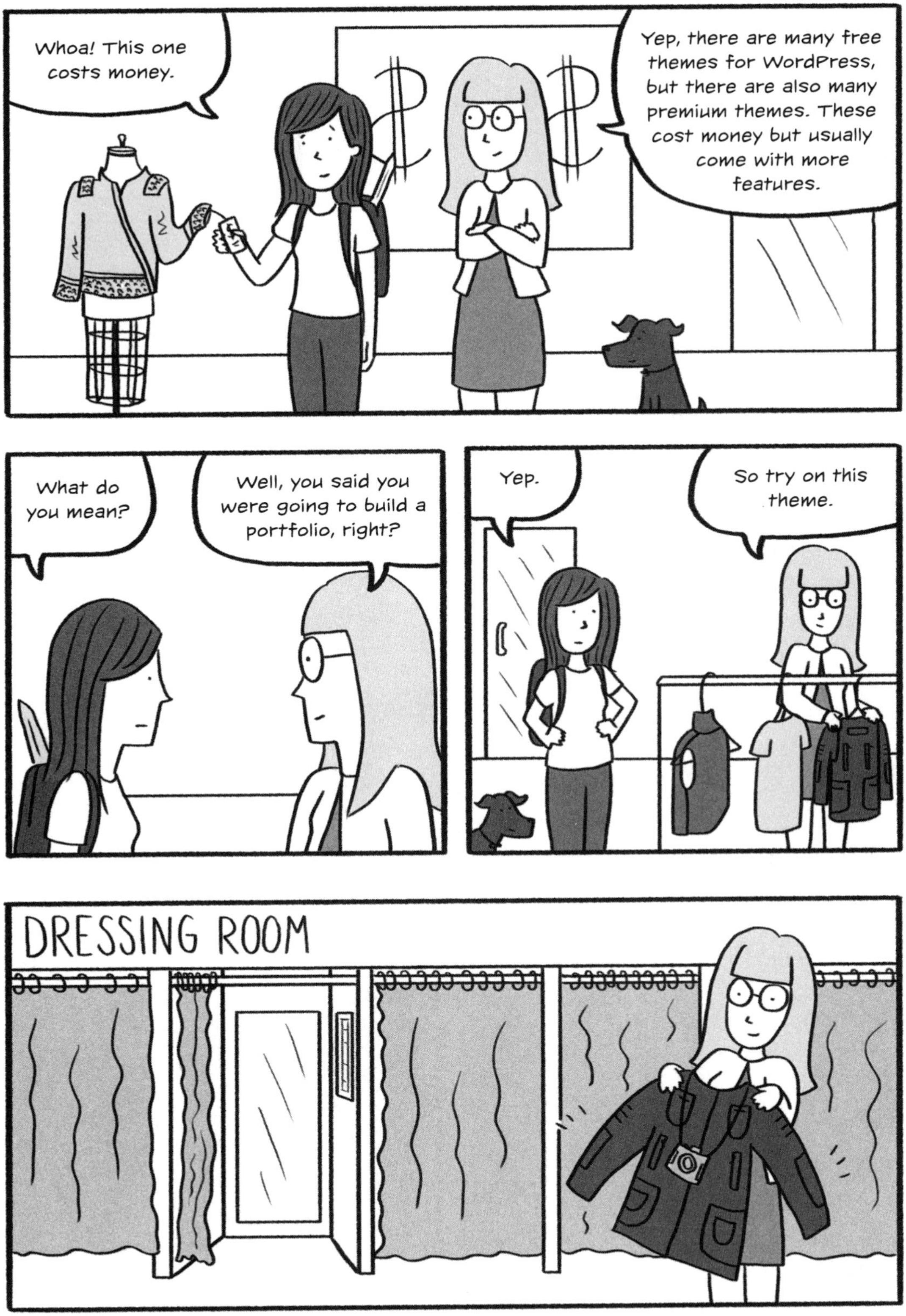
Whoa! This one costs money.
Yep, there are many free themes for WordPress, but there are also many premium themes. These cost money but usually come with more features.
What do you mean?
Well, you said you were going to build a portfolio, right?
Yep.
So try on this theme.
DRESSING ROOM

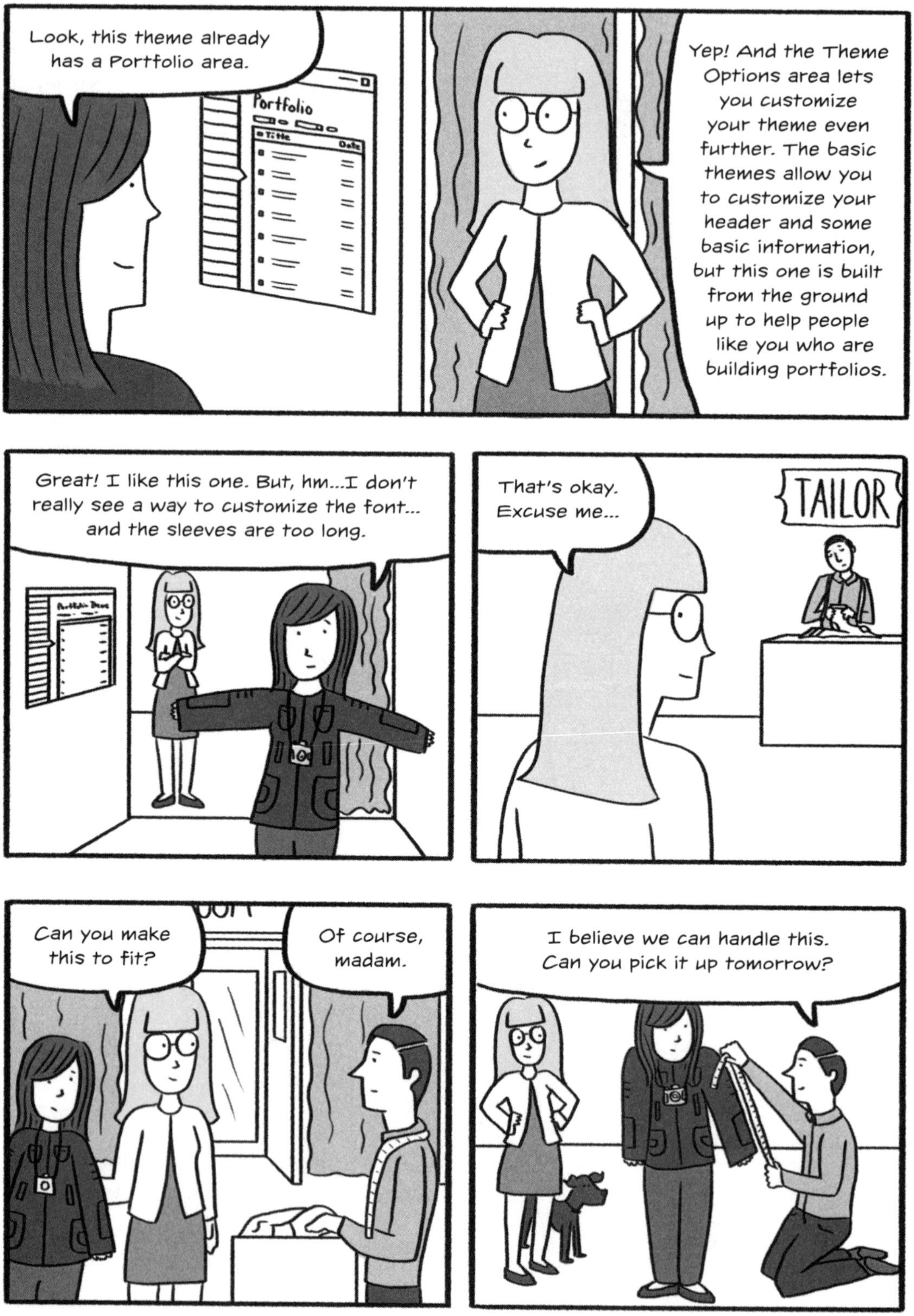
Look, this theme already has a Portfolio area.
Portfolio
Title
Date
Yep! And the Theme Options area lets you customize your theme even further. The basic themes allow you to customize your header and some basic information, but this one is built from the ground up to help people like you who are building portfolios.
Great! I like this one. But, hm...I don't really see a way to customize the font... and the sleeves are too long.
That's okay. Excuse me...
TAILOR
Can you make this to fit?
Of course, madam.
I believe we can handle this. Can you pick it up tomorrow?

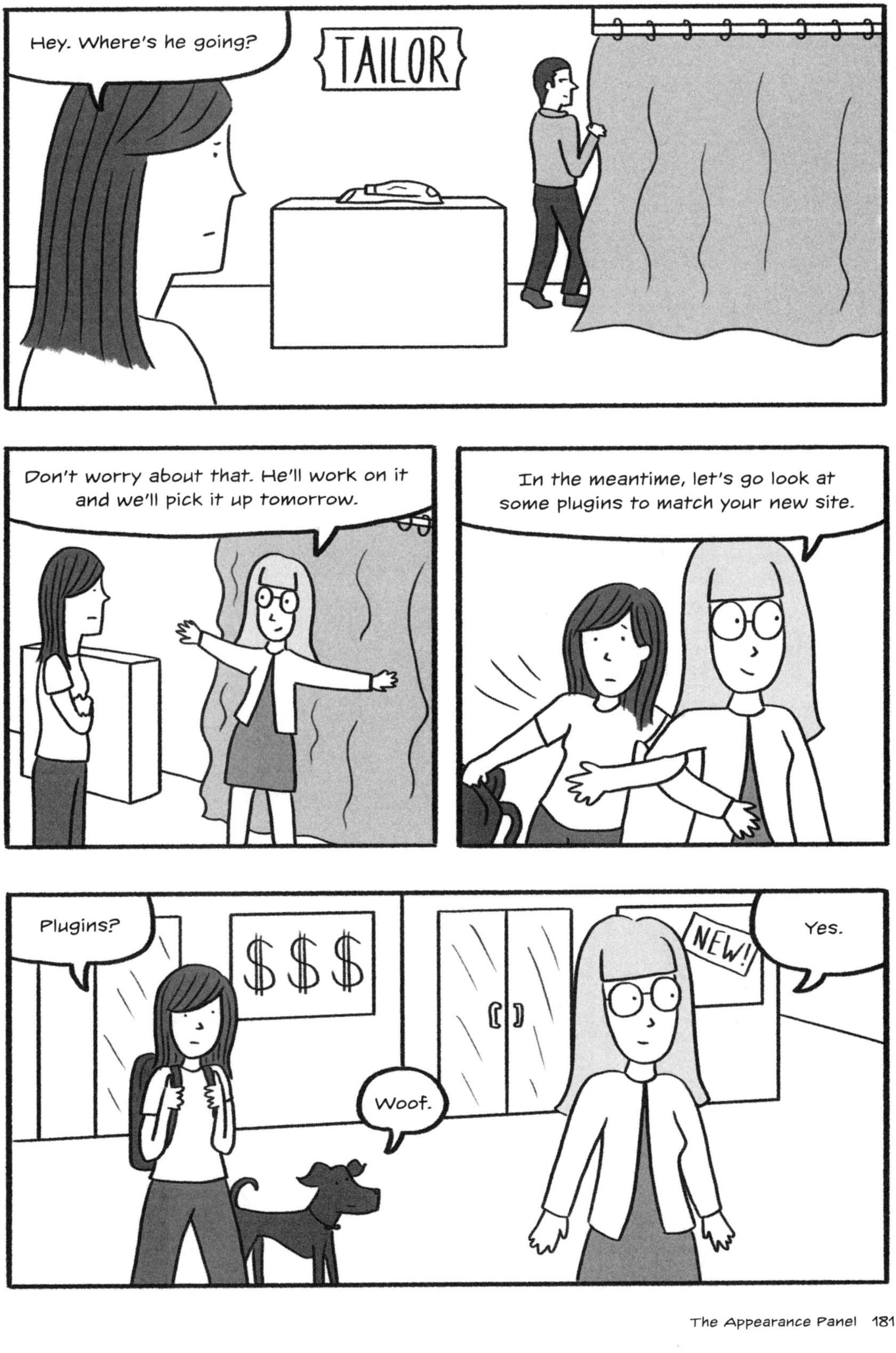
Hey. Where's he going?
TAILOR
Don't worry about that. He'll work on it and we'll pick it up tomorrow.
In the meantime, let's go look at some plugins to match your new site.
Plugins?
$$$
NEW!
Yes.
Woof.

Kim Superpowers Her Site with Plugins

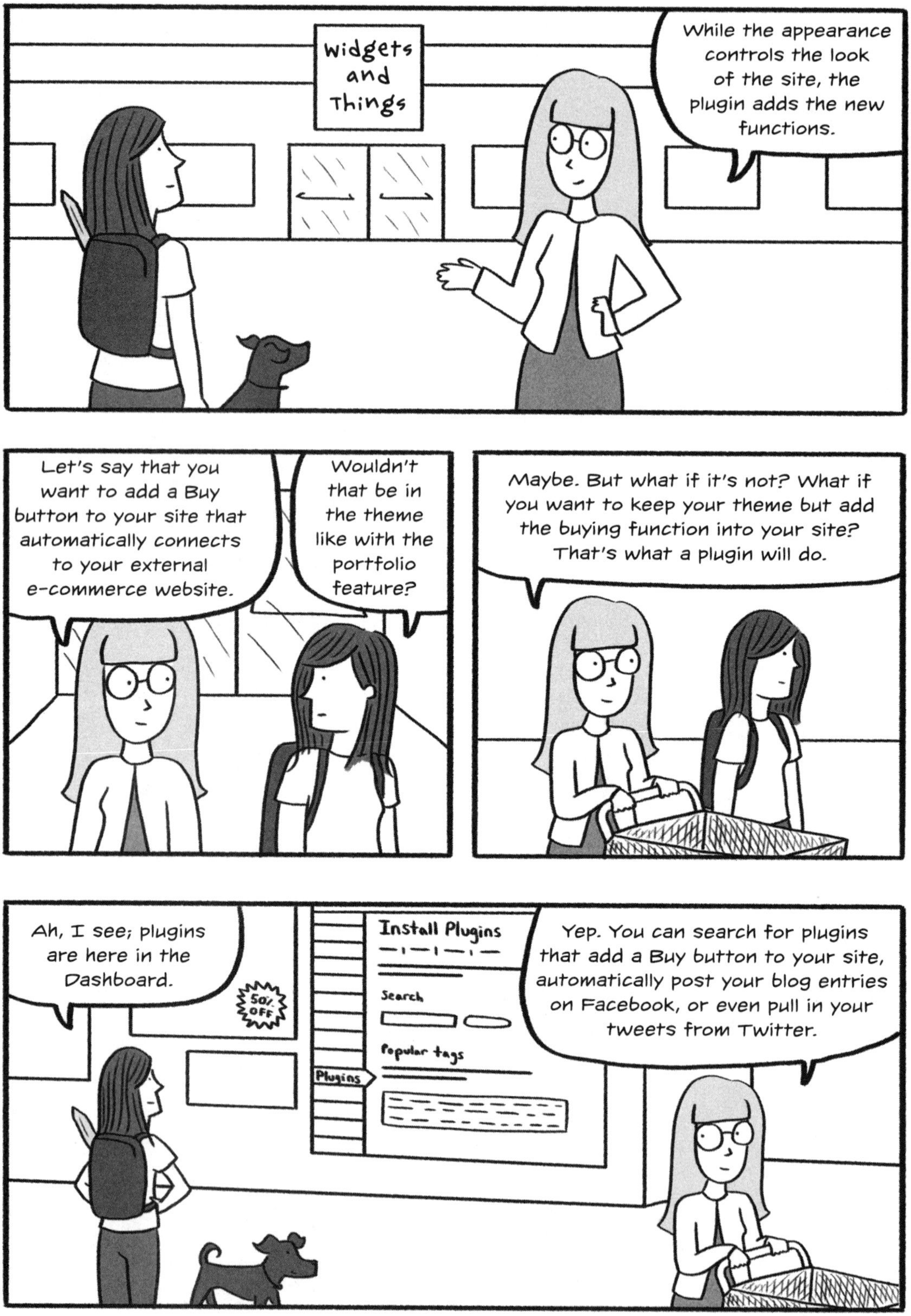
Widgets and Things
While the appearance controls the look of the site, the plugin adds the new functions.
Let's say that you want to add a Buy button to your site that automatically connects to your external e-commerce website.
Wouldn't that be in the theme like with the portfolio feature?
Maybe. But what if it's not? What if you want to keep your theme but add the buying function into your site? That's what a plugin will do.
Ah, I see; plugins are here in the Dashboard.
50% OFF
Install Plugins
Search
Popular tags
Plugins
Yep. You can search for plugins that add a Buy button to your site, automatically post your blog entries on Facebook, or even pull in your tweets from Twitter.

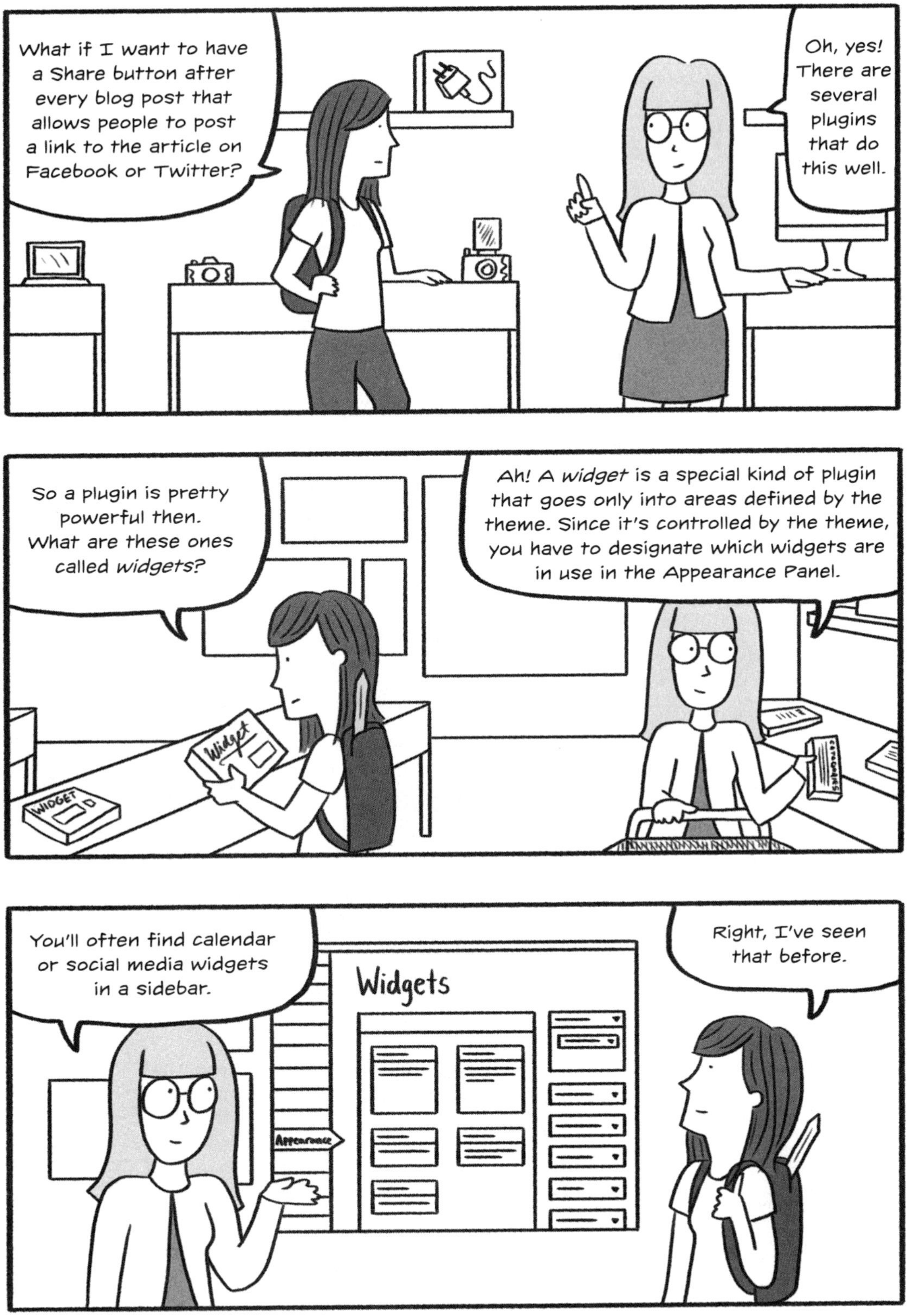
What if I want to have a Share button after every blog post that allows people to post a link to the article on Facebook or Twitter?
Oh, yes! There are several plugins that do this well.
So a plugin is pretty powerful then. What are these ones called *widgets*?
Ah! A *widget* is a special kind of plugin that goes only into areas defined by the theme. Since it's controlled by the theme, you have to designate which widgets are in use in the Appearance Panel.
WIDGET
Widget
CATEGORIES
You'll often find calendar or social media widgets in a sidebar.
Widgets
Appearance
Right, I've seen that before.

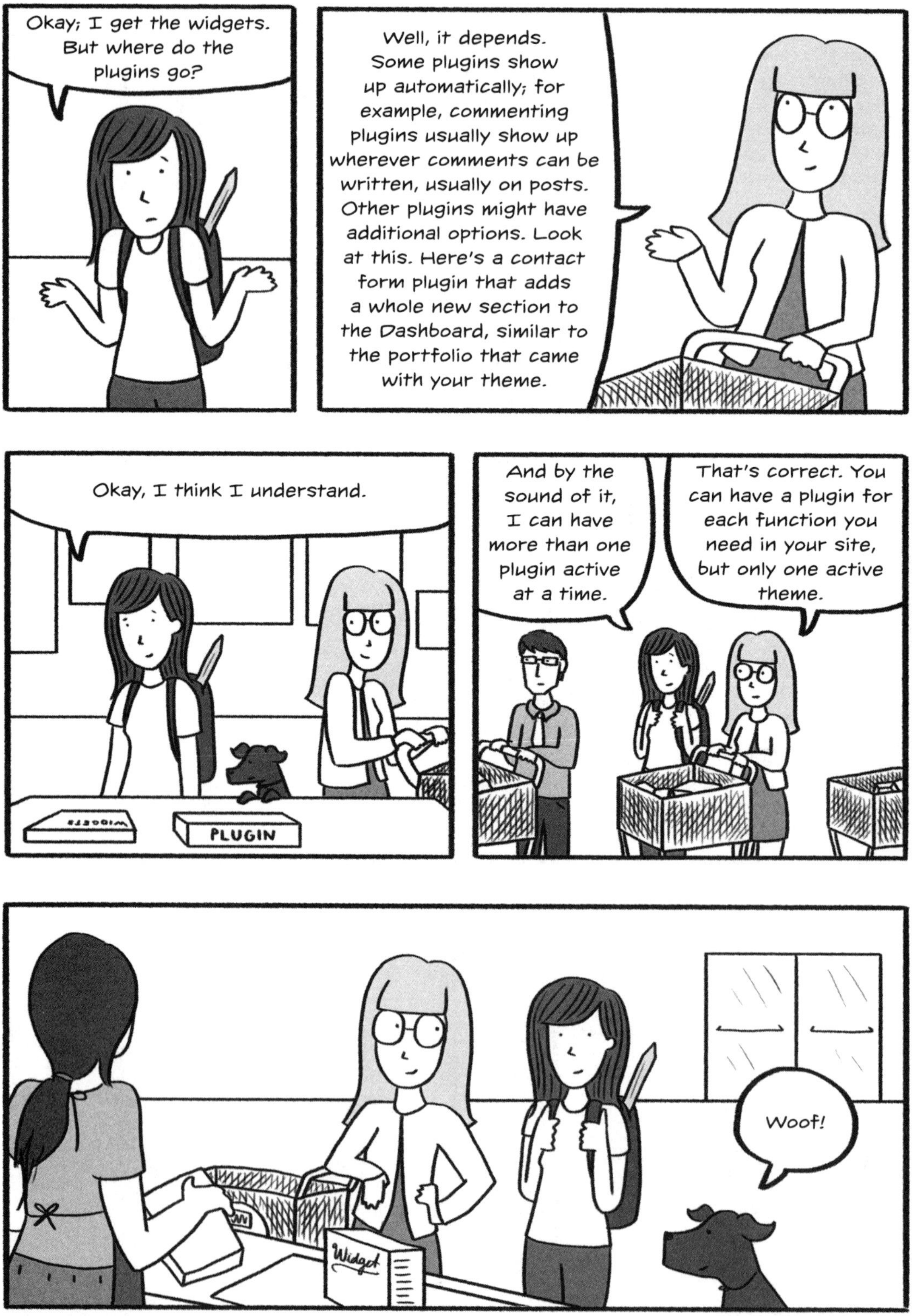

Okay; I get the widgets. But where do the plugins go?
Well, it depends. Some plugins show up automatically; for example, commenting plugins usually show up wherever comments can be written, usually on posts. Other plugins might have additional options. Look at this. Here's a contact form plugin that adds a whole new section to the Dashboard, similar to the portfolio that came with your theme.
Okay, I think I understand.
WIDGETS
PLUGIN
And by the sound of it, I can have more than one plugin active at a time.
That's correct. You can have a plugin for each function you need in your site, but only one active theme.
Widget
Woof!

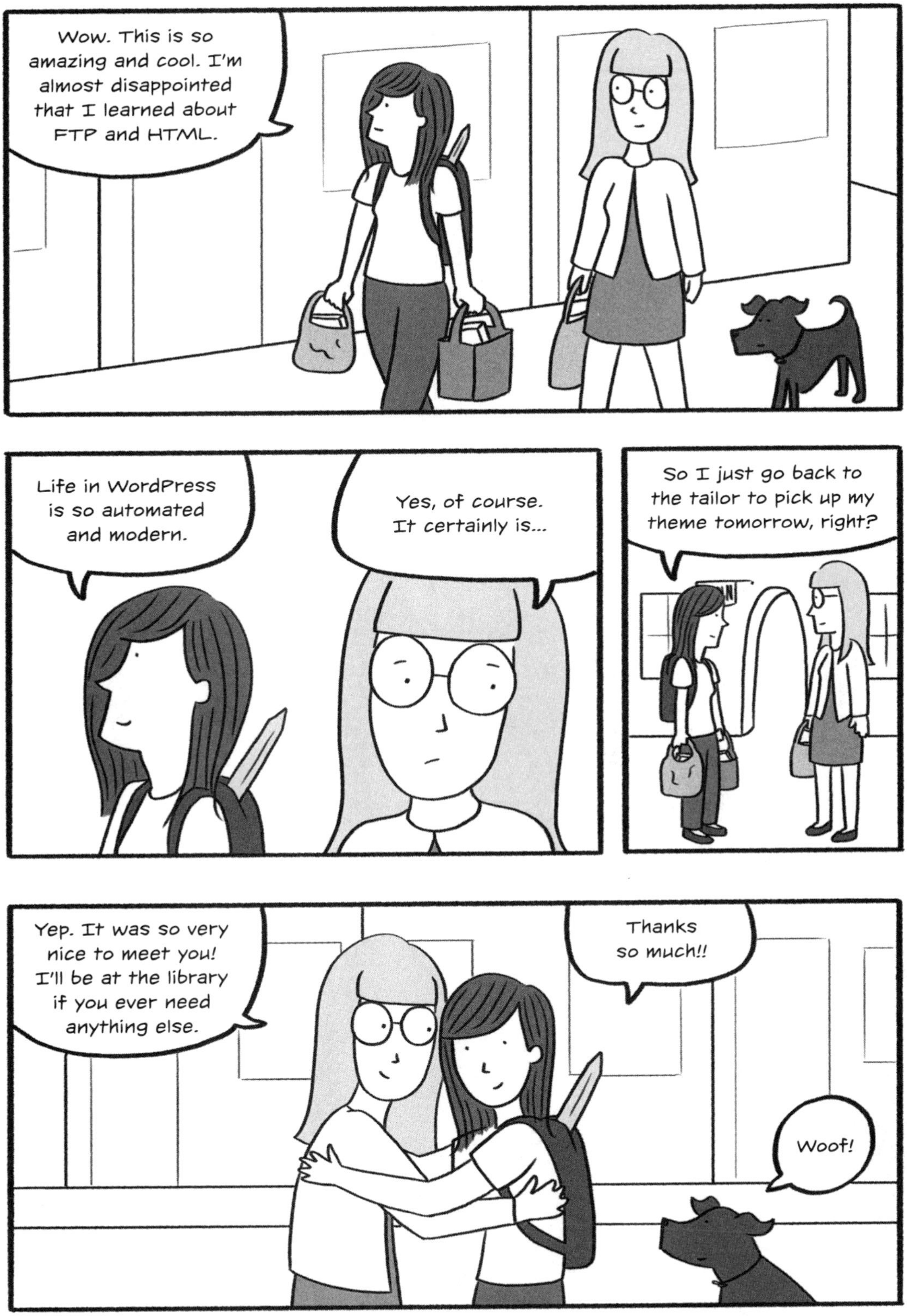
Wow. This is so amazing and cool. I'm almost disappointed that I learned about FTP and HTML.
Life in WordPress is so automated and modern.
Yes, of course. It certainly is...
So I just go back to the tailor to pick up my theme tomorrow, right?
Yep. It was so very nice to meet you! I'll be at the library if you ever need anything else.
Thanks so much!!
Woof!

Kim Goes Behind the Curtain

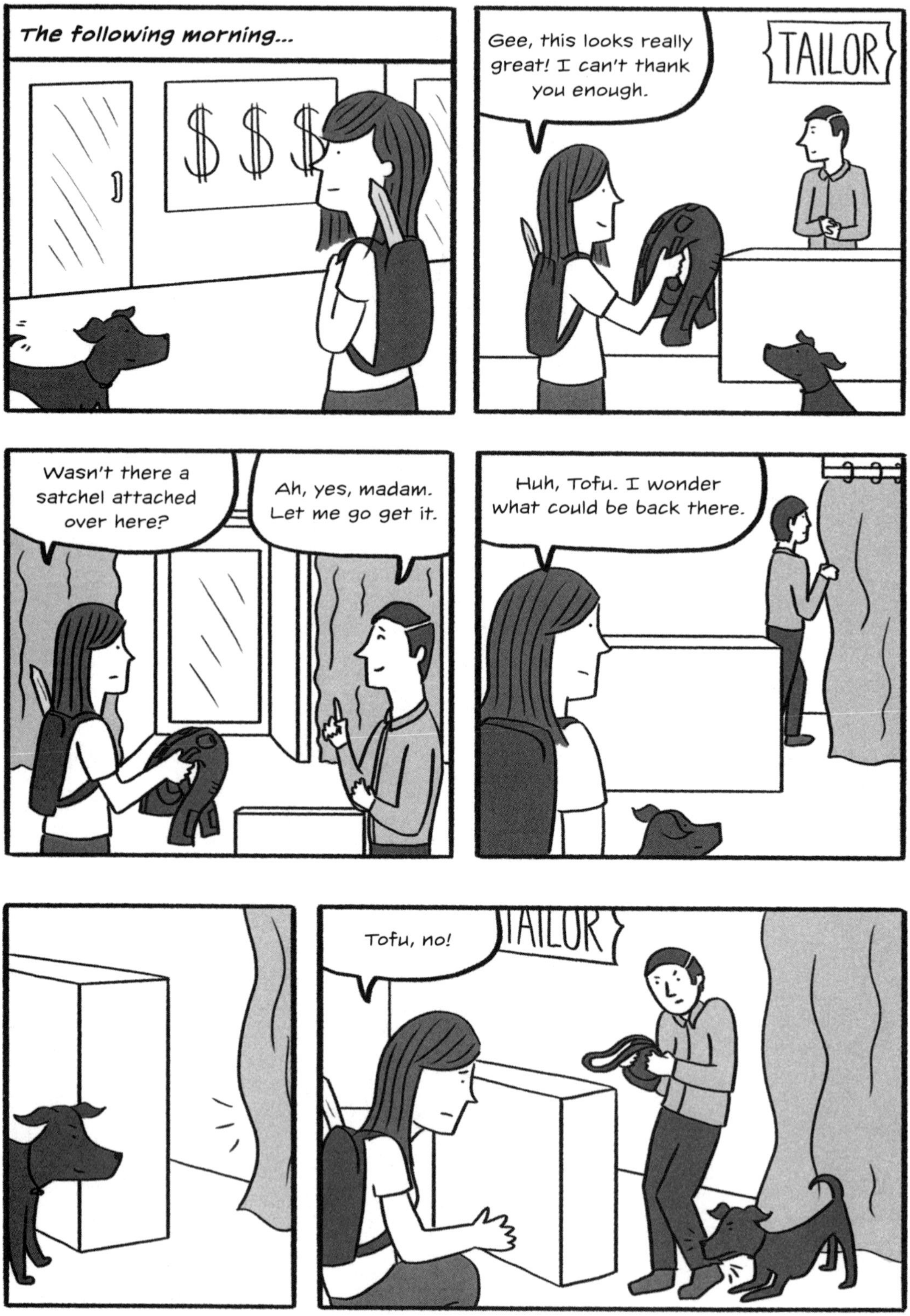
The following morning...
$$$
Gee, this looks really great! I can't thank you enough.
TAILOR
Wasn't there a satchel attached over here?
Ah, yes, madam. Let me go get it.
Huh, Tofu. I wonder what could be back there.
Tofu, no!
TAILOR

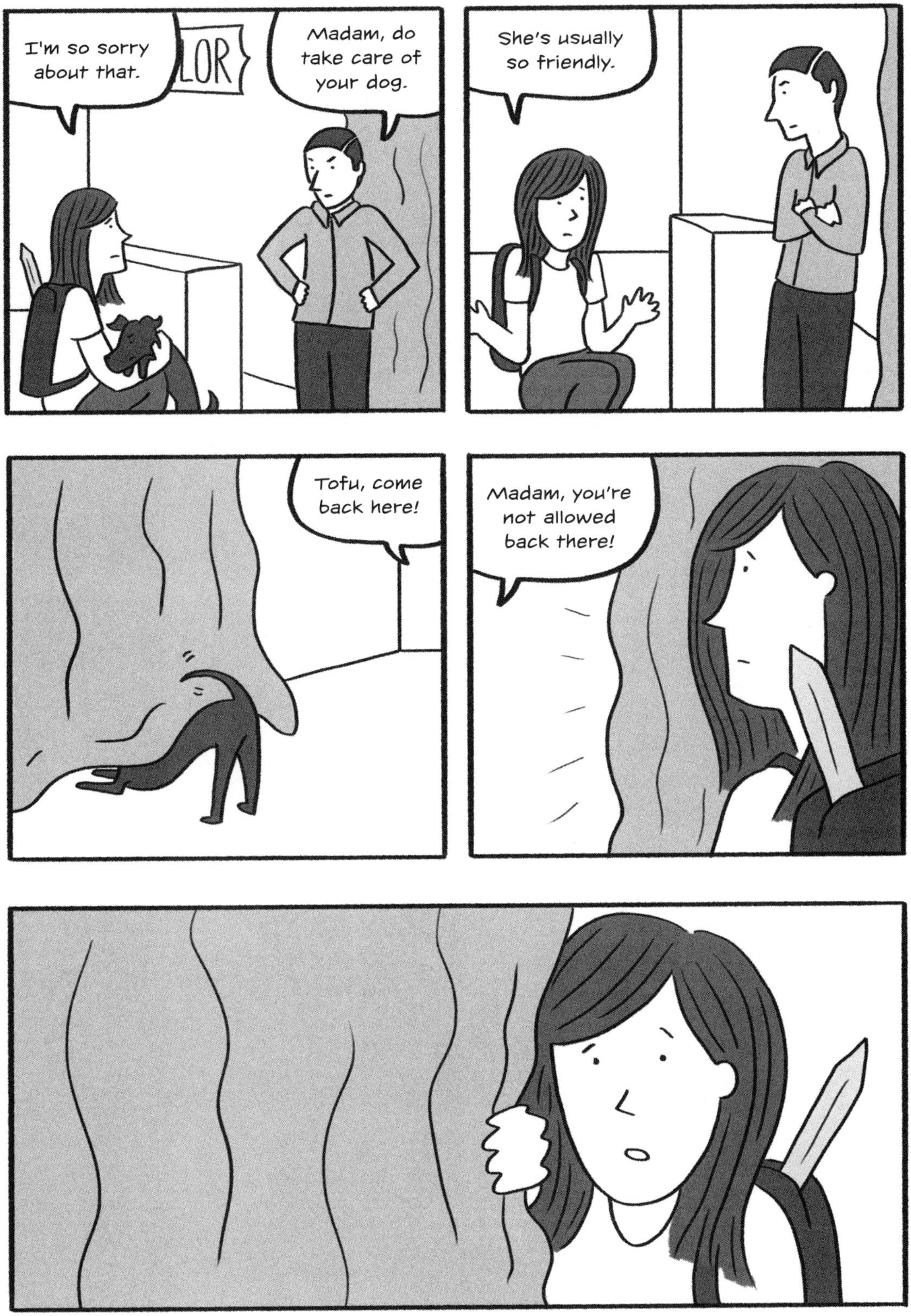
I'm so sorry about that.
LOR
Madam, do take care of your dog.
She's usually so friendly.
Tofu, come back here!
Madam, you're not allowed back there!

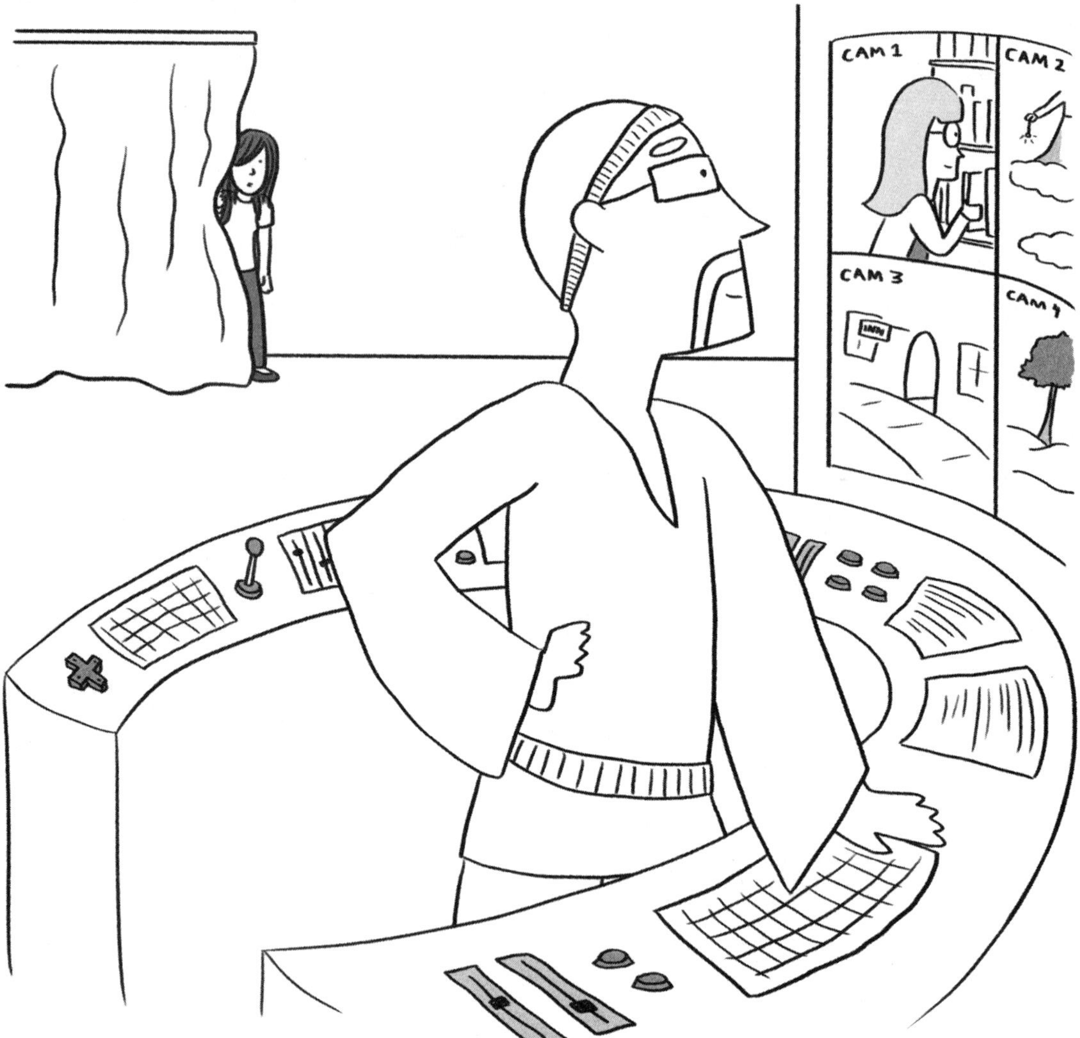
CAM 1
CAM 2
CAM 3
CAM 4

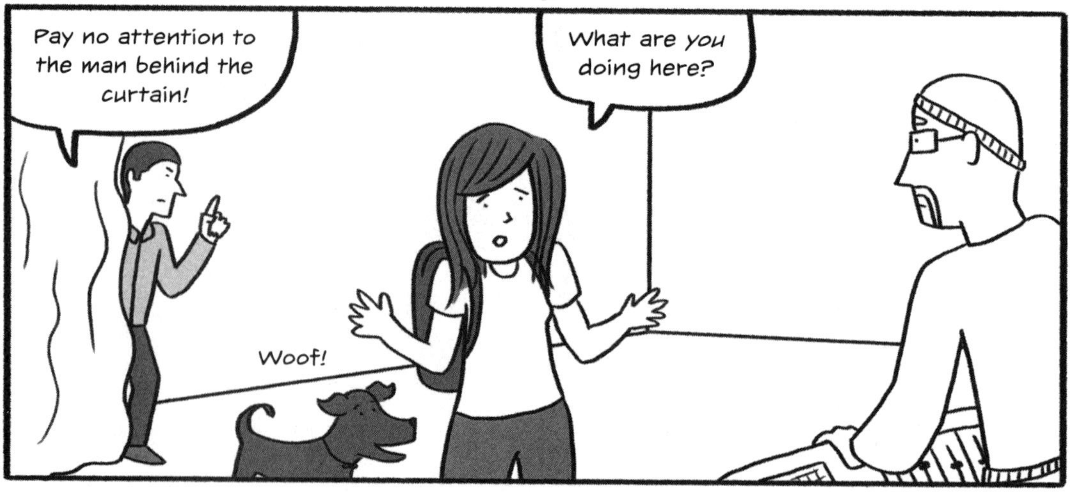
Pay no attention to the man behind the curtain!
What are *you* doing here?
Woof!

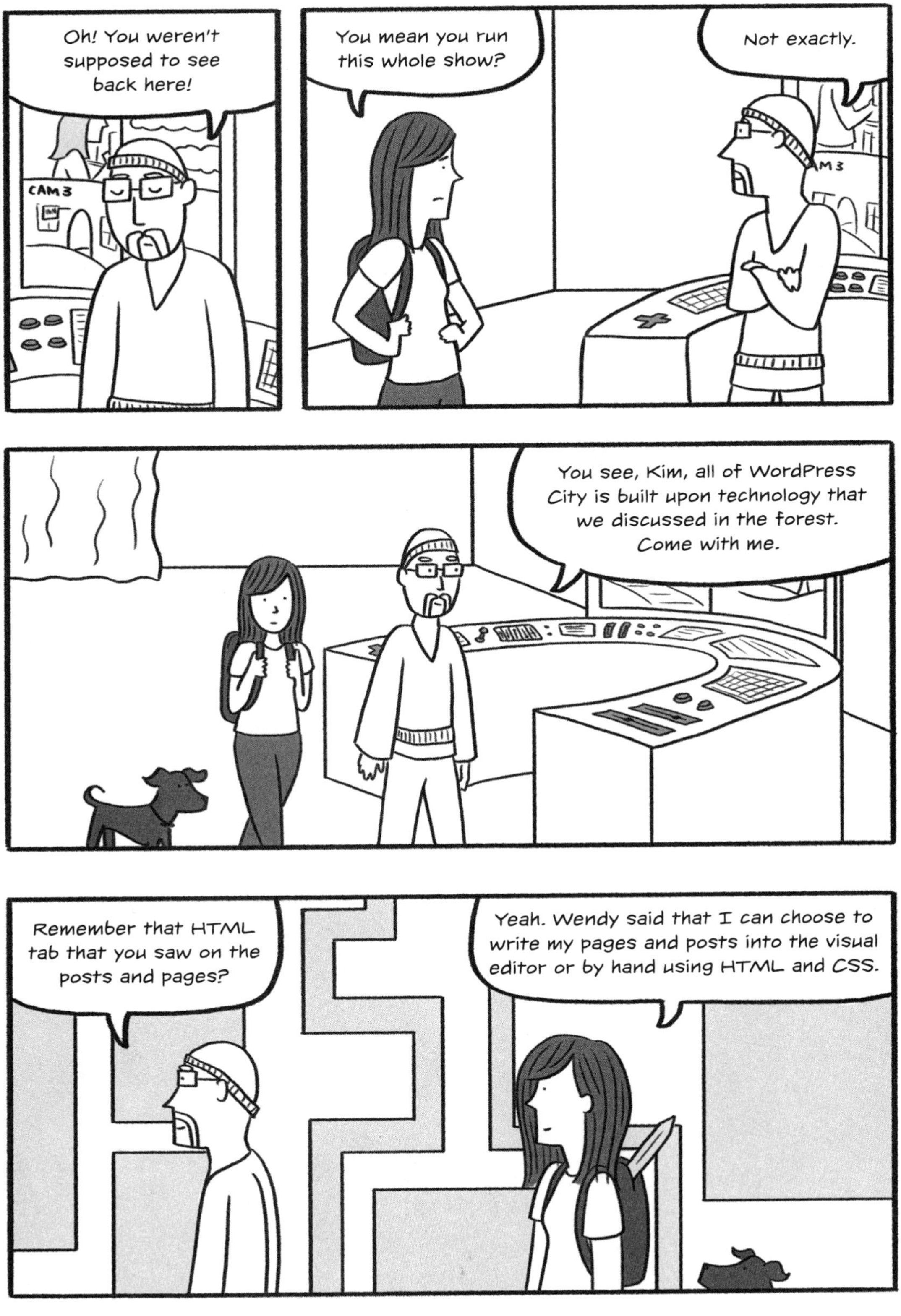
Oh! You weren't supposed to see back here!
You mean you run this whole show?
Not exactly.
CAM 3
You see, Kim, all of WordPress City is built upon technology that we discussed in the forest. Come with me.
Remember that HTML tab that you saw on the posts and pages?
Yeah. Wendy said that I can choose to write my pages and posts into the visual editor or by hand using HTML and CSS.

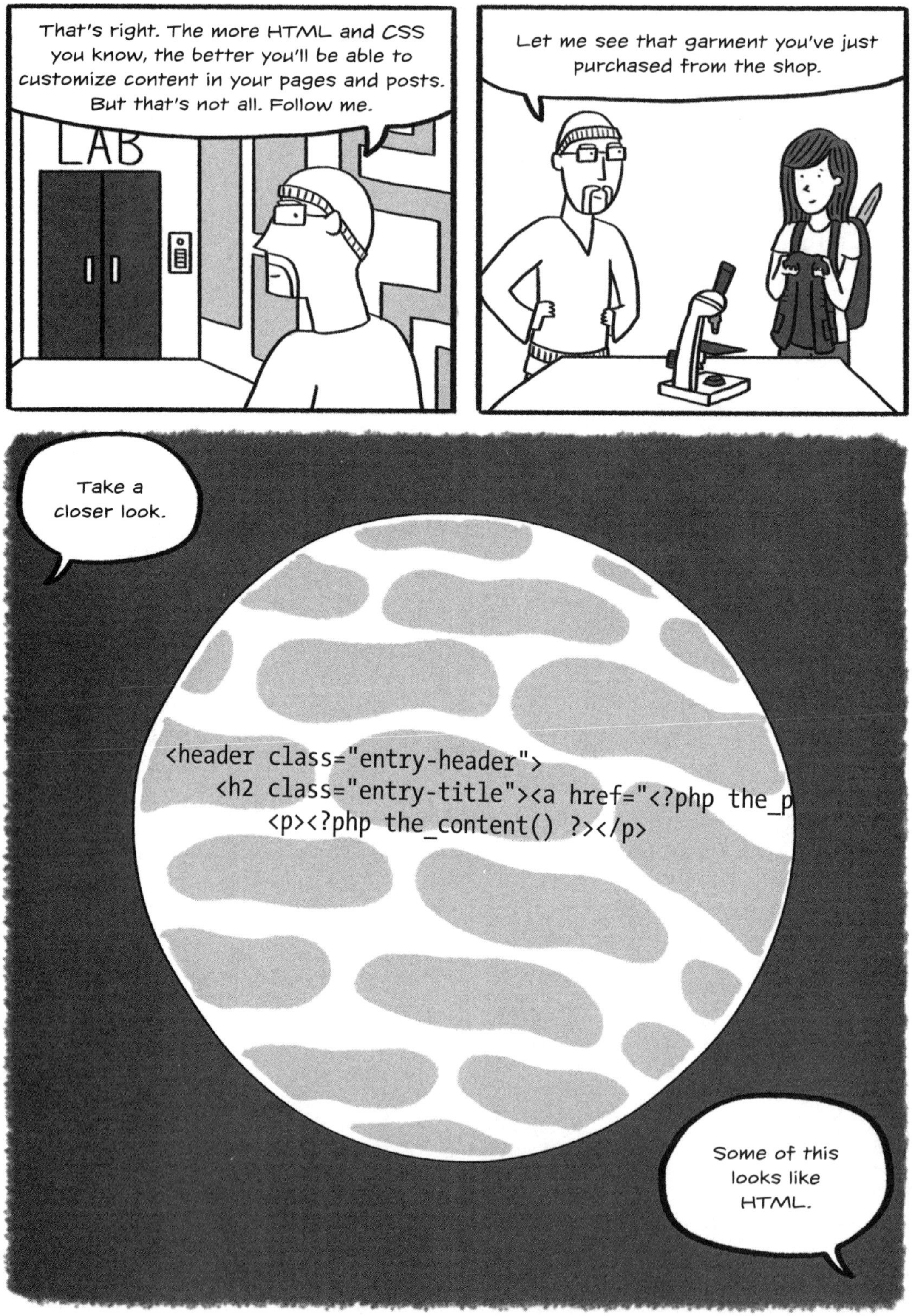
That's right. The more HTML and CSS you know, the better you'll be able to customize content in your pages and posts. But that's not all. Follow me.
LAB
Let me see that garment you've just purchased from the shop.
Take a closer look.
<header class="entry-header">
<h2 class="entry-title"><a href="<?php the_p
<p><?php the_content() ?></p>
Some of this looks like HTML.

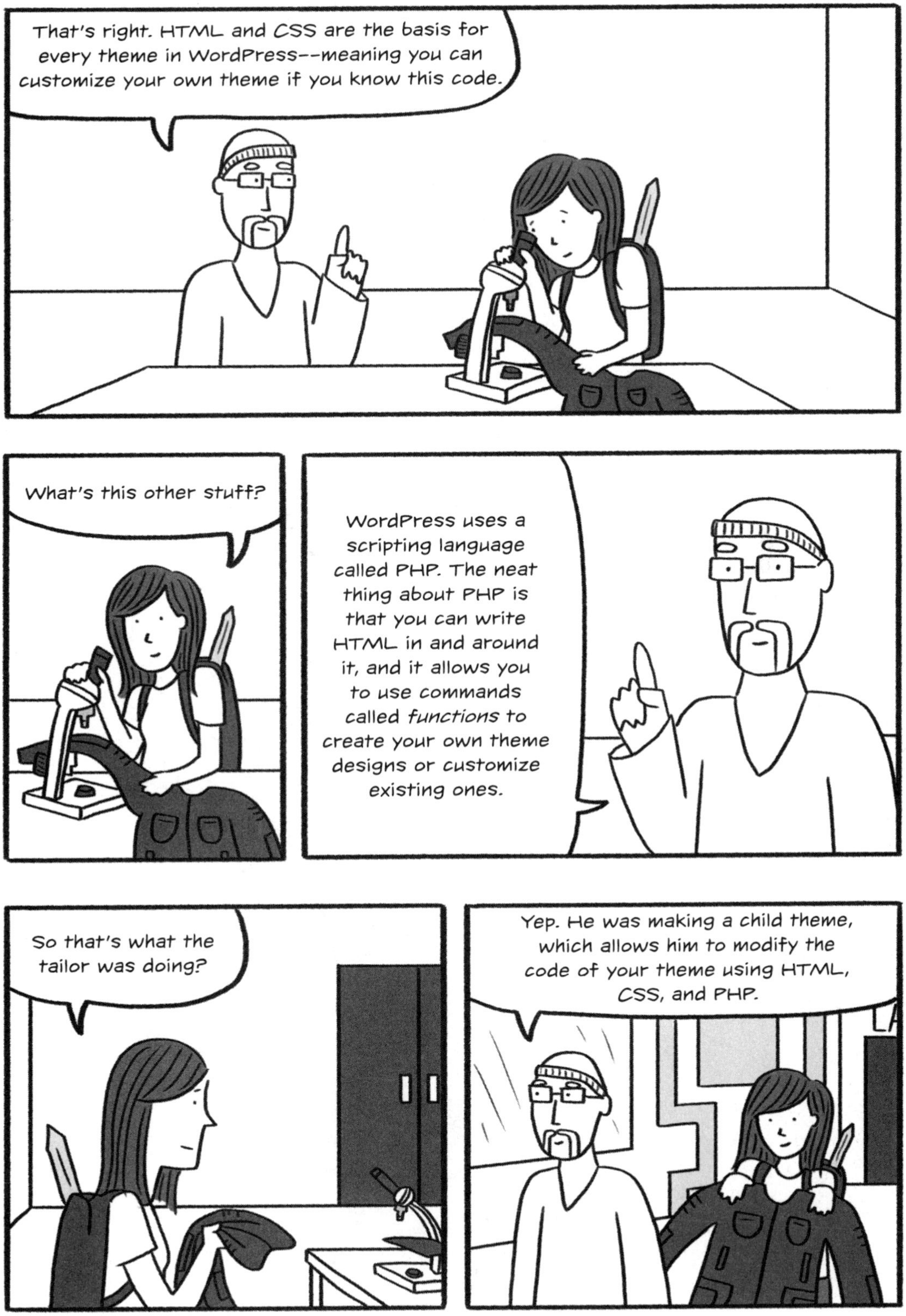
That's right. HTML and CSS are the basis for every theme in WordPress--meaning you can customize your own theme if you know this code.
What's this other stuff?
WordPress uses a scripting language called PHP. The neat thing about PHP is that you can write HTML in and around it, and it allows you to use commands called *functions* to create your own theme designs or customize existing ones.
So that's what the tailor was doing?
Yep. He was making a child theme, which allows him to modify the code of your theme using HTML, CSS, and PHP.

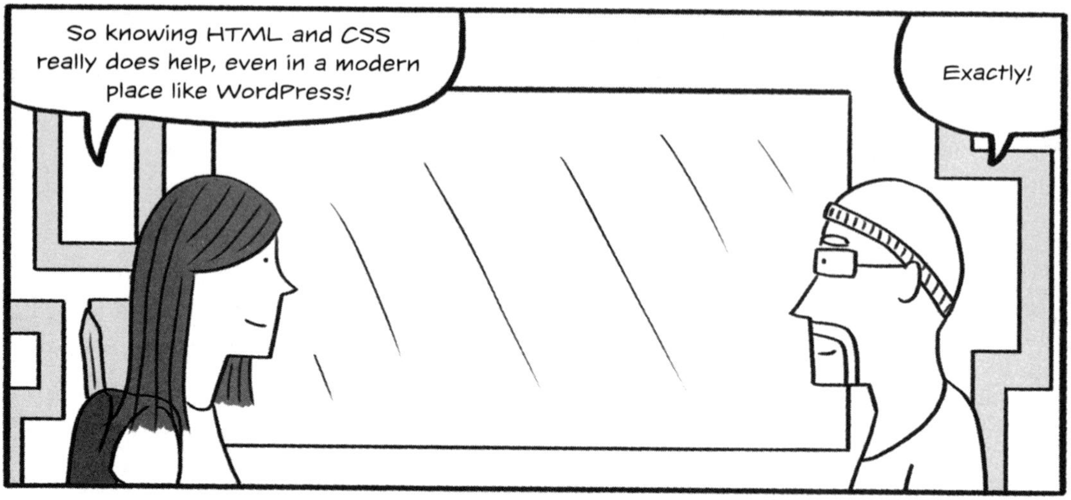
So knowing HTML and CSS really does help, even in a modern place like WordPress!
Exactly!

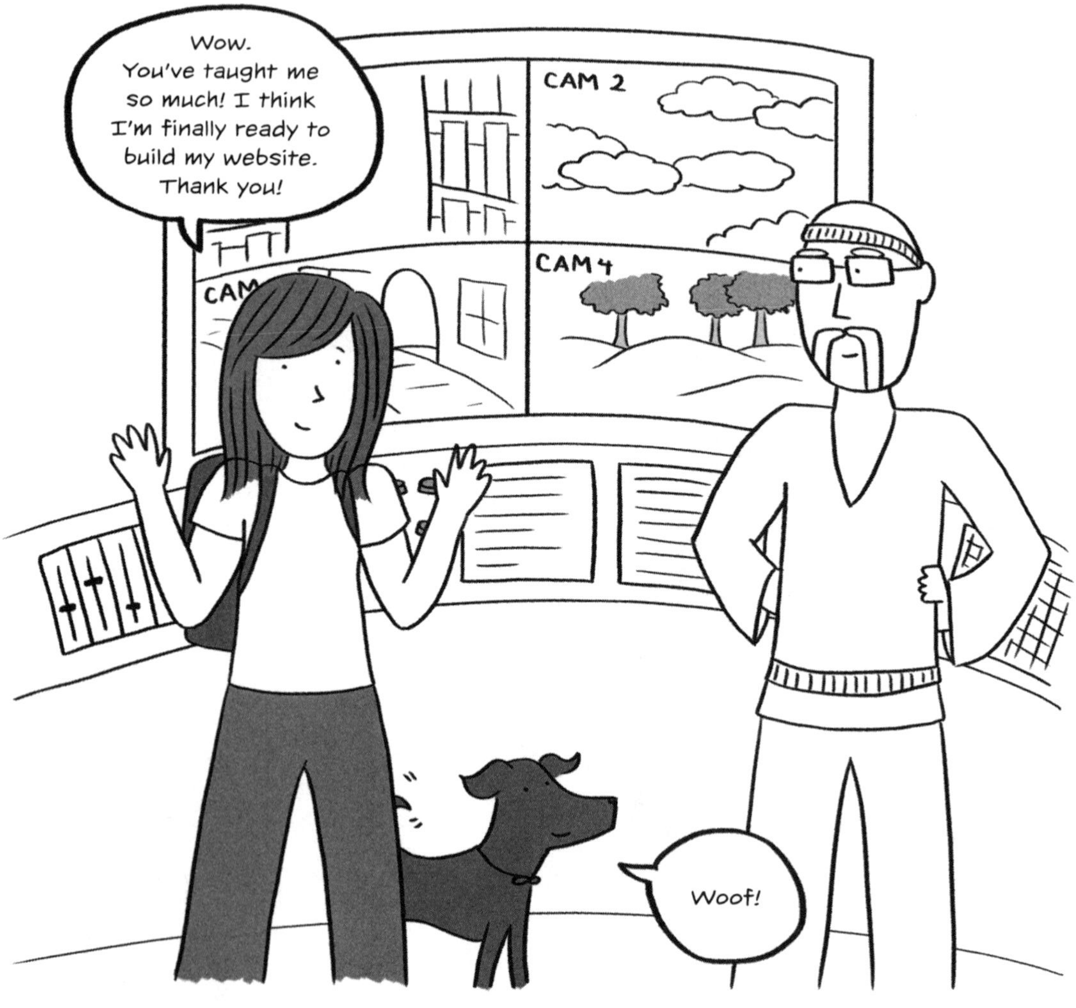
Wow. You've taught me so much! I think I'm finally ready to build my website. Thank you!
CAM 2
CAM 4
Woof!

Changing the Appearance: Theme Basics

Up to this point we've been focusing on content; that is, the words, links, and pictures that go into your pages and blog. Aside from a few basic formatting options like aligning images and breaking up paragraphs, we haven't been able to change the look of the site much. This is an intentional feature of WordPress. All of the appearance-related aspects of the site are stored in the *theme*, a template that determines the look and layout of your whole website. At any time you only ever have *one* active theme. There are millions of themes available, which can be a bit overwhelming at first, although it's nice to have so many options. You can even decide to build your own theme from scratch if you'd like.

In your Dashboard, go to **Appearance ▸ Themes** and you should see a list of themes organized in a grid, as shown in Figure 5-1. One of the biggest differences between a site hosted on WordPress.com and a self-hosted WordPress site is in the theme selection. On WordPress.com, you will see a wide variety of themes—some free, some for sale (the latter are called *premium*). What you *won't* see is any way to add a theme that isn't preselected by WordPress.

Dashboard
Store
Posts
Media
Links
Pages
Comments
Feedback
Appearance
Themes
Customize
Widgets
Menus
Header
Background
Custom Design
Mobile
Themes 256
Search themes...
Help
Trending
Popular
Newest
ALL
FREE
PREMIUM
Active: Reddle
Customize
Hemingway Rewritten
Tonal
Gridiculous Pro
Dashboard
Jetpack
Posts
Media
Pages
Comments
Appearance
Themes
Customize
Widgets
Menus
Header
Background
Editor
Plugins
Users
Tools
Settings
Collapse menu
Themes 3
Add New
Search installed themes...
Help
Theme Details
Active: Twenty Fourteen
Customize
Twenty Thirteen
Twenty Twelve
Add New Theme

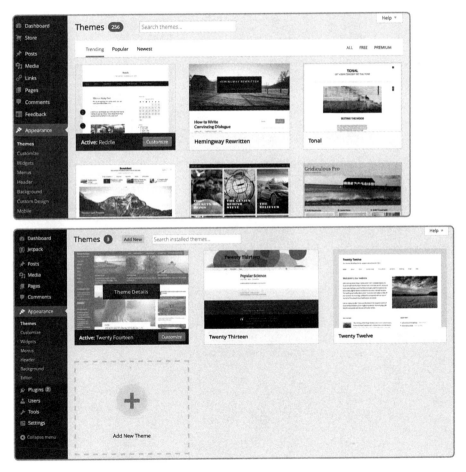

Figure 5-1: The Theme Chooser on WordPress.com (top) and a self-hosted WordPress site (bottom). You can pick out a theme in Appearance ▸ Themes.

Changing the look of your site in WordPress is as easy as activating a new theme. By activating one theme, you automatically deactivate the previous theme. However, activating a new theme doesn't erase your content (your posts, pages, and images); it just changes how your content looks. Try searching for themes by clicking the **Add New Theme** button. This will allow you to search through a free directory of themes on WordPress.org (see Figure 5-2). In our example, we're searching for a responsive theme. Once you find a theme you'd like to try, click the **Install Now** link. This will download the theme from WordPress.org and put it on your host for you.

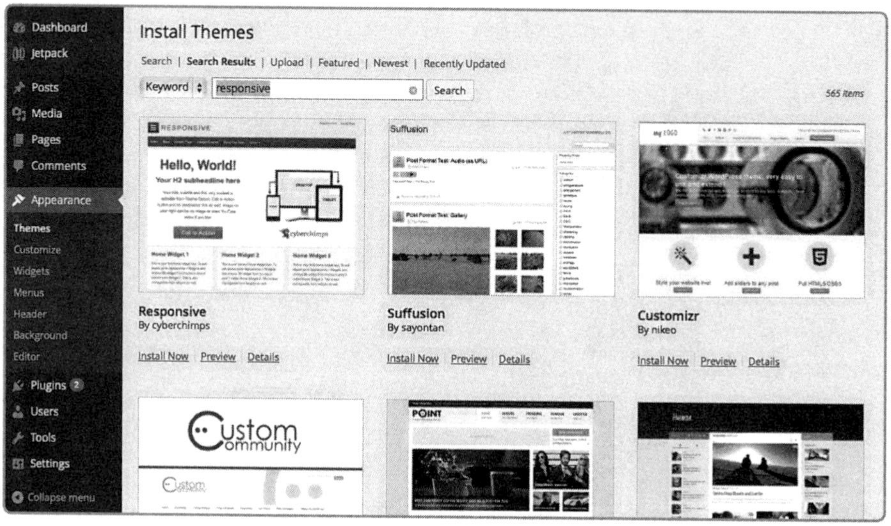

Dashboard
Jetpack
Posts
Media
Pages
Comments
Appearance
Themes
Customize
Widgets
Menus
Header
Background
Editor
Plugins 2
Users
Tools
Settings
Collapse menu
Install Themes
Search | Search Results | Upload | Featured | Newest | Recently Updated
Keyword
responsive
Search
565 items
Hello, World!
Responsive
By cyberchimps
Install Now
Preview
Details
Suffusion
By sayontan
Install Now
Preview
Details
Customizr
By nikeo
Install Now
Preview
Details
Custom community
POINT

Figure 5-2: By clicking Add New Theme and typing a search query, you'll be able to search for free themes hosted on WordPress.org.

Once the theme has been installed onto your host, you will need to *activate* it to make it your current theme (see Figure 5-3). Remember, themes can vary the look of your site tremendously. Check out Figure 5-4, which shows identical content with two different themes enabled. Look at the differences in how the quote post looks, and notice how the post below it with the featured image is displayed differently with each theme.

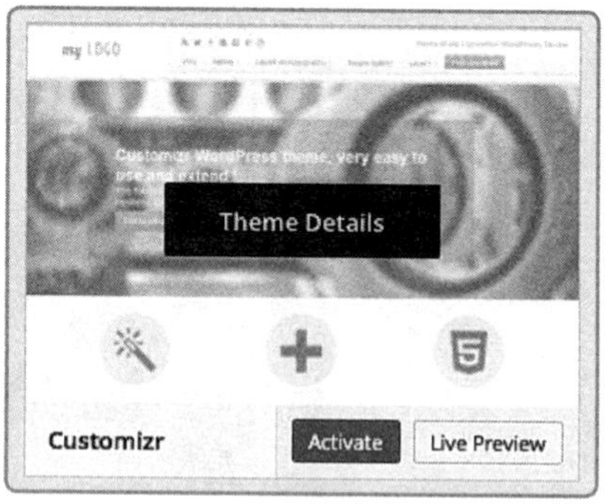

Theme Details
Customizr
Activate
Live Preview

Figure 5-3: Once a theme has been installed onto your host, you can activate that theme.

INSPIRATION
QUOTE APRIL 1, 2015 EDIT
"Creativity is knowing how to hide your sources" — Albert Einstein
"Creativity is knowing how to hide your sources" — Albert Einstein
A Beautiful Spring Day in NYC
Edit
"Today is the first day of the rest of your life!" someone said to me on my walk across the Brooklyn Bridge today. The smell of flowers was in the air, and a calm breeze reminded me the winter chill had not quite given up its hold on our city.

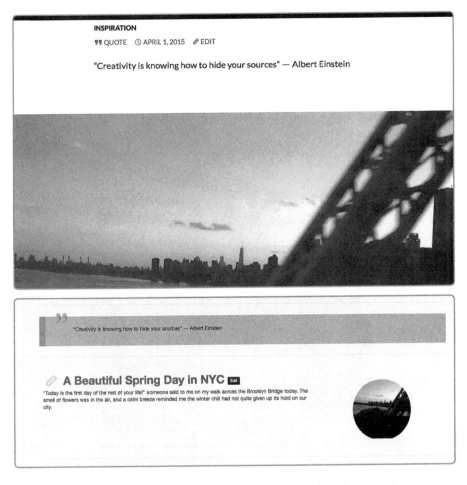

Figure 5-4: The same posts viewed with the Twenty Fourteen (top) or Customizr (bottom) themes active.

You may also wish to install themes that aren't included in the WordPress.org directory. There are several websites where you can find free themes or purchase themes for WordPress. One of the easiest ways to install a theme you downloaded from a third-party website is to upload a Zip file to WordPress and then activate the theme as just described. Be careful only to upload themes to your site that come from reputable developers. There are several high-quality marketplaces for themes, like ThemeForest (*http://themeforest.net/*), WooThemes (*http://woothemes.com/*), and StudioPress (*http://studiopress.com/*).

If you want to redesign your site, it's just a few simple clicks to activate a whole new theme. And because the content of your site is stored separately from the theme, you won't have to rewrite your pages or upload new photos when you make changes to your theme.

Customizing Your Theme

Of course, a theme is not necessarily going to look exactly how you want it to right from the get-go. Luckily, WordPress themes offer a wealth of options for you to tweak and customize your theme according to your needs and tastes. First, for some straightforward customization options, go to the **Appearance ▸ Header** section (see Figure 5-5). This allows you to style the fonts and colors of your header and even allows you to upload banner images that are displayed in the header of your blog.

Kim's Portfolio
2
New
Delete Cache
Howdy, Kim
Dashboard
Jetpack
Posts
Media
Pages
Comments
Appearance
Themes
Customize
Widgets
Menus
Header
Background
Editor
Plugins 2
Users
Tools
Settings
Collapse menu
Custom Header
Header Image
Preview
Kim's Portfolio
Select Image
You can select an image to be shown at the top of your site by uploading from your computer or choosing from your media library. After selecting an image you will be able to crop it.
Images should be at least 1260 pixels wide. Suggested width is 1260 pixels. Suggested height is 240 pixels.
Choose an image from your computer:
Choose File no file selected
Upload
Or choose an image from your media library:
Choose Image
Header Text
Header Text
Show header text with your image.
Text Color
Select Color
Save Changes

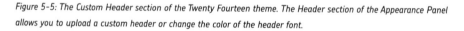

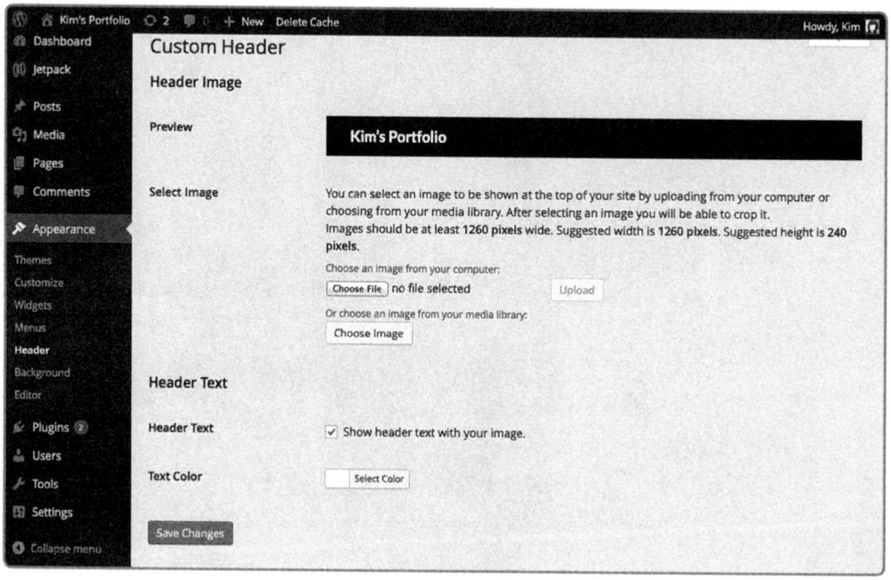

Figure 5-5: The Custom Header section of the Twenty Fourteen theme. The Header section of the Appearance Panel allows you to upload a custom header or change the color of the header font.

You can also design a logo and upload it to the header so that your site looks uniquely your own and is branded the way you'd like.

It's becoming more common for themes to have sections for Appearance ▸ Customize. Figure 5-6 shows the Customize section for the Twenty Fourteen theme. With it you can change some of the colors as well as set a background image for the frontend of your site. More complex (and often premium) themes might include a separate section called Theme Options, as shown in Figure 5-7, which allows for a wider degree of customization. For example, many modern themes include options for changing the fonts from a drop-down menu without needing to modify the code.

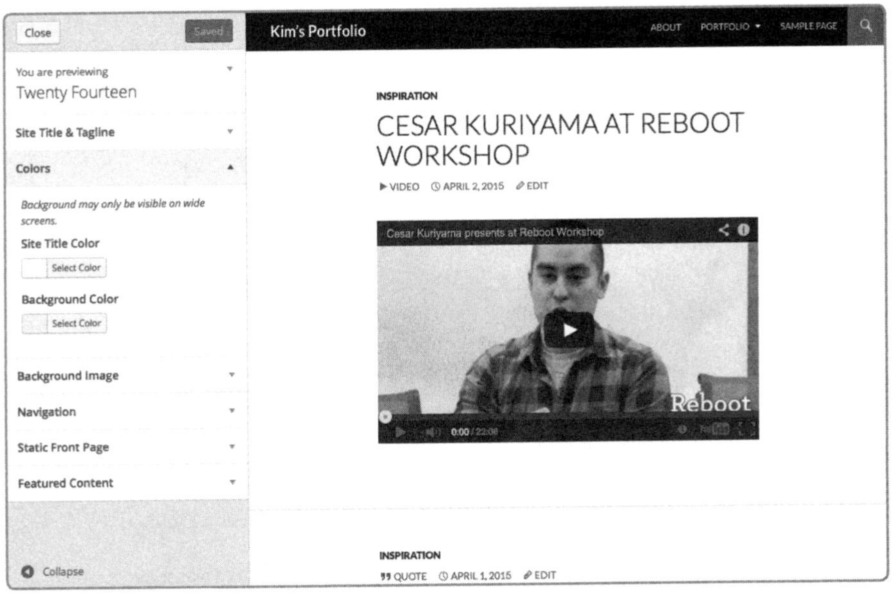

Close Saved Kim's Portfolio   ABOUT   PORTFOLIO ▾   SAMPLE PAGE

You are previewing
Twenty Fourteen

Site Title & Tagline

Colors

Background may only be visible on wide screens.

Site Title Color

Select Color

Background Color

Select Color

Background Image

Navigation

Static Front Page

Featured Content

Collapse

INSPIRATION

CESAR KURIYAMA AT REBOOT WORKSHOP

▶ VIDEO   APRIL 2, 2015   EDIT

Cesar Kuriyama presents at Reboot Workshop

Reboot

0:00 / 22:08

INSPIRATION

QUOTE   APRIL 1, 2015   EDIT

Figure 5-6: The Appearance ▸ Customize section of the free Twenty Fourteen theme that comes with WordPress. Use this section to tweak colors or add a background image. The Customize section will vary from theme to theme, so be sure to check this whenever you activate a new theme to see what options are available.

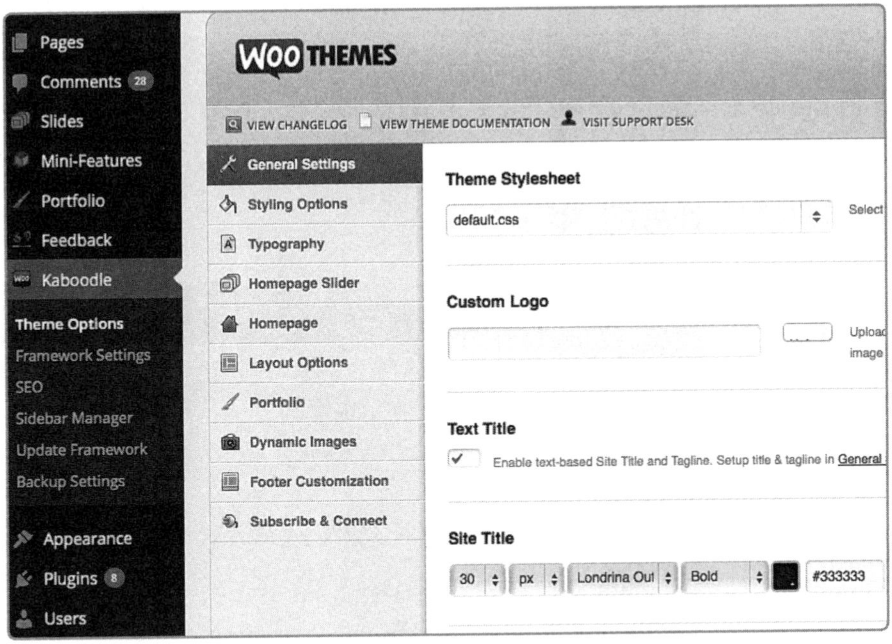

Pages
Comments 28
Slides
Mini-Features
Portfolio
Feedback
Kaboodle

Theme Options
Framework Settings
SEO
Sidebar Manager
Update Framework
Backup Settings

Appearance
Plugins 8
Users

WOO THEMES

VIEW CHANGELOG   VIEW THEME DOCUMENTATION   VISIT SUPPORT DESK

General Settings
Styling Options
Typography
Homepage Slider
Homepage
Layout Options
Portfolio
Dynamic Images
Footer Customization
Subscribe & Connect

Theme Stylesheet

default.css   Select

Custom Logo

Upload image

Text Title

✓ Enable text-based Site Title and Tagline. Setup title & tagline in General

Site Title

30   px   Londrina Out   Bold   #333333

Figure 5-7: The Theme Options section of a theme made by WooThemes. So-called premium themes often advertise a wealth of features that extend the functionality of WordPress, like the ability to change the font or layout without coding. You'll often find a Theme Options section included with these themes.

When you install a new theme, it will come with page templates, as shown in Figure 5-8, which allow you to customize the layout of certain pages. Twenty Fourteen comes with three page templates. Choosing Full Width Page, for example, will remove the right sidebar from that page, as shown in Figure 5-9. While Twenty Fourteen does not allow you to change these templates without going into the code, some themes will allow you to customize layouts in the Theme Options or Customize sections of the Appearance Panel. Once you've chosen a layout, you'll need to assign that layout to a page by going back to the visual editor and selecting that template in the Page Attributes box. This is the same place we set up child pages in Chapter 4.

Page Attributes
Parent
(no parent)
Template
✓ Default Template
Contributor Page
Full Width Page
0
Need help? Use the Help tab in the upper right of your screen.

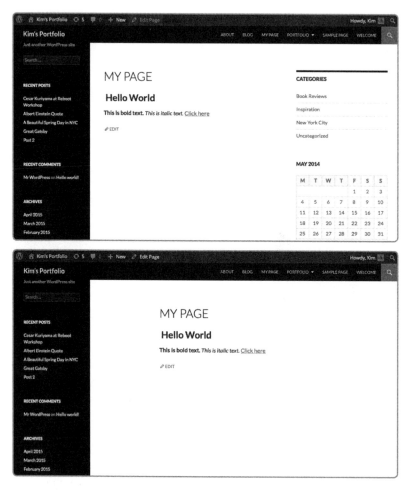

Figure 5-8: You can assign a page template to change the layout of that one particular page.

Kim's Portfolio
ABOUT
BLOG
MY PAGE
PORTFOLIO
SAMPLE PAGE
WELCOME
Howdy, Kim
RECENT POSTS
Cesar Kuriyama at Reboot Workshop
Albert Einstein Quote
A Beautiful Spring Day in NYC
Great Gatsby
Post 2
RECENT COMMENTS
Mr WordPress on Hello world!
ARCHIVES
April 2015
March 2015
February 2015
MY PAGE
Hello World
This is bold text. This is italic text. Click here
EDIT
CATEGORIES
Book Reviews
Inspiration
New York City
Uncategorized
MAY 2014

Figure 5-9: The Default Template (top) and the Full Width Page (bottom) from the Twenty Fourteen theme

If you're building a simple site or blog, using a free theme may be enough, but if you want to have a portfolio, highly customizable slideshows, or an e-commerce store built into your site, it's often very easy to find a premium theme that does the job for a one-time fee set by the developer.

Customizing Your Navigation Menu

In most themes, you'll also see a lot of basic customization options under Appearance ▶ Menus. Here you can choose what pages, posts, or other content you want to appear in the navigation menu on your site. Let's give it a try.

NOTE *If you see that the boxes on the left are gray, as in Figure 5-10, you need to create a menu first: Type* **Menu** *in the Menu Name field, and then click* **Create Menu**.

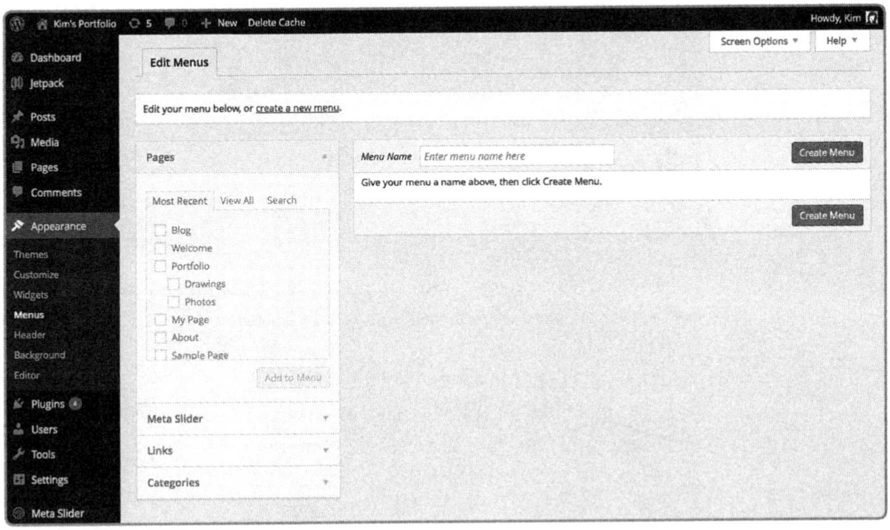

Figure 5-10: You'll need to create a menu before you can add items to it.

A custom menu allows you complete freedom to choose which tabs appear in the navigation bar on your site. Earlier we saw that when we added a page into our site it was automatically added to the menu. But this screen will give us complete control over what a user sees on our site.

To add pages to your navigation menu, simply check the box to the left of the item you want to add and then click the **Add to Menu** button (see Figure 5-11).

You may also want to give visitors quick access to other areas of your site—for example, a category of blog posts. You can add categories to a navigation menu just as easily as adding pages.

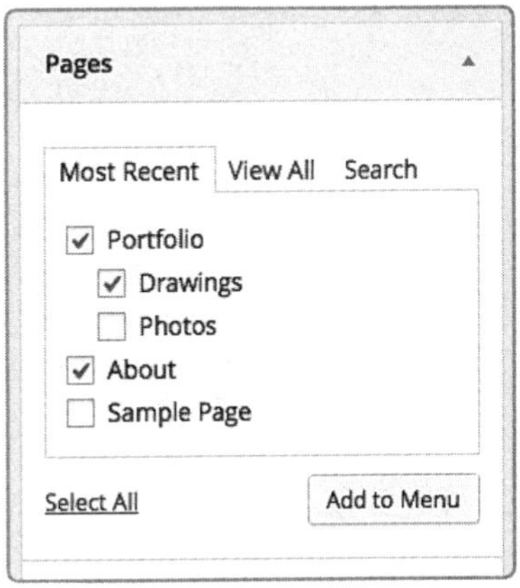

Figure 5-11: Add pages into the menu by checking the boxes next to the page name and then clicking the Add to Menu button.

In Figure 5-12, we see the Book Reviews category in our menu. That means users can now simply click that link and WordPress will show all of the posts filed under Book Reviews.

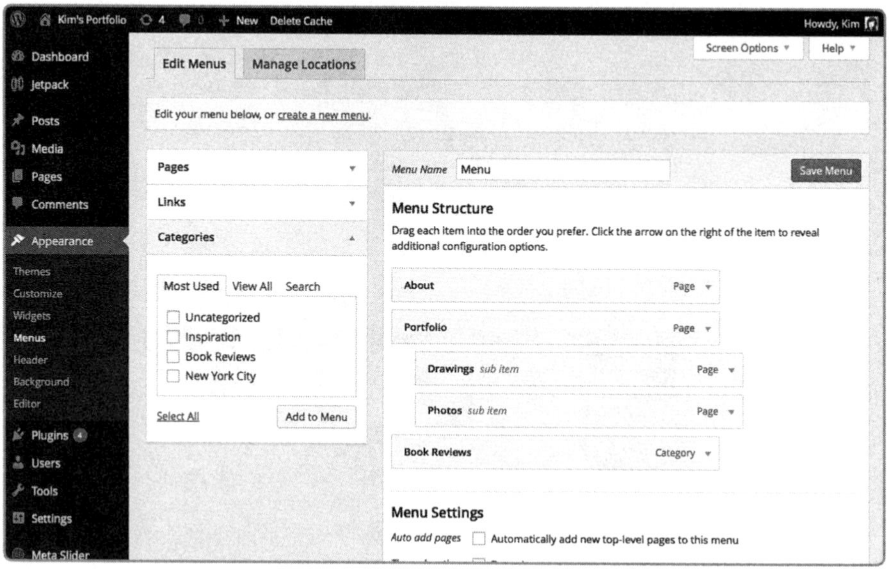
Kim's Portfolio
4
New
Delete Cache
Howdy, Kim
Dashboard
Jetpack
Posts
Media
Pages
Comments
Appearance
Themes
Customize
Widgets
Menus
Header
Background
Editor
Plugins 4
Users
Tools
Settings
Meta Slider
Screen Options
Help
Edit Menus
Manage Locations
Edit your menu below, or create a new menu.
Pages
Links
Categories
Most Used
View All
Search
Uncategorized
Inspiration
Book Reviews
New York City
Select All
Add to Menu
Menu Name
Menu
Save Menu
Menu Structure
Drag each item into the order you prefer. Click the arrow on the right of the item to reveal additional configuration options.
About
Page
Portfolio
Page
Drawings sub item
Page
Photos sub item
Page
Book Reviews
Category
Menu Settings
Auto add pages
Automatically add new top-level pages to this menu

Figure 5-12: When you create custom menus, child-parent relationships between pages are ignored. Dragging menu items to the right, underneath another item, creates a subitem.

You can even add custom links to external sites. For example, what if you have an Etsy or eBay store and you want to give visitors quick access to that in the menu? You can simply add a custom link and set the label to *Store* (see Figure 5-13).

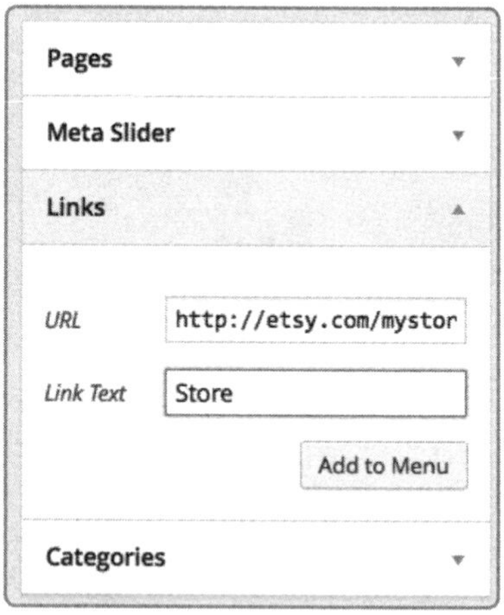
Pages
Meta Slider
Links
URL
http://etsy.com/mystor
Link Text
Store
Add to Menu
Categories

Figure 5-13: Adding a custom link to your menu

Note that your theme may support more than one menu. For example, some themes have a menu in the header and a different menu in the footer. Be sure to set where you'd like the menu to appear in the area labeled Theme Locations. *Theme locations* are specific areas of a web page where the theme allows you to place a menu. In Twenty Fourteen we have two theme locations, one in the header called *Top primary menu* and another in the sidebar labeled *Secondary menu in left sidebar*.

To test out our menu, let's check **Top primary menu**. You may also want to check the box labeled "Automatically add new top-level pages to this menu" (see Figure 5-14). This ensures that any time you publish a page it will automatically be added into your menu. Whenever you make a change, click the Save Menu button to update your menu.

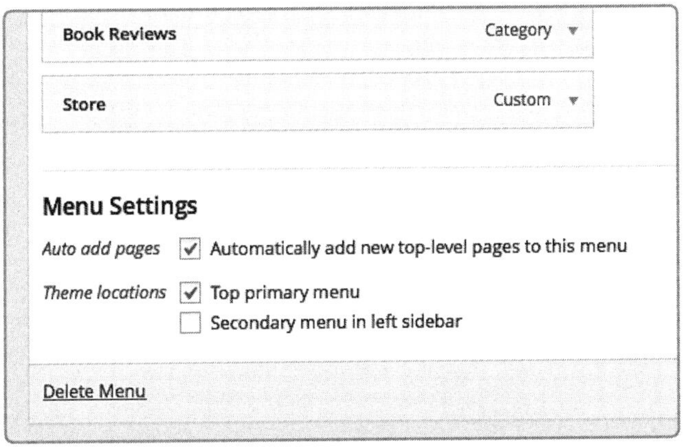

Book Reviews	Category ▾
Store	Custom ▾

Menu Settings

Auto add pages ☑ Automatically add new top-level pages to this menu

Theme locations ☑ Top primary menu
                   ☐ Secondary menu in left sidebar

Delete Menu

Figure 5-14: By assigning a theme location for your menu, you tell WordPress where the menu should go within the current theme. Twenty Fourteen has two possible menu locations, one called Top primary menu *and another called* Secondary menu in left sidebar.

If you haven't done so already, scroll down the page until you see the Pages section; check About, Portfolio, Photos, and Drawings; and then click **Add to Menu**, as shown in Figure 5-15.

After you click **Add to Menu**, you should see that the pages have been added to the menu on the right. The cool thing about custom menus is that you can drag and drop them to set the order. Try dragging the order around so that About is first, followed by Portfolio, then Drawings, and finally Photos, as shown in Figure 5-16.

Now click **Save Menu** and take a look at the frontend of the site. Notice how the first page in the menu in the Dashboard corresponds to the first page on the menu on the frontend. Drawings and Photos are sub items underneath Portfolio.

Did that work? Pretty cool, right? Now go back to your Dashboard and try to add the Book Reviews category and a custom link to your menu. If you are able to, great—but most likely you won't see the Categories or Links sections available. That's because you have to enable them in the *Screen Options* tab. More on that next.

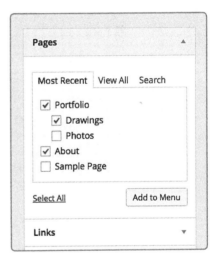

Figure 5-15: With custom menus, you specify which items you'd like to live within a menu rather than having WordPress automatically place all of the pages in the menu for you. You might have some pages that aren't in the menu at all but are still part of the site. This makes for clean navigation and more flexibility with organizing larger sites.

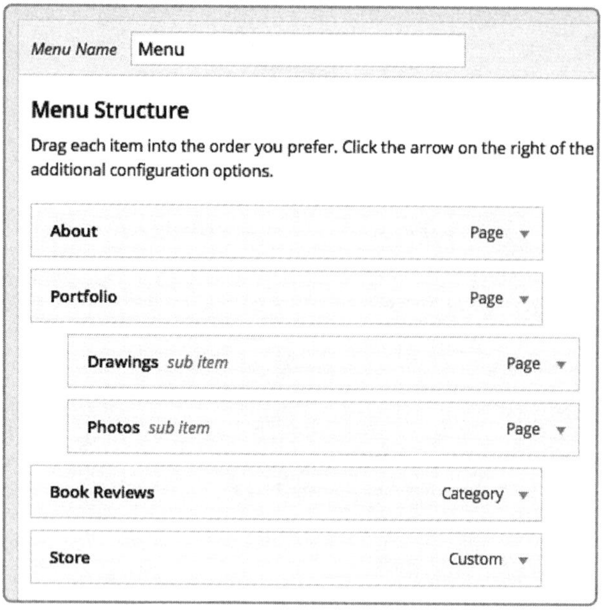

Menu Name	Menu

Menu Structure

Drag each item into the order you prefer. Click the arrow on the right of the additional configuration options.

About	Page ▼

Portfolio	Page ▼

Drawings *sub item*	Page ▼

Photos *sub item*	Page ▼

Book Reviews	Category ▼

Store	Custom ▼

Figure 5-16: Once pages have been added to a custom menu, you can drag and drop to reorder them.

Understanding the Screen Options Tab

Occasionally things may not be as they seem in the Dashboard; you think you should be able to do something but can't see an option to do it. In the previous section, we added a link to a hypothetical Etsy store, but what if we want that link to open in a separate window? It seems like we should be able to do that, but the option isn't apparent.

Go back to **Dashboard ▸ Appearance ▸ Menus**, scroll to the upper right, and click **Screen Options**, as shown in Figure 5-17.

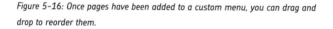

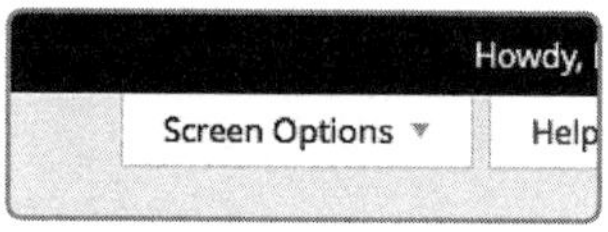

This tab, which appears at the top of every screen in the WordPress Dashboard, has lots of goodies in store. As we're editing the navigation menu, clicking this tab will provide some more options that don't show up on the main **Appearance ▸ Menus** screen. In this case, Screen Options shows us a list of elements with checkboxes (see Figure 5-18). If we were in the visual editor

Figure 5-17: The Screen Options tab in the upper-right corner of the Dashboard

for a post or if we were in the All Pages section, for example, we'd see a different set of options. When we check a box next to an option, we'll see that feature available to us in the navigation menu. For now, make sure the following are checked: Links, Categories, Pages, and Link Target.

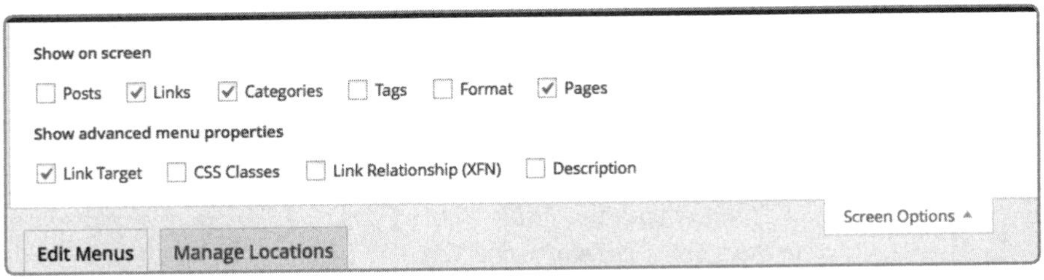
Show on screen
Posts
Links
Categories
Tags
Format
Pages
Show advanced menu properties
Link Target
CSS Classes
Link Relationship (XFN)
Description
Screen Options
Edit Menus
Manage Locations

Figure 5-18: The Screen Options panel allows you to enable or disable options for the current screen.

If you weren't able to add a link or category before, you should now see those options on the left as in Figure 5-13. Try adding a link to your menu: in the Links section under URL, type **http://etsy.com/mystore** and under *Navigation Label*, type **Store**. We should see an option underneath our Etsy link that says, "Open link in a new window/tab" (see Figure 5-19). If you ever find yourself in the Dashboard wondering why you can't figure out how to do something, check the Screen Options tab to see what you're missing!

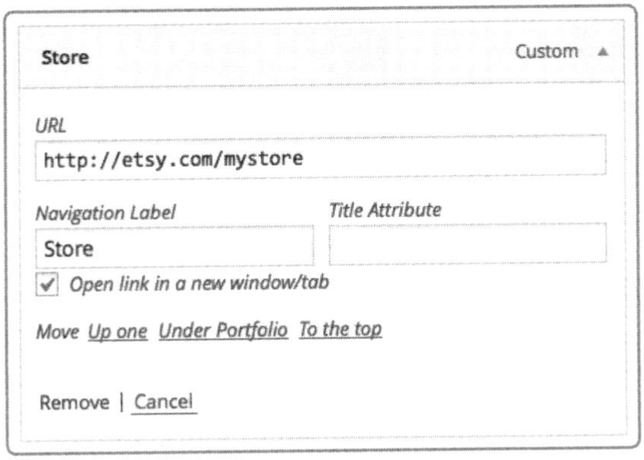
Store
Custom
URL
http://etsy.com/mystore
Navigation Label
Title Attribute
Store
Open link in a new window/tab
Move Up one Under Portfolio To the top
Remove | Cancel

Figure 5-19: Opening a link in a new window with the Link Target option enabled

Customized Settings

Moving further down along the left sidebar of the WordPress Dashboard, you should see a Settings tab, as shown in Figure 5-20. This is where you control options that affect the entirety of your WordPress site. There's a lot to this section, so let's just take a look at the "greatest hits," if you will, of the WordPress settings.

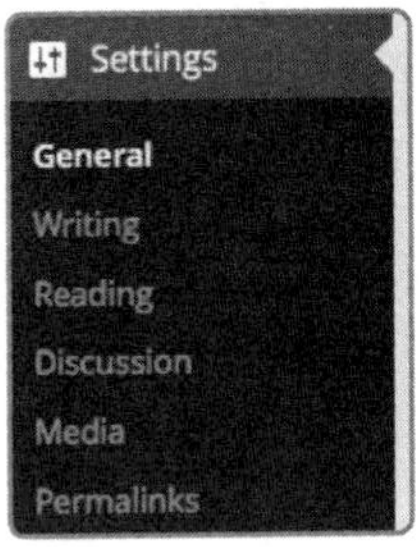
Settings
General
Writing
Reading
Discussion
Media
Permalinks

Figure 5-20: WordPress settings

Settings ▸ General is where you can change your site's title and tagline. The *tagline* is kind of like a slogan or one-sentence description of your site. Depending on your theme, it's usually visible beneath the title at the top of your pages on the frontend. If you don't intend to use a tagline, just delete

what's there and leave it blank (though leaving in a tagline is often good for search engine optimization). If you've made changes, you'll need to click the Save Changes button at the bottom of the screen.

NOTE *Many people never bother to change WordPress's generic tagline "Just another WordPress site" to something else. Just for fun, try googling "Just another WordPress site." You can see that there are millions of people who didn't bother changing it. Don't let that be you!*

Settings ▸ Reading is where you can change the structure of your site (see Figure 5-21). To see what I mean, go to **Pages ▸ Add New** and name your new page **Welcome**. Type a simple sentence in the content box, like **Welcome to My Site!**. Now click **Publish**. Next, add another page and call it **Blog**. Publish it as well. Under **Settings ▸ Reading**, you'll see that the site is set by default to display your latest posts on the front page. This means that the first page in your site is your blog page.

Reading Settings
Front page displays
Your latest posts
A static page (select below)
Front page:
Welcome
Posts page
— Select —
About
Blog
Portfolio
Drawings
Photos
Blog pages show at most
10
po

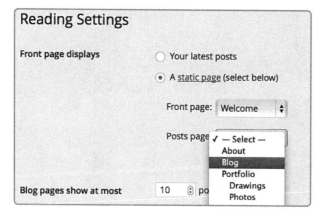

Figure 5-21: In Settings ▸ Reading, you can set the site to open up to a static page rather than your posts page.

What if you'd like to have a splash page on the first page and put your posts on that blog page we just created? Select **A static page**, and then from the drop-down menu select **Welcome**. Then for **Posts page**, select **Blog**.

When you click the **Save Changes** button, your site should be automatically reorganized. Go back to **Appearance ▸ Menus** and add the Welcome and Blog pages to your menu. Switch back to the frontend. You should see that the first page is the blank Welcome page that we've just created—not your posts. If you click Blog in the menu, you'll see your posts there.

There are a lot more options to play with here in the Settings tab, although I don't have space to describe each of them in detail. You can change everything from the default sizes of images to the settings for comments to the number of posts that show up on your blog's main page. If you are feeling curious, go ahead and experiment with some of these settings to see how else you can tweak your site. If you ever get stuck, there's plenty of documentation online that will help explain how each setting works (see "For More Help" on page 215).

Here is a quick rundown of the built-in settings and what you'll find there:

- **Settings ▸ Writing**: Customize your blog posts with different options, including proof-reading (WordPress.com and Jetpack only) and default post categories.
- **Settings ▸ Discussion**: Enable or disable comments. Get an email whenever a comment is made.
- **Settings ▸ Media**: Set default sizes for Thumbnail, Medium, and Large photos.
- **Settings ▸ Permalinks**: Change the structure of the page and post URLs (important for SEO and human readability).

Advanced Customization

If your website is hosted through WordPress.com, there are some limits as to how much you can customize your website. If you want to make changes that go beyond playing with the options and settings described already, you'll need a Custom Design upgrade. For an annual fee, this upgrade enables you to dig into the code of your site and write your own CSS into the theme. Otherwise, you are limited to the customization options already built in to the Dashboard for your theme.

If you are hosting your website yourself through your own host, there are no limits to how much you can customize your site. If you are self-hosting, you'll notice an additional option in the Appearance Panel of your Dashboard: Appearance ▸ Editor. This gives you full access to the underlying code of your theme. If you choose to build a custom theme or if you want to modify more than the CSS on your site, a self-hosted version of WordPress will give you almost unlimited abilities to do so. You can even use your knowledge of FTP to log in remotely and upload your own manual changes to the code—further proof that knowing HTML/CSS is important!

If you'd like to experiment, try changing the fonts for the paragraphs in your theme. At the bottom of the stylesheet, add the following code:

```
p { font-family: times, serif;}
```

This should change all of the paragraphs on your site to Times from Helvetica or Arial. Now it's just a matter of determining which element you'd like to change and then adding the appropriate CSS rules to change that element. As a challenge, see if you can change the colors of the links.

Even though tweaking code in the editor works, it's not considered a good practice. If you are planning on making code changes to an existing WordPress theme, you will likely want to explore the process of *child theming*. This is a way to make changes to the code of a theme without destroying the original code. You may also want to look at setting up testing sites locally on your computer. These options are all outside of the scope of this book, but you can find more information at *https://codex.wordpress.org/Child_Themes/* and *https://codex.wordpress.org/Installing_WordPress_Locally_on_Your_Mac_With_MAMP/*.

Plugins

Plugin is a broad term for a program that can be installed to add functionality to your website. For example, you might use a plugin to process credit cards if you're selling ebooks on your site. There are other plugins that speed up the performance of your site, called *caching plugins*. There are plugins to help with SEO and analytics (measuring how popular you are!). The variety and availability of plugins is one of the reasons WordPress is so popular.

NOTE *Plugins are available only if you are hosting the site yourself (i.e., using a host other than WordPress.com). If your site is hosted through WordPress.com, you won't be able to install any plugins. But WordPress.com does come with a lot of features preinstalled, sometimes eliminating the need for additional plugs.*

Adding plugins to your site allows you to do a number of things that you aren't able to do with a normal WordPress site. But if you start installing plugins, you'll need to stay on top of any future updates. Older, out-of-date plugins can cause security vulnerabilities and allow your site to get hacked. Don't worry too much, though. As long as you stick with standard plugins and are good about updating them, WordPress should remain a robust way of managing your site.

Scroll down on the left-hand side of your Dashboard, and you should see a Plugins tab, as shown in Figure 5-22. If you don't see that tab (and your site is self-hosted), make sure that you are signed in to an administrator account for the website.

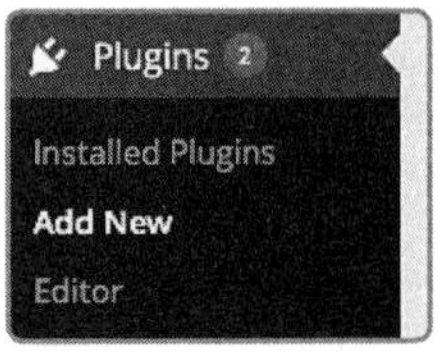
Plugins 2
Installed Plugins
Add New
Editor

Figure 5-22: Adding a new plugin to your site

Let's try to install a cool plugin called Meta Slider. This is a slideshow plugin that lets you create a gallery of images. Go to **Dashboard ▸ Plugins ▸ Add New** and type **slider** in the search field (shown in Figure 5-23). You should see a big list of slideshow plugins available. All of the plugins in this directory are free to install and try out, so if you are experimenting with something new you can always install it, try it, and then get rid of it if you don't like it.

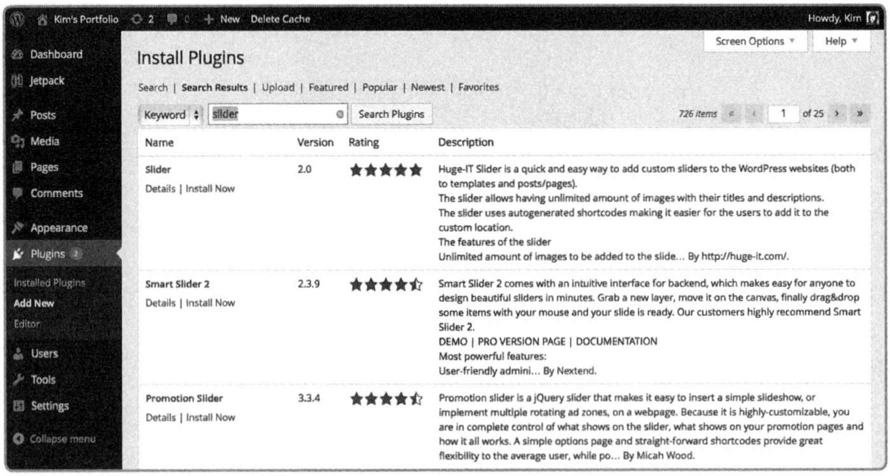
Kim's Portfolio
New
Delete Cache
Howdy, Kim
Dashboard
Jetpack
Posts
Media
Pages
Comments
Appearance
Plugins 2
Installed Plugins
Add New
Editor
Users
Tools
Settings
Collapse menu
Screen Options
Help
Install Plugins
Search | Search Results | Upload | Featured | Popular | Newest | Favorites
Keyword
slider
Search Plugins
726 items
1 of 25
Name
Version
Rating
Description
Slider
Details | Install Now
2.0
Huge-IT Slider is a quick and easy way to add custom sliders to the WordPress websites (both to templates and posts/pages).
The slider allows having unlimited amount of images with their titles and descriptions.
The slider uses autogenerated shortcodes making it easier for the users to add it to the custom location.
The features of the slider
Unlimited amount of images to be added to the slide... By http://huge-it.com/.
Smart Slider 2
Details | Install Now
2.3.9
Smart Slider 2 comes with an intuitive interface for backend, which makes easy for anyone to design beautiful sliders in minutes. Grab a new layer, move it on the canvas, finally drag&drop some items with your mouse and your slide is ready. Our customers highly recommend Smart Slider 2.
DEMO | PRO VERSION PAGE | DOCUMENTATION
Most powerful features:
User-friendly admini... By Nextend.
Promotion Slider
Details | Install Now
3.3.4
Promotion slider is a jQuery slider that makes it easy to insert a simple slideshow, or implement multiple rotating ad zones, on a webpage. Because it is highly-customizable, you are in complete control of what shows on the slider, what shows on your promotion pages and how it all works. A simple options page and straight-forward shortcodes provide great flexibility to the average user, while po... By Micah Wood.

Figure 5-23: Searching the plugin directory for slider

One good way to see if a plugin is worth trying is by clicking the Details button underneath the plugin name. Along with other information, this will give you some indication of what others thought of the plugin before you install it on your site, as shown in Figure 5-24.

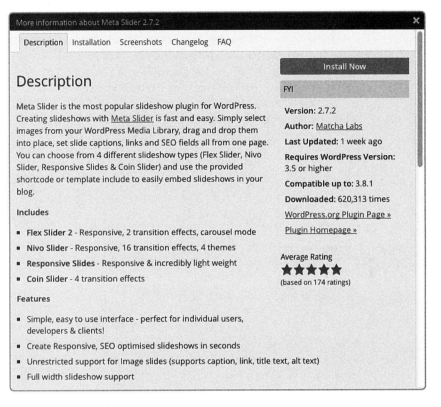

Description | Installation | Screenshots | Changelog | FAQ

More information about Meta Slider 2.7.2

Description

Meta Slider is the most popular slideshow plugin for WordPress. Creating slideshows with Meta Slider is fast and easy. Simply select images from your WordPress Media Library, drag and drop them into place, set slide captions, links and SEO fields all from one page. You can choose from 4 different slideshow types (Flex Slider, Nivo Slider, Responsive Slides & Coin Slider) and use the provided shortcode or template include to easily embed slideshows in your blog.

Includes

- **Flex Slider 2** - Responsive, 2 transition effects, carousel mode
- **Nivo Slider** - Responsive, 16 transition effects, 4 themes
- **Responsive Slides** - Responsive & incredibly light weight
- **Coin Slider** - 4 transition effects

Features

- Simple, easy to use interface - perfect for individual users, developers & clients!
- Create Responsive, SEO optimised slideshows in seconds
- Unrestricted support for Image slides (supports caption, link, title text, alt text)
- Full width slideshow support

Install Now

FYI

Version: 2.7.2
Author: Matcha Labs
Last Updated: 1 week ago
Requires WordPress Version: 3.5 or higher
Compatible up to: 3.8.1
Downloaded: 620,313 times
WordPress.org Plugin Page »
Plugin Homepage »

Average Rating
★★★★★
(based on 174 ratings)

Figure 5-24: Clicking the Details link gives you more information about the plugin, including ratings, screenshots, and FAQs.

Scroll down the list of slider plugins until you find the plugin Meta Slider and click **Install Now**. Just like when you're installing a theme from WordPress, this will download the plugin files to your host and make them available for use on your site. After the plugin has been installed, click **Activate Plugin**. Unlike with themes, you can have *many* active plugins running simultaneously, all performing different functions.

Once you have activated Meta Slider, you'll see a tab for it in your Dashboard underneath Settings. Not all plugins show up here—you'll want to read the instructions for each plugin to find out how to use that particular one.

Click the tab to find the settings for Meta Slider, and you'll be taken to the management screen for this plugin. Click the **+** button at the top of the screen to create your first slideshow, which we can then use in our site. You can name your slideshow by clicking **New Slider** and then typing a name.

Let's say we want to put a slideshow on our Welcome page. Give your slider the name **Welcome Slider**. Now we can add images into our slider. Click the **New Slide** button at the top. Meta Slider will look at our Media Library to choose images, or it will use the image uploader to allow us to add new ones. Add two or three images into your slider by selecting the images and clicking **Add to Slider**.

You've just created a slideshow! Click the **Save & Preview** button to see your slideshow in action. Below this button, you'll see a number of settings that will allow you to adjust the animation speed or the style of transitions. There's a lot to play around with. But how do we put the slideshow on our Welcome page? Meta Slider works with what's called a *shortcode*. If you scroll all the way down on the right-hand side, you'll see a box labeled **Usage** and within that a tab labeled **Shortcode** (see Figure 5-25).

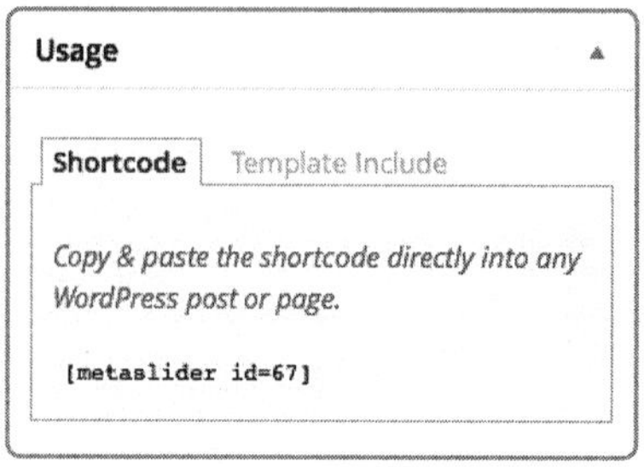

Figure 5-25: Shortcode for Meta Slider

A *shortcode* is a type of code that you can copy and paste into an area of your site that automatically references a plugin, widget (see "Widgets" on page 210), or theme element. Some themes come with shortcodes that allow you to instantly create buttons or other visual elements without having to write the code from scratch!

Copy the shortcode from the box and then navigate to your Welcome page by selecting **Pages ▸ All Pages** on the left side of the navigation (you can also insert the slider anywhere you like, if you don't have a Welcome page). Meta Slider also has an Add Slider button in the visual editor that will insert the shortcode. Because a shortcode isn't a general coding language like HTML, there's no need to insert the code into the text view. Instead, you can add it right into the visual editor as is. Create a line below the text that reads **Welcome to My Site!**.

Click the **Update** button and then click **View page**. You should see that the slideshow takes the place of the shortcode in your page, as shown in Figure 5-26.

Kim's Portfolio
New
View Page
Delete Cache
Howdy, Kim
Dashboard
Jetpack
Posts
Media
Pages
All Pages
Add New
Comments
Appearance
Plugins
Users
Tools
Settings
Meta Slider
Collapse menu
Screen Options
Help
Edit Page
Add New
Page updated. View page
Welcome
Permalink: http://testing.natecooper.co/kimsportfolio/welcome/
Edit
View Page
Get Shortlink
Add Media
Add slider
Visual
Text
Paragraph
[metaslider id=67]
Welcome to My Site!
Publish
Preview Changes
Status: Published Edit
Visibility: Public Edit
Revisions: 3 Browse
Published on: Apr 3, 2014 @ 21:58
Edit
Move to Trash
Update
Page Attributes
Parent
(no parent)
Template
Default Template
Order

WELCOME
Welcome to My Site!
EDIT

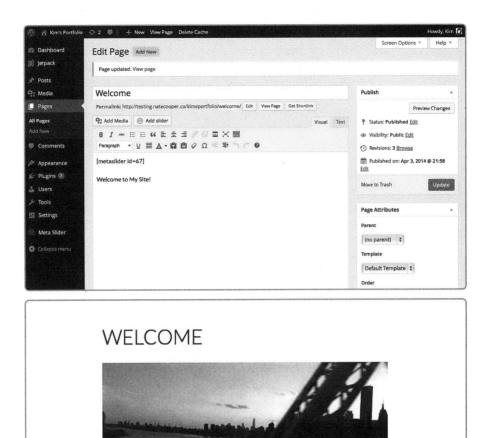

Figure 5-26: The Meta Slider shortcode in the Dashboard and the finished slider on the frontend of the site

Widgets

Widgets are a type of plugin that you can insert into your site to add a specific extra feature. But widgets tend to perform limited functions and can be slotted into only certain spots on a web page. For example, let's say you want to have your Twitter feed appear in your WordPress blog's sidebar. You can add the widgets just like you would add any other plugin by clicking Plugins ▸ Add New and then performing a search for *Twitter widget*. Or, if you don't have a Twitter account, try something like an image widget just to give it a try.

As with a plugin, we'll need to install and then activate our widget. Once the widget is installed and activated, navigate to the Widgets section of the Dashboard (see Figure 5-27). On the right side of the Appearance ▸ Widgets area is a list of where widgets can be placed in your current theme. Most themes have at least one sidebar that you can add widgets to, and some themes have several other areas where widgets can go as well, like a secondary sidebar or footer.

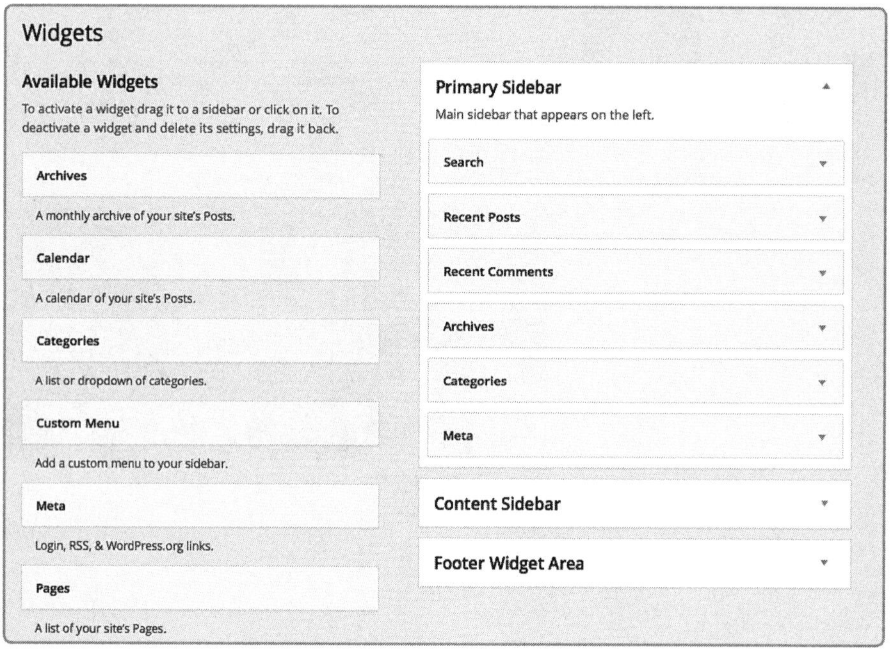
Widgets
Available Widgets
To activate a widget drag it to a sidebar or click on it. To deactivate a widget and delete its settings, drag it back.
Archives
A monthly archive of your site's Posts.
Calendar
A calendar of your site's Posts.
Categories
A list or dropdown of categories.
Custom Menu
Add a custom menu to your sidebar.
Meta
Login, RSS, & WordPress.org links.
Pages
A list of your site's Pages.
Primary Sidebar
Main sidebar that appears on the left.
Search
Recent Posts
Recent Comments
Archives
Categories
Meta
Content Sidebar
Footer Widget Area

Figure 5-27: Widgets allow you to include additional little functions into areas of your site like the sidebar. These are the widget areas for the Twenty Fourteen theme.

To the left of the Widgets area, you'll see all of the available widgets that you can choose to put into your sidebar. On the right, you'll see places your widget can go! To install a Twitter widget, simply scroll down until you see Twitter and drag it to the Primary Sidebar area, as shown in Figure 5-28. If you've got a long page and dragging is difficult, you can also just click the widget and then add it to the area of your choosing (see Figure 5-29).

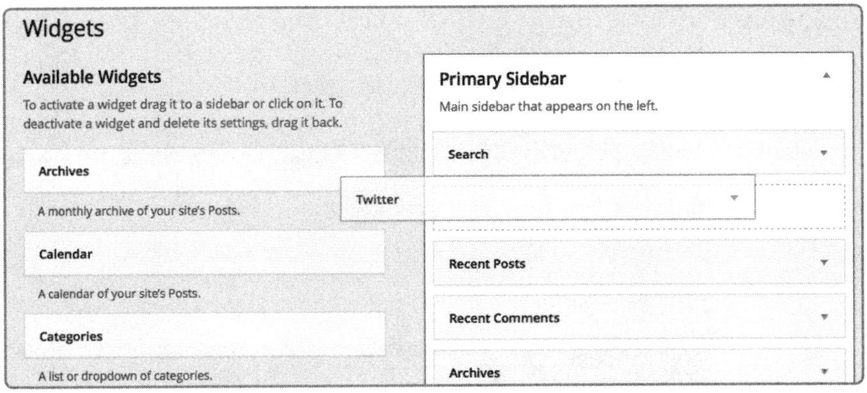

Figure 5-28: Installing a widget by dragging it to the Primary Sidebar

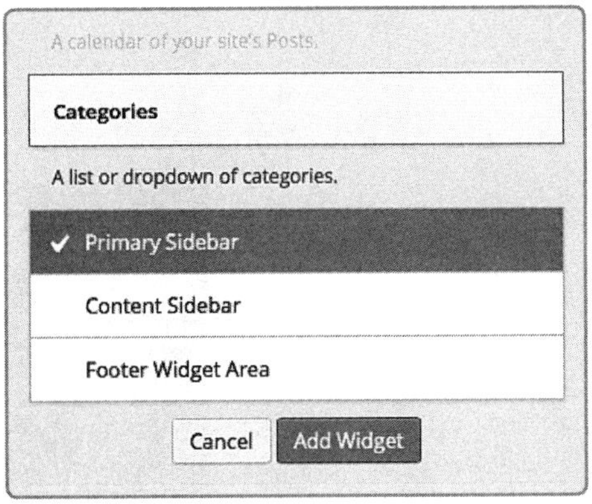

Figure 5-29: Installing a widget by clicking it and then choosing a location

Once you have a widget in your sidebar, you'll need to fill in some settings to get it to work (see Figure 5-30). Just click the triangle in the upper-right corner of the widget and fill in your username, select whatever other options you'd like, and then click **Save**.

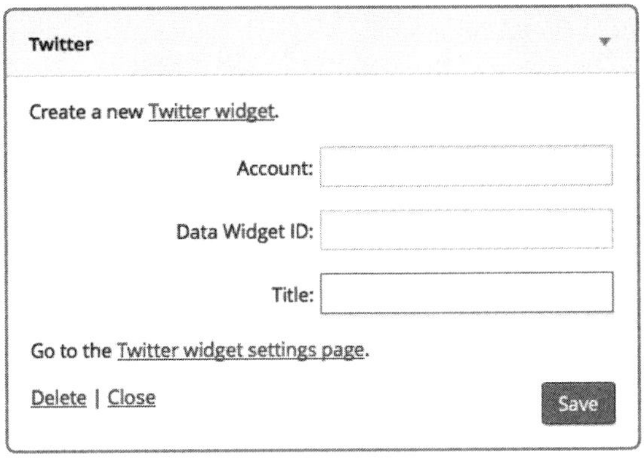

Figure 5-30: Setting up the Twitter widget

NOTE *You'll have to get a widget ID from the Twitter website. Click the Twitter widget settings page link to be taken to your Twitter account and create a widget there. The ID will be in the address bar of your browser (see Figure 5-31).*

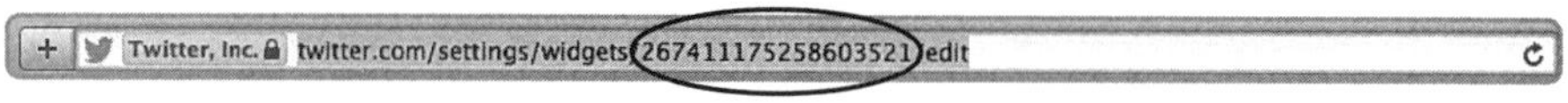
Twitter, Inc.
twitter.com/settings/widgets/267411175258603521/edit

Figure 5-31: The widget ID appears in the address bar.

When you look at the frontend of your site, you should see your tweets start to automatically show up in your sidebar, as shown in Figure 5-32.

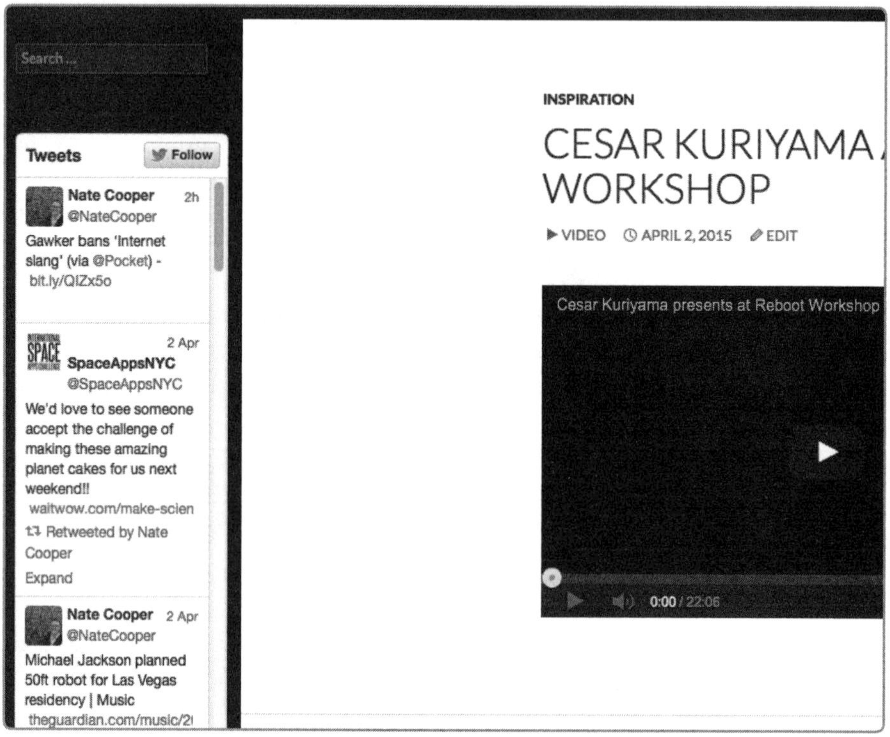
Search ...
Tweets
Follow
Nate Cooper 2h
@NateCooper
Gawker bans 'Internet slang' (via @Pocket) - bit.ly/QIZx5o
2 Apr
SpaceAppsNYC
@SpaceAppsNYC
We'd love to see someone accept the challenge of making these amazing planet cakes for us next weekend!!
waitwow.com/make-scien
Retweeted by Nate Cooper
Expand
Nate Cooper 2 Apr
@NateCooper
Michael Jackson planned 50ft robot for Las Vegas residency | Music
theguardian.com/music/2
INSPIRATION
CESAR KURIYAMA
WORKSHOP
VIDEO
APRIL 2, 2015
EDIT
Cesar Kuriyama presents at Reboot Workshop
0:00 / 22:06

Figure 5-32: A functioning Twitter widget

Let's say that we want to remove a widget. Go back to **Appearance ▸ Widgets**, and you can drag the widget out of the sidebar to anywhere on the left.

It disappears from the sidebar. If you'd like to put it back, you can simply find it in the middle again and drag it back to the sidebar. When setting up your site, you'll want to try out different widgets to get a feel for what's available so that you can customize your site just the way you'd like.

Testing Widgets

A great way to test out widgets and additional plugins is the Jetpack plugin. Jetpack is a package of useful widgets and plugins normally available only to WordPress.com users. Just connect your free WordPress.com account to use them; if you don't have one, you can create one when you install Jetpack.

Updates

Everything you add to your WordPress site will eventually have to be updated. Updates are important for your site's safety and security. You'll need to stay on top of updates to themes, plugins, and WordPress itself. Out-of-date copies of these items can expose your site to hackers and spammers.

As of WordPress 3.7, WordPress will automatically do smaller updates for you with no action needed on your end. But for now, themes, plugins, and larger WordPress updates will need to be run manually on your site. You can tell if there is an update needed any time a number appears under the Updates section of your site. To run an update, simply go to **Dashboard ▸ Updates**, as shown in Figure 5-33.

Kim's Portfolio
New
Delete Cache
Howdy, Kim
Help
Dashboard
Home
Updates
Jetpack
Posts
Media
Pages
Comments
Appearance
Plugins
Users
Tools
Settings
Meta Slider
Collapse menu
WordPress Updates
Last checked on April 3, 2014 at 10:46 pm.
Check Again
You have the latest version of WordPress.
If you need to re-install version 3.8.1, you can do so here or download the package and re-install manually:
Re-install Now
Download 3.8.1
Plugins
The following plugins have new versions available. Check the ones you want to update and then click "Update Plugins".
Update Plugins
Select All
Akismet
You have version 2.5.9 installed. Update to 2.6.0. View version 2.6.0 details.
Compatibility with WordPress 3.8.1: 100% (according to its author)
Jetpack by WordPress.com
You have version 2.8 installed. Update to 2.9.2. View version 2.9.2 details.
Compatibility with WordPress 3.8.1: 100% (according to its author)
Select All
Update Plugins
Themes

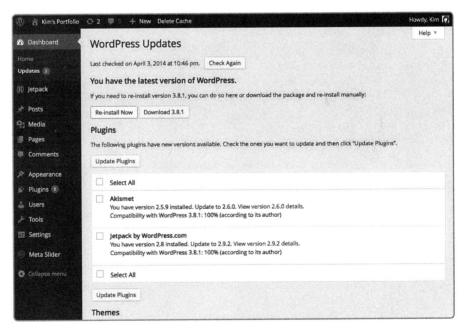

Figure 5-33: Under Dashboard ▸ Updates, you'll find all available updates for WordPress itself as well as any theme or plugin updates.

For each item that needs to be updated, you'll see a notice. If more than one item needs to be updated, you can check each one and then click the Update button for that section. Running these updates regularly is a good habit to get into.

If the theme is built normally and you use standard plugins, you shouldn't run into any problems. However, if you have a custom-built theme or plugin, you might want to check that your customized version will still be compatible before you update WordPress. Otherwise, updating to the latest version of WordPress may cause that element to stop working. You never want to put yourself in a situation where running regular updates to WordPress breaks your site.

Staying on older versions of WordPress is a security risk because it leaves your site vulnerable to hacking. If you aren't sure about the compatibility of a plugin or theme, check with the developer. Reputable theme and plugin developers will usually be aware of upcoming WordPress updates and test their products to ensure they will work with current versions of WordPress. It's rare that an outdated plugin or theme will completely break your site, however.

Moving Hosts using the Tools Panel

One cool thing about WordPress, whether you're using the free WordPress.com site or a self-hosted version, is that you're never stuck with one domain name or hosting provider. Under the Tools section, you can export your content (posts, pages, and images) and import them to another site (see Figure 5-34).

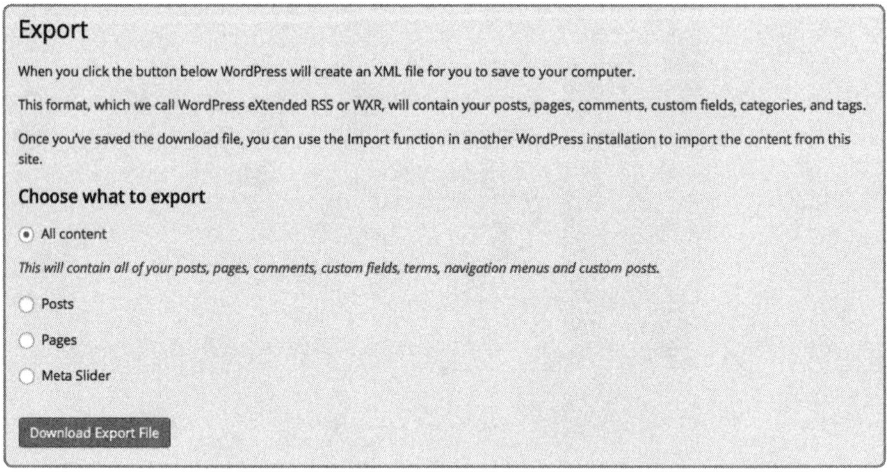

Export

When you click the button below WordPress will create an XML file for you to save to your computer.

This format, which we call WordPress eXtended RSS or WXR, will contain your posts, pages, comments, custom fields, categories, and tags.

Once you've saved the download file, you can use the Import function in another WordPress installation to import the content from this site.

Choose what to export

⊙ All content

This will contain all of your posts, pages, comments, custom fields, terms, navigation menus and custom posts.

○ Posts

○ Pages

○ Meta Slider

[Download Export File]

Figure 5-34: The Tools tab has an export option so that you can migrate or back up your WordPress site.

You can also import content from a number of other popular CMS tools (see Figure 5-35), so moving to WordPress is never difficult. When you choose Export, you'll get a file containing all of your content downloaded to your computer. When you have your new site set up, simply go to Import, and it brings back all of your stuff. Keep in mind that your theme won't be transferred over. On the new site, you'll have to choose the theme you'd like to use separately. But all of those posts you've spent days writing are there for you automatically once you import.

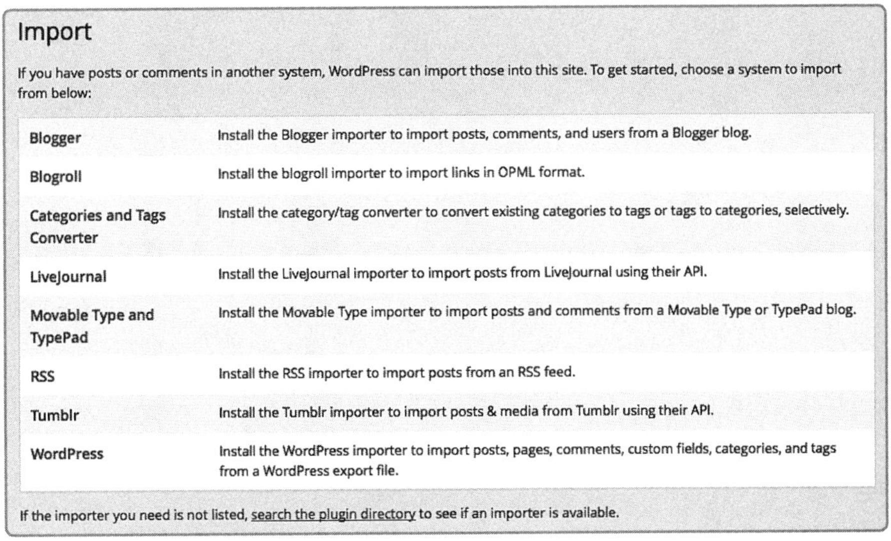

Import

If you have posts or comments in another system, WordPress can import those into this site. To get started, choose a system to import from below:

Blogger	Install the Blogger importer to import posts, comments, and users from a Blogger blog.
Blogroll	Install the blogroll importer to import links in OPML format.
Categories and Tags Converter	Install the category/tag converter to convert existing categories to tags or tags to categories, selectively.
LiveJournal	Install the LiveJournal importer to import posts from LiveJournal using their API.
Movable Type and TypePad	Install the Movable Type importer to import posts and comments from a Movable Type or TypePad blog.
RSS	Install the RSS importer to import posts from an RSS feed.
Tumblr	Install the Tumblr importer to import posts & media from Tumblr using their API.
WordPress	Install the WordPress importer to import posts, pages, comments, custom fields, categories, and tags from a WordPress export file.

If the importer you need is not listed, search the plugin directory to see if an importer is available.

Figure 5-35: WordPress allows you to import from several popular blogging platforms.

For More Help

If you're wondering where to get additional information on using WordPress and tinkering with your website, the best place to go is the WordPress Codex, which can be found at *http:// codex.wordpress.org/*. Most of the time when you google a question about WordPress, you'll end up here anyway. There's the regular WordPress documentation, and there are also helpful forums where you can see questions that others have asked about WordPress. Finally, there are also a number of good sites to learn about WordPress like *http://digwp.com/*, *http:// torquemag.io/*, and *http://wp.smashingmagazine.com/*. The best part about learning WordPress is that there's a wealth of free information out there and many, many people willing to provide help.

Now that you've gotten a good picture of what WordPress is *truly* capable of, go back and create an amazing plan for your site. What goes where? Organize it all and get blogging. The sky is the limit.

The Big Launch

There's No Place Like Your Web Host

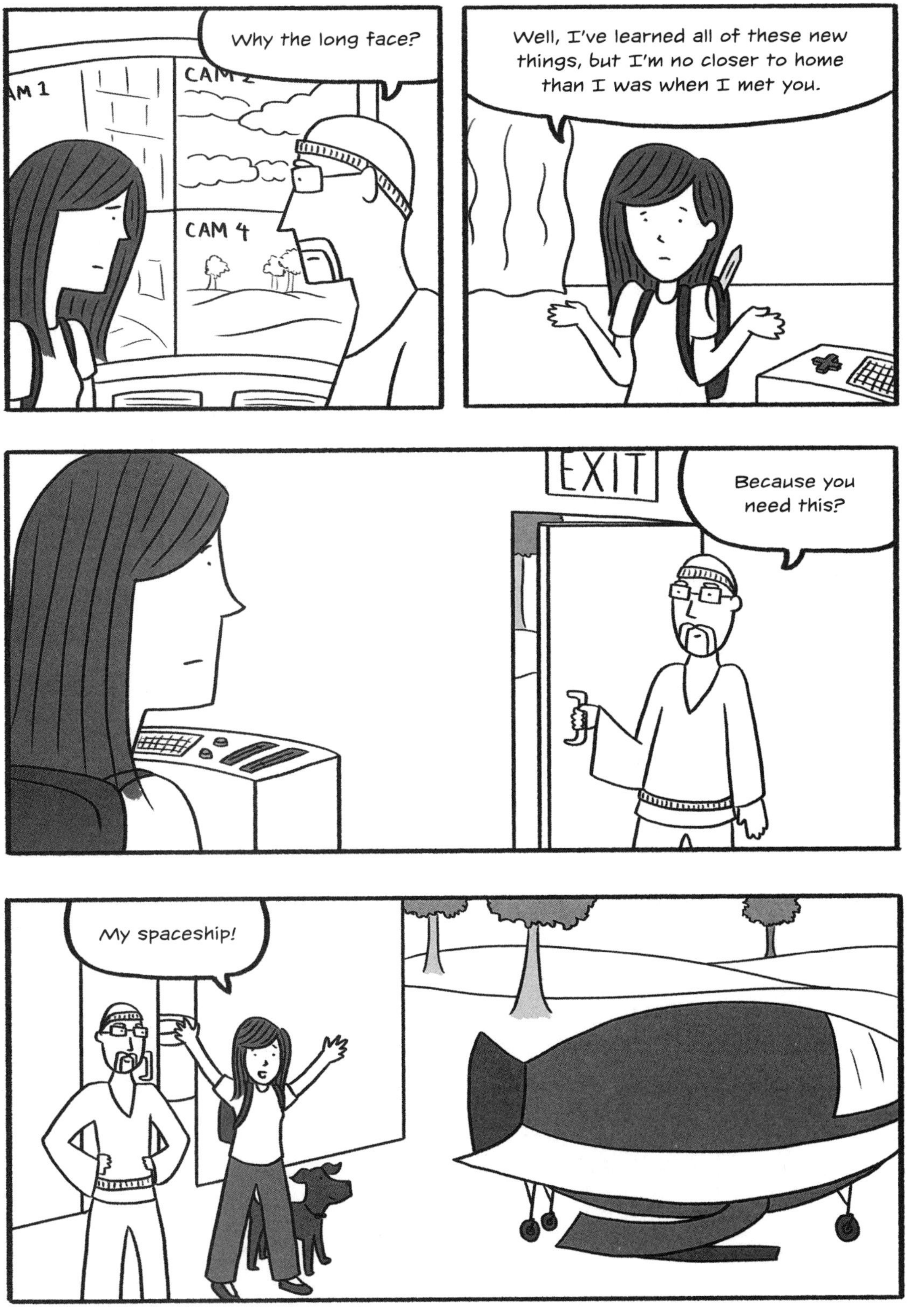
Why the long face?
CAM 1
CAM 2
CAM 4
Well, I've learned all of these new things, but I'm no closer to home than I was when I met you.
EXIT
Because you need this?
My spaceship!

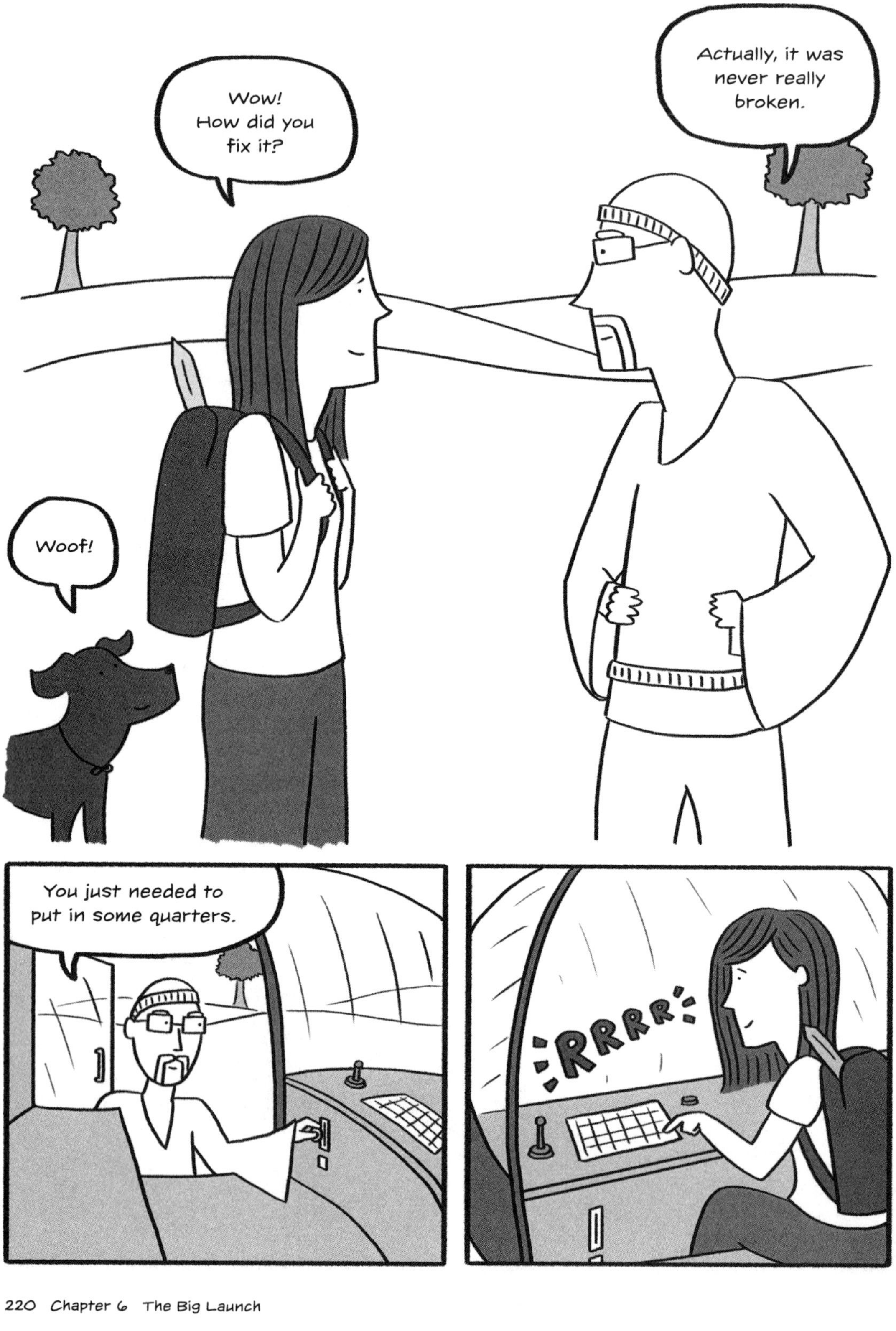
Wow! How did you fix it?
Actually, it was never really broken.
Woof!
You just needed to put in some quarters.
RRRR

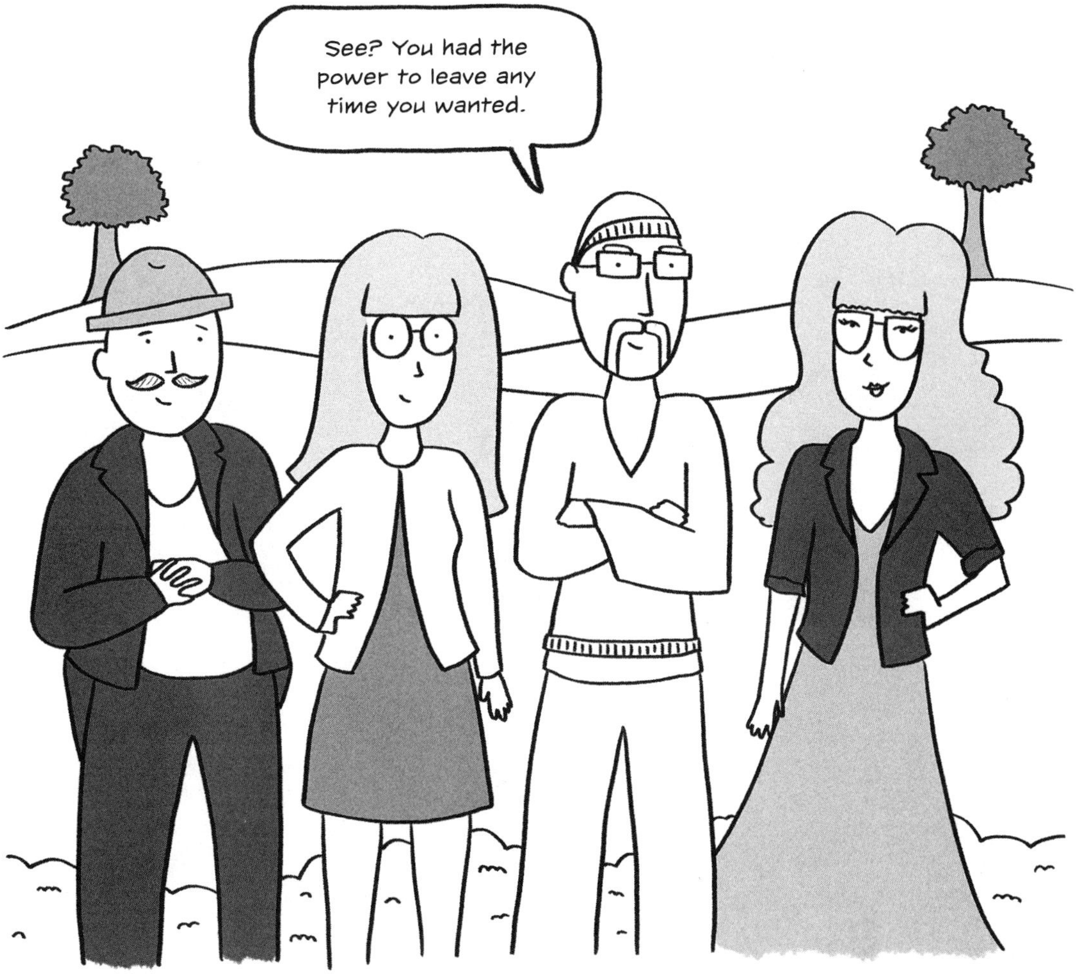
See? You had the power to leave any time you wanted.

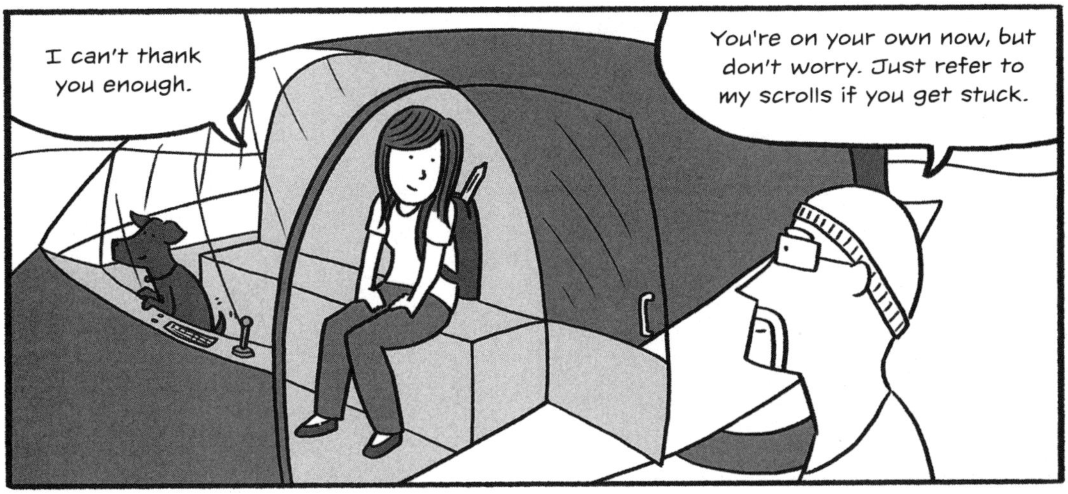
I can't thank you enough.
You're on your own now, but don't worry. Just refer to my scrolls if you get stuck.

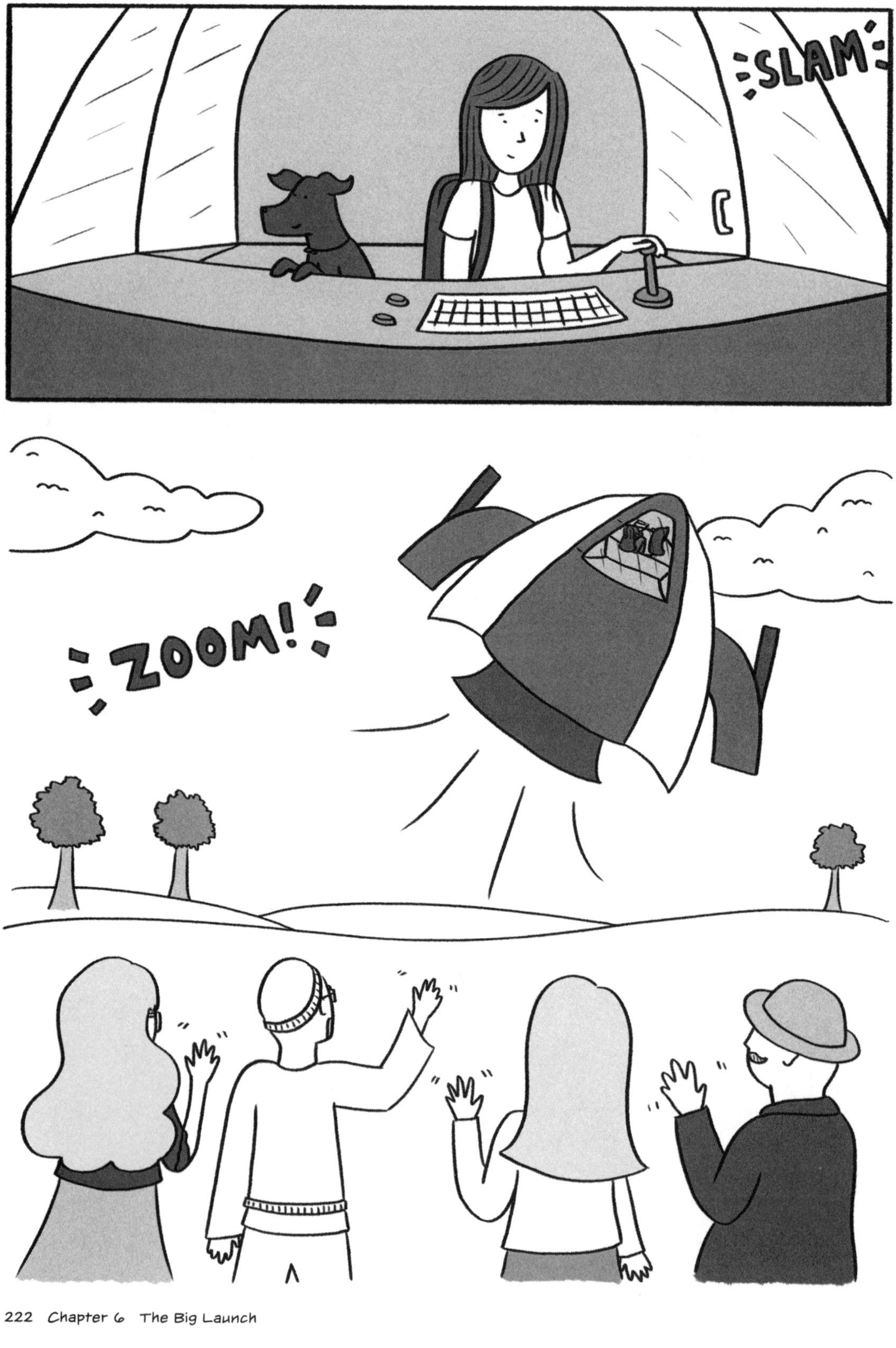
SLAM
ZOOM!

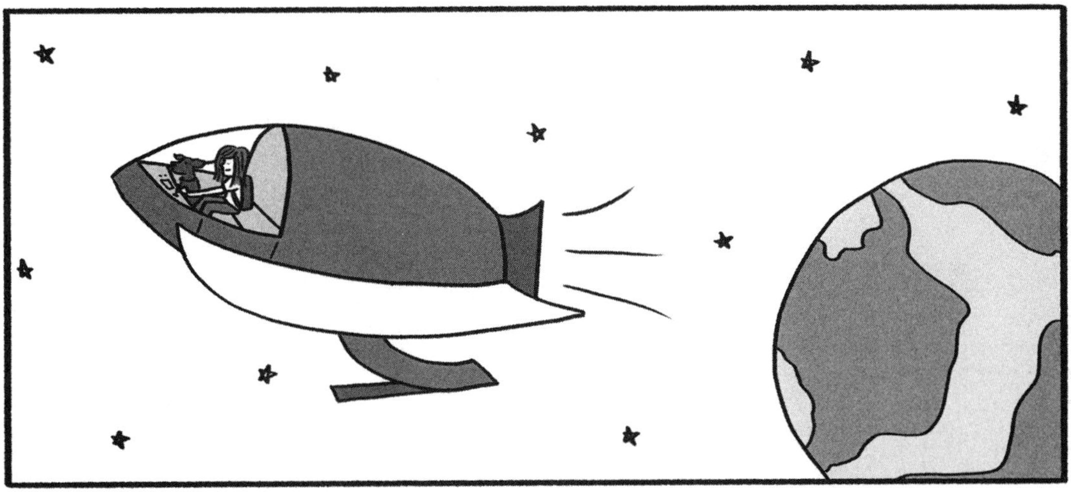

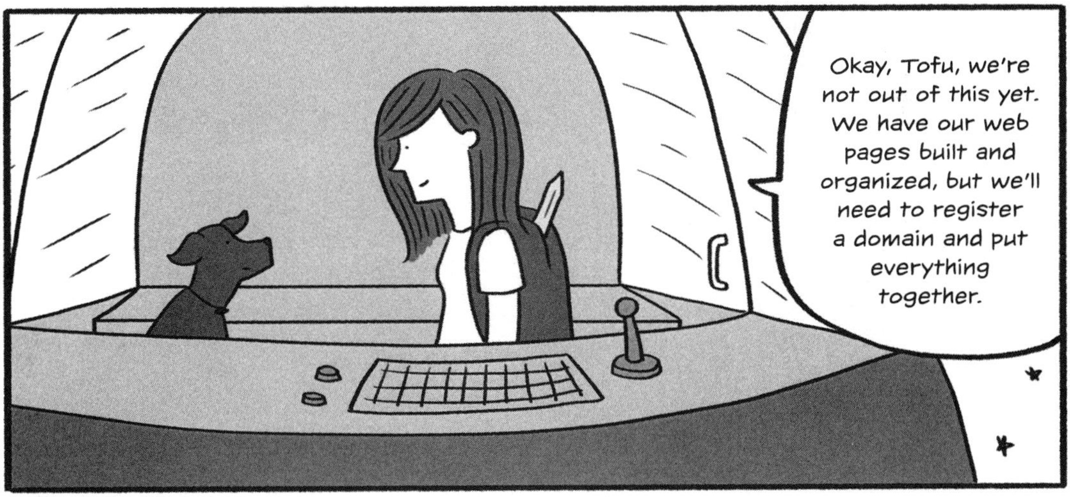
Okay, Tofu, we're not out of this yet. We have our web pages built and organized, but we'll need to register a domain and put everything together.

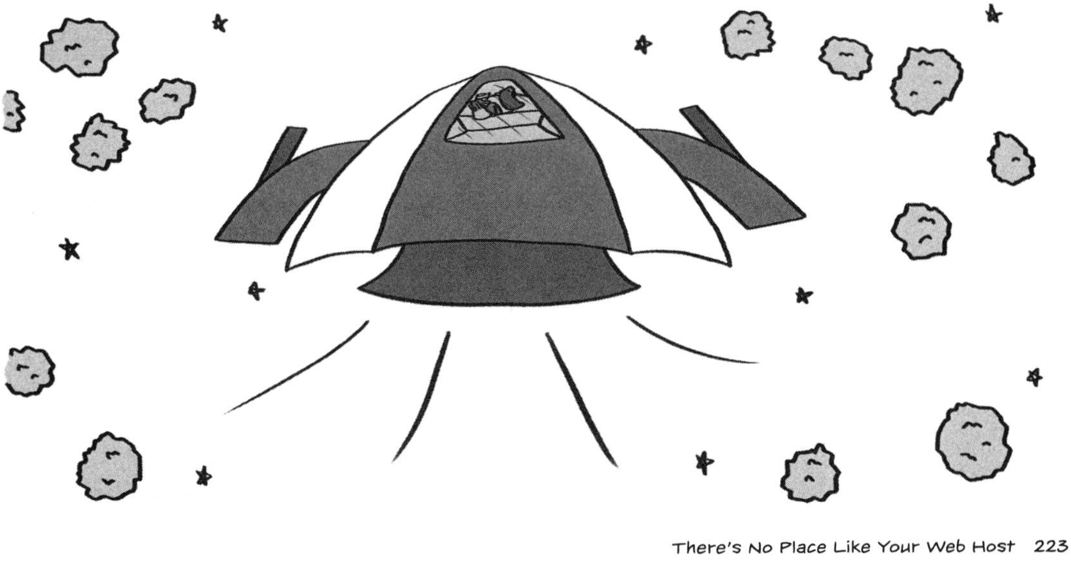

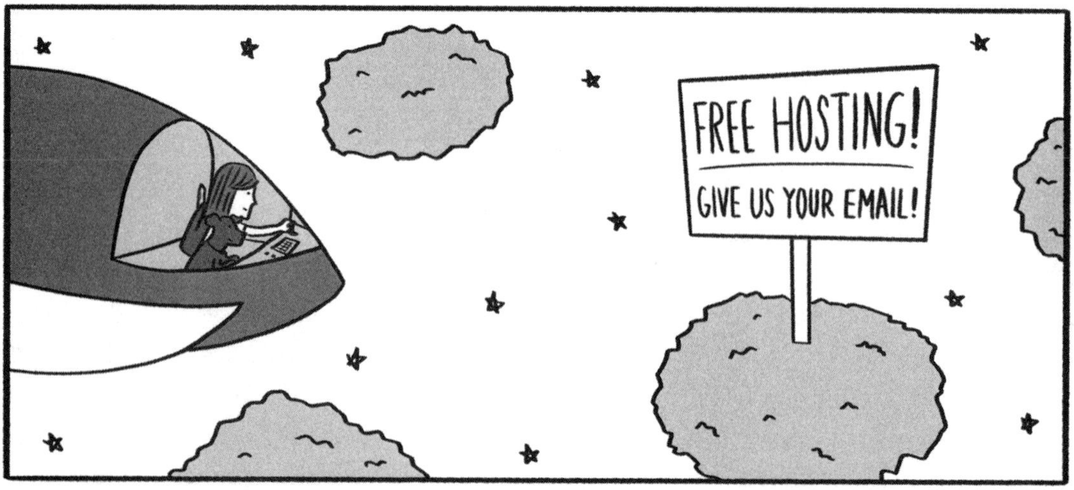
FREE HOSTING!
GIVE US YOUR EMAIL!

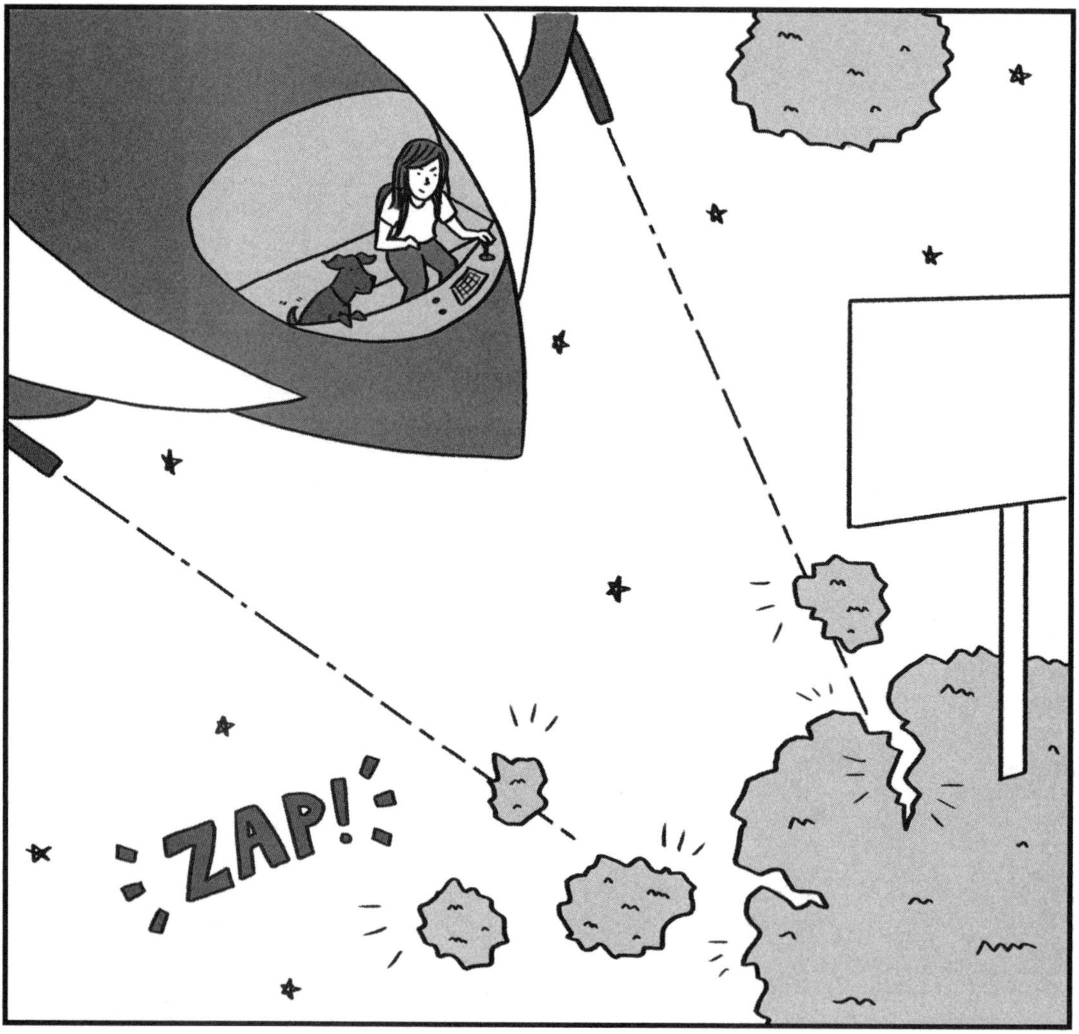
ZAP!

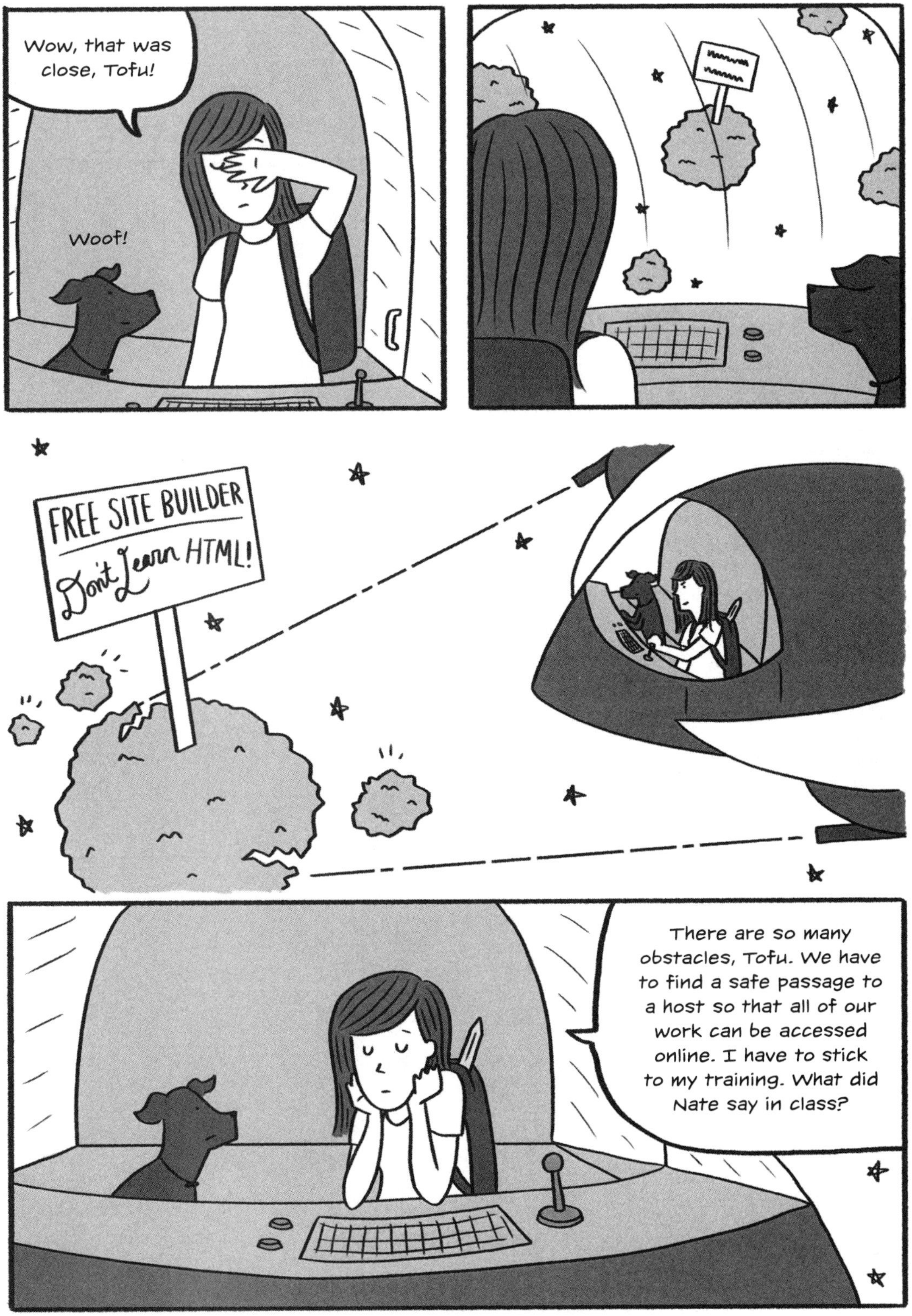

Wow, that was close, Tofu!
Woof!
FREE SITE BUILDER
Don't Learn HTML!
There are so many obstacles, Tofu. We have to find a safe passage to a host so that all of our work can be accessed online. I have to stick to my training. What did Nate say in class?

We're going to be learning how to build web pages using HTML and CSS, and eventually WordPress. If you know you'd like to build a blog from the very start, WordPress is a great option.

That's right; Nate said that although there are free hosting plans available, we should probably expect to pay for one that costs around $50 to $100 per year. To find a home for my portfolio, we'll have to find a hosting plan that will support WordPress and give me FTP access so I can edit the HTML and CSS directly, too.

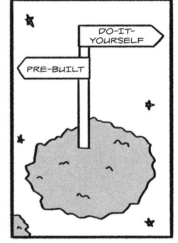

DO-IT-YOURSELF

PRE-BUILT

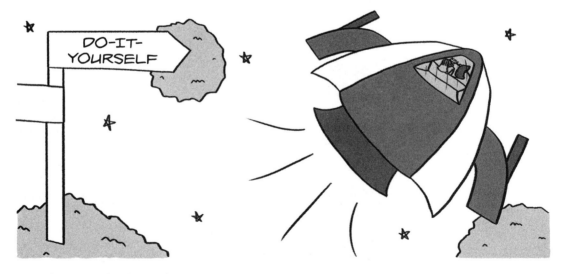

DO-IT-YOURSELF

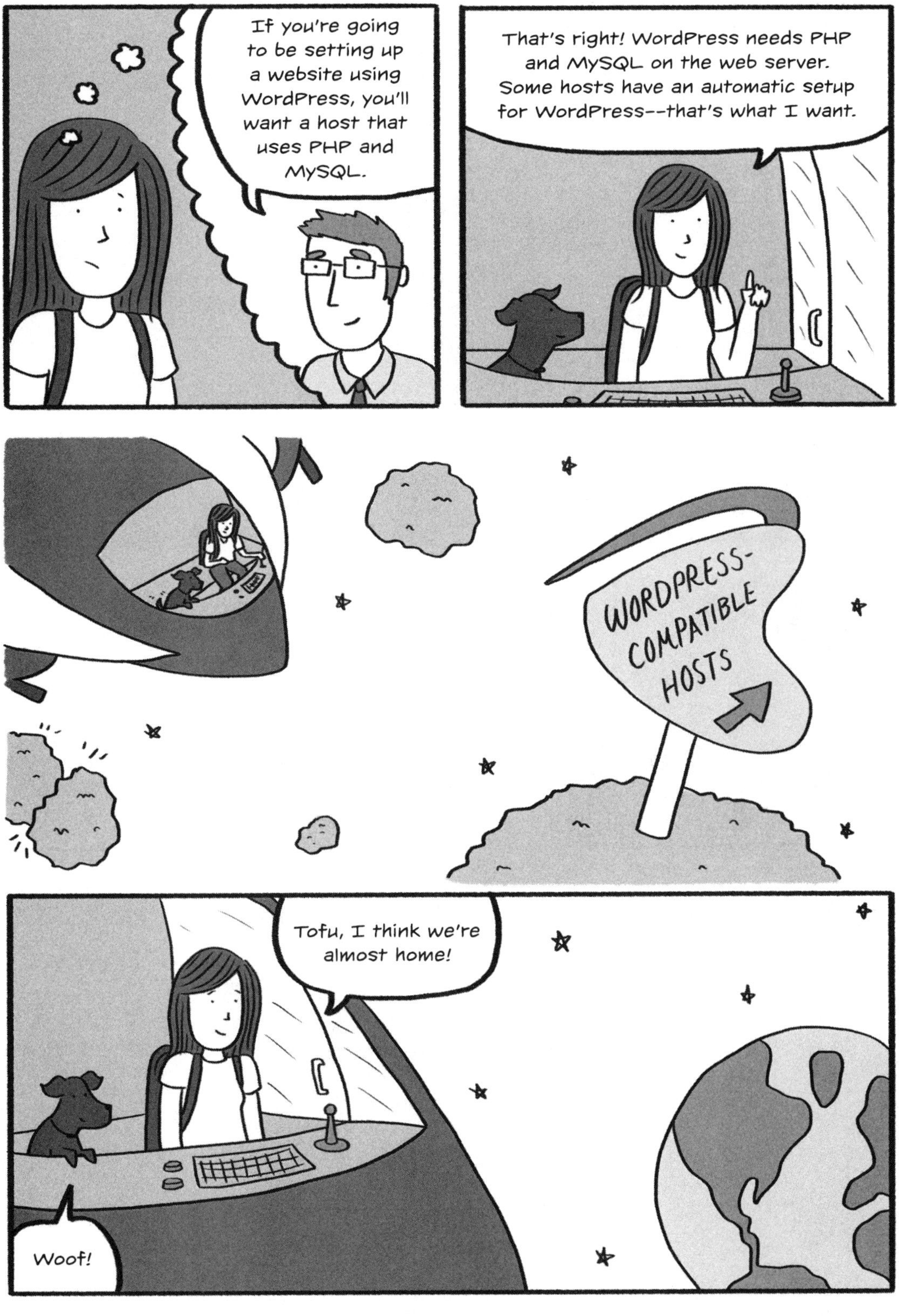
If you're going to be setting up a website using WordPress, you'll want a host that uses PHP and MySQL.
That's right! WordPress needs PHP and MySQL on the web server. Some hosts have an automatic setup for WordPress--that's what I want.
WORDPRESS-COMPATIBLE HOSTS
Tofu, I think we're almost home!
Woof!

Kim's Portfolio Finds a Home

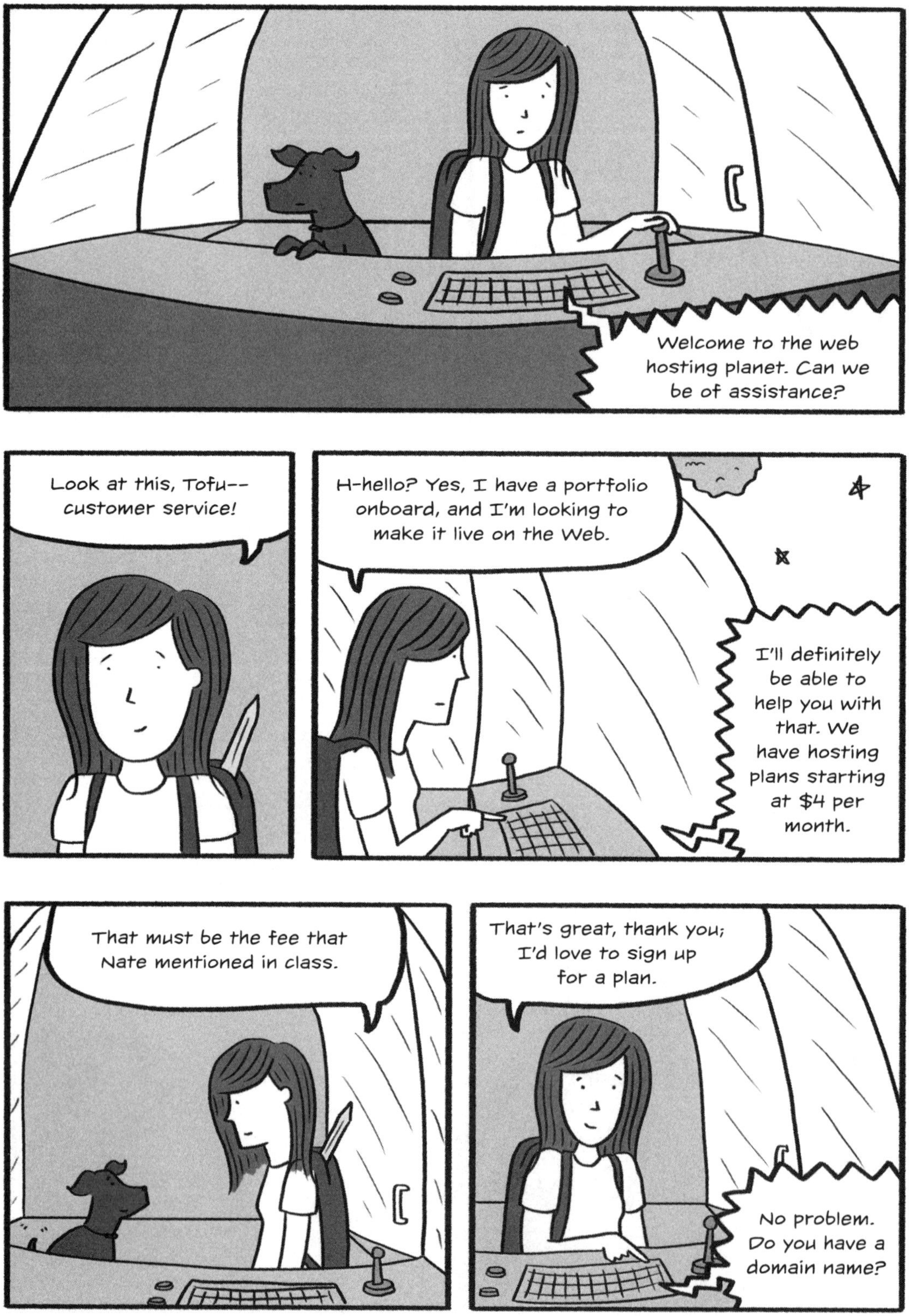
Welcome to the web hosting planet. Can we be of assistance?
Look at this, Tofu--customer service!
H-hello? Yes, I have a portfolio onboard, and I'm looking to make it live on the Web.
I'll definitely be able to help you with that. We have hosting plans starting at $4 per month.
That must be the fee that Nate mentioned in class.
That's great, thank you; I'd love to sign up for a plan.
No problem. Do you have a domain name?

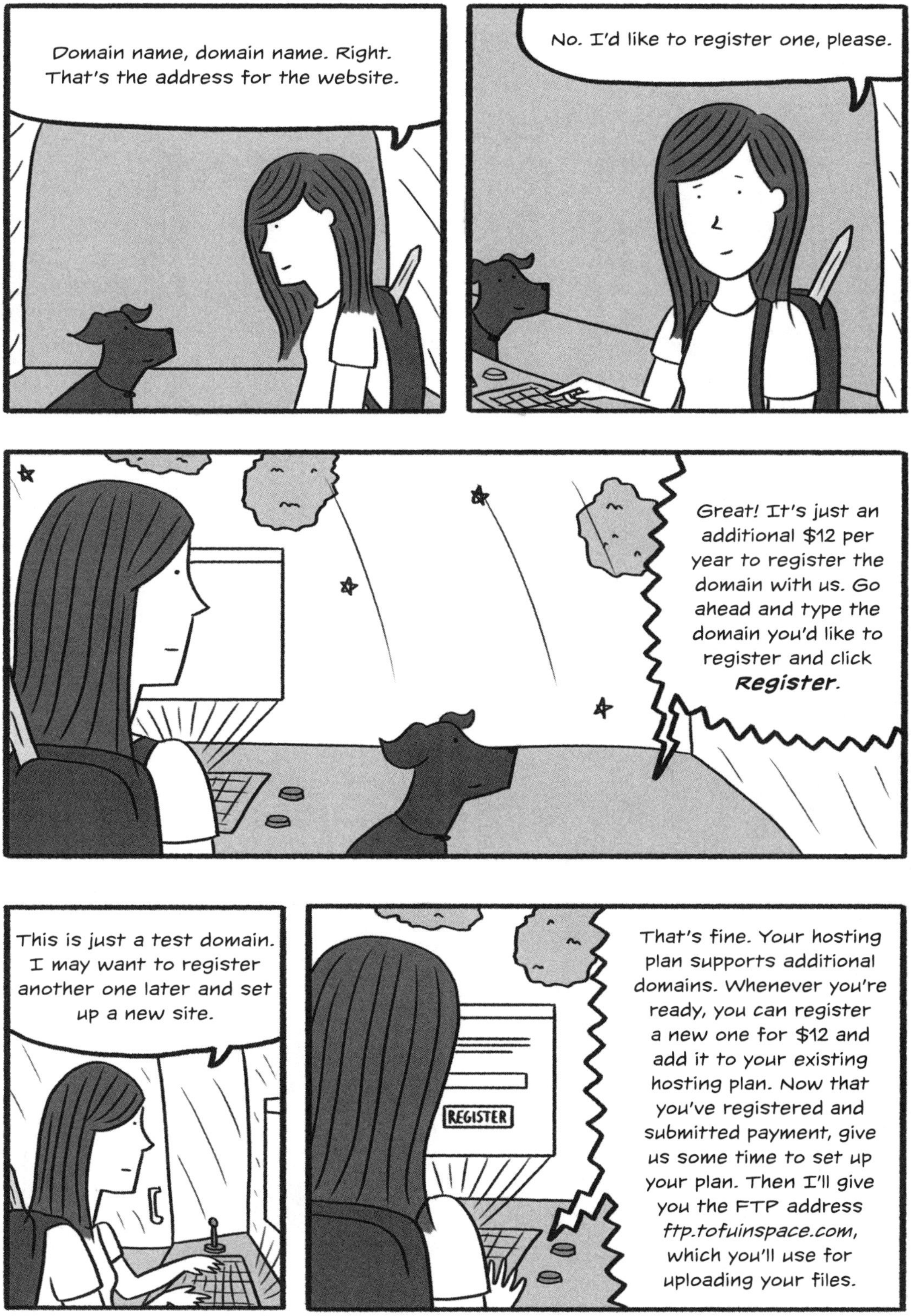

Domain name, domain name. Right. That's the address for the website.
No. I'd like to register one, please.
Great! It's just an additional $12 per year to register the domain with us. Go ahead and type the domain you'd like to register and click **Register**.
This is just a test domain. I may want to register another one later and set up a new site.
REGISTER
That's fine. Your hosting plan supports additional domains. Whenever you're ready, you can register a new one for $12 and add it to your existing hosting plan. Now that you've registered and submitted payment, give us some time to set up your plan. Then I'll give you the FTP address *ftp.tofuinspace.com*, which you'll use for uploading your files.

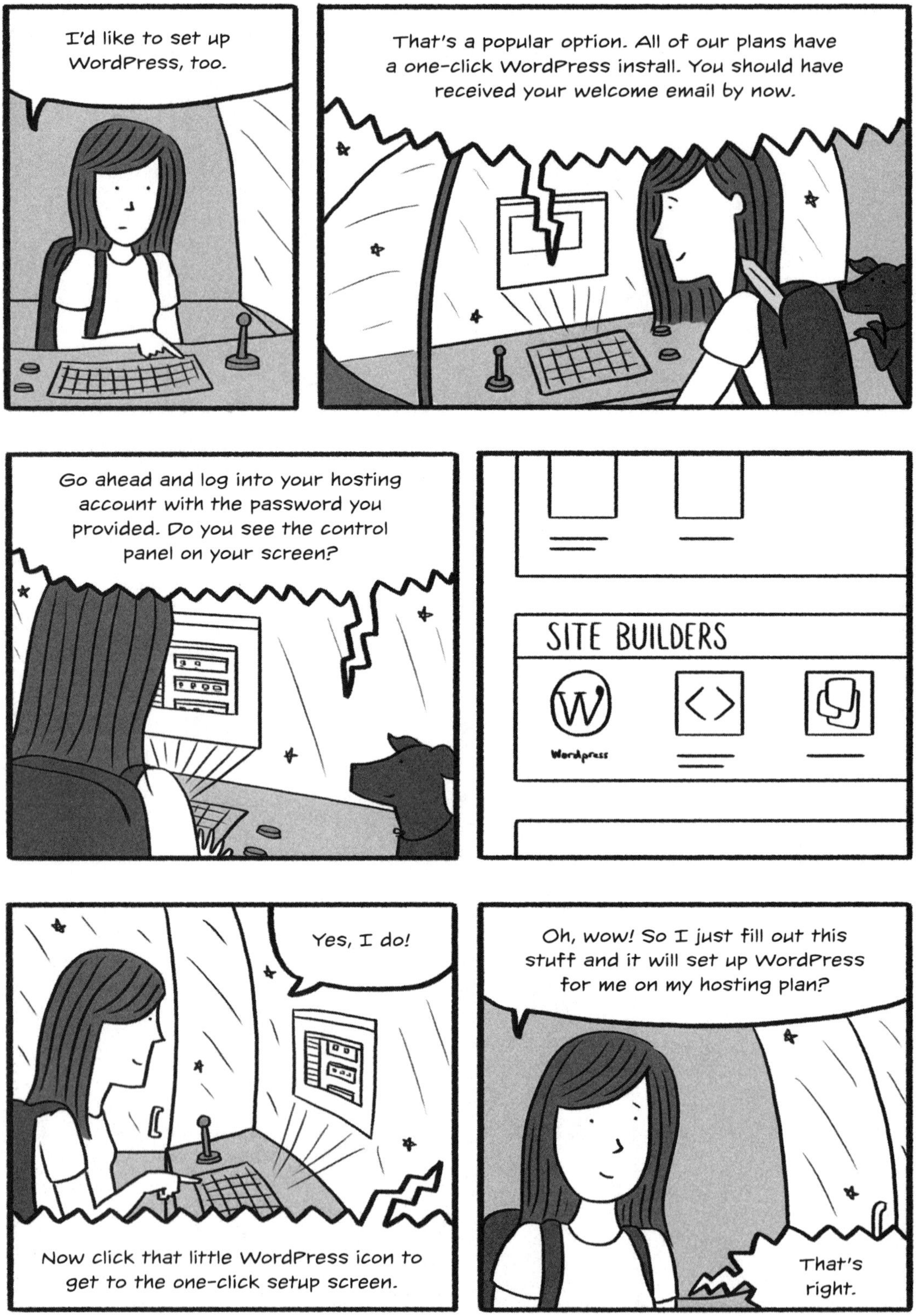
I'd like to set up WordPress, too.
That's a popular option. All of our plans have a one-click WordPress install. You should have received your welcome email by now.
Go ahead and log into your hosting account with the password you provided. Do you see the control panel on your screen?
SITE BUILDERS
WordPress
Yes, I do!
Now click that little WordPress icon to get to the one-click setup screen.
Oh, wow! So I just fill out this stuff and it will set up WordPress for me on my hosting plan?
That's right.

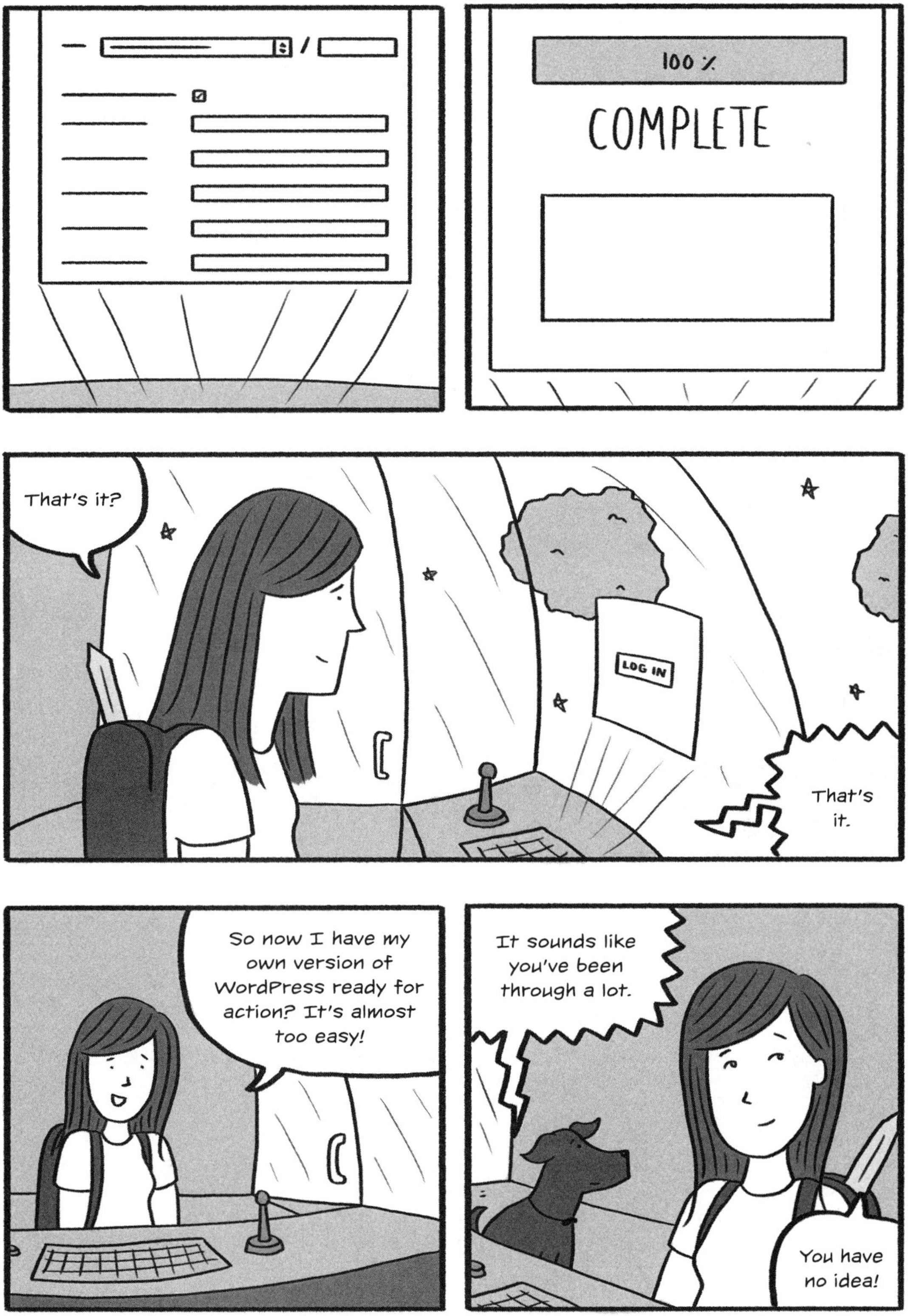
100 %
COMPLETE
That's it?
LOG IN
That's it.
So now I have my own version of WordPress ready for action? It's almost too easy!
It sounds like you've been through a lot.
You have no idea!

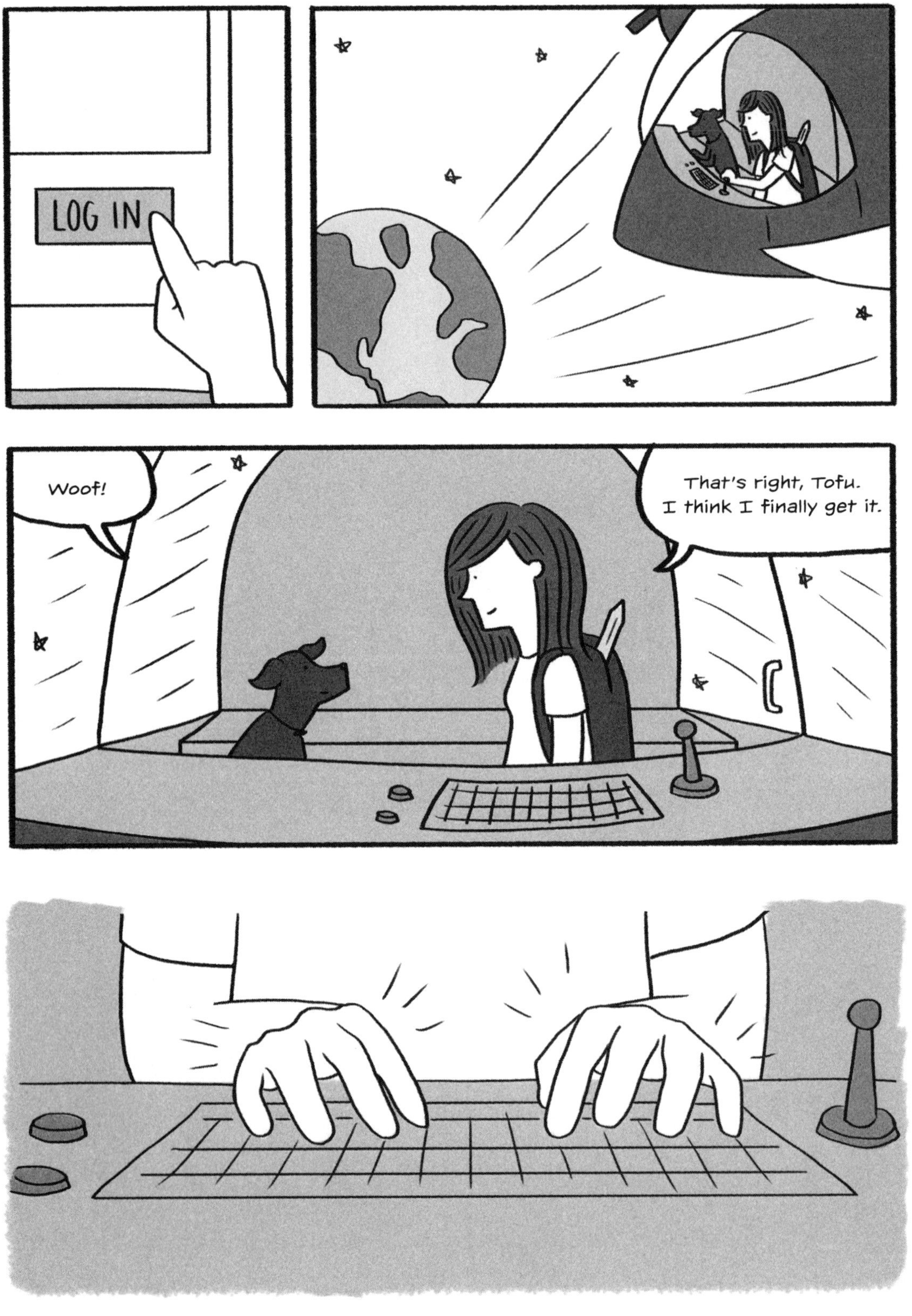
LOG IN
Woof!
That's right, Tofu.
I think I finally get it.

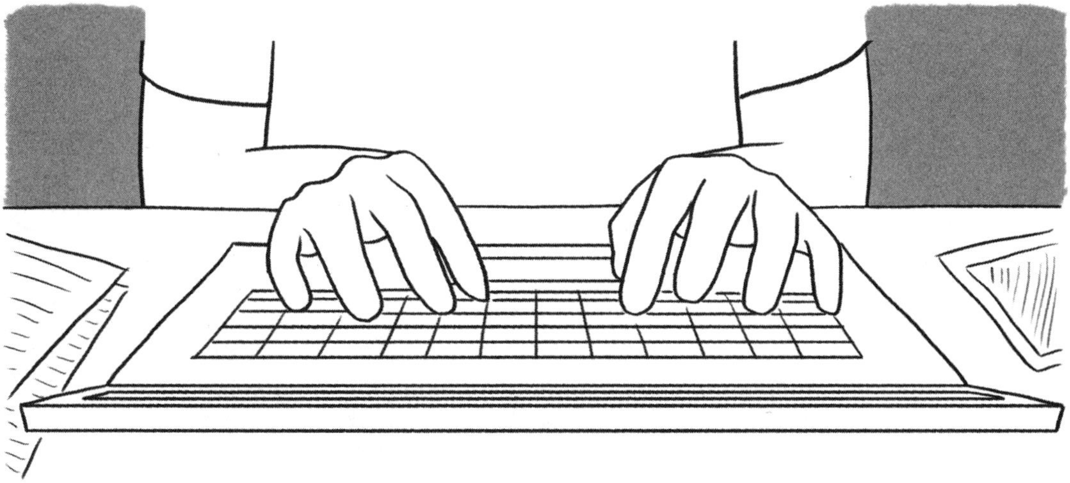

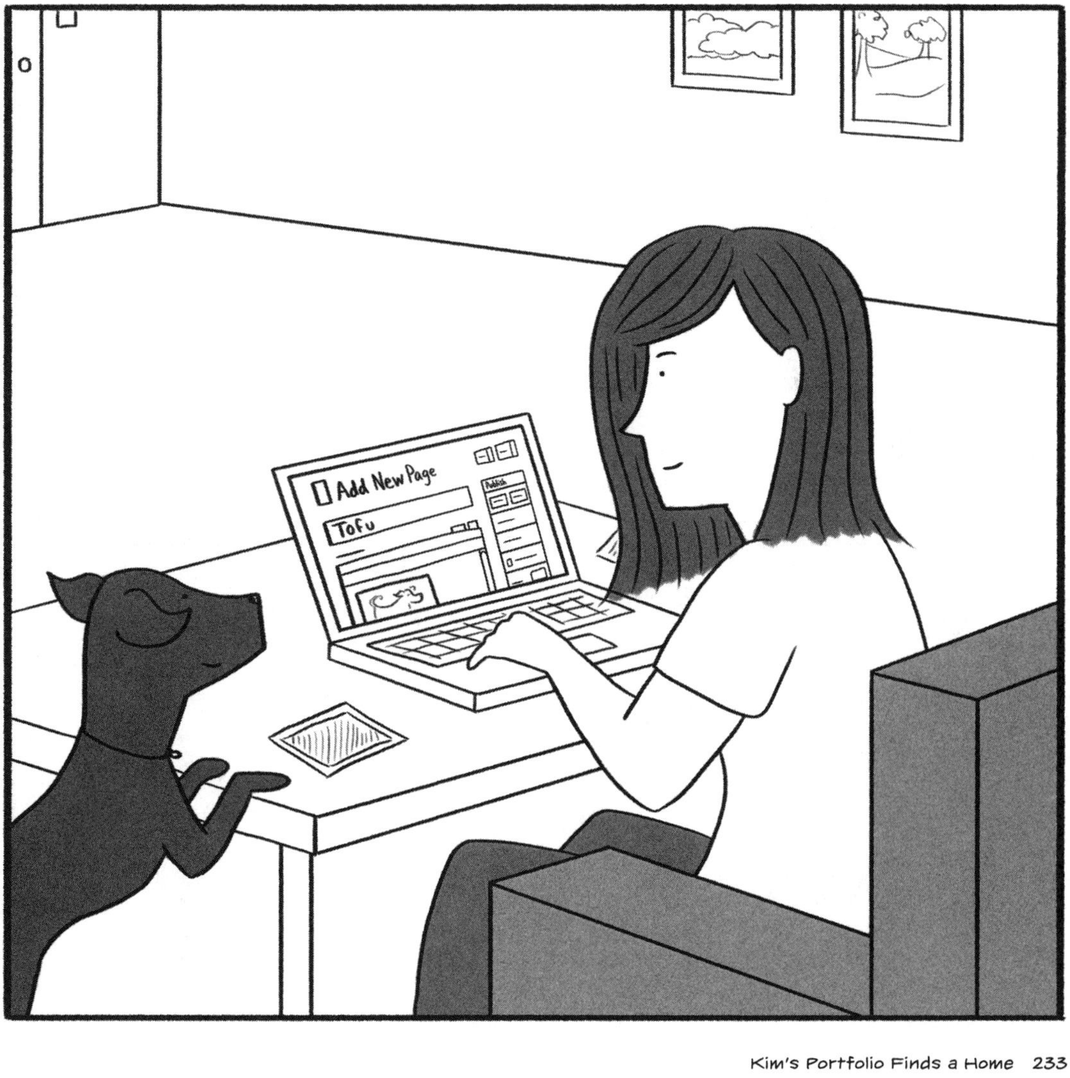
Add New Page
Tofu

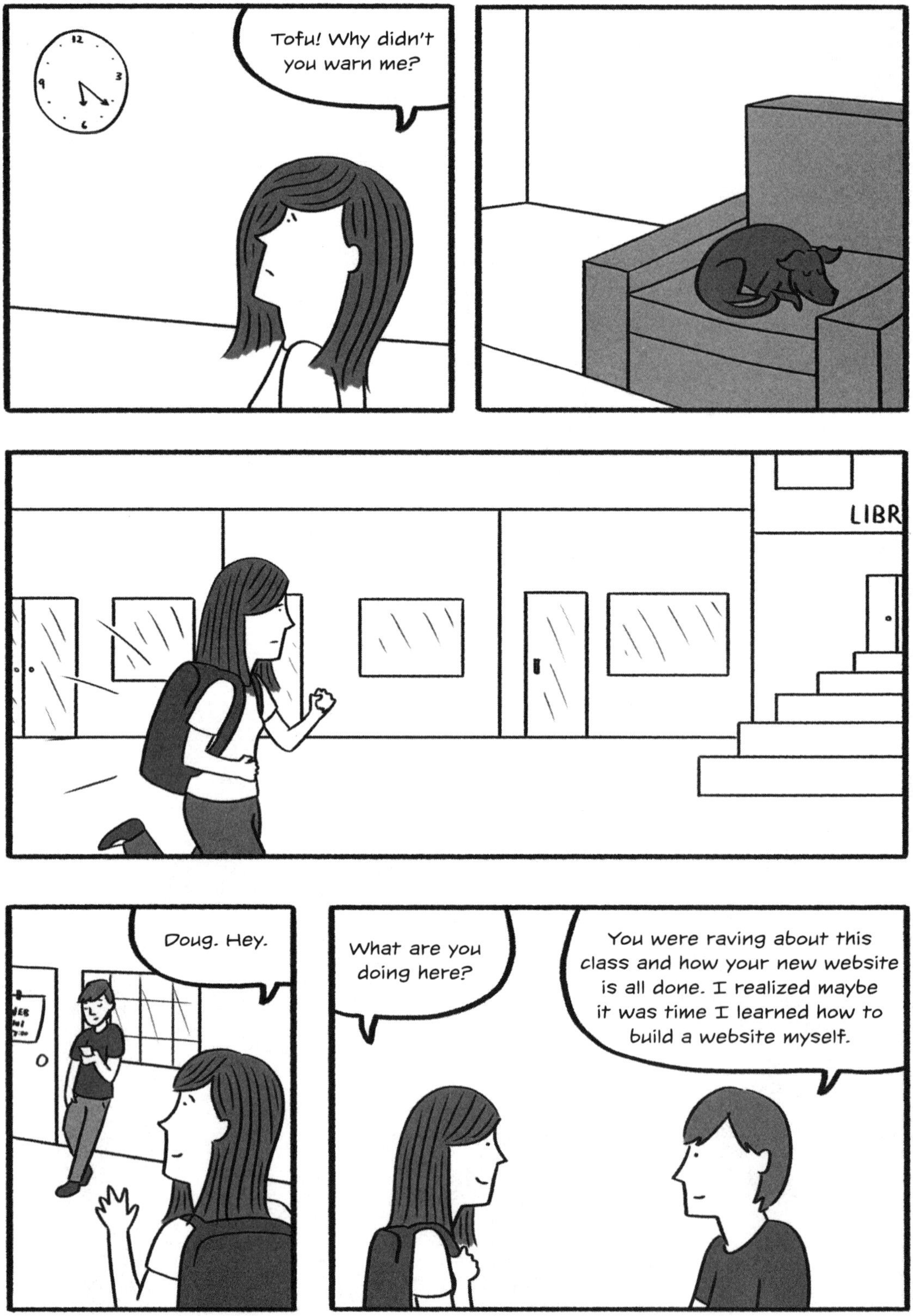
Tofu! Why didn't you warn me?
LIBR
Doug. Hey.
What are you doing here?
You were raving about this class and how your new website is all done. I realized maybe it was time I learned how to build a website myself.

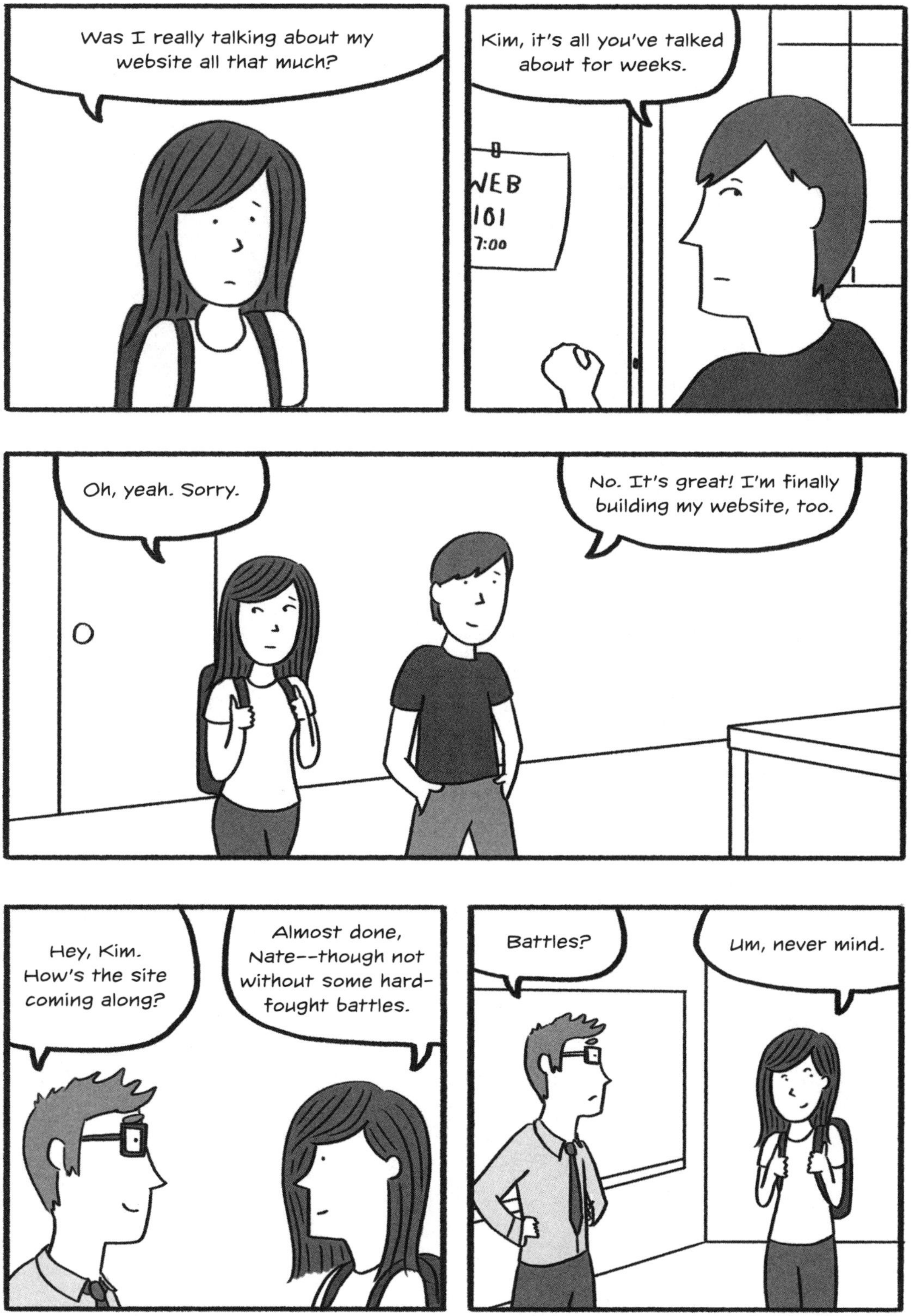
Was I really talking about my website all that much?
Kim, it's all you've talked about for weeks.
WEB 101 7:00
Oh, yeah. Sorry.
No. It's great! I'm finally building my website, too.
Hey, Kim. How's the site coming along?
Almost done, Nate--though not without some hard-fought battles.
Battles?
Um, never mind.

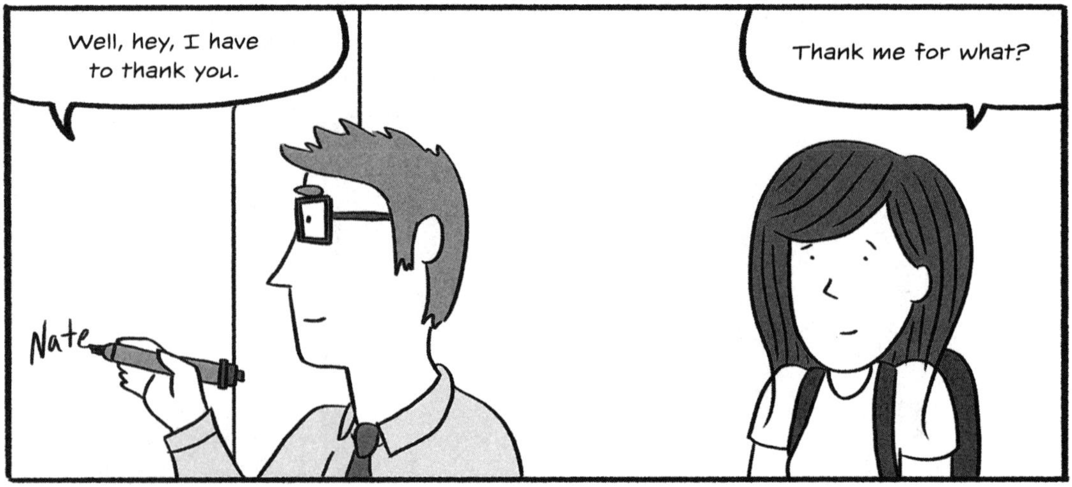
Well, hey, I have to thank you.
Nate
Thank me for what?

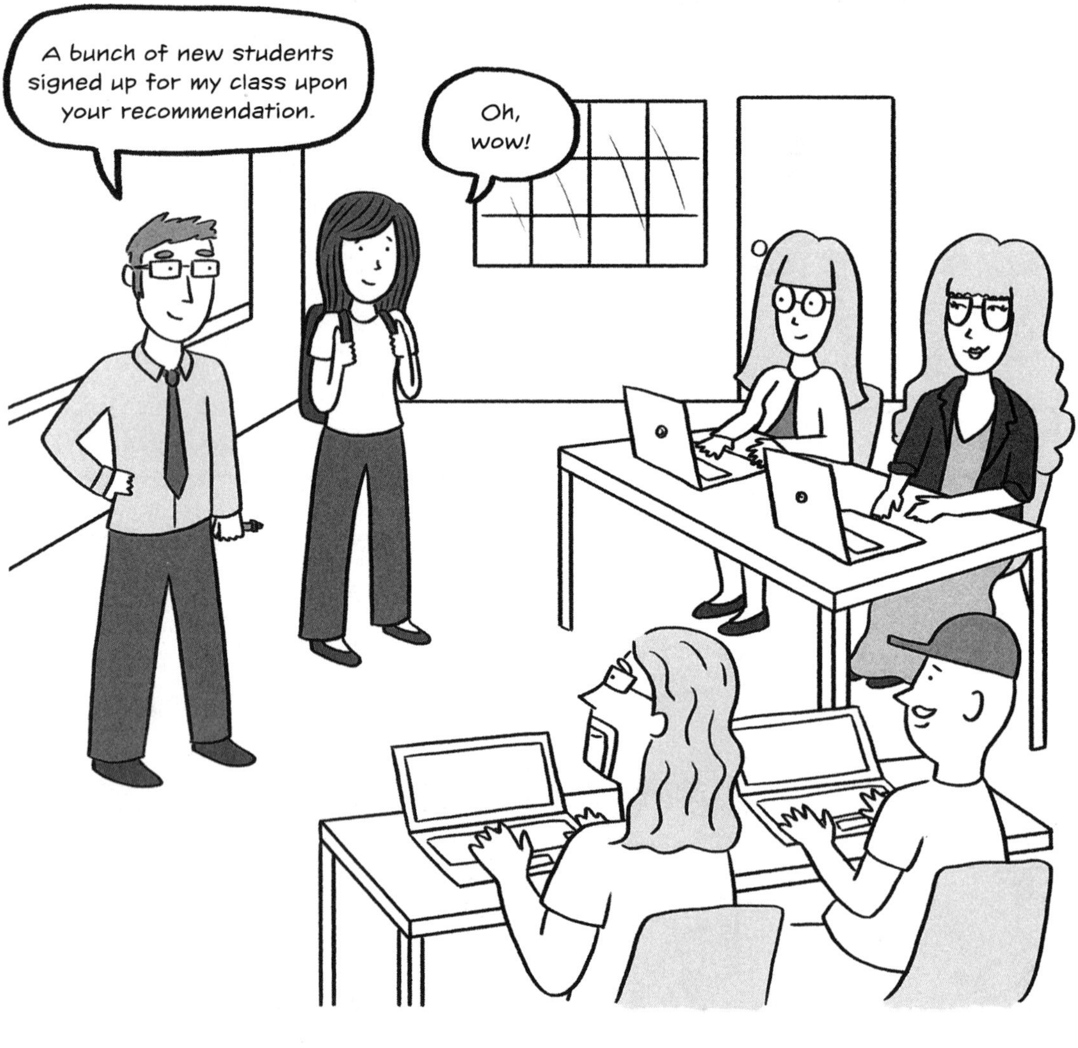
A bunch of new students signed up for my class upon your recommendation.
Oh, wow!

So You're Ready to Set Up Your Website

Building your website starts with a name. Before you can set up a host (where the files for your website will be stored), you need to register a domain name. The *domain* is the address that others will use to find your site online.

Registrars are companies that allow you to claim your desired domain. There are several thousand registrars online. You can register common top-level domains—like *.com*, *.org*, and *.net*—with most registrars. Visit a site like GoDaddy, BlueHost, or HostGator to get started (see Figure 6-1). You'll be able to check whether your domain name is available, and if it is, you can pay a fee to claim it. Think of this fee as a kind of rental. A domain is registered on a recurring basis, so you may choose to register a domain for a year or longer depending on your preference. You will need to pay the rental fee at the end of this time period to *renew* your domain.

There's only one name for each top-level domain available. So, for example, if you're trying to register *kimswebsite.com* and it's taken, you might check to see if *kimswebsite.co* or *kimswebsite.org* is available instead. You may need to get creative!

NOTE   *When your registration term ends, your registered domain goes back to the available domain pool and anyone can register it. If you want to ensure that your domain is never taken from you, be sure to stay on top of renewing your registration. Many registrars offer autorenewal.*

Wondering which kind of domain to register? Different groups tend to use different domains (though there aren't many hard-and-fast rules). The domain *.org* is often used by organizations and nonprofits, *.com* is used by companies, and *.net* (short for *network*) is used by lots of different types of groups. There are even reserved top-level domains for special purposes, such as *.edu* for schools, *.mil* for the military, and *.gov* for governments. Various countries also have their own unique top-level domains, and you can often register them even if you don't live there. For example, *.co* (Columbia), *.tv* (Tuvalu), and *.io* (British Indian Ocean Territory) are all domains that were originally available for a specific country but have been co-opted for use by companies wanting a cool-sounding domain name. These unique top-level domains often require you to work with a particular registrar, and may be more expensive than a more common domain name.

You may decide to register a domain even before you have a hosting plan so that no one else can register your awesome domain name. Remember that after you've registered a domain, it's *all* yours. This means you can take the domain you've registered and transfer it to another host should you wish.

Registering a domain is generally inexpensive. But owning the domain alone isn't enough to have a website. You'll also need to set up a host—a company that serves your website to your visitors. Hosts and domains are independent of each other, but you can often set them up using the same company to save some time and money.

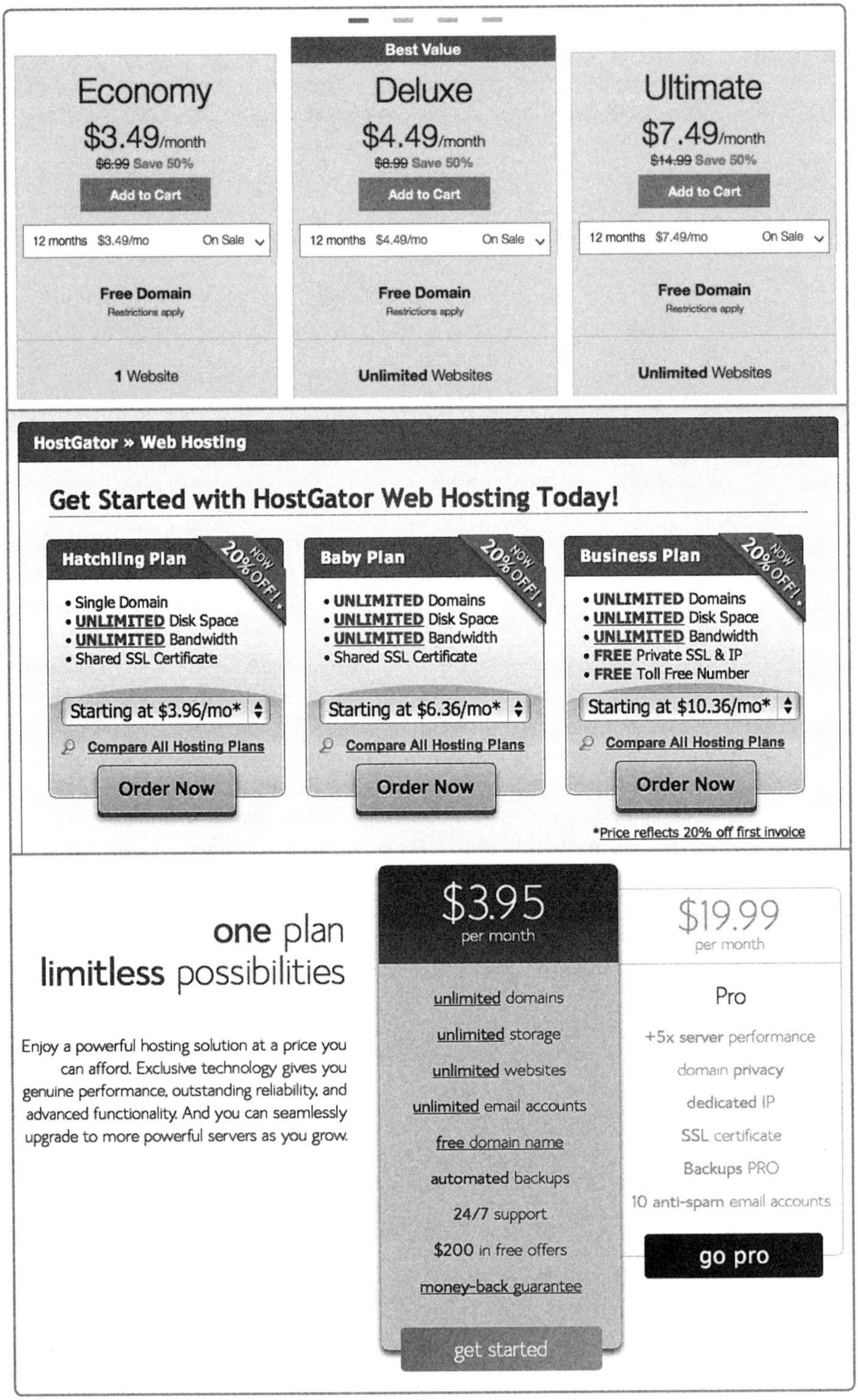
Best Value
Economy
$3.49/month
$6.99 Save 50%
Add to Cart
12 months $3.49/mo On Sale
Free Domain
Restrictions apply
1 Website
Deluxe
$4.49/month
$8.99 Save 50%
Add to Cart
12 months $4.49/mo On Sale
Free Domain
Restrictions apply
Unlimited Websites
Ultimate
$7.49/month
$14.99 Save 50%
Add to Cart
12 months $7.49/mo On Sale
Free Domain
Restrictions apply
Unlimited Websites
HostGator » Web Hosting
Get Started with HostGator Web Hosting Today!
Hatchling Plan
NOW 20% OFF!
• Single Domain
• UNLIMITED Disk Space
• UNLIMITED Bandwidth
• Shared SSL Certificate
Starting at $3.96/mo*
Compare All Hosting Plans
Order Now
Baby Plan
NOW 20% OFF!
• UNLIMITED Domains
• UNLIMITED Disk Space
• UNLIMITED Bandwidth
• Shared SSL Certificate
Starting at $6.36/mo*
Compare All Hosting Plans
Order Now
Business Plan
NOW 20% OFF!
• UNLIMITED Domains
• UNLIMITED Disk Space
• UNLIMITED Bandwidth
• FREE Private SSL & IP
• FREE Toll Free Number
Starting at $10.36/mo*
Compare All Hosting Plans
Order Now
*Price reflects 20% off first invoice
one plan
limitless possibilities
Enjoy a powerful hosting solution at a price you can afford. Exclusive technology gives you genuine performance, outstanding reliability, and advanced functionality. And you can seamlessly upgrade to more powerful servers as you grow.
$3.95
per month
unlimited domains
unlimited storage
unlimited websites
unlimited email accounts
free domain name
automated backups
24/7 support
$200 in free offers
money-back guarantee
get started
$19.99
per month
Pro
+5x server performance
domain privacy
dedicated IP
SSL certificate
Backups PRO
10 anti-spam email accounts
go pro

Figure 6-1: A comparison of hosting plans offered by GoDaddy (top), HostGator (middle), and BlueHost (bottom)

Setting Up Hosting: A Home Online

Picking a host can seem daunting at first because there are so many options available and the choices can be overwhelming. Don't worry! It's really hard to go wrong. And you can always change your host if you are unhappy with it. Start by thinking about what you want. Do you want WordPress? Pick a host with one-click WordPress installs. Or do you want just a basic HTML site to start?

Here are some questions for you to consider when shopping for hosting:

How many domains does your account support?

For each website, you'll need a separate domain. You'll need more than one domain if you are setting up several businesses, or if you want one site for your business and another for a personal website or blog.

How much storage is available?

This is mainly an issue of how many files you'll store online. If you are building a portfolio and storing a lot of high-quality images or videos, then you'll want to find a host that provides a reasonable amount of space. Many hosts now offer unlimited storage, so if you're concerned about space, look for a host that isn't limited.

What is the bandwidth limit?

Bandwidth (sometimes called *transfer*) refers to the amount of information that can be sent from your host to your audience per month. If you have a lot of visitors and they are accessing large files, then more bandwidth is used. Many shared hosting plans have unlimited bandwidth options, so look for those if you have concerns.

Is email hosting included?

While we won't be covering email in this book, most web hosts offer email hosting along with their regular hosting packages. Don't assume it always comes with your hosting packages, though; it may cost extra.

What kind of support is included?

Is there phone support available should you need to call the host? Does the host have an easy-to-access online chat service or customer support email? Customer service is often one of the major factors that sets hosting companies apart.

Once you've found a host that offers you what you need, the safe bet is to choose the plan that best fits your budget. It's not difficult to upgrade to a more expensive plan if you need to later. More expensive hosting packages may make sense if you have a particular goal in mind, like hosting two separate domains. For example, you may register one domain for a personal site and another domain for an unrelated business. Many hosting plans offer free addon domains with certain plans, as shown in Figure 6-2. This means you have one hosting plan fee but multiple domains pointing to different folders on the server.

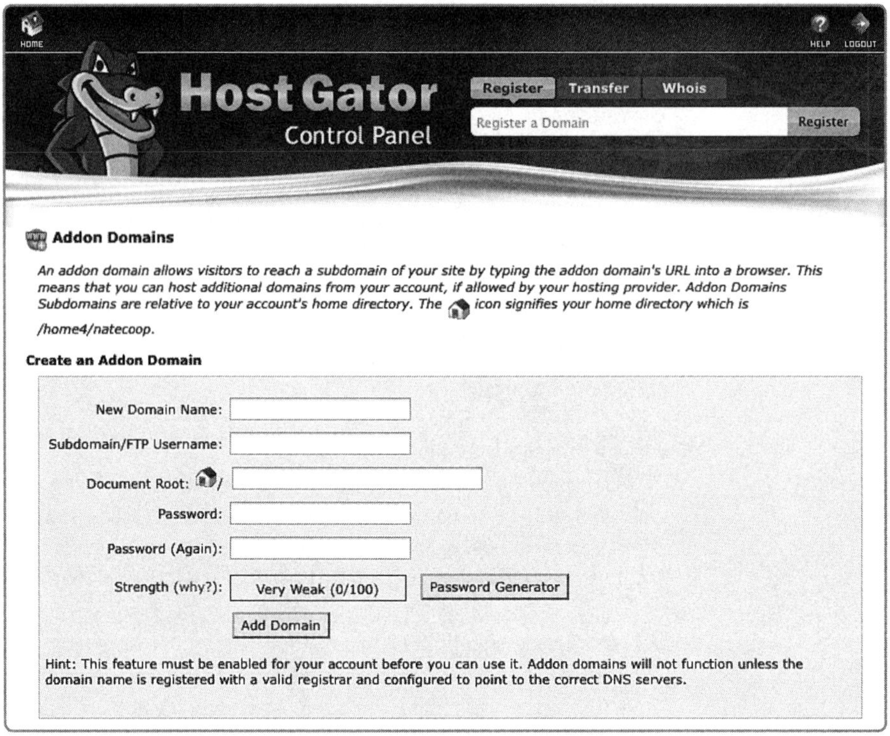

Figure 6-2: HostGator has a plan for so-called addon domains. You can attach a separate domain to the same hosting plan without having to set up another hosting plan.

Getting a Basic HTML and CSS Site Up and Running

Once you've decided on your plan and set up your domain and hosting, you should be given some information on how to log in. Your host may send this to you in an email. With this kind of hosting, you'll never actually see the computers that act as servers; you'll just work on them remotely using FTP or an *administrative panel* that you'll log into using a browser.

Follow the steps the host provides to log into your account. What you'll see now is an administrative panel. cPanel (shown in Figure 6-3) and Plesk are common examples of administrative panels.

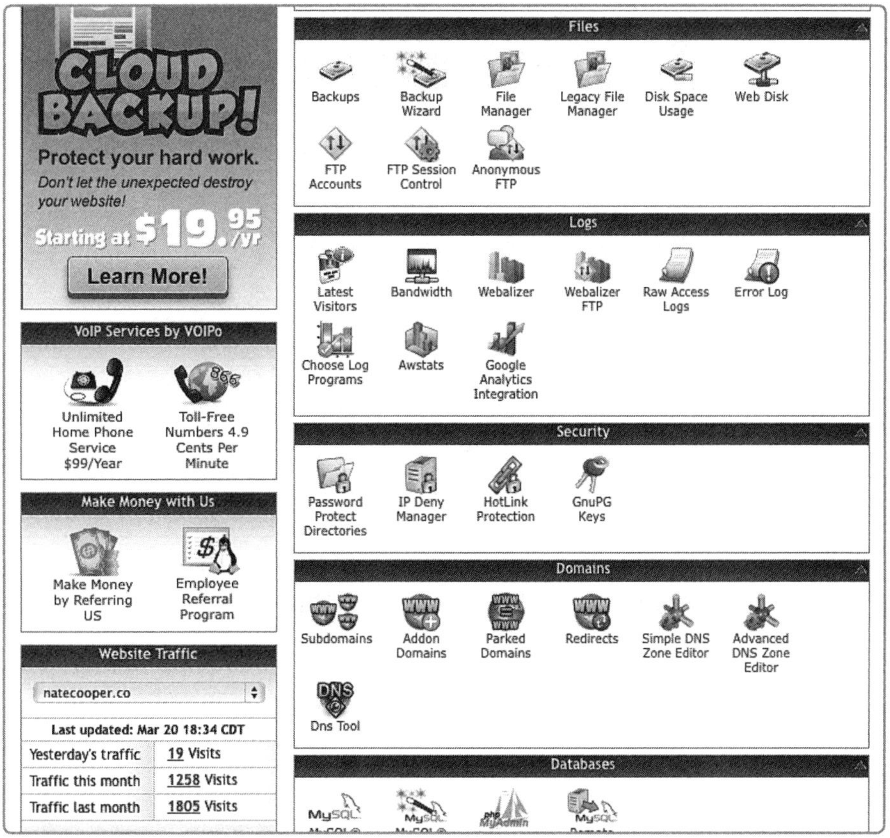

Figure 6-3: A cPanel screen on HostGator

Your host should also provide you with an FTP address, username, and password. (You may find this information in your administrative panel as well.) You'll need that FTP information to add files you create on your computer to the remote server.

Remember from Chapter 1 that you need two programs to build web pages by hand: a code editor and an FTP client. If you already followed the recommendation to download FileZilla (*https://filezilla-project.org/*), you can enter the FTP address, username, and password (provided by your host) to access your folder on your hosting plan, as shown in Figure 6-4.

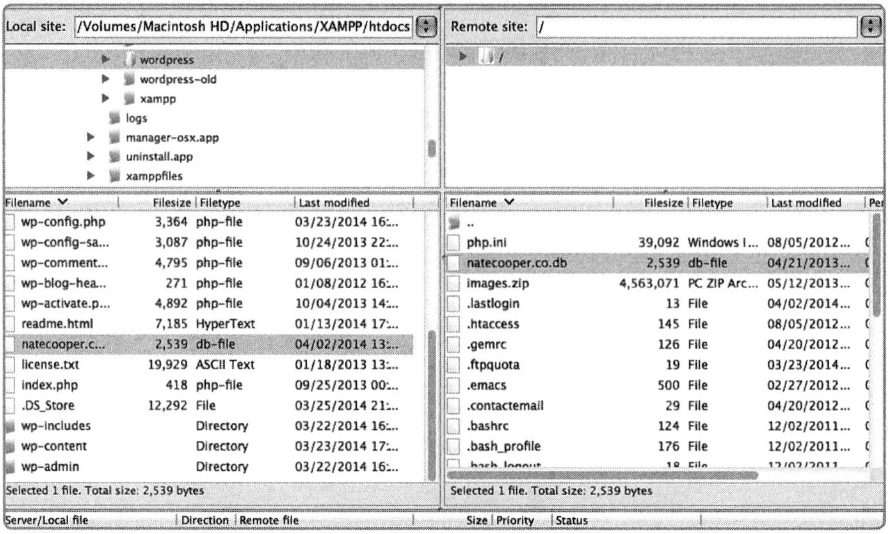

Local site: /Volumes/Macintosh HD/Applications/XAMPP/htdocs   Remote site: /

- wordpress
- wordpress-old
- xampp
- logs
- manager-osx.app
- uninstall.app
- xamppfiles

Filename ∨	Filesize	Filetype	Last modified
wp-config.php	3,364	php-file	03/23/2014 16:...
wp-config-sa...	3,087	php-file	10/24/2013 22:...
wp-comment...	4,795	php-file	09/06/2013 01:...
wp-blog-hea...	271	php-file	01/08/2012 16:...
wp-activate.p...	4,892	php-file	10/04/2013 14:...
readme.html	7,185	HyperText	01/13/2014 17:...
natecooper.c...	2,539	db-file	04/02/2014 13:...
license.txt	19,929	ASCII Text	01/18/2013 13:...
index.php	418	php-file	09/25/2013 00:...
.DS_Store	12,292	File	03/25/2014 21:...
wp-includes		Directory	03/22/2014 16:...
wp-content		Directory	03/23/2014 17:...
wp-admin		Directory	03/22/2014 16:...

Selected 1 file. Total size: 2,539 bytes

Filename ∨	Filesize	Filetype	Last modified	Per
..				
php.ini	39,092	Windows I...	08/05/2012...	
natecooper.co.db	2,539	db-file	04/21/2013...	
images.zip	4,563,071	PC ZIP Arc...	05/12/2013...	
.lastlogin	13	File	04/02/2014...	
.htaccess	145	File	08/05/2012...	
.gemrc	126	File	04/20/2012...	
.ftpquota	19	File	03/23/2014...	
.emacs	500	File	02/27/2012...	
.contactemail	29	File	04/20/2012...	
.bashrc	124	File	12/02/2011...	
.bash_profile	176	File	12/02/2011...	
.bash_logout	18	File	12/02/2011...	

Selected 1 file. Total size: 2,539 bytes

Server/Local file | Direction | Remote file   Size | Priority | Status

Figure 6-4: FileZilla shows both your local computer and the remote host via FTP so that you can easily keep track of your files in both locations. Just drag files from your local computer to the remote side to upload them.

Because you always work off of your computer, it's a good habit to create a folder for each of your sites somewhere on your hard drive. This folder should look exactly like the live version of your site. The folder acts as a backup and allows you to test changes you want to make *locally*; that is, before taking them live to your website. Once you are sure the changes you've made are working, you are ready to transfer them to your web host using FileZilla. Open FileZilla; type the host, username, and password from your host; and click **Quick-connect**. Once connected, you should see a local view (your computer) on the left side of the window and a remote site view (your web host) on the right side.

On the local side, you'll want to navigate to the folder where you keep the HTML and CSS files you created. On the remote side, you'll want to navigate to the folder where you'd like the files to go on your website. Remember, there is always a *root* of the site, from which you can create folders to branch off, just as Kim did to build her portfolio. When you are sure the files are in the location you're looking for, you can drag and drop them from the left (local) to the right (remote) side. This will copy the files to your remote host and keep a local copy for you.

The root of your site—where the live web pages live—is usually in a folder called *www* or *public_html*. Check with your host if you're unsure which folder is the root. If you're using WordPress to build your site, you don't really need a local copy. You can just create the site live on the host.

Setting Up WordPress

As you know from Chapter 4, WordPress is a content management system that runs on your host and allows you to create pages, post blog entries, and upload media (photos, videos, and so on) through the web browser. A content management system has lots of tools to . . . well . . . help manage your content. WordPress makes it easier for you to organize your site and make it look nice without having to code or manage your files using an FTP program.

Many hosts these days support WordPress natively and make setup a snap. WordPress itself is free, but you'll still need to pay for hosting to use it to manage your content. Your host stores the text, photos, and other site information, and then serves it to your visitors.

A Note on Buying WordPress Hosts

If you intend to set up your own hosting plan using WordPress to manage your content, look for a host that has *one-click install* to set up WordPress on your site (see Figure 6-5). One-click install scripts make setting up WordPress a cinch, because it means WordPress lives in a single folder on your host, like *<your-site>.com/wordpress* or *<your-site>.com/blog*. When you run the install script, it asks you where you'd like WordPress to live (see Figure 6-6). You can also point it to the root of your site so that the address is just *<your-site>.com*. The one-click install does all the heavy lifting by creating the WordPress database, installing a fresh copy of WordPress, and connecting it to the database for you automatically. If your host doesn't have a one-click install script, there are detailed instructions on how to set up WordPress in the online documentation: *http://codex.wordpress.org/Installing_WordPress/*.

Special Offers
Cloud Backup
SSL Certificate Service
SEO Gears - Promote your site
Beautiful Premium WordPress Themes
Sitelock: Protect Your Site from Hackers
Mojo Graphics & Logos
WordPress Themes & Templates
WordPress Plugins & Extensions
Get Started With WordPress Today
Cloud Desktop Storage
Bing Ad Credits
Accept Credit Cards with TransFirst

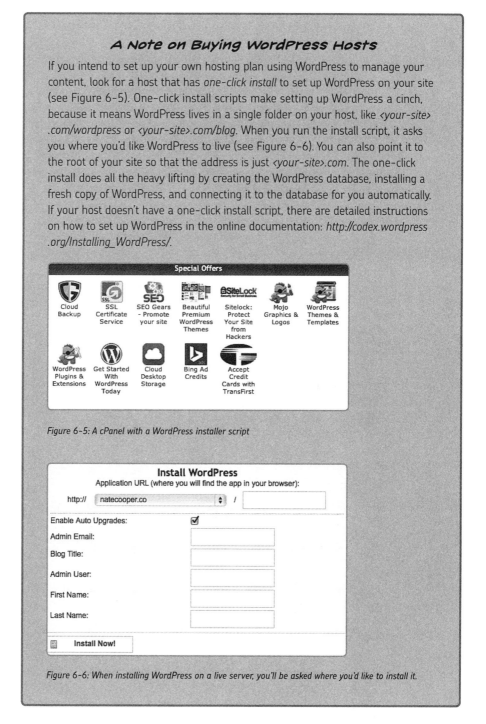

Figure 6-5: A cPanel with a WordPress installer script

Install WordPress
Application URL (where you will find the app in your browser):
http://
natecooper.co
/
Enable Auto Upgrades:
Admin Email:
Blog Title:
Admin User:
First Name:
Last Name:
Install Now!

Figure 6-6: When installing WordPress on a live server, you'll be asked where you'd like to install it.

Conclusion

And so we come to the end of our journey. You've learned a lot! You tackled the ancient code of HTML and the slick style of CSS. You defeated 404 dragons and learned the proper ways of the path. You got a tour of WordPress City and saw how modern content management works. You even tried on the best fashions with theme selection. Now you're ready to build your own website.

But really, this isn't the end of learning—it's the beginning. You've gotten a good start, but it's up to you to actually build something cool. It doesn't mean there won't be bumps on the road. Whenever you start something new, it's never as good as you imagined, but the secret is to keep at it. Try! Don't give up! If you get lost, come back to this book and review a section to get back on your path. The Guru, Kim, and Kim's friends will all be here if you need help, but from now on the adventure is yours!

Index

I

J

L

M

V

W

Build Your Own Website is set in Inkslinger, Chevin, and TheSansMono Condensed. The book was printed and bound by Sheridan Books, Inc. in Chelsea, Michigan. The paper is 60# Finch Offset, which is certified by the Forest Stewardship Council (FSC).

   The book uses a layflat binding, in which the pages are bound together with a cold-set, flexible glue and the first and last pages of the resulting book block are attached to the cover. The cover is not actually glued to the book's spine, and when open, the book lies flat and the spine doesn't crack.

Updates

Visit *http://nostarch.com/websitecomic/* for updates, errata, and other information.

More no-nonsense books from  **no starch press**

Python for Kids
A Playful Introduction to Programming
by JASON R. BRIGGS
DEC 2012, 344 PP., $34.95
ISBN 978-1-59327-407-8
FULL COLOR

JavaScript for Kids
A Playful Introduction to Programming
by NICK MORGAN
FALL 2014, 328 PP., $34.95
ISBN 978-1-59327-408-5
FULL COLOR

Ruby Wizardry
An Introduction to Programming for Kids
by ERIC WEINSTEIN
FALL 2014, 252 PP., $29.95
ISBN 978-1-59327-566-2
TWO COLOR

The Manga Guide™ to Databases
by MANA TAKAHASHI *et al.*
JAN 2009, 224 PP., $19.95
ISBN 978-1-59327-190-9

Learn to Program with Scratch
A Visual Introduction to Programming with Games, Art, Science, and Math
by MAJED MARJI
FEB 2014, 288 PP., $34.95
ISBN 978-1-59327-543-3
FULL COLOR

The Book of™ GIMP
A Complete Guide to Nearly Everything
by OLIVIER LECARME *and* KARINE DELVARE
JAN 2013, 676 PP., $49.95
ISBN 978-1-59327-383-5
FULL COLOR

phone 800.420.7240 or 415.863.9900 | fax 415.863.9950 | sales@nostarch.com | www.nostarch.com